A Practical Guide to Stage Lighting

A Practical Guide to Stage Lighting

Steven Louis Shelley

FOCAL PRESS

Boston Oxford Auckland Johannesburg Melbourne New Delhi

Butterworth–Heinemann supports the efforts of American Forests and the Global ReLeaf program in its campaign for the betterment of trees, forests, and our environment.

Library of Congress Cataloging-in-Publication Data
Shelley, Steven.
    A practical guide to stage lighting / Steven Louis Shelley.
        p.   cm.
    Includes bibliographical references and index.
    ISBN 0-240-80353-1 (paperback : alk. paper)
    1. Stage lighting.   I. Title.
PN2091.E4S52   1999
792'.025—dc21   98-43725
                                                        CIP

British Library Cataloguing-in-Publication Data
A catalogue record for this book is available from the British Library.

The publisher offers special discounts on bulk orders of this book.
For information, please contact:
Manager of Special Sales
Butterworth–Heinemann
225 Wildwood Avenue
Woburn, MA 01801-2041
Tel: 781-904-2500
Fax: 781-904-2620

For information on all Butterworth-Heinemann publications available, contact our World Wide Web home page at: http://www.bh.com

10 9 8 7 6 5 4 3 2 1

Printed in the United States of America

Table of Contents

List of Illustrations

Foreword

At last. The book that we in the theatrical lighting world have been waiting for. Whether you are a lighting designer on Broadway, off Broadway, in LORT theaters, for small or large dance companies who tour or give one time performances, or for any kind of theatrical venture, you will find a way to get a handle on your lighting process, both the craft and the design, in this book. It is totally comprehensive and written in such a way that accomplished designers as well as beginners can find information, know-how, and stimulating ideas written in an organized and easily understandable manner. It is staggeringly complete and therefore hardly a volume for one's back pocket but I am sure it will find it's way into many a workbox as well as the shelves of studios and classrooms alike.

In my experience as a teacher, I have learned that it is important for a student to learn one way well. Once that is done it becomes clear that any way—the student's way—is possible. Steve Shelley in *A Practical Guide to Stage Lighting* has dissected his own carefully devised process and generously presented it to the reader. He shows us every aspect of lighting and how it becomes a part of a total production. The emphasis is on craft but his experience in design allows us to see how the two go hand in hand. The how may well determine a large part of the what.

It is through the light onstage that theater communicates with an audience. Only when one has a richly developed and organized language, a clear way of speaking, can one begin to express the light with a nuance and subtlety that will reveal the depth of fine playwriting and acting. Once one has read and comprehended *A Practical Guide to Stage Lighting* one's ideas in light cannot help but become more organized, more systematic enabling one to communicate those ideas with greater depth and clarity. This organization coupled with a developed eye for composition is all that one needs to be a fine designer. I have no doubt that this book will make better lighting designers of us all. I have no doubt that this book will allow us all to see light better and therefore stimulate the making of better light onstage. Bravo!

Jennifer Tipton
Lighting Designer

Preface

This book has not been written for students just beginning a study of lighting design. Many other texts are available that more fully examine the basic concepts and principles discussed in Chapter 1. Rather, this text presumes that the reader already has some practical experience and understanding of the activities required to realize a lighting design, and wishes to know more. He or she understands theatrical drawings and has some hands-on experience with theatrical lighting instruments and the processes involved in mounting a design. The reader has a basic knowledge about the different types and kinds of lighting control consoles and has some experience working with them.

By the same token, *A Practical Guide to Stage Lighting* does not discuss topics considered by many to be advanced. It does not address touring, international, repertory, or Broadway lighting design. It doesn't include discussions of advanced or international lighting consoles, nor does it address programming techniques for moving light fixtures.

Effort has been made to explain or define the terms used in *A Practical Guide to Stage Lighting* to reduce the need to draw reference from other materials. The methods and techniques used are not absolute; they're merely the simplest ways that have been found in my experience to address and facilitate that particular activity. In many cases, ideas are merely presented as suggestions. Sometimes, they're strongly suggested. In particular cases, such as Golden Rules, the ideas are, in my experience, absolute.

Several icons were created for use in this book.

Checklist: This icon indicates a list of items. Though not every item is applicable to every situation, this list should be reviewed prior to addressing specific tasks.

Shelley's Notes: This icon indicates notes based on my own experiences. They're included so others don't have to make the same mistakes.

Sneaky Tip: This icon is used to present a piece of information that was a revelation when it was presented to me.

Shelley's Soapbox: This icon is used for my own personal opinion regarding a particular topic that I feel strongly about.

Golden Rule: This drawing of a tape measure with a halo is used to highlight a particular fact, situation, or method that I've found to be almost irrefutable.

Tales from the Road: This icon is used when telling a story that relates to the surrounding text. The icon is a picture of a headset under tire tracks, since that's often how one feels after learning a painful lesson.

Acknowledgments

Like all books, this book would not have been possible without the assistance and cooperation of several organizations, manufacturers, lighting rental shops, and individuals.

The organizations: United States Institute of Theatre Technology and Don Padgett at United Scenic Artists 829.

The manufacturers: Tony Sklarew and John Ryan at Altman Stage Lighting; Traci Kelliher, Sue Englund, Tony Romain, and David North at Electronic Theatre Controls; Tom Folsom and Keith Gillam at Strand Lighting; Joe Tawil at Great American Market; and Josh Alemany and Donna Nicol at Rosco Labs.

The lighting rental shops: Ken Romaine and Kori Hansen at Production Arts and Larry Schoeneman at Designlab Chicago.

The individuals: Pete Dillenbeck, George Darveris, Kevin Dreyer, David Fleming, David K. H. Elliott, Greg Goldsmith, Jim Griffith, Ellen Jones, Rolf Lee, Cindy Limauro, Jerry Lewis, Maureen Moran, Martha Mountain, Mitch Tebo, and Rhys Williams. Appreciation extended to the owners, staff, and patrons of Mimi's Macaroni.

Technical editing: Sabrina Hamilton.

Copyediting: Steve Shelley and Mitch Tebo.

For her guidance, knowledge, and high tolerance level, thanks go to Ms. Lorraine Ross Hall, who provided equal doses of encouragement and despair. For her assistance and even higher tolerance level, big thanks to Ms. Judith Schoenfeld. Many thanks to the two people who helped inspire me in this business: Ms.

Sara Boatman and Mr. Michael Orris Watson. This book is dedicated to my family and my friends. Without their support, I might still be delivering laundry.

A Practical Guide to Stage Lighting was written on a Power Computing 210 and an Apple Power Macintosh G3, using a Microtek E6 scanner. The following applications were originally used to create the text and graphics used in this book: Adobe PhotoShop, Colorit!, Filemaker Pro, MacDraw, Microsoft Office 98, and ScanWizard.

Material in Chapter 1 relied heavily on *Designing with Light*, by J. Michael Gillette, *Stage Lighting*, by Richard Pilbrow, and *Lighting Handbook*, by the Westinghouse Electric Corporation. Material in the shop order section made supplemental use of information from John McKernon's home page: http://www.mckernon.com

Images of Source Four instruments courtesy of Electronic Theatre Controls. Image of color scroller courtesy of Wybron, Inc. Image of gobo rotator and Rosco Designer Pattern #7733 courtesy of Rosco Labs. All other images of lighting instruments and reflectors courtesy of Altman Lighting.

Cover photographs taken with the gracious permission of the Joyce Theater and Garth Fagan Dance. Assistance in the photo session provided by Richard Koch.

All elements, concepts, and descriptions of *Hokey: A Musical Myth* by Steven Louis Shelley. All illustrations by Steven Louis Shelley.

All theatrical lighting symbols produced with the Field Template™ and SoftSymbols™. Field Template registered patent 5,033,333.

Visit the Field Template Home Page: http://www.esta.org/homepages/fieldtemplate

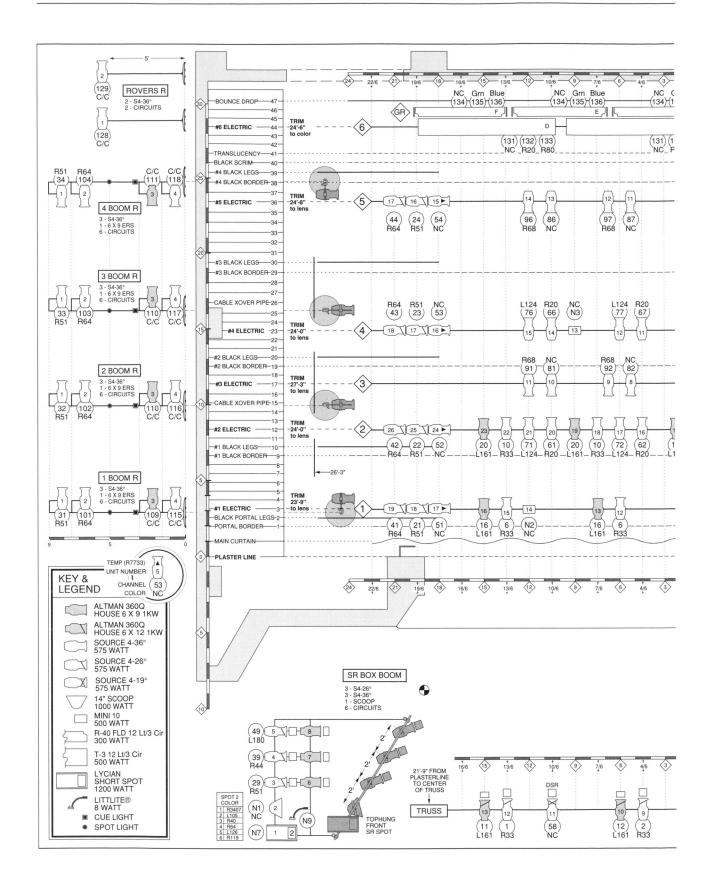

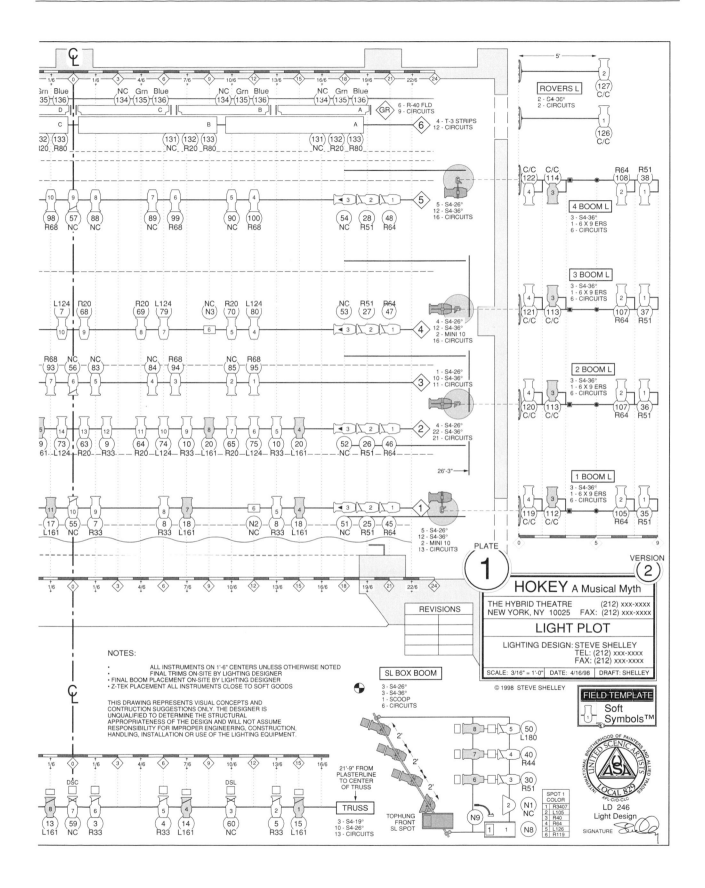

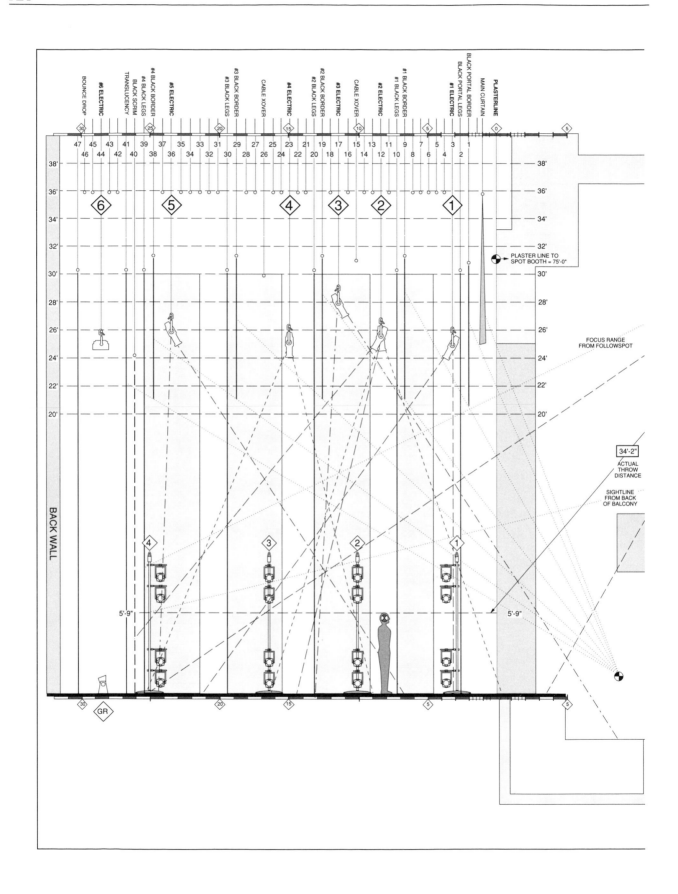

The Hybrid Theatre
New York City

APPROXIMATELY 7" CENTERS
GRID: 62'-0"
PIPE TRAVEL: 59'-6"
NO HOUSE MASKING GOODS
BLACK SCRIM: 28'-0"H X 50'-0" W

TRUSS

26° = 18' DIAMETER POOL

SL BOX BOOM

	PLATE		VERSION
	2	**HOKEY** A Musical Myth	**3**

THE HYBRID THEATRE   (212) 865-2969
NEW YORK, NY 10025   FAX: (212) 749-9117

SECTION LOOKING SL

LIGHTING DESIGN: STEVE SHELLEY
TEL: (xxx) xxx-xxxx
FAX: (xxx) xxx-xxxx

| SCALE: 1/4" = 1'-0" | DATE: 4/16/98 | DRAFT: SHELLEY |

Introduction

Although many texts explain the different styles, processes, and methods used to create light on stage, very few explain the purpose and use of the mechanical tools necessary to convert conceptual images into a lighting design for a production. From an analytical perspective, there are three very finite moments in any lighting design. The first moment is when the lighting designer is hired. The second moment is when the load-in starts and lighting instruments begin to get hung. The third and final moment is when the curtain opens to an audience. In between, processes and scheduled events occur that can be performed haphazardly or with expediency. Once in the theatre, however, all events take place within a scheduled framework that can be called *stage time*. And this will come as no great news: There's never enough. Time spent on stage trying to make a decision, rather than implementing a decision, is often wasted time that can never be regained.

When I was a younger student of lighting design, I wasted a lot of stage time. I had gone to classes and read books, but no one said anything about effectively using time. The classroom didn't address the need to streamline the lighting design construction process. Without a system or enough experience, I would unknowingly allow myself to be led by others through a production schedule that would frequently result in an unfinished product. Afterwards, I would attempt to analyze my disappointment resulting from unsatisfactory designs that remained unfulfilled because I had run out of time. Eventually I realized I had it backwards. I needed to analyze the situation first, construct a strategy, and create the tools prior to the load-in that would allow on-site decisions to be made. Rather than walking in the door and backpedaling through whatever situation was dictated to me, I began searching for ways to dictate the situation. My goal broadened to not only creating a design, but also to establishing the environment that would allow the design to be completed within the presented parameters.

When viewed from a perspective of time management, I've come to recognize that the creation of every lighting design requires a progressive sequence of tasks. Although every production is different (or the end result may be completely different from the initial plan), a progression of tasks and choices must be followed every time to complete a design. Some speed making choices and expediting those tasks comes from experience and common sense. Other elements of the speed, however, come from proper homework so that the entire design is understood and the proper tools are created. After years of watching and analyzing mistakes (both my own and others'), I believe I'm beginning to understand the relationships and progression of the steps. In doing so, I've created a general set of tools, methods, and techniques that I use to expedite the process.

By doing the homework and producing lighting designs based on realistic parameters, the entire production process has become an exercise in adapting a conceived design into a realized product, not just knee-jerk reactions to information that should have been analyzed, rather than ignored.

A Practical Guide to Stage Lighting is a "nuts and bolts" examination of some of these tools and methods. Part One, Review and Definitions, examines the elements, terms, and concepts within the theatrical environment, and explores the different boundaries that change and define a light plot. The second part, Preparing the Tools, examines the different documents used to define, communicate, and expedite a light plot. The final part, Using the Tools, discusses each task involved in the on-site creation of a lighting design and examines how the tools are applied to successfully and rapidly design light.

The purpose of this book is to illustrate one series of methods that I've used to utilize the precious commodity of stage time and create theatrical lighting designs. *A Practical Guide to Stage Lighting* presents tools and techniques that solely address the realities of crafting or recreating a light plot with minimal space, tools, or time. Or, to put it another way, how to get the best lighting bang for your buck.

Steve Shelley
New York
1998

part one

Review and Definitions

1

A Review

Generally, the purpose of a theatrical presentation is to entertain, educate, and communicate ideas. A typical presentation is comprised of a script or music, interpreted by both performers and elements of design, all unified by the director's overall concept. Lighting is only one of the production elements, and for a lighting design to successfully achieve this purpose it cannot take place in a vacuum. Instead, it must work in combination with the other design elements, the performers, and the directorial concept.

Similarly, the physical components of a lighting design must work in combination with various elements of the physical environment including the theatrical space, the lighting components, the personnel, and the schedule. The aesthetic objectives of the design may be of primary concern, but in order to effectively conceive, communicate, and coordinate those objectives, the lighting designer must also possess a practical knowledge of the physical and conceptual framework in which those objectives will be achieved. The purpose of this review is to examine and define the basic elements of this framework as they will be used in this text.

The first step in that review is to define the labels for the various architectural elements of the theatrical space.

THE THEATRICAL SPACE

The theatrical space is described with a combination of architectural nomenclature and historical terminology. In general, theatrical presentations or performances can't exist without a public to observe the proceedings. Most theatres have specific locations for the public to watch the performance, called the **audience**,
and locations where the performers perform, called the **stage**. The floor itself is also sometimes referred to as the "**deck**."

The arrangement that allows an audience to view the stage from one side as through a "picture frame" is known as a **proscenium** configuration. The arrangement that allows the stage to be viewed by an audience from either side of the stage is known as an **alley** configuration, and the arrangement that allows the audience to view three sides of the stage is known as a **thrust** configuration. The arrangement that allows the audience to view the stage from all sides is known as an **arena** configuration, sometimes referred to as "in the round." Arrangements that intertwine the stage and audience seating are often referred to as an **environmental** configuration. Since there are many possible combinations and variations of these configurations, one generic phrase used to describe a space used for theatrical presentations is **performance facility**. Although many of the discussions in this text have application to other arrangements, the proscenium configuration is the principal environment that we consider.

Another term for the area containing audience seating is the "**house**." The main curtain, which may be used to prevent the audience from viewing the entire stage until a designated moment, is often located immediately behind the architectural "picture frame" that divides the house from the stage area, called the proscenium. In many cases, the proscenium isn't a rectangular shape; instead, the top horizontal frame edge curves into the two vertical side elements, creating the **proscenium arch**.

The "back side" of the proscenium arch, concealed from the audience's view, is known as the **plaster line**. The plaster line is often used as an architectural plane of reference. If the proscenium opening is

3

divided in half, that bisected distance produces a point on the stage. This point can be extended into a single line perpendicular to the plaster line called the **centerline**, which is used as a second architectural plane of reference. The point where the centerline and the plaster line intersect on the stage is a point of reference called the **groundplan zero point** or the **zero zero point**.

Two types of drawings are most commonly used to present the information about each space. One perspective looks down onto the performance space, compressing every object into a single plane. This drafting is called a **groundplan view**. The cross-section, commonly referred to as the **sectional view**, is the perspective produced after the entire space has been visually "cut in half" like a layer cake, often on centerline. After half of the "cake" has been removed, the inside of the remainder is viewed.

Theatrical Stage Nomenclature and Notation

The area between the plaster line and the edge of the stage is often referred to as the **apron**. In some theatres, a gap exists between the edge of the stage and the audience. This architectural "trench," acoustically designed to accommodate musicians and enhance sound, is often referred to as the **orchestra pit**. The area of the stage not concealed by masking and available for performers is known as the **playing area** or the **performance area**. The rest of the stage, which is often concealed from the audience's view, is known as **backstage**.

Stage directions are used as a basic system of orientation. Their nomenclature is often thought to stem from the time when all stage floors were raked, or sloped, toward the audience. Modern stage directions can be illustrated from the perspective of a person standing at groundplan zero facing the audience. From this perspective, moving closer to the audience is movement **downstage**, while moving away from the audience is movement **upstage**. **Stage left** and **stage right** are in this orientation as well. Moving toward centerline from either side is referred to as movement **onstage**, while moving away from centerline is movement **offstage**. Up and downstage **light lines** are imaginary boundaries where light on performers is terminated. The upstage light line is usually defined to prevent light from spilling onto backing scenery, while the downstage light line's placement may be established by a combination of factors. Its location may be

the edge of light beam coverage, the edge of the performance space, or established to prevent light from spilling onto architecture. A point on centerline midway between the light lines is often known as **center center**. While standing on this point, moving directly toward the audience is movement down center. Moving to either side is thought of in terms of movement offstage left or right. Moving directly away from the audience is movement toward upstage center. Diagonal movement uses a combination of terms, upstage left or downstage right being two examples.

Other terms are used to provide a general system of orientation relative to centerline. If a person stands on stage left, for example, all objects stage left of centerline can be referred to as **near** objects, or being on the **near side** of the stage. All objects on the opposite side of centerline, in this case stage right, are **far** objects, or exist on the **far side** of the stage. Objects on the far side can also be referred to as being on the **opposite side** of the stage. This orientation remains constant until the person moves to the stage right side of centerline, in which case all of the terms reverse. The same objects that were near are now far, and vice versa. Opposite is always on the opposite side of centerline.

Theatrical Rigging

Objects hung in the air over the stage are typically referred to as "**goods**," which are divided into two categories. Backdrops, curtains, and velour masking all fall under the heading of "soft goods," while built flattage, walls, and other framed or solid objects fall under the heading of "hard goods."

In most proscenium theatres, the area above the stage contains elements of the **fly system**, which allows goods and electrical equipment to be suspended in the air. Most modern fly systems are counterweighted; meaning that the weight of the load suspended in the air is balanced by an equal weight in a remote location. Since many lighting instruments are often hung in the air over the stage, it's prudent to understand the basic components and mechanical relationships in a fly system.

Figure 1.1 shows a **counterweight fly system**. Goods are typically attached to **battens**, which often consist of lengths of steel pipe. The battens are held in the air by **system cables**. The system cables each trace a unique path up to the **grid**, which is typically a steel structure that supports the entire fly system and anything else that hangs in the air. Once in the grid, each

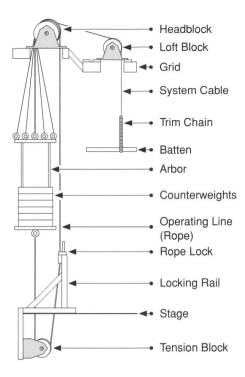

Figure 1.1 A Counterweight Fly System

system cable passes through a single unique pulley called a **loft block** or a **sheave**. After passing through the sheaves, all of the system cables for one batten passes through a multisheaved pulley called a **head block**, and then terminate at the top of the **arbor**. The arbor, when loaded with sufficient **counterweight**, balances the weight of the goods attached to the batten. Rope tied to the arbor describes a loop, running from the bottom of the arbor down through a tension pulley near the stage, then up through the **locking rail** to the head block in the grid, and then back down again to the top of the arbor.

Pulling the rope (or **operating line**) adjusts the height of the arbor and, conversely, alters the height of the goods on the batten. Since the weight is counterbalanced between the batten and the arbor, the **rope lock** on the locking rail merely immobilizes the batten's location. Though not entirely accurate, this entire assembly which controls a single batten is often called a **lineset**.

Theatrical Backdrops

Large pieces of fabric that prevent the audience from viewing the back wall of the theatre are known as **backdrops**. Although they are usually located at the upstage edge of the playing area, any large piece of fabric "backing" a scene in the performance area is referred to as a backdrop or, simply, a drop. Several drops hung adjacent to each other upstage of the performance area are often referred to as the "**scenic stack**."

Often the visual objective of a backdrop is to provide a surface that appears solid or unbroken by wrinkles. To achieve this, most drops constructed of fabric have a sleeve sewn across the bottom, known as a pipe pocket. The weight of pipe inserted in the pocket provides vertical tension to reduce the severity or number of wrinkles seen by the audience. Additional weights may be placed on top of the pipe pocket to increase this tension. Clamps called stretchers may be attached to the side edges of the drop to provide horizontal tension. The combination of tensions attempts to achieve a smooth unbroken surface.

Backdrops can be constructed from a variety of materials, including canvas, muslin, plastic, bobbinette, or scrim. Backdrops that possess no visual design element are often lighted with washes of color. These drops are often referred to as **cycloramas**, or **cycs**. The techniques used in their construction often determine the method in which they are lit. Drops constructed of horizontal strips of fabric are often lit only from the downstage side (or the **front** of the drop), since the silhouettes of the horizontal seams will be seen if lit from the upstage side (or the **back**). Other drops are constructed from a single piece of material. This more expensive drop is known as a **seamless**, and, since there are no shadow lines created by horizontal seams, they may be lit on either the front or the back.

Viewing different types of backdrops is one way to illustrate the three different levels of visible transmission. When a fabric backdrop is painted so that the tiny holes between the fabric are filled with paint, light can no longer openly pass through the fabric. Light projected onto the back of the drop will not be seen by the audience. In this first condition, the drop is considered **opaque**. An unpainted fabric backdrop, on the other hand, allows light to pass through the tiny holes. Light projected onto the back of the drop will be seen by the audience. In this second condition, the drop is considered **translucent**. (This term is often used as another name for a seamless drop. It can also be called a **translucency**.) A drop constructed of a loosely woven fabric material called **scrim** can be used to illustrate the third level of transmission. If light falls only on an object that is positioned upstage of a scrim, the audience can clearly see the object through the fabric. In this condition, the scrim is considered **transparent**. The method used to weave a scrim, however, allows light to change its visible transmission. If the upstage light is removed and replaced by a high angle wash of light projected onto the front of the scrim, the object disappears, and the scrim is now visually opaque.

Translucent drops are typically lit from behind with rows of lights. To make the drop as bright as possible, the rows of lights are sandwiched between the translucency and a second light-colored backdrop hung further upstage, which acts as a reflector. Although the audience doesn't see this upstage drop, it contains and bounces all available light into the back of the translucency, thus its name, the **bounce** drop.

Theatrical Masking

The common convention in theatre is to hide the technical elements from the audience with large pieces of fabric or built flats generally called **masking**. Although many different types of fabric are used for masking, it's generally accepted that black velour reflects the least amount of light. If the masking is unframed and can be folded for storage, it's generally categorized as "soft." If masking or scenery is framed or stiff, it's known as "hard." Pieces of vertical masking hung on either side of the stage are called **legs** or **tormentors**, while units of horizontal masking hung above the stage are called **borders** or **teasers**.

Legs and borders are often hung adjacent to each other to create **masking portals** that mirror the proscenium arch. Masking portals prevent the area above or to the side of the performance area from being viewed by the audience. When fly systems are involved, a pair of masking legs of equal height is typically hung on a single batten. To hide the leg batten from the view of the audience, the accompanying masking border is typically hung on a separate batten downstage of the legs. Utilizing two exclusive battens allows the height of the border to be adjusted without altering the vertical placement of the masking legs. The two masking linesets are often hung adjacent to each other to allow room between portals for electrics or other flying pieces.

Additional scenery is often hung in this same area. If scenic legs are a part of the design, they are often hung on a separate batten between the two masking linesets, so that the border hides the batten containing the scenic legs. By hanging scenic legs adjacent to the masking legs, light can be cut off both sets of legs while providing optimum coverage. Midstage drops or scrims are often assigned to linesets immediately upstage of the masking leg battens. The masking border hides the batten, while the masking legs conceal the side edges of the drop.

The word "opening" can have two meanings when used in conversations regarding masking. The left and right distance between two legs hung on the same batten is often referred to as the "**width of the opening**" or the "**leg opening**." The up and downstage distance between two legs on the same side of the stage, on the other hand, is referred to either as the "**depth of the opening**," or an "**in**." The "in" label is used to distinguish each opening, each of which is numbered starting at plaster line. "Stage Left In 1" is the first leg opening upstage of plaster line on stage left, and so on. If the entire performance space is masked in black velour legs, borders, and a black backdrop, the combined masking creates a "**black surround**."

Theatrical Performance Surfaces

Performance surfaces are often used to cover the deck and create a surface that's easily installed, transportable, and uniform in appearance. Large pieces of canvas, often painted, are called **ground cloths**. Rolls of vinyl flooring, generically referred to as **dance floors**, may also be used to cover the stage. Or, platforms may be used to cover the entire playing area, which are collectively referred to as **stage decks**. (Stage decks are often used to conceal mechanical devices, which power turntables or other moving scenery.) On the other hand, rather than any of these, the stage may merely be painted.

THE HANGING POSITIONS AND FOCUS

Within the theatrical space the lighting designer must have a grasp of the terms that describe the locations specifically designed to house the lighting instruments used to illuminate the performers and the other elements of the production. These locations are generically called **hanging positions**. When lighting instruments are being targeted at specific points for use in a live presentation, the act of maneuvering and shaping each beam of light is referred to as **focusing** the instrument, which has its own vocabulary.

Hanging Position Names and Nomenclature

To prevent confusion, each hanging position or location has a unique name. The nomenclature is defined by the architectural location, the type of mounting position, and the relative location to groundplan zero.

The initial division defining hanging position name is relative to plaster line. Hanging positions downstage of the plaster line are generically known as front of house positions. Although they may have many names, they're usually found in three locations. The position parallel to plaster line over the audience that provides the highest angle of light to the stage is usually known by an architectural feature; the **cove**, the **catwalk**, the **beam**, or the **slot**, to name a few. Hanging positions on the sides of the audience providing diagonal frontlight are often named for their adjacency to the audience box seating. These positions are usually called **box booms**. The position providing the flattest angle to the stage is often found in front of the balcony closest to the stage. This hanging position is usually called the **balcony rail**.

Hanging positions upstage of plaster line above the stage may be known as **overhead pipes, electrics, catwalks**, or, in large theatres with moving catwalks, **overhead bridges**. The electric closest to plaster line is the first electric. The further away from plaster line, the higher the position number. Likewise, if there is more than one front of house hanging position from approximately the same angle, the hanging position of each type closest to the plaster line is listed first.

The hanging positions on either side of the stage are identified by their degree of permanence, their appearance, or their function. Hanging positions permanently accessible by architectural catwalks on either side of the stage are often called **galleries**. Structural frameworks temporarily suspended from the grid in that same approximate location may be referred to as **ladders**, since their typical appearance resembles that device. Permanent vertical hanging positions built into or adjacent to the proscenium are often called **torms**. Temporary structures that sit on the stage providing vertical hanging positions are often referred to as **booms**. Individual lighting instruments mounted on movable structures that sit on the stage are known as **stands, rovers**, or **floor mounts**. Lighting instruments attached to pieces of scenery are often referred to as **set mounts**. Positions contained in the deck, creating a gap in the stage, are often known as **troughs**. A trough in the stage running parallel to the downstage edge of the apron is often referred to as a **footlight trough**, while the same gap upstage containing instruments used to illuminate backdrops is often called a **cyc trough**.

All hanging locations not intersecting centerline are often subnamed by their location relative to centerline. Ladders, booms, and such are divided between stage left and stage right. The hanging locations are then numbered by their relative proximity to plaster line. The stage left boom closest to plaster line, for example, is known as 1 Boom Left. Each boom further from plaster line receives the next higher whole number.

A numbering system is employed to identify the instruments at each hanging position. Each instrument is given a unique whole number to speed identification. The first instrument at each position is usually labeled as unit number 1, and continues in whole numbers to the end of the position. Over time, the terms have become interchangeable; instruments are often referred to as units. The act of "counting the instruments" has historically been performed while standing on stage, facing the audience. Because of that, the numbering of the instruments starts from the left orientation, and runs from stage left to stage right. When instruments are stacked vertically, unit numbering is related to height and proximity to plaster line. The typical convention is to number the units from top to bottom. When pairs of instruments are on the same level, the numbering starts with the downstage instrument and proceeds upstage. Paired units stacked in box booms are often numbered starting from centerline and proceed offstage.

Additional electrical devices are often represented in a light plot, which may or may not be controlled by the light board. To avoid confusion, each separate device requiring line voltage or a control signal receives a unique unit number. If the electrical device is an attachment altering the beam of an instrument, it will often not receive its own whole number, but rather the host instrument's number and an alphabetical letter. For example, unit 22 may have a color scroller. The color scroller would be identified as unit 22A. Alphabetical letters are also used for instruments added after initial numbering of the position has taken place. As an example, an instrument added between units 7 and 8 is often labeled as unit 7A. Since letters serve in two capacities, numbering the units at each hanging position is one of the final tasks performed while the plot is being drafted, so that each instrument can be assigned a whole number.

Focus and Function Nomenclature

When lighting instruments are focused for a production, a set of terms is used to describe the characteristics of the light beams. A different set of terms describes the function that each instrument is assigned to perform in a lighting design.

Almost every lighting instrument produces a **beam** (or pool, or cone) of light containing several characteristics that are referred to when a lighting design is being constructed and when an instrument is being focused. Figure 1.2 shows a side view of an instrument's beam targeted at a designer. The overall size of the light beam is called the **beam spread** and is usually measured in degrees. The beam spread created by some types of instruments is referred to in three distinct areas. The beam spread is also called the **field angle**, which is technically defined as the outer cone where the light diminishes to 10% of the center intensity. Approximately half of the field angle is referred to as the **beam angle**, which is defined as the internal cone where the light is 50% of the center intensity. The center intensity, which is the brightest portion of the beam, is commonly referred to as the **hot spot**.

The hot spot is the portion of the light beam often targeted at a specific location. The location on the stage where the lighting designer stands to act as a target is often referred to as a focus point. This term is also used to refer to the targeted space occupied by the designer's head. In general, however, a **focus point** is defined as the location on the stage, scenery, or in space where the hot spot of the instrument's beam is pointed. The amount of light that is produced by any instrument increases in size and decreases in intensity the farther the light has to travel. The **actual throw distance** is the measured distance between the instrument and the focus point, which is used to calculate the size and intensity of light beams.

When a single instrument is focused to either a specific location or purpose, that instrument is labeled as a **special**. Multiple instruments, equipped with the same color filter, may be focused to cover more than one area of a stage. When they are activated and used together, they can be collectively referred to as either specials or a **system**. A system is often comprised of at least two instruments that are used together, focused to different or adjacent areas of the stage. When multiple instruments of matching color are focused so that their overlapping beams create a consistent hue and intensity over a portion or all of a performance area, they're collectively referred to as a **wash**. The two terms are often used interchangeably, but while a system may be composed of several instruments focused to different areas of the stage, a wash implies a smooth blend of instruments in a matching color.

Systems and washes of light are often the fundamental tools used in a light plot to create lighting on the stage. They're often hung and focused in such a way that multiple bands of light are created across the width of a stage. A single band of light aimed at focus points equidistant from plaster line, so that the overlapping beams create a consistent intensity across the width of a stage, is called a **zone**. Overlapping zones are often used to create a wash, allowing a performer's face to remain a consistent intensity beyond the depth of a single light beam while moving up or downstage.

Systems are typically identified relative to a person standing on the stage facing the audience. They are often identified by the degree of angle from centerline, their hanging position, or by the relative height to the person's head. Light striking the front of a person's body is often referred to as **frontlight**. If the instruments are hung so that their focused beams travel parallel with centerline, the system is referred to as **straight frontlight**, while light striking a person's body from approximately a 45° angle from centerline is often called **area frontlight**. If a frontlight wash originates from the box boom position, the system can be called a **box boom wash**. Light striking a person's body from approximately a 90° angle on either side of centerline is called **sidelight**. If the source of the

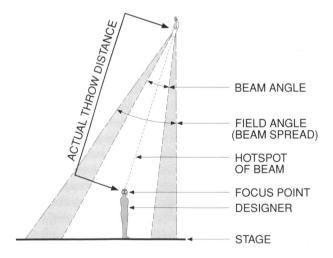

Figure 1.2 The Different Portions of a Light Beam

light is from the overhead electrics, it can be referred to as **overhead sidelight** (or high sidelight). Instruments close to the stage, on the other hand, can be referred to as low sidelight, or referred to by their hanging position as **boom sidelight**. Light from overhead electrics focused directly down onto the top of a person's head is often referred to as **toplight** or **downlight**, while light striking the upstage side of a person's body is often called **backlight**. Backlight hung so that the focused beams travel parallel to centerline is often called **straight backlight**, while focused backlight striking a person's body from approximately a 45° angle from centerline is often called **diagonal backlight**.

Creating these systems is achieved by understanding the different concepts and components of theatrical light. This understanding begins by examining the properties and control of electricity, the form of energy that allows theatrical lighting to exist.

ELECTRICITY AND DISTRIBUTION

Electricity is a fundamental law of nature that is created by the movement of atomic particles called electrons. The need to manipulate electricity in the theatre has given rise to the role of the lighting designer. From a fundamental point of view, the lighting designer's function is to control the amount of electricity to each lighting source. Although the designer is typically not required to have a detailed knowledge of electricity, he or she should have a basic grasp of this law of nature. The designer must have a comprehension of how to control electricity, if for no other reason than one of safety.

Basic Electricity

A basic electrical circuit is comprised of three components: a **source** of electricity, a **load** using the electricity, and **circuitry** providing a path between the two. There are two basic types of electricity: **direct** and **alternating current**. Every electrical system uses one of these two types. A demonstration of direct current can be seen in a typical flashlight. The electrical flow moves in a single direction of polarity from the positive terminal of the battery (the source), through the bulb (the load), and back to the negative terminal of the battery to complete the circuit. In today's world, low-powered direct current is seen in batteries and is used to internally power computer devices. High-

powered direct current, on the other hand, is rarely seen by the consumer.

Most electrical power provided to the consumer, ranging from entire cities to common household outlets, is alternating current. This type of electricity is created by large generators which essentially consist of fixed magnets surrounding a rotating shaft carrying three coils of insulated wire. The rotation of the shaft within the magnetic field generates pulsing electrical current in each of the three coils. The pulsing current reverses direction, or alternates polarity, 60 times a second, thus the term **60-cycle alternating current**. The individual current produced by each of the three coils is called a **phase** (or a "hot"). Three-phase 60-cycle alternating-current is the standard distributed throughout the United States, but the actual number of phases installed in any building or performing facility may vary. Regardless of the number of phases, an additional wire is present which completes the circuit back to the generator, called the **neutral**. In many installations, another wire is also included as a safety precaution, called a **ground**.

Electricity has three related electrical attributes: amperage, wattage, and voltage, which are measured in amps, watts, and volts, respectively. An **amp** is the unit of measurement for electron flow from one point to another, which can also be interpreted as the amount of electrical flow possible through a wire. A **watt** is defined as a unit of measurement expressing the amount of electrical energy consumed by a device or a load. A **volt** is defined as unit of measurement expressing electrical pressure to form a current, which can also be interpreted as the electrical "force" of current through a wire. 220 volts "pushes" twice as "hard" as 110 volts. (Although typical United States voltage is 117 volts, the number is often "rounded off" to 110 volts.)

One analogy used to explain the three attributes uses the image of a water hose and a pump. Amperage is the amount of water (or electricity) available to pass through the hose to the pump. Wattage is the amount of water (or electricity) that must be pulled through the hose to power the pump. Voltage is the pressure at which the water (or electricity) is pushed through the hose.

Two primary types of circuits are used to distribute electricity from the source to the load. An illustration of a **parallel** circuit can be seen when several cliplights are plugged into a plugging strip. Two wires, a hot and a neutral, run to each bulb. Although all of the loads are connected to a single source, if one of the cliplights burn out, the rest of the lights will still continue to operate. This is the type of circuit commonly found in households and theatrical lighting installations.

A **series** circuit, on the other hand, is wired so that electricity "daisy-chains" and follows a single path that connects each of the lights to each other and the source. Like some common strings of Christmas tree lights, when one of the lamps burns out, the circuit is broken, and the other lights in the string no longer function. Although this type of circuitry isn't commonly used in theatres, an example can be seen in striplights using low voltage MR-16 lamps. Each lamp is designed to require only 12 volts of electricity, but the combined voltage of 10 lamps wired in a series circuit is 120 volts. The voltage is equally divided between the lamps. Just like the Christmas tree lights, however, a single burned out lamp results in the loss of the entire circuit.

The Electrical Path

To manipulate light in a theatrical setting, the lighting designer separately controls the voltage supplied to each electrical device. To provide this separation, each device has its own **electrical path**. Figure 1.3 is an example of the four points in the electrical path for an instrument in a computer lighting system. The four points are the device, the circuit, the source, and the control.

Electricity is supplied to a device, in this case, a **lighting instrument**. The electrical source is a **dimmer**, which regulates the amount of voltage conducted to the lighting instrument, is commonly connected by a circuit. A circuit usually refers to a **cable** containing wires that bridge the electrical gap between the dim-

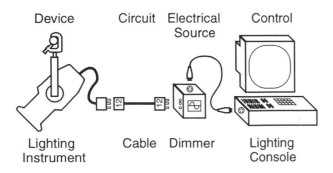

Figure 1.3 The Electrical Path

mer and the instrument. The dimmer allows the instrument's light output to get more or less intense. In this example, the dimmer is controlled by a computer lighting console. In general, **control** often refers to a device that controls the dimmer and is a requirement for every dimming system.

The electrical path must remain unbroken for the lighting instrument to receive controlled voltage and function correctly. Understanding each point in the path allows the lighting designer to properly control the electricity supplied to each device or lighting source.

Dimmers

Historically, direct current was the first type of electricity installed in theatres. The **resistance** dimmer, powered by this current, was the standard device used to control the voltage fed to lighting instruments. Dimmers were assembled in mechanical groups called **piano boards**, so named because their appearance resembled an upright piano. A typical piano board was constructed so that all of its dimmers could be controlled by a single overriding handle called a **grand master**. The number of dimmers required for a light plot directly translated into the same number of individual moving handles, which in turn would define the number of light board operators. The amount of control available to a light plot was often determined by labor cost or the amount of backstage space available for the piano boards.

The **autotransformer** dimmer was introduced as alternating current became more available for theatrical use. Although these light boards were comparably more compact and generated less heat, a separate handle still manually manipulated each dimmer.

Other types of dimmers were introduced, but they failed to gain wide acceptance. It was the innovation of the electronic silicon-controlled rectifier (or **SCR**), that was soon seen as the device that would replace both the resistance and autotransformer dimmer. Instead of being controlled by a mechanical handle, the SCR altered the voltage sent to the instrument by receiving low-voltage signals from a separate control device, which in turn triggered a relay within each dimmer. Not only did this mean that less space was required for the dimmers, but that many more dimmers could be controlled by fewer board operators. Initially, the SCR dimmer was controlled by manual preset light boards, which will be examined later in this chapter.

Modern SCR dimmers consist of a silicon-controlled rectifier, an "amperage rise controlling device," electronic controls, and a circuit breaker. Several dimmers are often combined into a single unit containing specific shelves (or racks) and internal wiring called a **dimmer rack**. A dimmer rack requires an electrical source to distribute power to the individual dimmers. Thick cables called **feeder cables** are often used to bridge the gap between a power distribution box, or PD (the line side) to a dimmer rack. Cables or wires then run from the dimmers to the individual instruments (the load side). Large circuit breakers or fuses protect the line side, while individual circuit breakers or fuses protect each dimmer on the load side.

Sometimes a light console is assigned to control electrical devices that cannot be dimmed; doing so can damage their internal electronic components. In these situations, some dimmer racks can be equipped with a device called a **non-dim**. Often inserted in place of a dimmer and controlled by the console, the unit is absolute. Any device circuited to the non-dim receives either full voltage or no voltage. Non-dims are often used to safely control motors or transformers.

Improvements in technology have reduced the size of individual dimmers while inversely increasing the complexity of the devices. Although a single light board can now control numerous dimmers, additional devices may also be required. Devices that translate the low-voltage signal can include "D to A's" (short for digital to analog converters), and other devices such as opto-isolators can be included to safeguard the electronics within the dimmers. An **opto-isolator** protects the low-voltage components from the higher voltage supplied to the instruments, and may also divide the control signal into multiple fragments. These additional devices should be treated with respect, since their exclusion or failure can result in nonfunctioning dimmers.

The control signal from the light board to these devices or the dimmers usually runs through relatively small cables. If the cables don't work, the dimmers don't function. As such, these small cables should also be treated with extra care.

When constructing a light plot, attention must be paid to the number of dimmers that will be used and their amperage capacity. When the number of existing dimmers doesn't provide the amount of flexibility required to produce a lighting design, circuits may be replugged (or **repatched**) during the performance.

Repatching will be examined in Chapter 6. Other situations may allow additional dimmer racks (sometimes called **road racks**) to be installed in the performance space for the show. Before any installation is considered, a knowledgeable electrician familiar with the space should be consulted.

Circuitry

Although instruments, dimmers, or electrical devices can be mounted anywhere, an electrical route must be provided to conduct electricity between them to complete the circuit. This electrical route is collectively called **circuitry**, and each separate route is often referred to as a single **circuit**. Circuitry usually consists of three elements: **Wires** conduct the electricity, **insulators** cover each wire to contain and separate electrical flow, and **plugs** installed on both ends of the wires make certain that the electricity in the wires is connected in the proper arrangement. The construction and diameter of the wire determine the amount of current it can safely carry, which must be larger than the current required by the load. If this basic rule is not followed, an overload will occur, and the circuit will be disrupted.

Plugs are constructed to either be male (conductors sticking out of the plug), or female (conductors concealed inside the plug). To reduce the possibility of confusion or electrocution, the established standard is to always have the female contain the source of electricity. In practical terms this means that instruments are always wired with male plugs, while dimmers are always wired with female plugs.

Circuitry is often broken into two categories, either preinstalled or added. **Preinstalled circuitry**, part of the permanent electrical infrastructure of a performance facility, is often contained in conduit and terminates at metal enclosures known as **raceways**, **plugging strips**, **plugging boxes**, **floor pockets**, or **drop boxes**. Some facilities are equipped with an intermediate point between permanent dimmer racks and preinstalled circuitry. These **circuitry transfer panels** allow the circuit's path to the dimmers to be interrupted and routed instead to road racks.

Since the hanging positions for the instruments may vary between productions, **added circuitry** may be installed. It often consists of cables that are plugged between the instruments and the preinstalled circuitry or dimmers. Cables usually consist of at least a pair of wires covered with insulation, but more typical are three wires enclosed in a single rubber skin or jacket with plugs at both ends. Several forms of cable may be employed to rapidly install additional circuitry in performance facilities. Initially, the path and total distance from each hanging position to the dimmers is determined (the "**run**"). If added circuitry is used exclusively to route electricity from an instrument to the dimmers, that cable is often referred to as a **home run**. If the electrical path between the dimmer and the instrument is broken, the instrument will not work. To reduce the opportunities for that type of separation, additional circuitry is usually assembled to include as few plugs as possible. A group of cables taped together is often referred to as a **bundle**, the plugs of which are labeled at both ends. Using bundles during installation means that the same amount of effort required to install a single circuit will instead result in the installation of several circuits.

In many cases the wire size of cables is large enough to supply electricity to more than one instrument. When two instruments are assigned to share the same circuit, a **two-fer** can be used to complete the connections. A two-fer usually consists of two female plugs connected to cables that join into a single male connector. When three instruments can be safely connected to a single circuit, a **three-fer** can be used.

It is worth noting that several different types of plugs are available for theatrical use. Although plugs allow for rapid connection of wires, they must be compatible with each other. If the plugs of additional circuitry don't match the existing plugs of the preinstalled circuitry, **adapters** must be utilized to bridge the gap.

A second form of added circuitry employs several groups of wires enclosed in a single jacket, known as **multicable**. Multicable can terminate either in several plugs at each end, or with a single connector. The plugs are then contained in a separate modular unit with a matching connector, called a **breakout**. Since multicable employs a single outer jacket, the overall size and weight of a length of multicable is much less than a comparable bundle, which makes it easier to transport, handle, and install.

The overall bulk of cable installed during a load-in can quickly increase the overall weight and dimension of any hanging position. As such, additional cable is often installed by initially being attached to the instruments at the hanging position. As the cable is installed, it's tied out of the way as much as possible. Following this method results in any extra lengths of cable being collected out of the way near the dimmers.

If there's any possibility that the placement of the instruments or the hanging position may need to be adjusted, though, an additional portion of the cable should be initially allocated to the hanging position. Otherwise, any movement on the part of the instruments or the hanging position may result in the addition of short cables to complete the circuit and introduce additional plugs to those routes.

Determining the paths and amounts of cable required for an installation is a responsibility typically assumed by the production electrician, since he or she is ultimately responsible for the installation, maintenance, and functionality of the lighting package. In many cases, enough circuitry exists that there's no need to know the number of available circuits at each hanging position. Other situations may require the lighting designer to be acutely aware of the existing circuitry inventory, since he or she will ultimately decide the final placement of the hanging positions.

Load Calculations

It has been said that all electrical devices require some amount of amperage to operate. If a device such as an instrument draws more amperage than a cable can handle, the result will be an **overloaded circuit**. In which case, the protective device, such as a **fuse** or a **circuit breaker**, should break the continuity of the circuit. If the total number of instruments plugged into a dimmer draws more amperage than is supplied to the dimmer, the result will be the same, but the entire dimmer may become disabled. Although the production electrician hypothetically checks all of the electrical demands required by the light plot, lack of time or knowledge may result in power problems that can result in a loss of stage time.

To ensure that scenario doesn't occur, **load calculations** are performed before a light plot is mounted. These calculations determine the amount of electricity required by the plot when every instrument is at its highest intensity. They are often performed as the light plot is being designed. Otherwise, one may discover that the amount of amperage required by a completed plot may exceed the amount of electricity available in the performance space. Although many different formulas and charts can be used to express electrical relationships, the power formula and a wire gauge chart are the two pieces of information typically utilized by the lighting designer to perform load calculations.

The **power formula** (or the "West Virginia" formula) is based on the three related attributes of electricity: amperage, wattage, and voltage. The formula, usually displayed in three variations, show the relationships between these three attributes:

$W = V \times A$ Wattage equals voltage multiplied by amperage. This arrangement is how the formula is often memorized (W. Va.).

$A = \dfrac{W}{V}$ Amperage equals wattage divided by voltage.

$V = \dfrac{W}{A}$ Voltage equals wattage divided by amperage.

If two of the factors are known, the third attribute can be determined by using these formulas.

The second piece of information is a **standard lamp and extension cord current capacity chart.** The American Wire Gauge (AWG) system assigns a number to each size of wire and establishes the amount of current that each wire size can safely carry. Most cable used for temporary theatrical circuitry is either #12 or #14 wire gauge. The identification number is often marked on the cable.

Wire Gauge	10	12	14	16	18
Amp Capacity	25	20	15	10	7

Although the rated current capacity for any wire gauge can vary greatly due to the type of metal in the wire or the number of wires in the cable, this small chart shows a generic sampling of wire gauges and capacities. A #12 (or 12-gauge) wire can safely carry 20 amps, while a #14 wire can only carry 15 amps. The specific wire gauges and capacities for each cable type employed should be determined prior to any load-in.

In practical terms, the power formula and the current capacity chart are two tools used by the lighting designer to make certain that no circuits, dimmers, or PDs can possibly become overloaded. Here are two examples of how the two pieces of information are used to perform basic load calculations.

Example 1: Is it possible to plug three 1000-watt instruments (or 3 kilowatts, or 3 kw) simultaneously into a single #12 cable? Multiplying the individual wattage by 3 results in the total wattage being considered (1000 × 3 = 3000 watts). Since the voltage is given (110 volts), the second version of the power formula is used. Divide 3000 watts by 110 volts, resulting in 27.27 amps, much more than the 20-amp rating assigned to the #12 cable. The answer is no; three 1000-watt instruments should not be plugged into a single #12 cable. Two 1000-watt instruments, on the other hand, equal 18.18 amps, and could be plugged into the #12 cable without exceeding its amperage rating.

Example 2: The dimmer is rated to handle 30 amps. How many 750-watt instruments can be plugged into that dimmer? This question could be determined in two ways. The first method would use the second version of the power formula to convert 750 watts into amperage, and then divide the 30 amps by that result: 750 watts divided by 110 volts equals 6.8 amps. Thirty amps divided by 6.8 equals 4.4 instruments. In theory, the dimmer could safely carry 4.4 instruments, but practically, it can only carry four 750-watt instruments. The second method would use the first version of the power formula to convert the 30-amp dimmer into wattage. Thirty amps multiplied by 110 volts equals 3300 watts. If that result is divided by 750 watts, the result is again 4.4 instruments. Either method arrives at the same result.

One rule of thumb often used is the general assumption that each 1-kw instrument is roughly equivalent to 10 amps. Based on that, a fully loaded 12-pack of 20-amp dimmers (2.4 kw) draws approximately 24,000 watts, or 240 amps. In another example, fifteen 1-kw instruments total 15,000 watts, or roughly 150 amps.

Whenever possible, checking the electrical loads on a dimmer system by the production electrician should be a double-check of prior calculations made by the lighting designer. If the lighting designer possesses a basic knowledge of electricity, he or she will be able to make certain that the designed light plot can be physically realized without on-site power limitations imposing last minute restrictions to the design.

Since electricity is the element that allows theatrical lighting to occur, it's involved in every lighting design. The lighting designer and all members of the lighting department must be aware of its attributes and the fact that it is dangerous. Electricity can cause injury or death. Knowledge, caution, and common sense are the basic tools that should always be kept in mind during any time spent on a stage. This text has presented some of the basic laws and principles regarding electricity, but other texts more closely analyzing this topic are worthy of examination.

CONTROL

Two general terms are applied in theatrical situations to the control of voltage to dimmers. **Manual control** implies physical movement of a handle, lever, dial, or slider to affect a dimmer. An autotransformer light board is an example of this type of control. The single physical handle directly affects the voltage supplied to an instrument. "Handle" has now become a generic term that can refer to anything that affects the intensity of an instrument. **Computer control**, on the other hand, implies an electronic interface with the dimmer rather than a physical one. In most cases the dimmers are affected by commands issued from a remote device called a computer light board or a computer lighting console.

Another use of the term "control" describes the numerical arrangement of the channels or dimmers that regulate the intensity of the instruments. When a light plot is constructed, the lighting designer decides which instruments will operate together, separately, and how they numerically relate to each other. Their arrangement is documented in a form called a **hookup**. The word "hookup" is an anachronism carried over from the days of manual road boards. The action of plugging bundles of cables into the dimmers meant the cables were being "hooked up" or "patched" to the dimmer boards.

The word is still used today, but when used in conjunction with lighting systems controlled by computer boards, the word "hookup" may also refer to the action of electronically assigning dimmers to control channels. This action is also referred to as **softpatching**. That's resulted in a "linguistic back construction" for the action of plugging the cables into the dimmers, which is now referred to as **hardpatching**.

As a result, a lighting system using a manual light board merely requires the act of hardpatching to provide control to a lighting instrument. The instrument is plugged into a cable or circuit, which is then hardpatched into dimmer 1. When the handle for dimmer 1 is manually brought up, the instrument turns on. With computer light boards, the same instrument plugs into the same cable. In this situation, however, that plug can be inserted into *any* dimmer, which can then be assigned to *any* channel. For this example, the cable is plugged into dimmer 2. The next step is to program the computer, instructing it that *dimmer* 2 should be assigned to *channel* 1. Now, when the computer light board is instructed to bring up *channel* 1,

channel 1 will instruct *dimmer* 2 to activate, and that same instrument turns on.

Since computerized lighting systems control dimmers electronically, it's possible for a single channel to control more than one dimmer. The same instrument is still hardpatched into dimmer 2. Another instrument is plugged into dimmer 3. Now the computer light board is programmed so that both dimmer 2 and dimmer 3 are assigned to be controlled by channel 1. Bringing up channel 1 activates both dimmers, and both instruments will be brought up together. Therefore, it's possible for any number of dimmers or instruments to be controlled by any channel. For the ultimate flexibility, every instrument is hardpatched into a separate dimmer, and then the dimmers are softpatched into any control channels.

Manual Control

Three main types of manual light boards are commonly used in today's theatre. Autotransformer and resistance boards (or piano boards) are similar in that they both utilize levers which are mechanically attached to dimmers. Manually moving the levers directly affects the amount of voltage passing through the dimmers to the instruments. On the other hand, a **preset light board** contains rows of sliders, knobs, or levers that electronically control the voltage passing through the dimmers to the instruments. Instead of a mechanical connection, the preset light board is connected to the dimmers by an electronic cable. Although the dimmers are controlled electronically, this light board is still considered a manual device, since controlling the voltage to an instrument's light can only be accomplished by a manual movement of some mechanism on the board. Usually each slider in one row controls a single dimmer. Each row (or preset or bank or scene) of sliders duplicates control to the same dimmer. Slider 1 in the top row controls the same dimmer as slider 1 in the following rows. While one row is "active" (controlling the dimmers), the sliders in the following rows are manually "preset" by an operator for subsequent lighting states (or looks or cues). Movement between lighting states is accomplished by "cross-fading" from one row to another.

Most preset light boards have a **scene master** that controls each row of sliders. The X and Y **cross-fader** determines which row of sliders is active. Some preset light boards have switches above each slider, allowing control of the dimmer to be separated from the X, Y, or scene masters to an **independent master**, which often supercedes the other masters. Almost all preset light boards, however, contain a **grand master**, which overrides all other control.

Computer Control

Instead of an arrangement of sliders on a manual light board, computer lighting consoles activate channels through sliders or by using keypads and software commands. The channels and other information about the light cues are often viewed on monitor displays. The intensity levels of all dimmers controlled by the channels are stored in recorded software units called **memories**. The consoles communicate this intensity information to the dimmers using a form of digital language or "protocol." **DMX 512** is one of the recognized standards in this form of communication, and is often the language used to communicate between consoles, dimmers, and other electrical devices.

Rather than cross-fading from one scene to another, the computer lighting console "plays back" different memories by loading them into a **fader**. Consoles often have the capability to assign a predetermined length of time to each memory. This **time duration** is the length of time that occurs when a memory is loaded into a fader. Many consoles contain several faders so that several memories can be played back simultaneously. Instead of independent masters, most computer lighting consoles have physical handles called **submasters** that control assigned channels. Software "handles" are provided on many consoles in the form of **groups** which can also control assigned channels. Most current software allows sequences of repetitive keystroking to be programmed into a single keystroke called a **macro**. All of these functions are discussed more thoroughly in Chapter 5, but the manual for any console is the most accurate source of information describing the capabilities of that particular light board.

Many computer lighting consoles can be equipped with additional devices to increase their flexibility. **Alphanumeric keyboards** can be connected to several consoles, allowing typed labels to be attached to a memory and providing it more identification than just a number. **Remote focus units** are small keypads that can be connected to the console, allowing basic tasks to be performed from a remote location. **Printers** are often seen as a necessity to provide hard copy of the information programmed into the console. **Off-line edit-ing programs** are software applications that provide the look and functions of specific lighting consoles to be mimicked on personal computers, thus reducing the time spent working directly with the console.

Computer Memory Storage

Computer lighting consoles are designed to store information about the memories and other functions on storage media including microfloppy disks, floppy disks, and hard drives. To utilize the capabilities of a computer lighting console, the lighting designer must have a basic understanding of how computer information is stored. There are two basic elements involved in computer memory storage. The first element is **random access memory** (RAM), where information can be changed, like thoughts in a brain. The second element is **storage media**, often a floppy disk or a hard drive, where information can be written down, like a book.

To change information in a book, the book must first be read. Reading the book transfers all of the information from the book to the brain. Then the thoughts about the book can be altered and changed in the brain. Afterwards, all of the thoughts, both old and new, can be written back into the book. If changes are made in the brain, but the brain sleeps before writing the changes back into the book, then all contents of the book will be forgotten. The brain must read the book again before the thoughts can be changed.

The RAM in a computer light board is much like that brain. To be able to change information in a computer console, the information must be transferred from the floppy disk or hard drive into the RAM of the console. Once the information is in RAM, the information can be changed or altered. After the information is changed it can be written back onto the floppy or the hard drive. If the RAM of the computer reboots, it's the same as the brain going to sleep. All of the changed information has been forgotten. Whatever information has been changed in the RAM since the last transfer back to the floppy disk or hard drive has been lost. For information to be written (or stored), it must be transferred to the storage media. This topic is discussed further in Chapter 8.

Computer Lighting Console Logic

Examining the methods and reasoning used to execute light cues on older light boards can assist in our understanding of the logic employed by modern computer lighting consoles. Initially, light boards were collections of dimmers mechanically controlled by a series of handles. A piano board, for example, consisted of several handles. Each handle controlled one dimmer. All of the handles in one board could be mechanically "locked in" and controlled by a **grand master** handle. When the grand master moved up or down, the other affected handles moved as well. The term "grand master" is now commonly applied to a fader that "masters" and overrides all other intensity output in a light board.

Every light cue on a piano board was achieved by manually grasping the handles and moving them at a predefined speed. As an example, if light cue 1 was recorded as dimmer 1 fading up to full in seven counts, then the handle for dimmer 1 would be moved to its final position in 7 seconds. If a light cue consisted of the movement of several handles, the movement of that light cue might involve more than one person. Typically the timing of the light cue was coordinated by one of the board operators who would count the seconds out loud to the rest of the operators.

After light cue 1 was complete, the board operators would refer to their cue sheets to prepare for light cue 2, which might involve a completely different set of dimmers. Some dimmers would fade up, other dimmers would fade down, while inactive dimmers would remain stationary through the action of the cue. The action of fading dimmers both up and down in a single action became known as a **cross-fade**. Rather than show the inaction of the stationary dimmers, the cue sheets would only list the dimmers in light cue 2 that had to change position. When the stage manager called the light cue, the affected dimmers would be moved in their proper direction to their new levels in the allotted time counted by the leader. The rest of the stationary dimmers would remain untouched, "tracking" through the light cue.

Manual preset light boards introduced a new way of cross-fading between light cues and a new method for the cues to be recorded. Preset boards consisted of rows of matching sliders, levers, or dials representing the same dimmers. Although there was still only a single dimmer 1, the control slider for dimmer 1 would be duplicated into each of the rows or scenes. A basic preset light board had two scenes. While the first scene (light cue 1) was active, the sliders of the second scene (involving the same dimmers) would be "preset" for light cue 2. When the stage manager called light cue 2, a single cross-fade handle transferred control from the first scene to the second scene, and the dimmer intensities moved appropriately up or down.

With the second scene now active in light cue 2, the first scene would then be preset for light cue 3. Before the sliders were preset for light cue 3, the operators would first move all of the sliders down to zero. By moving the sliders to zero, there was no possibility for errant sliders to be left active at levels from the previous cue (light cue 1). Then they would preset the sliders to match the intensities written on preset sheets. The preset sheets had to list the intensity of every slider to make certain that the preset sliders matched the written paperwork.

The thought processes shown in these examples provided the basis for the two types of logic used in today's computer lighting consoles. As a matter of fact, the original code name assigned to the Strand Palette lighting console was the "4PB6E," which was shorthand for "four piano boards, six electricians." The logic employed in the console design was an emulation of the actions and logic used to run those light boards. Both logics are based on the fact that "looks," or light cues, can be recorded by being assigned a memory number. When the GO button is pressed, a command is sent to the light board, which "loads" the memory into a fader. After the memory has been loaded, the handle of the fader can be used like a grand master. Typically, only one memory can be loaded into a fader at one time. Many light boards are equipped with more than one fader, so that more than one memory can be executed simultaneously.

Each memory or lighting state in a **computer preset console** is recorded as an individual snapshot like a manual preset board. The channel intensities are individually addressed in every memory. The **computer tracking console**, on the other hand, sees light cues like a piano board. It records the same memories, but will only alter channel intensities that are different from the previous memory. Unaddressed channels will track through the memory. For further explanation, consider this next example.

Five memories are created on both types of light boards. Channel 1 is brought up to full in memory 1, and is recorded at that intensity through memory 5. After all five memories have been recorded, the decision is made to reduce the intensity for channel 1 to 50% in all five memories. On the computer preset console, this means that each of the five memories will be accessed, channel 1's intensity will be reduced to 50%, and each memory will be re-recorded.

The computer tracking console, on the other hand, was programmed with a single command for channel 1. In memory 1, it was instructed to bring channel 1 to full. In the rest of the memories, the channel has been stationary, or tracking. To make the same intensity change, memory 1 would be accessed, the intensity for channel 1 would be reduced to 50%, and memory 1 would be re-recorded "**to track.**" Since the computer tracking console has now recorded a new initial (or hard) command for channel 1, it will track that reduced intensity through the following four memories.

There's a second function in a computer tracking console that separates it from the computer preset console. Returning to the five cues, it has now been decided that channel 1 will need to be brought up to full, but only in memory 3. To make that change in the computer preset console, memory 3 would be accessed, channel 1 would be brought up to full, and memory 3 would then be re-recorded.

That sequence could be duplicated on the computer tracking console, but after re-recording memory 3 "to track," channel 1 would track at full through memory 4 and 5. To confine the intensity change solely to memory 3, the computer tracking console is equipped with a function allowing the change to be re-recorded in memory 3 "**cue only.**" This command instructs the light board to not only record channel 1 at full in memory 3, but also to automatically revert channel 1's intensity back to its previous level in the following memory. After re-recording memory 3 "cue only," memory 4 would have a hard command to revert the intensity of channel 1 back down to 50%. Memory 5 would follow that command, and track channel 1's intensity as 50% as well.

A **hard command** (or **hard level**) is an intensity command given to a channel which establishes a point of tracking, as opposed to an intensity level that merely tracks through a memory. The hard command given to channel 1 in memory 4 initiates a tracking change in channel intensity. Once the channel's intensity is changed and recorded into memory, the hard command forces the channel to remain at that intensity through all subsequent memories until another hard command is encountered to alter the intensity level. In this example, channel 1 will remain at 50% until a memory is loaded into the fader that has a hard command, forcing channel 1 to a different level.

To create memory 6 as a fade to black (FTB), all active channels from memory 5 would be programmed

to 00% and recorded "to track" as memory 6, effectively stopping any tracking intensities. If memory 7 is then recorded, it will contain no active channel intensities, since no levels are tracking into the memory. The hard command zeros in memory 6 block the path of any intensity information that may be tracking from hard commands given in memories 1 through 5, and are known as **blockers**. To ensure that a memory designated as a "fade to black" doesn't later have intensity information track into it from prior memories, the FTB memory is often programmed with all pertinent channels containing hard command zeros. The FTB memory can then also be referred to as a **blocker cue**, since all tracking intensity information is being stopped at that memory.

This is a basic explanation of the logic used in the two primary types of computer light boards. Certainly, there is much more complexity regarding command structures than can be discussed in this text. Knowing the logic, command language, limitations, and work-arounds of a given computer lighting console can be critical to achieving a successful design. Understanding the differences can affect how the memories are constructed, stored, or manipulated. If there are any questions or unfamiliarity with a particular console, the advice is simple: Be prepared. Acquire information from every possible source, including board operators, lighting rental shops, or manufacturers, to name a few. Don't presume that the board operator will have a full understanding of or grasp the implications of actions taken while programming the console. If the lighting designer doesn't have a complete understanding of functions or commands, hours of work can be quickly destroyed.

Cues and Memories

The word **cue** has two meanings. It is often defined as a command (usually given by a stage manager) at a specific moment to initiate a specific action. It is also defined as the specific desired effect that is predetermined to take place as a result of that command. A spoken command given during a show, or a **called cue**, results in an action, or the cue, being taken. While other types of cues may occur during a performance to affect scenery, sound, or other facets of the production, a **light cue** often implies a change in dimmer or channel intensities from one "state" or "look" to another. When manual light boards are used, a completed light cue usually refers to a single arrangement of dimmers or channels to produce a single look.

When computer light consoles are involved, the unit of RAM containing a recorded arrangement of channel intensities is called a **memory**. A cue is a command that activates a memory. As computer light boards have become more commonplace, however, the distinction between these two terms has blurred. Nowadays, memories may often be referred to as cues.

When referring to light cues, nomenclature is used to identify the type of cue being discussed. Whereas called cues are initiated by the stage manager's spoken command, additional cues may be programmed to automatically begin without a second command. A stage manager's call book will list the called light cues, but there may be many uncalled **follow cues** programmed "in the background" to initiate additional lighting changes, preset moving light fixtures, activate special effects, or control other devices. Technically, if a follow cue begins the instant that the first memory completes its fade, the second cue is referred to as an "autofollow." Here are other names given to types of light cues:

- A **preset cue** often refers to the lighting state seen on stage prior to the beginning of a show or the opening of the main curtain.
- A **fronts up cue** typically adds only frontlight to a preset cue. This term is often applied to the first light cue called after the main curtain has been removed to begin a performance.
- A **fronts out cue** typically subtracts only frontlight from the previous cue. This term is often applied to the final cue called before the curtain flies in at the end of an act or a performance.
- A **base cue** is the name given to the first cue in a scene, upon which other less substantial cue changes within the same scene are made.
- An **effect cue** involves a programmed series of actions typically involving a collection of channels, which activate in a sequential pattern.
- A **fade to black cue** fades all of the lights completely out, resulting in darkness.
- A **blackout** is the same action as a fade to black cue, but the fade typically happens in a zero count (a bump).
- A **bow cue** is the look used during curtain call when performers take their bows. Though it may often be a copy of a cue seen earlier in the show, its main intent is to make certain that the faces of the performers can be seen.

- A **bow preset cue** is often used when a closed main curtain prevents the audience from seeing the performers move to their position onstage prior to the bows. It's usually the same as the bow cue, but without any frontlight. When the cue is active, no light is seen on the curtain.
- A **bow ride cue** adds frontlight to the bow preset cue when the main curtain opens for bows. It's designed to be piled onto the bow preset cue, so that it can be removed or added as the curtain opens or closes. When the bow ride cue is removed, the bow preset cue remains on stage.
- A **restore cue** is a copy of a previously used cue. One example may be seen during bow sequences at the end of a show, when the stage quickly fades to black, followed by the lights fading back up and restoring the same previous lighting state.
- A **postset cue** is the lighting state seen by the audience as they leave the theatre after the bows. This cue is often used when the main curtain is not closed and the stage is exposed to the audience's view.

There is also nomenclature for series of cues that occur close in time to one another:

- An **opening sequence** often begins with the house lights fading to 50% (or **half**) and ends with the lighting state that establishes the first "look" in the show.
- A **transition sequence** usually begins with the final cue of the first scene, and ends with the lighting state that establishes the second scene.
- A **final sequence** often begins with the first cue changing the last established look in the show, and ends with the bow preset cue.
- A **bow sequence** often begins when the curtain is raised for the bows. This sequence is often a combination of a fronts up cue and a series of blackouts and restores.

Computer Lighting Console Language

For many computer lighting consoles, spoken words or phrases are interpreted by a board operator and typed into a keypad to achieve the desired result. On many computer lighting consoles, a specific area of the computer monitor, known as the **command line**, reflects these programmed keystrokes as numerals or symbols as they are typed in (or "entered"). The command line provides a simple visual confirmation that the correct programming sequence of instructions has been executed. Although programming sequences (or **command structures**) may vary wildly between lighting console manufacturers to achieve the same result, many typographical symbols have been adopted as a shorthand for English words. Many lighting designers write their notes and corrections using this shorthand, so that the symbology matches between the written notes and the command line to confirm accurate programming modification.

For example, the ">" and "@" characters are often employed, respectively, to display the selection of a continuous range of channels and their intensity activation. If channels 1 through 10 are simultaneously activated, the ">" symbol is shown on the command line in place of the word "through"; the command line displays "1 > 10." If the same channels are set to a matching intensity of 50%, pressing the "at," "5," and "0" buttons often results in the command line displaying "1 > 10 @ 50." For the purposes of this text, the ">" symbol will be used to indicate any continuous series of numbers, and the "@" symbol will be used in place of the word "at." In another example, the "+" symbol is often used to represent "and" or "plus," while the "-" symbol is often employed to represent "minus" or "less." If channels 1 through 10 and channel 15 are set to a matching intensity of 25%, the command line might read "1 >10 + 15 @ 25." If channels 1 through 5 and channels 7 through 10 are all set to 70%, the command line may read "1 > 10 - 6 @ 70."

Depending on the manufacturer and model of computer lighting console, all of these command lines may successfully achieve the desired action. On the other hand, there will inevitably be the unique console that will not accept the structure of these commands. In order to understand and control the programming that is being reflected on the command line, the lighting designer must understand the language and command structure employed by that particular lighting console.

Time Fades

Understanding time fades is fairly simple. On a manual light board, the time fade assigned to a cue indicates the amount of time that should occur between the stage manager's call and the moment the fade is complete. Dimmers assigned to move in a light cue can be divided into two categories: dimmers that move up

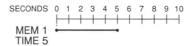

Figure 1.4 A Basic Time Fade

(an upfade) and dimmers that move down (downfade). Cues that are solely considered upfades are cues employed to fade a scene up from a darkened stage. Cues that are solely considered downfades occur when the lights fade out to complete darkness, a fade to black.

When discussing a computer light board, a **time fade** is defined as the duration of time that occurs between the moment the GO button has been pressed (to load a memory into a fader) and the moment the fade is complete (the memory is completely loaded). In most computer lighting consoles, every memory used as a light cue can be assigned a single time fade, which determines the amount of time that will occur for all of the channels to complete their movement. If memory 1 is assigned a 5-second time fade, it might be illustrated with a "time map," as shown in Figure 1.4.

The numbers across the top shows the number of seconds. The time fade of memory 1 is shown as a line with a dot at each end. The 5-second time fade starts at zero, when the GO button is pushed, until the fade is complete.

Some light boards have the ability to "**split**" the time fade. All of the channels that move up can be assigned a different speed than all of the channels that move down. If memory 1 is assigned an upfade time of 5 seconds and a downfade time of 10 seconds, most consoles would display that time duration as "5/10." Figure 1.5 shows a time map of how that time fade might look. Memory 1 is shown as a split time fade. Although the channels moving up still take 5 seconds, the channels moving down in the same memory take 10 seconds to complete the fade.

Waits and Delays

Understanding waits and delays can be a bit more confusing. Both of these terms also refer to durations of

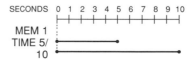

Figure 1.5 A Split Time Fade

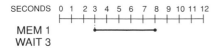

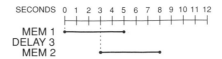

Figure 1.6 A Time Fade with an Assigned Wait

Figure 1.8 Two Time Fades with an Assigned Overlapping Delay

time, but they are separate from a time fade, and the definition of the terms change among the manufacturers of different lighting consoles. These additional time durations can be assigned to any memory used as a light cue. Consider two memories, memory 1 and memory 2, both assigned a time fade of 5 seconds each. On a generic console, for example, a **wait** is often defined as the amount of time that occurs between the moment at which the GO button is pressed and when memory 1 actually loads into a fader. The wait affects only the memory to which it's assigned. Figure 1.6 is a time map that shows the effect of assigning a wait of 3 seconds to memory 1. After the GO button is pushed, 3 seconds will elapse before memory 1 begins its timed fade. The overall elapsed time is 8 seconds. The value of this function is discussed later in Chapter 10 when part cues are examined.

A delay, on the other hand, always implies a "link" to another memory, usually the next memory in sequence. On a generic console, a **delay** is defined as the amount of time between the moment at which the GO button is pressed (loading memory 1 into a fader) and when the cue that it is linked to (in this case memory 2) automatically loads into a fader. The GO button is only pressed once to complete the two fades. Figure 1.7 is a time map that shows the effect of assigning a 5-second delay to memory 1. After the GO button is pushed, memory 1 immediately begins its timed fade. Five seconds later, memory 2 automatically begins its timed fade. The overall length of time for both cues to complete their fade is 10 seconds. In that example, the length of the delay was the same as the fade time of memory 1.

Figure 1.8 is a time map that shows the effect of assigning a 3-second delay to memory 1. After the GO button is pushed, memory 1 immediately begins its timed fade. Three seconds later, memory 2 automati-

cally begins its timed fade. The overall length of time for both cues to complete their fade is 8 seconds.

The terms "time fade," "wait," and "delay" can vary in their meaning, depending on the manufacturer of the console. Not only can the terms imply different functions between manufacturers, the terms can also have unique implications for different lighting consoles created by the same manufacturer. Though the semantics may be interchangeable or completely different, most computer light boards are designed to provide these functions. Knowing which terms apply to a specific console will affect the language the lighting designer uses while assigning durations time to memories. Since the semantics can vary between consoles, cautious designers often write definitions of the terms directly on paperwork they keep close at hand while they create the light cues to eliminate confusion.

LIGHTING INSTRUMENTS

The lighting instrument is a device typically containing a lamp that receives electricity to produce light. To provide the desired illumination, the lighting designer must be able to select the proper lighting instrument. That selection should be made based on knowledge of the different characteristics of each type of instrument. The characteristics of the instruments are determined by their individual components.

Components of Lighting Instruments

Theatrical lighting instruments usually consist of three components contained within a housing. These components are lamps, reflectors, and lenses.

The Lamps
Most modern theatrical lighting instruments produce a beam of light using a lamp as a source. Different lamps create different colors, intensities, and types of light. Modern lamps contain a **filament** and an inert

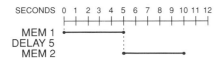

Figure 1.7 Two Time Fades with an Assigned Delay

Figure 1.9 This is an HPL lamp designed to be used in a specific theatrical lighting instrument. While this lamp can be "burned" (or turned on) regardless of its physical position, some lamps must be turned upside down (or burned "base-up") to ensure proper lamp life.

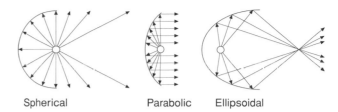

Spherical   Parabolic   Ellipsoidal

Figure 1.10 Spherical, Parabolic, and Ellipsoidal Reflectors

gas, both of which are enclosed in a transparent **bulb** or envelope mounted on a **base**. Electricity passing through the filament produces light. Not only does the base secure the lamp to the socket and conduct electricity to the filament, bases often prealign the filament in the proper relationship to a reflector within an instrument.

The two main types of lamps used for modern theatrical stage lighting are **incandescent** and **tungsten-halogen** lamps. Both of these types of lamps are manufactured in a variety of wattages and produce a range of color temperatures. Distinctions between the types and wattages of all lamps are designated by three-letter codes assigned by the American National Standards Institute (ANSI), which provides a system to identify different lamps produced by various manufacturers. Among other attributes, the ANSI code identifies the type of base, the wattage, the filament location within the bulb, and the amount of foot-candles that it produces. A **foot-candle** is roughly defined as the amount of light measured one foot from the flame of a single candle.

Often the design of a lamp is specific to a particular instrument. If the proper lamp isn't used, the light output may be hampered, the lamp may have a prematurely shortened life, or, in some cases, the lamp may explode. The proper lamp should be placed in the proper instrument.

In most cases, any oil, grease, or foreign matter left on the bulb can drastically reduce the life of the lamp. Any fingerprints or smudges on a bulb should be removed.

The Reflectors

The light that is created by most lamps is cast in all directions. Theatrical instruments are designed so that a lamp is typically contained within a mirrored reflector to direct as much of the light as possible toward the lens. Three different shapes of reflectors are used in theatrical lighting instruments, as shown in Figure 1.10.

The **spherical reflector** on the left-hand side of Figure 1.10 redirects light that would otherwise be lost in the housing back through the source toward the lens. Though not all of the light is efficiently used, the reflector dramatically increases the amount of light coming out of the front of the instrument. This reflector is used mainly for plano-convex and Fresnel instruments.

The **parabolic reflector** in the center directs the beams of light in a more controlled fashion. When the source is placed at the proper point, the beams of light reflected from a parabolic reflector are essentially parallel. This reflector often uses no lens to concentrate or direct the light.

The **ellipsoidal reflector** on the right-hand side is shaped like a football with one end cut off and a small hole for a lamp cut in the other. This reflector redirects light more efficiently than the first two and is considered the most efficient. The diagram shows that the beams of light cross in front of the reflector.

The Lenses

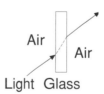

Air

Air

Light Glass

Figure 1.11 Lenses refract or redirect light. The amount of refraction is a result of the amount of curvature and thickness molded into the lens, and the angle of the light source in relation to the lens. Some amount of light passing through a lens is transformed into heat. Because of that, thicker lenses absorb more heat and are more susceptible to heat fracture. Lenses in theatrical instruments are constructed from either glass or plastic to control the beam of light created by the lamp inside the housing.

Figure 1.12 shows three basic types of lens surfaces. The **convex** lens on the left-hand side bulges out, while a **concave** lens in the middle cuts in. A convex lens cut in half results in a plano-convex lens ("plano" means flat), shown on the right-hand side. This is the basic lens configuration employed in most theatrical lighting instruments.

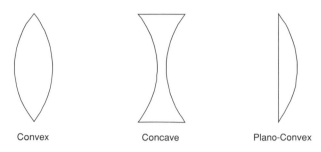

Figure 1.12 Convex, Concave, and Plano-Convex Lens

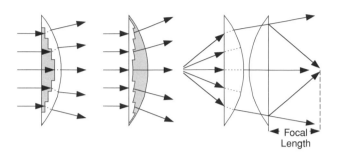

Figure 1.14 Step Lens, Fresnel Lens, and Double Plano-Convex Lens

Depending on its orientation to the light source, the plano-convex lens redirects a beam of light such that it either spreads or concentrates to a point. The left-hand side of Figure 1.13 shows light from a source passing through the plano side of a lens, equally spreading the beam. The right-hand side shows parallel beams passing through the convex side of the lens, which directs the beams to converge to a single point. In this case, the distance from the lens to the convergence point is often referred to as the **focal length** of the lens.

The left-hand illustration in Figure 1.14 shows parallel beams passing through a **step lens**. The shaded area represents the glass area that has been "cut away" from the plano side of the lens. Although the effect of the lens has been retained, the elimination of the glass has reduced the weight and the amount of heat absorption.

The center illustration of Figure 1.14 shows parallel beams passing through a **Fresnel lens**. The shaded area represents the portion of glass that has been "cut away" from the convex side of the lens. This type of lens produces a more diffused, softer edged beam of light.

The right-hand illustration of Figure 1.14 shows beams of light passing through a **double plano-convex**

lens system. In addition to light passing directly through the lenses, a convergence point where the beam crosses establishes the focal length for the lens system.

The Individual Instruments

Lamps, reflectors, and lenses are combined in different housings to create theatrical lighting instruments. They are generally categorized by type, wattage, and the degree of beam spread that is produced.

Figure 1.15 The **beam projector**, or BP, consists of a parabolic reflector mounted in a housing without a lens. The lamp and a small spherical secondary reflector, which blocks direct light from escaping the housing, move together on a carriage relative to the reflector. The carriage movement alters the size of the beam spread. If the beam is focused too wide, however, the secondary reflector blocks the center of the beam, creating a "doughnut" of light with a dark hole in the middle. BP light is often described as "shafty," and is typically used to create "sunlight." Controlling the edges of a BP beam can be very difficult.

Figure 1.16 The **plano-convex** instrument, or PC, is comprised of a housing containing a lamp and a spherical reflector. The beam spread is controlled by a single plano-convex lens mounted in the housing, with the flat side of the lens facing into the lamp. The lamp and reflector move together on a carriage closer or further away from the lens, allowing the cone of light coming out of the instrument to become larger (or **flooded**) or smaller (or **spotted**). The edge of the beam can be shaped using external accessories such as barndoors. The PC beam has a harder edge than that of a Fresnel lens.

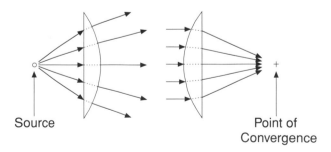

Source   Point of Convergence

Figure 1.13 Light Passing through a Plano-Convex Lens

Figure 1.17 The **Fresnel** instrument also has a lamp and a spherical reflector mounted on a carriage like the PC. Because of that, the Fresnel's beam spread can also get larger or smaller, and the edge of the beam can be shaped using barndoors. The main difference in the instruments is the Fresnel lens, which has a softer edge than the PC lens.

Figure 1.18 The parabolic aluminized reflector, or **PAR**, is a sealed-beam lamp like a car headlight. The filament, reflector, and lens are combined into a single unit. The housing, or PAR can, merely holds the lamp, color, and any external hardware. The size of the elliptical beam produced by the lamp depends on the type of facets that are molded on the lens. The light beam has "punch," but retains a soft edge.

Figure 1.19 The **ellipsoidal reflector spotlight**, also known as an **ellipsoidal** or an ERS, utilizes the ellipsoidal reflector and a double plano-convex lens system. Some versions of ellipsoidals use a single step lens instead of the double plano-convex lens system. The reflector inside the ellipsoidal directs the beams of light from the lamp to invert, or "flip-flop," before reaching the lenses. An opening inside the housing, known as the **gate**, is located close to this inversion point. The gate is where pieces of metal called **shutters** may be used to internally shape the edges of the beam. The beam can also be shaped with other devices, which are discussed in the accessory hardware section later in this chapter. The ERS design enables the instrument to project concentrated beams of light over an extended distance. For this reason, the instrument is often chosen to project controlled or shaped light over long distances. The lenses are contained in a tube, or **barrel**. Adjusting the tube, or "running the barrel," moves the lenses closer or farther away from the reflector, and the light beam becomes sharper or softer.

Figure 1.20 Although many ERS instruments are designed with a fixed beam size, some versions have the ability to change the relationship between the lenses. This allows the beam spread of the instrument to be altered while retaining the ability to shape the beam with shutters. These instruments are often generically referred to as **zoom ellipsoidals**. Since they can change beam size, they can be assigned to tasks that would otherwise be assigned to several different types of fixed beam ellipsoidals. Though applicable to a variety of tasks, zoom ellipsoidals typically have larger housings and are heavier in weight.

Figure 1.21 As lamps have become more efficient, the design of the housings have become smaller and more lightweight. This means that more instruments can be installed in the same hanging location without a massive increase in weight. Many of the newer instruments utilize a lamp equipped with four filaments, which often produces a beam output exceeding lamps of higher wattage while requiring less electricity. These features often make them more economical. Because the instrument produces a bright, easily shaped beam, the ellipsoidal is the chosen workhorse for many lighting designers.

Figure 1.22 Housings containing a row of multiple lamps are called **striplights**, whose main purpose is to create a smooth band of light. Striplights are usually internally wired to produce more than one wash of light from a single unit. Each wash, or **circuit**, is typically equipped with a uniform color. Changing the intensities of the circuits allows the different washes of color to be mixed. While striplights are often hung in a row across a batten, lighting backdrops or areas of the stage, they can also be placed on the apron and used as footlights. A row of striplights placed on the deck to light backdrops is often referred to as a **groundrow**. The size, weight, number of circuits, and types of lamps available in striplights are extensive.

Figure 1.23 Other instruments are designed specifically to provide light onto backdrops or cycloramas. Since this is their designed intent, they're often referred to as **cyc lights**. This illustration shows a four-circuit (or four-cell) cyc light. When plotting these instruments, the general rule of thumb is to provide one foot of distance between the cyc light and the backdrop for every foot of side-to-side coverage desired on the backdrop.

Figure 1.24 **Followspots** are used to highlight a performer or an area of the stage. Their basic design is similar to that of an ellipsoidal. The housing contains a lamp, a reflector, and a series of lenses. In addition to those basic elements, however, followspots are typically equipped with additional manual controls, including an iris (to alter beam size), a douser (to alter intensity), and the ability to easily change colors. The characteristics and methods of control are unique for every manufacturer. Since the light can move, followspots can be used to highlight any static or moving point of focus, but they typically require an operator to be fully utilized.

There are many other sources and types of instruments that can be utilized in any lighting design. Instruments containing metal halide lamps (HMI) produce a high color temperature beam of light, but require knowledge to safely mount the instrument and control the beam. Blacklights (UV) can be used to "pop" chemically treated colors on stage, or to provide eerie visual effects. Scenic projectors can project spinning patterns, moving clouds, flame, rain, and numerous other images.

Although specialized lighting instruments can be viewed as increasing the flexibility of a light plot, the devices can also increase the complexity of a lighting package. These instruments can produce exceptional visual effects, but they can also become a time-consuming headache if they are not installed or utilized properly. Trial setups and a thorough understanding of the components and their purpose can speed the time required for setup and execution.

Likewise, moving light instruments can be viewed as a simple solution to limited resources, since these instruments can be remotely focused, colored, and sometimes patterned. The addition of these instruments to a light plot, however, can add extensive complexity to any lighting package configuration and logarithmically compound preshow programming. Potential problems can be significantly more complex without an experienced moving light board operator. While they may initially be seen as a panacea for the lighting designer, the inclusion of moving lights to a light plot should be carefully considered. This technology is changing rapidly, and is sufficiently complex to be outside of the scope of this text.

Housing and Hanging Hardware

The housing of most lighting instruments is designed to shape or alter the beam of light, and is usually equipped with hardware to secure the instrument.

Figure 1.25 shows the different hanging and housing hardware terms for an ellipsoidal. Instruments are often mounted using a **c-clamp** assembly bolted to pipe. The c-clamp assembly includes a c-clamp bolt, a yoke bolt, and a pan nut used to secure the instrument to a hanging position. The c-clamp is attached to a **yoke**, which is a U-shaped bracket that wraps around the instrument. The yoke is compressed to the sides of the instrument housing by two **locking handles**. Not shown is a piece of aircraft cable with a loop at one end and a snap hook at the other, commonly referred to as a **safety**. Safeties are often connected to create a loop around the yoke and the hanging position as a precautionary measure.

Ellipsoidals contain specific hardware to shape their beam. A **template slot** is a gap in the housing, which is adjacent to the internal gate. Devices inserted into the slot internally shape the beam of light. **Shutters** are also contained within the gate, and commonly consist of four pieces of metal that can be used to shape the beam.

The front of most instrument housings are equipped with brackets of metal called **color frame holders**. These are primarily used to hold color media mounted in **gel frames**. They're also used as a mounting position to hold other external accessories which are designed to slide into the brackets. Housings that are designed to alter the size or focus of the light beam are equipped with a **focus knob** for that purpose.

Accessory Hardware

Accessory hardware includes devices added to lighting instruments to alter or shape the beam of light. Typically, they fall into two categories. Most accessories alter the beam of light after it has left the lens, while other devices can fit inside instruments to internally alter the beam. Internal devices are typically limited to equipment that is specifically designed to fit inside ellipsoidals. These include irises, templates (or gobos), and gobo rotators.

The left-hand illustration of Figure 1.26 is an **iris**. When inserted into the template slot of an ellipsoidal, the handle extending above the device can be moved to contract the size of the hole. This reduces the diam-

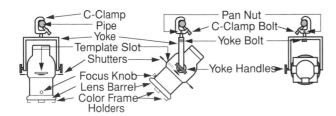

Figure 1.25 *Hanging and Housing Hardware Terms*

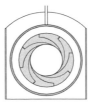

Figure 1.26 *An Iris, a Template, and a Gobo Rotator*

eter of a light beam while maintaining its circular shape. While many irises are built into ellipsoidals, other irises can be easily inserted into compatible instruments specifically designed to accept them.

Templates (or gobos, patterns) are thin pieces of metal with holes in them. When they are inserted into the gate of an ellipsoidal, light escapes through the lens of the instrument in the shape of the holes. Although templates can be made from aluminum pie plates purchased from a store, a wide range of designs in different sizes and shapes are available from several manufacturers. The center diagram of Figure 1.26 is an illustration of a Rosco Designer Pattern 7733 called Dense Leaves. Running the barrel of the ellipsoidal alters the edge of each hole to appear sharp or soft.

Templates can be combined with another device that allows the patterned light to move. The right-hand illustration of Figure 1.26 shows a **gobo rotator**. When the device is equipped with a template and inserted into the template slot of an ellipsoidal, the patterned light from the instrument spins in a circular fashion. Some gobo rotators are designed to accept two templates, which can then be controlled to spin in opposite directions in a variety of speeds.

Mechanical devices that attach to the front of instruments to affect the light beam include tophats, halfhats, color extenders, barndoors, donuts, and scrollers. The left-hand illustration of Figure 1.27 is a **tophat**, which looks like a piece of stovepipe attached to a gel frame. It is used to reduce **halation**, or scattered light falling outside of the primary beam of light. Tophats are also used when the lenses of ellipsoidals are focused towards the eyes of the audience. If a border is not used to conceal a backlight electric, for example, the first rows of the audience may be able to see the inside of the barrels through the lenses of the instruments. Although the instruments may be shuttered so that no direct light is hitting the audience's eyes, the first row may be distracted by the glints of light bouncing off the inside of the barrel. If a tophat is inserted into the color frame holder, the stovepipe

may mask the inside of the barrel from the audience's view, and eliminate that visual distraction.

Sometimes, however, a full tophat may not be a complete solution. Rather than looking at the barrel glint, the audience may instead be distracted by the portions of light bouncing off the inside of the tophat. The center illustration of Figure 1.27 is a **halfhat**, so named because half of the stovepipe has been removed. Once inserted in the color frame holder, the halfhat may block the barrel glint from the audience's view. The absence of the other half prevents any portion of the beam from being seen.

The right-hand illustration of Figure 1.27 is a **color extender**, which is essentially a color frame holder attached to the end of a tophat. The purpose of this device is to move the color away from the heat coming out of the instrument. Doing so attempts to retain the dye in the color media and reduce the need to replace burned-out color media.

The left-hand illustration of Figure 1.28 shows a four-door **barndoor**, which is often used to shape the light beams of Fresnels, PAR cans, or PCs. The design of many barndoors allows the entire assembly to be rotated after being inserted in an instrument's color frame holder, so that the doors can "cut" the beam to a desired angle. Since a set of barndoors can occupy all of the space provided in an instrument's color frame holder; some versions include a slot for color media.

Sometimes the ambient light produced inside an ellipsoidal will produce unwanted light outside of the beam. One solution used to reduce this halation is a piece of metal known as a **donut**, illustrated in the center of Figure 1.28. The outside shape of a donut is the same size as the color frame for an ellipsoidal. The centrally located hole in the middle of the donut is roughly the same size as the diameter of the gate inside the ellipsoidal. The donut is also used to "clean up" the beams of ellipsoidals that are equipped with templates.

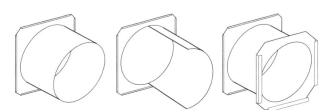

Figure 1.27 A Tophat, a Halfhat, and a Color Extender

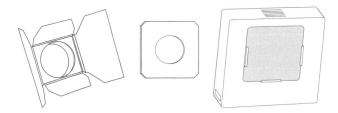

Figure 1.28 Barndoors, a Donut, and a Color Scroller

The right-hand illustration of Figure 1.28 shows a **color scroller**, which is a digital color changer. When inserted into an instrument's color frame holder, this device allows a single instrument to project numerous colors. Colors are assembled into a long strip (a gel string) and inserted in the scroller. The scroller is then digitally assigned to a control channel in a computer lighting console, separate from the channel that controls the intensity of the instrument's lamp. Altering the "intensity" of the scroller's control channel directs the gel string to move to different positions, exposing different colors in the gel string to the instrument's beam. The number of colors, along with the power components, control constraints, and amount of cooling fan noise, varies between manufacturers. Although color scrollers can increase the flexibility of a light plot, the lighting designer should be well versed in the additional computer programming these devices require before including them in a lighting design.

COLOR

In most theatrical presentations, color media is placed in front of the lighting instruments to change the color of the light beams. To effectively use this property of light, the lighting designer must have an understanding of the concepts and physical elements of color. Understanding color begins by understanding the physical nature of light and how we see it.

Light is the very narrow portion of the **electromagnetic spectrum** that is visible to the human eye. Light possesses several characteristics; it travels in straight lines unless modified by reflection, refraction, or diffusion. Light waves pass through one another without alteration; a beam of red light will pass directly through a beam of green light unchanged in direction or color. Finally, light is invisible passing through space, unless a medium (such as dust or mist) scatters it in the direction of the eye.

Color is merely different wavelengths of light within the visible portion of the electromagnetic spectrum, measured in units called nanometers. The span of the **visible spectrum** can be seen when white light is separated into colors by a prism. The "slow" visible wavelengths start with red, and increase their speed through orange, yellow, green, and blue, finishing with violet. Wavelengths slower than red include infrared, television, and radio waves, while wavelengths faster than violet include ultraviolet, X-rays, gamma rays, and cosmic rays. The human eye contains two specialized nerve cells in the retina called rods and cones. While **rods** in the human eye perceive light and dark, the **cones** of the eye are divided into three groups of receptors that are sensitive to red, green, or blue wavelengths of light. The cones are the cells in the eye that actually perceive color.

Defining Color

Hue is the quality that differentiates one color from another. **Primary colors** are defined as hues that cannot be created from any other colors. While the primary colors of pigment are red, blue, and yellow, the primary colors of light are **red, blue,** and **green**. The entire spectrum of color is often represented on a **color wheel**, which visually illustrates the interrelationship between the three primary colors. An equal combination of the three primary colors of light hypothetically results in white light. An equal mix of the three primary colors of pigment, on the other hand, results in the color black. The equal mix of two primary hues of light produces three **secondary** colors: Red equally mixed with green results in **amber** (or yellow), red equally mixed with blue creates **magenta**, and green equally mixed with blue results in **cyan** (or blue-green).

Complementary colors are often defined as being opposite each other on the color wheel. When two complementary colors of light are equally mixed together, the hypothetical result is white. When two complementary colors of pigment are equally mixed together, on the other hand, the result is black.

Color **saturation** refers to the amount of hue in a color mixture. A pale blue has much less saturation than a primary blue. The **value** of a hue is defined as the lightness or darkness of a color. The pale blue color has a much higher value than a dark green color. A **tint** is defined as a color of high value mixed either with white pigment or light, while a **shade** is a color of low value, mixed with black. A color mixed with both white and black simultaneously is known as a **tone**.

Color Temperature

Although **color temperature** can be confused with degrees of heat or cold, it defines color only, and is a comparative measurement of different wavelengths of light. A spectrometer is a device used to produce these wavelength measurements in degrees of Kelvin (K). The color temperature of a household incandescent bulb, for example, is much lower than the color temperature of sunshine on a sunny day.

When mixing colors using theatrical instruments, the typical objective is to begin with beams of light that are equally white before adding color media. Although all standard theatrical instruments produce beams that can be considered "white," the comparative color value between two uncolored beams from different instruments can be distinctly unique to one another. The quality or type of lamp, lens, and reflector alters the actual wavelength, or color temperature, of the light produced.

Equipped with two different types or wattages of lamps, the color temperature of light beams between two otherwise identical instruments can also be wildly different. For that reason, inventories may separate the same kind of instrument into groups defined by different manufacturers, wattages, or lamp type. Provided with this information, lighting designers often allocate instrument groups of similar type and color temperature to the same system. By making this assignment, they hope to achieve a uniform color temperature of light before any color media is added.

Color Perception

All people react to color, and each person's reaction to color may be unique. One person might find a particular green "comforting," while another person might find the same color "repulsive." Tests have shown that this reaction or perception may be either conscious or subconscious; people can have different emotional reactions to color without being consciously aware of them. Color used in theatre often attempts to capitalize on conscious or subconscious reactions held by the majority of a viewing audience to help telegraph the production concept or transmit the emotion of a specific moment on stage.

Color perception is also based on comparison. A blue paint chip held next to a red wall might be perceived differently than that same blue chip held in front of a green wall. Since color perception is variable, "warm" and "cool" light can refer to the tint and shade of colored hues relative to one another. It can also refer to the perception of that filtered light by an observer.

Light colored in the red and yellow hues is often perceived as "warm," possibly connected to firelight. Blues and greens, on the other hand, are often perceived as "cool," possibly connected to night. This basic perception is often employed as a guideline in theatrical productions. Comedy is warm and bright, while tragedy is cool or dark.

The color palette chosen for a lighting design can be affected by the genre of the production. While productions set in natural surroundings often employ a tinted or less saturated color scheme to reinforce the show's "natural" setting, the style of musical comedy or opera often uses a more saturated palette in keeping with the heightened nature of the performance.

Colors for light may be chosen to reinforce the color palettes employed by the scenic and costume designer. Filters can also enhance skin tone, subconsciously allowing the eye of the audience to watch an extended performance without growing tired. The colors chosen by the lighting designer can be emotional, symbolic, or iconographic, all selectively chosen to heighten the message being delivered to the audience by the action on the stage.

Mixing Color

Additive color mixing in light is the result of different individual hues being transmitted by the eye and interpreted (or "mixed") by the brain. The typical demonstration employs three overlapping pools of light focused onto a neutral or white surface. Each pool is colored in a primary hue: green, red, and blue. Where two colors overlap, additive mixing produces a secondary color. At the center point where the three beams overlap, additive mixing produces white light on the surface.

Another example of additive color mixing uses a piece of red fabric placed on the surface. The red light will make the color of the fabric more pronounced, the blue light will alter the fabric to some shade of lavender, while the green light will subdue the value of the colored fabric. The color of the light additively mixes to change the value of the hue in the surface of the fabric.

Subtractive color mixing in light is typically demonstrated by the insertion of any colored filter in front of an uncolored beam of light. The physics of color filters allows only their own hue to pass through the filtered medium. The filter absorbs all other wavelengths of the visual spectrum. When a beam of light is colored with a primary blue filter, for example, all other colors in the visual spectrum are absorbed by the filter and physically transformed into heat. The only wavelength passing though the filter is the blue hue.

If a second lighting instrument is focused to the same surface colored in the complementary color of amber, the additive color mix between the two pools would result in white light. If the same amber color filter is placed in front of the first beam of light already containing the blue filter, however, the subtractive quality of the amber filter will stop the remaining blue wavelength. The combined filters will stop all wavelengths of light, and no light will come out of the instrument.

Color Media

Color media often refers to anything placed in front of an instrument's lens that changes the properties of its light beam. In the past, color media primarily referred to thin translucent sheets, manufactured from animal gelatin or acetate and colored with dyes, that were used to color light. Today's color media, in addition to changing the color, can also diffuse, shape, or alter the color temperature of a light beam. Instead of a gelatinous base, the "body" of current color media can be made of glass, polyvinyl chlorides, polycarbonates, polyesters, Mylar, or "spun" filters.

The creation of plastic media falls into one of three manufacturing processes. In the first process, the hue (contained in a dye) is "surface coated" (like paint) onto a clear base. In the second process, the hue is "co-extruded" (or mass-dyed), which means that the hue is essentially sandwiched in between two clear bases. In the third process, called "deep-dyed," the chemical containing the hue is molecularly linked with the clear base. This means that the clear base is heated to open molecular pores in its surface, and then the dye is applied. The hue is "stained" into the clear base. Although many different materials are used for the base in colored filters, they're still often generically referred to as "**gel**." When color media is inserted in front of an instrument's lens, it is often kept rigid by being packaged in a gel frame.

Because all wavelengths of the visual spectrum stopped by color filters transform into heat, a more saturated color filter will absorb a greater amount of heat. Under intense heat, dyes "move away" from the hot center, resulting in a faded gel. Since the saturated color will get hotter faster, the hue of the color will comparably fade more rapidly than a less saturated filter. Saturated greens and blues absorb the most infrared energy, so they're the colors most susceptible to lose their hue due to heat. Technological improvements in lamp design have increased the intensity and temperature output of instruments. This has resulted in numerous tactics being adopted to reduce the amount of heat absorbed by the color media in an effort to retain the hue.

One tactic begins with color selection. Some color manufacturers suggest choosing filters that transmit high amounts of light in the 700-nanometer wavelength range. The nanometer range is shown in the spectral energy distribution curves included in most color swatchbooks. Other color manufacturers suggest reducing the intensity of the hot spot in light beams by altering the relationship between the lamp and reflector of ellipsoidals, also known as aligning the instruments to a "flat field."

All color manufacturers recommend increasing the distance between the lens and the filter, or providing airflow between the two objects. Sometimes this can be achieved by taping the color onto the front of a tophat or barndoor, or utilizing a color extender. Another practice commonly employed involves adding a piece of media between the lens and color media commonly known as "heat shield," which is constructed of Teflon™. Although some manufacturers claim that "heat shield" has a higher melting temperature that absorbs much of the convected heat, others contend that there is no significant drop in beam temperature when the material is added. If the material is added in front of the beam, air space must be maintained between it and the color media. Regardless of that debate, all agree that the most effective heat shield is a special dichroic glass filter. Dichroic glass products actually reflect infrared and ultraviolet energy away from the color filter, and also protects the color filter from convected heat. Since this form of heat shield is very expensive, however, a combination of the other suggestions is often employed to reduce the loss of hue in the color filter.

One difficulty often encountered with many ellipsoidals is achieving a barrel focus that produces an equally soft edge on both the shuttered and unshuttered portions of the light beam. Although the barrel focus can be adjusted to many different positions, in many cases a soft edge on one side of the beam will result in a sharp edge on the opposite side. Many different diffusion materials known as "frosts" can be employed that alter the entire edge of the beam to have an edge of equal softness.

Technology and innovation is so swift in this facet of the industry that keeping track of the changes and improvements is difficult. Although swatch books give some indication of the wide range of tasks that media can perform, experimentation by the lighting designer in the light lab or the lighting rental shop is the true test to determine accurate application and success.

THE LIGHT PLOT

A **light plot** is a map that graphically presents the physical components of a lighting design, showing the position and electrical assignment of all of the instruments and electrical devices used to provide illumination for a production, and their physical relationship with the other elements of the production. Although the actual physical equipment that is represented on the light plot can be referred to as the **lighting package**, it is often called the light plot as well.

In addition to identifying the type, wattage, and electrical assignment given to each instrument and device, the light plot specifies their location in the performance space and allocates a unique identity to each unit.

Construction of a Lighting Design and a Light Plot

The process of constructing a lighting design and the resulting light plot is individual to every lighting designer. One method, commonly and successfully employed, begins by a thorough study, research, and analysis of the script, the production, and all related matter. Visualizations are discussed in initial production meetings, which provide a forum for communication between the director and the design team, to cooperatively shape the emotional and physical concepts of the entire production. All of the concepts are eventually defined and embodied by the **production concept** and production meetings are held with the rest of the production staff to plan translating the concept into the reality of the physical situation.

Beginning with this portion of the design process, the lighting designer attempts to develop and express the visual objectives of the production concept utilizing the properties and objectives of stage lighting design.

Properties of Light

Virtually all texts agree that light possesses four controllable properties: brightness, color, distribution, and movement. The **brightness** or intensity of a light is directly affected by the contrast between that light and the surrounding environment. The surroundings may range from beams of light from other instruments to the relative color and texture of the objects being lit. The **color** of light can change the emotional perception of a scene. As an example, it's been said that warm colors are often associated with comedy, while cool colors are associated with tragedy. It is also often noted that desaturated colors are normally perceived as more realistic, while saturated or stronger colors are associated with more dramatic or stylized stage moments. The form, angle of origin, and coverage all refer to the **distribution** of the light. The speed at which any of these three properties of light changes from one moment to another is referred to as the **movement** of the light. The faster the change occurs, the more likely that it will be consciously perceived.

Objectives of Light

Most lighting texts also agree that stage lighting is said to have four objectives. The first is to **achieve visibility**. Since the eye is naturally drawn to the brightest point of a picture, a successful lighting design provides the proper visual focus for each member of the audience. It is often said that what can't be seen can't be heard, so the visual focus is often directed to the acoustic source, such as the speaking performer. Conversely, the lack of illumination in a lighting design deflects attention from areas of the performance that should not concern the audience member.

A single source of low-angle frontlight can result in a flat perception of the stage. Since most of what might be shadows is "filled in," all objects may appear to be compressed onto a single visual plane. In contrast, a scene utilizing numerous sources from a variety of angles provides a plasticity, or a sense of form and mass, which sets the performer apart from surrounding scenery. This is an illustration of the second objective of lighting, **providing illumination in a three-dimensional form** of light and shadow.

Visually painting the stage with intensity, color, and distribution of light achieves **composition**, the third objective of light. Any number of paintings created by the great masters provides demonstrations of successful composition. The successful integration of these objectives creates **mood**, the fourth objective.

The properties and objectives of light are used as the basis for the construction of visual images for a production. After the broad visual concepts of the production have been determined, the smaller components of the show can be defined. First acts, then scenes, and finally moments within the production are visually imagined. Various methods are used to record these "looks" or "snapshots" in a sequential order, so that they can be easily remembered or communicated. Often the method used is based on the medium of the performance. If the medium is music, looks may be noted in a score. If the medium is drama, on the other hand, ideas may be noted in a script. Sometimes the images are separately listed in a spreadsheet format, or the list takes shape in a series of sketches.

Once the looks are initially defined, they are then often listed on a separate document, allowing all of the looks for the entire production to be in one visual location. Each look is then broken down into the separate lighting sources required to create that look. The use of each source is considered, and decisions are made regarding the amount of stage coverage and intensity for each source. The source may need to be only a single instrument concentrated on a small performance area, or several instruments that wash the entire stage. The amount of coverage determines the number of instruments that comprise each system of light. Determining which portion of that coverage needs to be activated to achieve the mental images defines the amount and separation of control required for each system.

It is during this process that the mental images must be adapted to the reality of the specific production, requiring the recognition of the parameters that surround each show. There are many physical boundaries that define a lighting package, including the number of instruments, the amount of control, the other design elements, or the performance facility. Many other parameters can affect the final lighting design, which will be examined in Chapter 2. Designing several interrelating systems of light is achieved by combining the proper number of instruments necessary to provide the intensity, coverage, and control required to realize all of the lighting designer's mental images for the use of light in the production.

Constructing a Beam Section

The process used to determine appropriate instrumentation and properly position systems of light is another process that is individual to every lighting designer. Most methods are based on calculating the intensity or size of an individual beam of light from a given hanging position. These attributes are determined by drafting a **beam section**, which determines the actual throw distance from each instrument to its focus point. Once the actual throw distance has been defined, it is then possible to determine the size and foot-candle output of each instrument's beam pool. To create a beam section, the direct distance and the relative height between the focus point and the instrument in question should be known, along with the presumed beam and field angle of the instrument.

In the example of Figure 1.29, a beam section will be created for a 26° ellipsoidal located 28 feet, 0 inches above the stage, focused as an overhead sidelight. Constructing a beam section requires four steps. The first step, diagrammed in Figure 1.29A, shows the **direct distance** measurement made between the instrument and the focus point in groundplan view (33'-0"). The direct distance line also defines the viewing plane of the beam section.

Next, the beam section is constructed in Figure 1.29B; initially, the scaled direct distance (33'-0") is drawn as a horizontal line. The height of the instrument's **hanging position** (28'-0") and the **focus point** (5'-9") are lines drawn rising vertically from either end of the direct distance line. (The focus point height approximates the top of an average performer's head.) The line drawn between the two points is the approximate **actual throw distance** (40'-0") of the light beam.

The third step, illustrated in Figure 1.29C, begins by using a protractor to measure matching angles of 13° on either side of the actual throw distance line. Lines representing the instrument's **field angle** of 26° are then drawn as shown in Figure 1.29C. The distance between the two field angle lines is measured perpendicular to the actual throw distance line at the focus point (17'-0"). This distance is the **field angle**

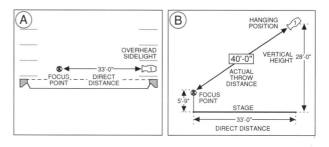

Figures 1.29A and B The First Two Steps in the Creation of a Beam Section

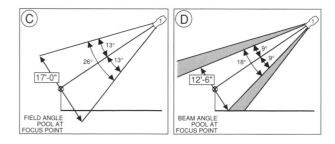

Figures 1.29C and D The Final Two Steps in the Creation of a Beam Section

pool that will be created by the 26° ellipsoidal at the focus point.

Once that distance is determined, some rules of thumb are used. One rule of thumb states that the pool diameter should be no greater than 15'-0", while another relies on photometric data from manufacturer's data sheets to determine that a light beam's intensity will be greater than 60 foot-candles when it arrives at its focus point. In this example, the photometric data shows that from a 40'-0" throw, 90 foot-candles will be produced by the beam, which is more than acceptable.

The fourth and final step begins by using the protractor to measure matching angles of 9° on either side of the actual throw distance line. Figure 1.29D shows lines representing the instrument's **beam angle** of 18° drawn through those measurements. The distance between the two beam angle lines at the focus point is 12'-6". This distance is the **beam angle pool**, or the inner cone of light, that will be created by the 26° ellipsoidal at the focus point. This means that the performer's face will be most brightly lit 6'-3" on either side (or upstage and downstage) of the hot spot of the beam. To provide proper coverage from the same angle and distance, conventional wisdom states that the next focus point should be no greater than 12'-6" away from the example focus point for the beam angles to overlap.

Beam sections are one method used to calculate the number of instruments required for each system or wash in the light plot. This topic is examined more closely at the end of Chapter 9.

Define Systems

Although beam sections are one tool used to determine the number of instruments required for each wash, defining the number of systems in any given light plot is often a situation involving give and take. One technique used during this process begins by categorizing the full stage systems of light in one column, and the partial or special coverage systems of light in a second column. The number of instruments and the way they are divided up into channels of control is determined for each system, often utilizing a combination of groundplans, sections, beam sections, and manufacturer's cut sheets to construct a preliminary light plot showing the contents and physical relationships of instruments in different systems.

In addition to those tools, graphic groundplans and a basic list of channels and their purposes allow the lighting designer to visualize the completed light plot. At the same time, spreadsheets show the distribution and usage of the instruments, the circuitry, and the dimmers. During this process, the need to retain discrete control over each instrument in one system may force the designer to group instruments in another system to a single channel of control. Providing enough instrumentation to achieve the desired intensity and coverage in one system may force the designer to reduce coverage and the number of instruments in another system.

After including all of the system and special components needed to realize the mental images of the proposed lighting design, the lighting designer may add spare instrumentation, dimmers, and channels to provide flexibility and the ability to rapidly produce unforeseen visual requests. Allocating and distributing these as yet unknown production needs is sometimes based on instinct, but anticipating requests is an attempt to support any conceptual or practical additions that might arise as the production develops and react to them in the shortest amount of time.

 ## Shelley's Notes: Avoid the Box

As the light plot construction process is nearing completion, experienced lighting designers build in a cushion to avoid constraint and provide flexibility. Assigning spare instrumentation and channels addresses these concerns within the plotting process, but allocating spare circuitry and dimming in a light plot should also be considered to allow some "room for growth." Discovering a lack of "reserves" in the middle of the rehearsal process forces reanalysis of priorities, taking time away from the actual realization of the design. Retaining a reserve avoids being "boxed in," forcing the lighting designer to constrain the design during the rehearsal process sooner than necessary. Having reserves means that when the need for another special is suddenly discovered, the structure is in place to add the special, rather than spending time reviewing the plot in search of equipment or a channel that can be stolen from another assignment.

Peripheral Lighting

In addition to all of the instruments and devices that will be used to create a lighting design, the light plot often shows peripheral light that may used in addition to, or instead, of the theatrical lighting instruments. **Worklights** may be included in the light plot, which are often controlled by switches on the stage manager's console, rather than by the show's dimmers. Not only does this allow them to be turned on regardless of the state of the dimmers, it also means that, in union situations, worklights can often be turned on without involving additional personnel.

If there's a possibility that the production will have blackouts or involved offstage activity during the course of a show, **running lights** may need to be included in the light plot. The term applies to offstage lights used during performance to provide visibility backstage, and may range from cliplights to lighting instruments dedicated to this function. If sidelight booms are used, small colored "golf ball" lamps may be attached to each boom and circuited to remain on throughout the performance. This means that the sidelight boom positions will always be seen, even in blackouts.

If the performance includes dance or the need for performers to know the location of centerline without referring to tape marks on the deck, **spotting lights** may need to be included in the light plot. These small lights are often placed on the balcony rail, at the back of the audience, or wherever performers need to "spot" their dance turns or orient themselves while facing the audience. To prevent confusion, spotting lights are often assigned a different color than the exit lights in the theatre.

An involved production may have several cues requiring commands given by a stage manager that occur in a remote location without a headset station. **Cue light systems** often use small colored bulbs circuited to a main switchbox at the stage manager's console. If there are several different types of cues, cue lights in different colors may be used at the different locations to identify the action.

Once the give-and-take assembly of the systems, specials, spares, and peripheral lighting has been considered and deemed adequate, the light plot is ready to be drafted.

THE STAFF OF A PRODUCTION

The role of the lighting designer exists within a framework of other personnel, and the designer must understand his or her role within this framework. Every production has a staff that executes specific tasks. Although the titles may change or the responsibilities

may shift from show to show, the tasks must still be accomplished.

The broad descriptions that follow are merely to indicate the general responsibilities and functions of each role. Depending on the level of complexity, detail, or the amount of time or money, the size of the production staff may increase, so that the individual responsibilities may be parceled out in a manner that ensures that each technical aspect of the production receives adequate attention. The actual allocation of responsibility and the amount of coordination between the positions are unique to every production.

The Administrative and Creative Staff

In professional for-profit productions, the administrative staff consists of, at least, a **producer** whose responsibility is to recruit investors who supply the capitalization, while the **general manager** oversees the collection and budgeting of those monies. A **company manager** is most frequently the general manager's on-site representative, and oversees on-site expenditures, box office income, and addresses any offstage needs of the performers or production staff. These responsibilities may be delegated to other members of the management staff.

The creative staff includes the **director**, **scenic designer**, **costume designer**, and **sound designer**. These people comprise the collaborative artistic core that creates and implements the production concept for the show.

The Production Staff

The **production manager**, who supervises all technical elements and stage personnel for the production, heads the production department. Because the production manager is ultimately responsible for the successful mounting of the production while adhering to the budget, he or she must have a detailed knowledge of each facet of the concept, design, labor, and scheduling of the show and, therefore, is usually responsible for creation and oversight of the production schedule.

The **technical director** is responsible for the overall on-site success of the production schedule. He or she oversees and coordinates all of the technical departments for each work call. To execute these responsibilities successfully, the technical director often works closely with the production manager to coordinate each element and the time framework involved.

The **stage manager** oversees the performers and coordinates their interaction with the technical aspects of the production. Whenever performers are involved in rehearsals or performances on stage, the production stage manager is in charge.

The **production carpenter** oversees all aspects of the preparation, installation, and maintenance of the scenic package, and supervises the carpentry crew. If the overall design involves equipment suspended over the stage, a **head flyperson** may be assigned the task of making certain that all goods that fly in the air are safely secured, balanced, and functional. If pieces of the scenic design or other elements will require square footage on stage, the **deck carpenter** oversees the assemblage, movement, or placement of those pieces.

The **production electrician** oversees all aspects of the preparation, installation, and maintenance of the lighting package. Often, objects pertaining to the show that require electricity, such as properties, may fall under his or her jurisdiction, or at least require his or her involvement. Not only does this include the elements of the light plot, it may also include peripheral equipment requiring coordination of the overall use of electricity within the performance space.

A **production properties head** is often hired to facilitate numerous tasks, principally overseeing the preparation and use of any properties carried by performers during the production. He or she may also oversee preparation, installation, and maintenance of any covering that tops the stage. Other tasks may include installation of equipment into the orchestra pit and the wardrobe area.

The **production sound head** is responsible for preparation, installation, and maintenance of all aspects of the show involving sound. This includes installation of the sound console, playback devices, amplifiers, and speakers for producing sound to the audience and all other areas that need to monitor the show. The production sound head is also often responsible for headsets and any visual communication, including cameras and video monitors. If the production involves live sound, microphones specific to each task must also be installed and maintained.

The **wardrobe head** oversees the preparation, installation, maintenance, and execution of any elements that cover the performers' bodies during a production. This often includes all clothing parts and any head coverings, but may also include makeup and coordi-nation of other elements used with costumes, including wireless microphones or storage of hand properties.

The Lighting Designer

The lighting designer is responsible for the design, implementation, execution, and documentation of all lighting and effects associated with the production. Along with the other designers, the lighting designer is responsible for the creation of the visual and visceral environment for the production. While dealing with the realistic limitations of time, space, money, or labor, he or she strives to provide illumination, assist direction of stage focus, and reinforce the concepts of the production. To achieve these goals, the lighting designer draws on many talents to produce a well-lit show. He or she has to have a passion for light, and be a combination of artist and realist, seeing what could be, while being aware of what will be required to produce it. The lighting designer often needs to simultaneously utilize several skills:

- Collaborate on the production concept and conceptualize the part lighting will play in the performance.
- Analyze, direct, and realize concepts in light that reinforce the production concept.
- Visualize the images and colors based on the concept and work with the other designers.
- Communicate; be able to express lighting ideas using verbal or graphic skills. Be able to listen, to understand ideas, and to respond to them.
- Coordinate and orchestrate the lighting with the other production elements.
- Make certain the lighting can be accomplished within the existing parameters.

THE PRODUCTION SCHEDULE

The document that details the order and predicted amount of time required for activities involved in producing a theatrical presentation is called a **production schedule**. A typical production schedule may include many production meetings and deadlines that take place over the course of several months. This text, however, is principally directed towards the period of time in the life of a production that begins when work concerning the show begins on the stage, and ends with the beginning of the first performance. This relatively small period of time between those two finite moments is defined as **stage time.**

The events that have to take place during stage time differ for every production. Although the name, sequence, and amount of time required for each activity can vary, in almost all cases the basic events that must take place to mount any production are universal. Stage time usually officially begins with the period of time solely devoted to unloading all of the technical equipment related to the production into the performance space. Although there are many other titles given to this initial period of time, for the purposes of this text, it will be called the **load-in.** (When equipment is transported to the space from remote locations, it is "loaded in"). The load-in continues in periods of time known as **work calls** until all of the components are assembled and "preset" in the locations where they'll be used during the production.

The production schedule is often constructed so that initially any goods that will eventually live in the air above the stage are assembled, attached to the battens of the fly system, and "flown out" into the air and out of the way. While the carpentry department hangs these scenic goods, the electrics department mounts the instruments, electrical devices, and cable onto battens. This process is usually referred to as **hanging the plot** or just **the hang.** Once the instruments for an entire hanging position have been mounted and circuited, the functionality of each instrument's electrical path is checked or "**hot tested**" to determine and solve any problems.

At an appropriate time during or after the installation of the overhead equipment, the stage is usually cleared, swept, and then often topped with a deck, canvas, or vinyl covering generically referred to as the performance surface. Once the performance surface is in place, the stage can be used again as a work area. Additional scenery and properties are assembled and stored. Through this entire process, the sound equipment is distributed to its proper locations throughout the theatre, after which it is connected and tested.

Once the overhead equipment is installed, a period of time is spent placing the goods and electrics in their performance positions. Each piece is either shifted to a predetermined height above the stage or visually sighted from a viewpoint in the audience, establishing its proper relationship to the other goods in the air. This process of adjusting the scenery and electrics to performance positions is often referred to as "**setting the trims.**" The "**trim height**" is usually de-

fined as the vertical height required to produce the necessary beam spread and focus range of the instruments, or the adjustment made to flying goods so that the audience views the desired stage picture. Often trim heights are established so that the masking prevents the audience from seeing the instruments in the overhead electrics. Once the proper performance "trims" are established, their locations are marked so they can be moved when need be and subsequently returned to their performance positions. This activity is known as "spiking the trims."

Once the overhead goods and electrics are trimmed and spiked, the **focus session** takes place. This period of time is dedicated to pointing the light beam of each instrument to a location on the stage or onto scenic elements. While the focus session occurs, scenery or properties involved in the focus may be placed on the performance surface and their locations marked (or "spiked") as well. Offstage of the playing area, storage positions for scenery and properties are established, and the backstage area is cleaned.

After the instruments are focused, a separate period of time is dedicated to creating the light cues that will be used during the performance, often called the **light cue level setting session.** The lighting designer sits at the production table and constructs each "look" for the show. Once the light cues are created, the scenery placed, the performance surface installed, the sound cues set, the headsets and monitors operational, and the backstage area clean and clear, the space is deemed safe, and performers are introduced to the space.

During the **technical rehearsal,** or the **tech,** performers and production elements are added to the stage and the timing of every technical cue is established. Once the sequence and flow of the show has been determined, costumes, makeup, and wigs are added to complete the stage picture, a period of time known as the **dress rehearsal,** or the **dress.** Following the final dress rehearsal, the house is cleared of all equipment in preparation for the audience. Before the show, the preshow checks and presets are completed, and then the production is presented to an audience (the **performance**). In many cases, the initial performances are called **previews,** which allow the director and the designers an opportunity to view the completed production with an audience, and make adjustments to the show. Finally, a performance is given for an audience that includes invited critics who then review the show (the **opening**).

Though the amount of time and the sequence of these events may vary from show to show, some form of each of these fundamental activities is usually required to produce a theatrical presentation. In some cases, activities may overlap; it may be possible to set trims while the performance surface is being installed. In other cases, the time and order of each activity must be discrete; the focus session must occur first, before the cue level setting session can take place.

SUMMARY

This concludes a review of the various physical and conceptual elements that form the basic framework of practical knowledge required. The next step is to examine how this basic framework and the creation of a lighting design interacts with variables specific to each production.

2 Define the Parameters

In the creation of any lighting design, there is a specific point at which the conceptualizations and concepts are defined, and the actual construction of the light plot begins. Before any decisions or judgments are made regarding the physical nature of the light plot, however, the harsh instruction of experience strongly suggests that the lighting designer should analyze the different elements that surround any production and define the parameters within which he or she must work. This chapter discusses in some detail several perceived parameters and the ramifications that can occur if they are ignored.

Determining the unique physical, conceptual, and financial limits of any production will prevent assumptions from being made that may later be realized as critical errors in judgment. Decisions based on ignorance create compound problems that didn't need to exist in the first place. Determining the parameters of any given production recognizes its realities, and will reduce the effort expended in redoing tasks that were planned or performed before the parameters were defined.

Another way of saying this is: Ask questions. If there's information that's unknown, don't patiently wait for the information to arrive. Ask. Although, defining the parameters sets limitations, it also introduces structure and saves time. Knowledge and preparation are two basic tools that prevent on-site judgments from becoming erroneous snap decisions.

First, it is important to define the expectations and obligations of the lighting designer. In a professional setting, this is expressed in a **contract,** which informs the lighting designer about the responsibilities that will be assigned and what to expect in return.

The production will also be defined by the **budget,** which outlines the size of the production staff and the number of additional people employed to mount the lighting package and run the show. It states the number of hours projected to complete the work, and defines the amount spent on the rental and purchase of lighting equipment. If the production has to travel, the budget also states the costs to house, transport, and feed the production staff.

The **type** or **size** of the production affects the lighting package. The **origin** of the show, whether it is an original presentation or a remount of a prior production, can affect how the light plot is designed. The **movement** of the production, whether it's a tour or a transport to a single theatre, affects the design and flexibility of the lighting package. The cubic limitations of the **mode of transport** may affect the size and preparation methods employed to create the lighting package.

The parameters provided by the **production facility** often constrain the size, preparation, or placement of the components of the light plot. An examination of the existing **house lighting system** will define the amount of additional equipment that may be required. Information about the **house light board** allows the lighting designer to judge its suitability to the lighting package. The **production schedule** influences the lighting package, especially if insufficient time is available for its preparation.

Successfully creating a lighting design while recognizing the parameters is a challenge. Knowing

36

what questions to ask, and how to ask them, is the first step.

DEFINE THE CONTRACT

Regardless of whether the agreement is through a union or is merely a written letter of agreement, the basic elements of a contract must be defined. Every unspoken assumption can open the door to misunderstanding, which can lead to conflict. Ideally, the contract is the first order of business that is addressed. Some unions, on the other hand, require their members to file the contract before any work can begin. From this perspective, all other agendas regarding the production are usually delayed until a mutual agreement has been clarified. At least two copies of that agreement are signed, so that the lighting designer retains a copy.

The first part of a lighting design contract usually defines the dates of employment. Typically, there are at least two of them: the date the contract is signed, and the date on which the show opens to a paying public. The second part of the contract states the compensation (the money) and explains how and when it will be paid. Union agreements often break the fee into thirds. The first third is paid upon signing the contract. The second third is paid when the plot and support paperwork are submitted. The final payment is made on opening night. Non-union work, on the other hand, is often handled in a single payment, or broken into weekly checks.

The third part of a contract often addresses other monetary issues. If the show opens in a city that is remote to the lighting designer's home, the topics of housing, transport, and per diem need to be addressed. Other discussions should include ownership of the light plot, insurance, liability, arbitration, union payments, benefit payments, and how the income will be reported to the government. In some cases, royalties and the right of first refusal are also discussed.

Other money issues that should be discussed include petty cash, which is typically defined as "usual and customary expenses incurred by the lighting designer related to the production." This discussion should also include the method and speed of reimbursement or advancement of those monies. Typical items that fall under the heading of petty cash include phone bills, fax bills, shipping and overnight delivery expenses, transport to and from meetings, duplicating costs (photocopy and blue lines), and tools or perishables that will then belong to the production.

Occasionally, assistants are required. The discussion may include the length of their contract, the amount of money they'll be paid, the payment of their union benefits, and reimbursement for any out-of-town expenses they incur.

For the agreed-on compensation, the contract usually states that the lighting designer is responsible for the following:

- Provide a finished light plot, all support paperwork, and any additional drawings to complete special electrical construction.
- Adhere to the lighting budget.
- Monitor the stage progress, direct focus, set lighting levels, and attend all technical rehearsals, dress rehearsals, and production meetings.
- Establish and adhere to the schedule and deadlines for the lighting department.

DEFINE BY THE BUDGET

One of the primary factors that will define the size and shape of the lighting package is the budget, which defines the amount of money allocated toward the rental or purchase of lighting equipment. The budget is usually in place before the lighting designer is engaged. Though an incredible light plot can be generated ignoring this parameter, the lighting budget will typically not be expanded to allow that plot to be realized. Additional time will be wasted in reanalyzing and regenerating an abridged version of the lighting design.

On the other hand, if the theatre has an existing inventory, the lighting designer should consider incorporating that equipment into the light plot. Investigations made to determine the accurate amount and quality of the house inventory will allow the lighting designer to make an informed choice as to its use. If the decision is made to exclude the house equipment from the lighting package, the reasons leading to that choice should be reported to the lighting designer's employer. Ignoring a minimal or substandard inventory may seem insignificant to the lighting designer when compared to the overall scope of the project, but dismissing the use of existing equipment without investigation may taint the employer's perception of the lighting designer's ability and intent. If the reasons for this action aren't properly communicated, it may be interpreted that the lighting designer has no interest in adhering to the budget, and isn't striving to reduce the overall cost of the production.

Additional financial limits that may affect the size of the lighting design relate to labor. The budget's creator and the production manager have presumably determined the number of bodies that will staff the production. A portion of that staff will be the size and the length of contract for the electrics department, which includes the production electrician and any assistants. Some light plots may be small enough to warrant only a production electrician. As the size and complexity of the lighting package increases, however, the need for additional support personnel employed by the production to service the package may be magnified. If the lighting package will be rented from a lighting rental shop, the entire electrics department (or at least the production electrician) should be on salary to participate in the preparation of the lighting package. Another question of labor relates to the number of electricians that will be contracted for each performance. If the director wants followspots, for example, providing the instruments may have no impact on the design. If no money has been allocated for followspot operators, however, this contradiction must be resolved before the final version of the design can be produced.

One portion of the budget may address the issue of perishables or consumables. In a broad sense, these are any items that, once opened or altered, cannot be returned. Common examples include color media or templates. Once the sheet of color has been cut, or the template burned inside the instrument, it belongs to the show. Perishables can also include scene machine disks, color scroller gel strings, fluids or powders used in special effects, and spare lamps. Some lighting shops expand the definition of perishables to include worklights, special types of adapters, or specialized hardware. Defining what falls under the category of perishables eliminates one possibility of unanticipated costs.

DEFINE BY TYPE AND SIZE OF PRODUCTION

The type of presentation can affect the size of the design, the lighting package, and the size of the staff. Knowing the size or type of presentation involved can provide an immediate grasp of the amount of lighting equipment that will be required. Labels placed on productions can immediately assist with an understanding of the scope of a project. For example, "Broadway," "Off-Broadway," "National Tour," or "Regional Theatre" are all labels that have different connotations as to the physical size, the length of production schedule, the mode of transport, and the budget involved for each type of production. If nothing else, a short description of the size of the performance space can be used to convey the amount and type of equipment that may be required. If the production is a small jazz concert on a 30-square-foot outdoor stage seen by 200 people, for example, the size of the light plot can reflect that intimacy. If the jazz concert is to occur on an 80-foot-square stage with an audience of 5000, the amount and type of equipment necessary to provide visibility for the performance space will be completely different.

A musical, for example, usually implies a large cast of performers. Directing the focus of the audience to the proper performers during group scenes immediately suggests followspots and the electricians to operate them. The musical form often involves representing several different locations, which requires additional lighting equipment that might not be needed in a less complex presentation. A realistic drama, on the other hand, may not require the use of followspots to direct focus, but the scenic design may require more individual hanging positions to provide illumination, or successfully reinforce the time of day. The complexity of the scenery could potentially increase the amount of time and money required for proper installation of the lighting package.

DEFINE BY ORIGIN

If the show is an original production, rather than a revival, the lighting package will need to be adaptable. Being able to rapidly react to sudden requests may be essential, so the light plot must be constructed with as much flexibility as possible. If a production is being remounted, on the other hand, the need to respond to change should not be as severe. In that case, the challenge is to regenerate the "looks" of the production. Sometimes, however, a remount may open the door for "improvements." Being asked to "improve" the existing show can imply many things. Reinventing the wheel can be very expensive. Be certain that the director requests the change and the employer approves any additional costs that may result.

If the production is to have a life following its present incarnation, more time may be required to produce accurate, precise documentation archiving the different aspects of the show. Creating that archival packet may need to occur as the production is mounted, requiring additional assistance to record the evolution of each lighting element.

DEFINE BY MOVEMENT

A production planning to load-in to a single venue can be tailored to that specific theatre. On the other hand, if the show will be touring to several different locations, the flexibility of the lighting package may need to be emphasized. The equipment assigned to different hanging positions may need to quickly and simply shift or adapt to each performing facility. The number of dimmers included in the lighting package may need to be greater than required by the light plot, so that existing circuitry within each performance facility can be incorporated into the lighting package.

DEFINE BY MODE OF TRANSPORT

If the lighting package is transported from a remote site to the performance facility, the type of transportation can affect the size or configuration of the light plot. If a small truck has been allocated to transport the entire plot, for example, its cubic size may determine the size and scope of the lighting package. If one truck is utilized for several loads of equipment, the package will need to be prioritized, so that the proper equipment arrives on site in the proper sequence. On the other hand, to maintain the production schedule, the time allowed for transportation of the equipment may force the size of the lighting package to be reduced.

If the production will be performed in several different venues, the cubic size of the transport may constrain the lighting package. If the lighting package won't physically fit into the mode of transport, some portion of the design will be left sitting on the loading dock.

DEFINE THE PERFORMANCE FACILITY

The performance facility can affect a lighting package in many ways. The size, shape, and permanent features of the facility must be recognized, since it often forces an adaptation to the design. Choosing to ignore the spatial limitations of a performance space, for example, could result in an attempt to fit 15 overhead electrics into a stage possessing 20 feet of depth. This would be viewed by many as an example of overkill, or a desire to be added to the quixotic lighting hall of fame. Acquiring information about the spatial dimensions of any performing space, prior to the inception of a design, allows the lighting designer to make informed choices that won't require reevaluation. Obtaining data about the existing electrical infrastructure allows the designer to accurately determine the amount of existing equipment that can be used to complete the lighting package.

If access from the street to the stage of a performing facility is a labyrinth, the preparation of the light plot may be affected. Though mounting individual instruments may be seen as a slower means of hanging the plot, prehung units on bars or trusses may consume even more time being transported via alternate routes to the stage. If the latter method isn't reflected in the production schedule during the load-in, time constraints may ultimately affect the success of the lighting design.

Presumably the facts about the performance facility are cataloged in a packet of information referred to as the **technical specifications**, or "**tech specs**." Although most facilities update the information on a regular basis, the possibility always exists that the data may be out of date. Each piece of information accepted on face value without confirmation has the possibility of being the single item that could potentially hinder the success of any design. Verbal confirmation of the facts by a technical representative from the facility will allow the lighting designer to construct a lighting design based on fact, not fiction.

Some form of groundplan and section usually accompanies the tech specs. The scale used to produce these drawings often involves the percentage of reduction provided by a photocopy machine, making them impossible to be traced in a scaled drafting. The reason for this is simple; in most cases, the initial purpose of technical specifications is to provide potential clients with information about the facility so they can analyze the suitability of that facility for their particular presentation. With that in mind, the reduced drawings are included merely to give a general indication of the facility's dimensions. To reduce effort and cost, scaled drawings are often not included in the generic package of information. A phone call to the technical representative of the performing facility is often all that is required to acquire scaled draftings of the facility.

Effort made to acquire these scaled drawings before the light plot is drafted can pay unexpected dividends. Study of the scaled draftings may alert the lighting designer to discrepancies between them and the facts listed on the tech specs. This might lead to the discovery, for example, that the length of the battens is much shorter than originally thought. That simple typographical mistake could potentially disrupt the plot's installation during a constrained amount of time. Discovery of the error before committing to a course of action means that the design can be adjusted to the space before the load-in, rather than in the middle of it.

Whenever possible, an on-site visit to the performance facility should be part of the lighting designer's initial agenda. If that's not geographically possible, an extended conversation with the house electrician may clarify any misunderstandings that could be made about the facility. If needed, additional drawings, pictures, videotape recordings, or sketches may provide greater understanding about complex physical relationships of elements in the space.

☑ A Basic Checklist to Consider That May Assist the Definition of the Performance Facility:

- The type of theatre: proscenium, thrust, arena, outdoors, or other. The number of seats may also assist understanding the scope of the facility.
- The height and width of the proscenium. For thrust or arena, the size of the playing area.
- If there is a main curtain, its location relative to plaster line. Does it part in the center as a draw curtain, rise up as a guillotine curtain, or combine the movement, like a tableau curtain? What is the speed of the movement from full open to full close, in seconds? If the main curtain's action is guillotine, does it have a split in the middle for performers to pass through during bows?

- The depth of the stage, from plaster line to the last lineset, to the back wall, to the front edge of the apron.
- The width of the stage, indicated in the distance from centerline to each side wall. Any interesting architectural challenges, either on the stage or in the air. The location of any traps or lighting troughs in the deck.
- The location of the sight lines in the audience (if not indicated on the draftings of the facility; this information is required to determine accurate electric and border trims).
- The identity of all front of house lighting positions, and the number of balconies.
- The type of fly system, along with the number, length, and location of the battens. The load limit above batten weight (which will determine the number of instruments possible on each batten). If not a fly system, the pipe or catwalk layout over the stage. The accessibility and hanging methods to same.
- The size, numbers, and condition of the house soft goods; legs, borders, blackout drops, or backings. (If the show plans to use the house masking goods, it's critical to know the height of all of the legs. This will directly affect the height of the border trims.)
- Anything specific to the production; an alternate crossover other than the upstage portion of the stage, booms that need to be lagged into the deck, traps in the stage, to name a few.
- Existence and specifics of the following: height, portability, and description of an overhead focusing ladder, the type of headset system, and the approximate size of production table.
- The size, access, and adjacency of the loading door to the stage.
- Names of other productions that have been presented there in the recent past. Names of the lighting designers or production managers, who, when contacted, may provide additional insight to the facility or personnel.

Define the House Lighting System

Defining the size, attributes, and quality of the existing electrical infrastructure can have a direct effect on the construction of the lighting design. The technical specifications should include the **house inventory**, which lists the number and type of dimmers, the number and type of instruments, the light board, and any additional hardware or accessories included in the space. An accurate house inventory allows the lighting designer to make choices regarding the need or amount of additional equipment that may be necessary to produce the light plot.

✅ **A Basic Checklist to Consider That May Assist the Definition of the House Lighting System:**

- The type, wattage, and number of all functional lighting instruments, along with any hardware accessories (such as gel frames or c clamps).
- The manufacturer, type, wattage, location, and number of color frames in each functioning followspot.
- The number and location of all working circuits, including location, wattage capacity, and portability. The location, plug type, and circuit identity of any circuitry transfer panels.
- The actual throw distance to all front of house lighting locations, and the number of instruments that can be safely mounted at each position. The current instrument inventory, if any, in the positions. Are the front of house instruments included in the first inventory?
- The number, physical location, and identity of functional dimmers: manufacturer, type, wattage, and number and type of inputs.
- A general sense of the amount, wire size, plug type, and length of functional stage cable.
- A general sense of the number of functional two-fers and three-fers, along with their wire size and plug type.
- The existence of lifts or ladders to focus the lighting instruments at each lighting position. The top height possible for the ladder used to focus overhead lighting positions.
- The location of the company switch (power dedicated to additional dimmers), including amperage, phase, and any existing plugs.
- Any additional hardware: sidearms, pipe, boom stands, floor plates, or pipe construction hardware.
- Solutions used for common problems in the past. Any history of unusual activity in the electrical power entering the facility.

- Names of other productions that have been presented there in the recent past. Names of the lighting designers or production electricians, who, when contacted, may provide additional insight to the facility and personnel.

Define the House Light Board

Initially, every piece of information gleaned about the type, identity, history, and condition of the **house lighting console** (or house board) is knowledge that may define its suitability for the overall lighting design. It is improbable that the house electrician will know all of the parameters of the console in question. Any unknown console should be investigated by contacting manufacturers, lighting rental companies, production electricians, board operators, or other lighting designers. If the choice is made to use the console, the knowledge of its capabilities, potentials, and limitations will allow the lighting designer to plan as much flexibility and function for its use while preparing the lighting design.

✅ **A Basic Checklist to Consider That May Assist the Definition of the House Computer Lighting Console:**

- The manufacturer, model name, and software version of the console.
- The actual condition of the console, including any history of problems and the last date the console was serviced.
- The largest number of dimmers that the console can address. The number of dimmer outputs located on the back of the console.
- The largest number of channels that can be controlled at any one time by the console.
- The largest number of cues contained within each RAM allocation (or disk).
- Is the light board a tracking or preset console or both? Can cues contain hard zeros?
- The ability of point cues to be inserted.
- The number of channels seen on each row of the channel intensity screen and the number of channels seen on each page of the channel intensity screen.
- The number of cues (listed with time durations) seen on the cue list screen.

- The number of split faders. The number of cues that can simultaneously occur.
- The number of physical submasters and their possible attributes. If the capability exists, the number of pages.
- The number of possible groups.
- Number of monitors required for fully functional system (showing channel intensity and cue list information).
- The existence and type of monitors for the production table (black and white, or color). The existence, condition, and length of monitor cable. Typical path and destination of monitor cable runs in recent past.
- The existence of a functioning alphanumeric keyboard to label the cues.
- The existence of a functional printer, and a printer cable to interconnect with the light board.
- The existence of a focus remote. Its typical location, condition, and history of problems.
- The typical location of the light board in the theatre. The distance to the stage, to typical rental dimmer rack locations, to the center of the house. The location of any DMX locations within the theatre.
- Any history of the console's use with any off-line editing programs. If so, can such a program be used?
- Names of other productions that have used the console in the recent past. Names of the lighting designers or production electricians, who, when contacted, may provide additional insight to the console or the personnel operating it.

✓ A Basic Checklist to Consider That May Assist Definition of the House Manual Light Board:

- The type, manufacturer, and model name of the light board.
- The actual condition of the light board, including any history of problems and the last date the board was serviced.
- Number of personnel required to run the light board.
- The number of functional scenes. The number and identity of nonfunctioning sliders, handles, or knobs in each scene.

- The number of scene masters. The number of scenes that can be simultaneously active.
- The number of functional dimmers.
- Any specific switching requirements needed to allow for independent control of the scenes.
- The typical location of the light board in the theatre. The distance to the stage, to rental dimmer racks, to the center of the house. The type of plug connected to the cable controlling the dimmers.

If the condition or functions of the house lighting console initially seem inadequate to the needs of the production, the entire situation should be carefully analyzed before the choice is made to reject that console and replace it with a different board. If installing a replacement console is viewed as "breaking new ground," the issue of compatibility in every connection and protocol must be seriously reviewed. The apparent advantage of working with a more powerful console may not be worth the additional cost, effort, and potential time that may be lost making the replacement board function within the house system. If this seems to be a possibility, it may be prudent to consider the adage "if it ain't broke, don't fix it," and every work-around allowing the house lighting console to be used should be considered. The replacement console can easily become a disruptive element to a previously functional system.

Other situations may preclude this issue. When a production utilizing color scrollers is to be presented in a performance facility that has a two-scene preset light board, there's no question that the house board will be unable to control the scrollers and create the cues required. The performance will require the use of both the house board controlling the house dimmers and the board traveling with the company (the road board) controlling the scrollers. If the scrollers are critical to the success of the production, other options may require that the road board control the scrollers and also interface with the system to control the house dimmers as well.

Another common example may be found when productions, scheduled in several venues, involve extensive cueing. The amount of time and effort required to recreate the same cues on each house light board may be less painful than somehow adapting the signal from the road board to control each house system. The choices that need to be made regarding this issue are wholly dependent on the mutual judgment of the lighting designer and the production electrician.

DEFINE THE PRODUCTION SCHEDULE

The **production schedule** lists each activity that occurs during stage time. Anticipating potential problems in the schedule begins by recognizing potential conflicts of interest. Sometimes, addressing those conflicts may result in a reassessment of the methods used to prepare or execute the lighting package. Unfortunately, if the constrained schedule can't somehow expand, the only solution may be to reduce the scope of the lighting design.

Consider this scenario: The schedule and the amount of labor have been defined before the lighting designer has been hired. The aspirations of the director, however, have not been curbed. When the director demands a lavish production, the lighting designer may be placed in a conundrum. Attempting to produce a lavish production within a constrained schedule can prove difficult. Opening an unfinished lavish show can be much more painful than opening a clean, simple show. In addition to that, it must be kept in mind that the overall budget is finite. There may be a healthy collaboration between the director, lighting designer, and the rest of the design team. The financial squeeze being felt by the lighting designer, however, may be shared by the other designers as well. Everyone involved may be battling for larger portions of the same money to produce their contributions to the show. The director's desires need to be balanced with the financial realities of the schedule and the budget. The lighting designer must negotiate a middle ground in the lighting design. If the parameters have been predetermined and are unchangeable, the size of the lighting design may need to be reduced to fit within this structure. A production meeting may be required to help define that middle ground.

In other cases, the schedule may not have been addressed by the time the lighting designer enters the situation. The only dates known may be the first day of the load-in and the date of the opening. Meetings may be held in which the lighting designer may be expected to help define the production schedule. To provide intelligent input into a scheduling discussion, the lighting designer needs to have a grasp of the production concept, the other elements of the production's design, the anticipated complexity of the show, the budget, and the planned amount of labor. Understanding these other elements will allow the lighting designer to provide an informed opinion and be certain that there is enough time to prepare the lighting for the production.

DEFINE THE COMMUNICATION

Understanding the parameters is wholly dependent on the ability to communicate. Contact sheets, phone books, and little black books are the tools that provide the means to accelerate that understanding. Realizing what questions need to be asked is an important skill, but knowing whom to contact to receive the missing piece of accurate information is just as important. Some basic documents list the personnel involved in the production, while other lists are culled from personal experience. Even if contact sheets aren't initially available to the lighting designer, the contact information should be determined and recorded.

The **production contact sheet** lists the staff assembled for the production. This list includes the rest of the design team and the production staff, including their phone numbers, fax numbers, addresses, pagers, and e-mail addresses. Sometimes the theatre's staff is different from the staff for the production. When that's the case, a copy of the theatre's contact sheet should be obtained as well. It is possible that additional numbers may be listed that aren't tied to the office phone answering system, like a pay phone in the basement or the lobby. The contact sheet should also list all phone and fax numbers, along with the mailing address, shipping address, and overnight delivery address for the theatre. Consider the possibility that these may be three separate addresses. Presumably, the theatre's contact sheet also lists all pertinent phone numbers for medical emergencies.

Personal contact numbers often include people that can provide backup, support, perishables, or equipment. If a lighting rental company is being used, every office number, fax number, "inside" line, weekend emergency number, pager number, and home number should be acquired. Lighting designers often compile phone, fax, and e-mail information for light board operators and troubleshooters (who know the light board), dimmer manufacturers and troubleshooters (who know the dimmers), or special effect specialists (for that weird new effect the show is using).

Depending on the scope, budget, or time constraint of a given project, it's wise to acquire any courier or overnight shipping account numbers that belong to the production. Many lighting designers also have their own accounts for times of extreme emergency.

A stress-saving list may be a compilation of phone numbers for vendors in each time zone. Some vendors have 800 phone numbers. With this list at hand, needs that become apparent after business hours on the East Coast can still be fulfilled by vendors on the West Coast without a loss of time. The decision to order support equipment can wait as late as 7:45 P.M. Eastern Time, and still be placed from a pay phone before the end of the business day on the West Coast. Using an overnight delivery service, the equipment can be delivered on-site the next morning. If the possibility of late night rehearsals is foreseen, consider acquiring phone numbers for vendors in Hawaii as well.

DEFINE THE PRODUCTION: *HOKEY*

Hokey: A Musical Myth is an imaginary musical theatre piece synthesizing movement, speech, song, and dance. Originally workshopped in a small downtown space, for the purposes of our learning, it is now going to blossom into a full production at the 800-seat Hybrid Theatre in New York City. It will be presented in three acts, consisting of three scenes in each act. The workshop production was well received by the critics. Anticipation runs high.

The Story

Hokey is loosely based on the song *Hokey Pokey*. Hokey is a timeless fictional tale that traces the travails of two lovers, Hokey and Pookie. Act 1 begins with the two lovers celebrating their relationship. Suddenly, they are separated in a storm that has been conjured by the antagonist Tee-boo. He kidnaps Pookie, leaving Hokey alone.

In Act 2, Hokey searches for Pookie in the forest, where he is joined by the Knotty Piners, a band of woodland fairies. One night, as he sleeps by the beach, Hokey sees Pookie in his dreams. She shows him where she has been confined by the evil Tee-boo, in the Sandbox of Snakes. Then she teaches her lover the Dance of Hokey and Pookie. When Hokey awakens, it is dawn. Hokey and the Knotty Piners travel to the Rock O' Thought, and with the rock's help, they rescue Pookie from her dungeon.

Act 3 begins with a party celebrating Pookie's safe return. In the midst of their celebration, Tee-boo ap-

pears to reclaim his former prisoner and descend into Hell. Hokey and Tee-boo engage in a furious battle. Their struggle takes them to the Precipice of Doom. As Tee-boo is about to claim victory, Hokey challenges him to follow the Dance of Hokey and Pookie. Tee-boo attempts to follow the movements indicated in the song, but being dyslexic, missteps, and falls into the abyss. The lovers are united, and the tale ends.

Casting The cast is made up of 16 singers and dancers who can act. Although there is a small live orchestra, additional sound cues are used, along with wireless microphones.

Scenery The basic scenic look will be black legs and borders, with a black scrim and translucency upstage. A main curtain will be used. A staircase will be used in Act 3. Aside from those elements, small set pieces and hand props will be used.

Costumes The costumes will consist of colored leotards and tights. Additional pieces will be added to identify the lead characters.

Lighting The lighting for *Hokey* will define the locations throughout the production. It will be presentational and colorful.

Hokey: A Quick Analysis

All of the parameters that have been discussed can now be applied to this hypothetical production of *Hokey: A Musical Myth*. The size and physical limitations of the Hybrid Theatre will define the hanging positions used for the show. The size of the budget has defined the crew size, the production schedule, the inclusion of house equipment where possible, and the size of the rental package. That package will include a lighting console, instrumentation, and dimmers which will supplement the house inventory.

In initial meetings with the director, the images that have been presented are that the production should feel "other-worldly" or "fantasy comic book-like," and that the show should move rapidly, like a "will-'o-the-wisp in a hurricane."

As production meetings begin, the basic information about *Hokey* can provide initial structure to the lighting design. The lack of flying scenery indicates that all of the overhead electrics will be able to be located to their best advantage. The note stating little deck scenery suggests that there may be enough space for sidelight booms. If booms can be used, they'll be able to illuminate and provide dimensionality on the performer's bodies, while the overhead systems can color the floor and isolate the areas. It's been noted that the lighting will define the location for each scene. A translucency is indicated, so presumably the scenic designer's intent is to use the translucency to help telegraph the different locations in the story.

There are three distinct scenes in each act. Presumably, the first act will begin with a "brighter," more normal look. This will help contrast the transition to the storm sequence, when the lovers are separated. If the storm also signals Tee-boo's first entrance, the colors used in the storm may become the colors used to signal Tee-boo's presence in the final act. Detailed discussions should certainly take place to determine the look of the storm. Should it be literal, with strobes for lightning? Or should it be more stylized? Presumably, after Pookie's kidnapping, the scene will restore to the initial look of the show, but more subdued or depressed.

The first scene in Act 2 introduces the Knotty Piners. Since this seems to indicate some sort of forest "look," a foliage template system may be warranted. The Scene 2 "night on the beach" look will need to contrast with the internal dream sequence. What devices will be necessary to help telegraph the "dreaminess" to the audience? A downstage black scrim or floor fog may be initial choices, dependent on the transition sequences into and out of the dream. How much time will there be from the end of the dream, until the final scene of Act 2, which is a sunrise "look"? Attention to timing will be carefully observed during rehearsals.

In the third act, the celebration will be brighter than the first act. Again, this will help contrast the transition for Tee-boo's entrance. Another area of discussion will be about the stairs and ways to show the entrance of Hell. Hokey's battle with Tee-boo will certainly need to be dramatic. The area of the stage used for the dance challenge will need isolation, to define the Precipice of Doom. The precipice will need a different look; the number of people on stage during that sequence may determine how the look is approached.

Combining the cast size, the indication of group scenes, and the note indicating wireless microphones infers that there will be solos, and the possible need for isolation in crowd scenes. That conclusion indicates the possible need for followspots, or at least a number of specials. Based on that assumption, the size of the crew should be checked to see if the budget includes enough electricians to operate the instruments.

Between the battle, the storm, and the "otherworldliness" of the show, it may be assumed that shafts of light would be useful. If that assumption is accurate, some sort of haze will be needed. Depending on the type of stylization, some kind of fog may be required as well.

As the production meetings between the director and the design team continue, the relationships between the lighting and other aspects of the production evolve. The more that *Hokey* is defined, the more the relationship between the lighting, scenery, costumes, and sound becomes intertwined. The wireless microphones, for example, will require pockets to be sewn into specific costume pieces to contain the base packs. The type of material carried by cast members for the storm will need coordination between the lighting and scenic designer to make certain the right fabric is chosen to ensure the success of the effect.

The agreements, language, and ideas expressed in these meetings form the basic conceptual understandings and communication for *Hokey* that won't be realized for months. Due to the fact that the piece may be evolving while several other productions are being executed by the members of the design team, clarity in communication and accuracy in documentation reduce the amount of potential misunderstanding.

SUMMARY

Now that the parameters and the concept of the production are known, the creation of the lighting design can begin. The mental images can be conceived, listed, discussed, and defined. The performance space can be analyzed for scenic, spatial, and electrical consideration. The different lighting systems can be constructed, colored, and separated in control, resulting in the creation of the light plot.

part two

Preparing the Tools

3 Paperwork Overview

This chapter provides an overview of the paperwork associated with a lighting design. Chapters 4, 5, and 6 then provide details about lighting design paperwork by examining a variety of the documents that complete, display, or monitor a lighting design. Each of these documents provides information that can be used in specific ways.

Although the lighting department is often accused of creating too much paper, a lighting design requires many different documents to retrieve, modify, and record the information about it. Since the lighting package for any production exists in spatial relationships with many other technical elements, documents are required that explain those relationships as well. Although the primary goal of any paperwork is to legibly communicate information, a secondary goal is to present that information in the most compact format to the broadest audience requiring the fewest documents. It is worth noting that the amount of paperwork produced by the lighting department to document a production can be heavy. Fewer documents means less strain on the back.

There are three categories of paperwork. The first category is graphic diagrams. If they provide information to other individuals, such as the light plot, the documents include keys and legends to provide explanation. Other diagrams are created by the lighting designer for his or her own personal use, so they require no explanation. The magic sheet and the cheat sheet are examples of this personal paperwork.

The second paperwork category contains information in a spreadsheet format. The search criteria for the document is usually assigned to the left-hand column of the documents, where the English-speaking eye is naturally drawn first. The remaining columns are sorted in a specific order, so that logical comparisons can be made between the columns. These documents range from the instrument schedule to the hang plot. Additional columns containing related information may reduce the need to consult other sources of information.

The third category of paperwork is comprised of forms that, when filled out, provide a record of actions taken. These documents are designed so that all relevant reference information is included on each form. When the forms are filled out, the only marks made on the form are specific to that particular action. These documents include the light cue sheets, the followspot cue sheets, and the board operator sheets. By including all pertinent reference information in the layout, each filled-out form can not only provide information about that specific action, it can also be used as an independent reference tool, reducing the need to consult separate documentation.

Deciding which documents are necessary for any production is a judgment made on a show-by-show basis. Although it is important to present the proper information in the simplest format, the question "What information needs to be seen by whom?" may bring about the realization that a fewer number of documents will be required. In some cases it may be possible to combine the information from two documents into a single piece of paperwork. If that seems feasible, it should be explored. One less document to construct is one less document that will eventually require an update. Every time a document is updated, the possibility of human error can occur. The fewer documents to update the better.

Brilliantly designed paperwork is useless if the people who use it can't understand it. In many cases, the lighting designer constructs a paperwork's layout so that he or she can read it. After the document's release, however, the lighting designer may rarely refer to it again. If the document is reference material used by other people, the lighting designer needs to ignore personal instinct or tastes. Discuss the layout and content of the paperwork with the people who will use it, and tailor the document's design to their preferences.

In the ideal world, a complete lighting paperwork package is compiled, revised, and distributed long before the load-in. The more time spent analyzing and solving potential problems prior to the load-in means that there is much more time available during stage time to actually complete the tasks.

Regardless of each document's layout, a "title block" of information should be included. This information may not be located in a specific area; it may instead be presented as a "header" or a "footer" in a spreadsheet document. At the very least, it should include the name of the show, the creation or revision date, and the purpose of the document. Other logistical information may include the lighting designer's name, contact information, and the facility where the show will be produced. Additional information may be specific to a particular document. One method to determine what reference information might be useful in a paperwork's "title block" is to imagine analyzing a document that has been separated from the rest of the paperwork package. Does enough information exist in the "title block" to use the document for its intended purpose without having to search for information from other documents?

THE PAPERWORK PACKETS

Paperwork generated for any production can be separated into three different packets, reflecting the different periods of time in the implementation of a lighting design. The **light plot,** the **section,** and the **support paperwork packet** present the mechanical view of the design. Not only is it the primary source of information about the lighting package, it is also used to gauge the cost and labor that will be involved. The **load-in and focus packet** includes the paperwork used to implement and focus a light plot, creating an operational lighting package. The **cue construction packet** includes the paperwork used to create, record, and monitor the cues of the lighting design.

Though all of the packets are constructed prior to the load-in process, the final version of any of these documents won't exist until the production is "frozen" and no other changes in the show will be made. Once frozen, the last updated version of the documents will produce the **archival packet,** which will reflect the final state of the design. Even though updating may not seem that important to the lighting designer, one responsibility that comes with the job is to provide accurate documentation that can be used following his or her departure. In many cases, these records will be stored in an archival file for future regeneration. It seems inevitable that whenever accurate documentation of the archival packet is skipped, it will later be required. One document that can't exist until the show is frozen, however, is a **final light board printout,** documenting the contents of the computer lighting console.

Upon examination, the reader may determine that these paperwork examples don't always suit his or her particular situation, and that's to be expected. The documents examined in this and next three chapters are specific to the production of *Hokey*. These documents are presented as a starting point to be adapted to individual circumstances.

The Document Distribution Chart

As the lighting design evolves, the identity, purpose, and number of documents required to communicate and expedite that design can be monitored by initially creating a **document distribution chart.** This list is often unique for each production. It illustrates the destination and number of copies required for each document. It can also act as a diary to track the creation and distribution of the paperwork. Kept updated, this list can also be used to ensure proper distribution of revised documents. Discussion with the rest of the production staff regarding the number and identity of documents required not only clarifies the total amount of copies that will be needed, it may also reveal the fact that someone else intends to produce their own version of the same document. This may result in one less document that the lighting designer has to create or maintain.

Figure 3.1 shows the document distribution chart for *Hokey*, laid out in a spreadsheet format. The rows are divided between the four main packets of information: the light plot, section, and support paperwork packet, the load-in and setup packet, the cue construction packet, and the archival adds packet.

Hybrid Theatre 1998 *Hokey* Document Distribution Chart Date: 4/30/98

	Date	Rev	DOCUMENT	Electric		Other Departments							Total
				LD	PE	SD	SM	PM	TD	PC	Prop	Sound	
Light Plot, Section, and Support Packet			Light Plot	1	3	1	1	1	2	2	1	1	13
			Section	1	3	1	1	1	1	1	1	1	11
			Instrument Schedule	1	1								2
			Hookup	1	1								2
			Dimmer Schedule	1	1								2
			Circuit Schedule	1	1								2
			Color Cards	1	3								4
			Floor Cards	1	3								4
			Instrument Spreadsheet	1	1			1					3
			Circuitry/Dim Spreadsheet	1	1			1					3
			Shop Order	1	2			1					4
			Perishables List	1	2			1					4
Load-in and Focus Packet			Hang Plot	1	1	1	1	1	2	2			9
			Headset Layout Diagram	1	1		1	1	1		1	1	7
			Disk Master	1	1								2
			Infrastructure Cues	1	1								2
			Groups	1	1								2
			Submasters	1	1								2
			System Spike Ground Plan	1			1	1			1		4
			Focus Document	1									1
			Focus Chart	1									1
Cue Construction Packet			Magic Sheet	1	2		1	1					5
			Cheat Sheet	1	2		1	1					5
			Cue Master	1			1						2
			Light Cue Sheets	∞									∞
			Followspot Cue Sheets	∞									∞
			Board Operator Sheets	∞									∞
			Repatch Sheets	∞									∞
			Worknote Sheets	∞									∞
Archival adds			Light Board Printout	1									1
			Track Sheet	1									1
			TOTAL	**26**	**32**	**3**	**8**	**11**	**6**	**5**	**4**	**3**	**98**

Lighting design by Steve Shelley.

LD = Lighting Designer, PE = Production Electrician, SD = Scene Designer, SM = Stage Manager, PM = Production Manager, TD = Technical Director, PC = Production Carpenter, Prop = Props Head, Sound = Sound Head, ∞ = Infinity.

Figure 3.1 The Document Distribution Chart

The "Date" and "Rev" columns on the left side of the chart can be filled in to track the completion and initial revision dates of each document. If the lighting designer is preparing paperwork for more than one production at the same time, remembering what paperwork for which show has been completed can be frustrating. Keeping an updated version of this document for both shows allows the designer to see at a glance what documents for either show have been completed. The document column lists each piece of information that will be produced. The columns immediately to the right show their destinations within the electrics department, while the rest of the chart shows the destination and number of copies required for the rest of the production staff. The final column on the right-hand side ("Total") shows the total number of copies that will be needed for each document, while the total number of documents that need to be supplied to each individual is shown in the "total" row on the bottom of the document. The forms at the bottom of the cue construction packet are marked with ∞, a symbol meaning infinity. The number of blank cue sheets for light cues, followspot cues, board operator cues, repatch sheets, and work note sheets is a judgment made based on the anticipated complexity of the show.

The act of copying, collating, and distributing all of these documents can be very time consuming. Since the need for additional copies may not be recognized until the middle of a load-in, consider making spare copies where seen fit. After moving into the theatre, designate an area out of harm's way as "the library," where the originals and spare copies can be stored. When updated documents are added to the library, hide the outdated versions. If copies are taken from the space in the designer's absence, they will match the current version in use. Retaining the "outdated" versions provides a record if the production reverts to that interpretation of the show.

4 The Light Plot, Section, and Support Paperwork Packet

The basic document of almost every lighting design, and the basis for the initial paperwork packet, is the **light plot.** Without the visualization of a plot, it is almost impossible to define a basis for the remaining information. Often a sectional view, or a **section,** is created that shows how the hanging positions relate to the surrounding elements of the production and the performance space.

Seeing the graphic presentation of the instruments used in the light plot shows only a portion of the information about each instrument. The detailed information about the instruments comprises the lighting database, which is presented in different forms of **support paperwork.** These forms usually include the **instrument schedule,** the **channel hookup,** the **circuitry schedule,** and the **dimmer schedule.**

If elements on the deck change focus, color, or channel identity during the production, **color cards** and **floor cards** are created to instruct and document the progression of those changes.

The components of the light plot often need to be reduced to a list of raw numbers defining the elements that will be required to construct the lighting package. The **instrument spreadsheet** and **circuitry and dimmer spreadsheet** are two documents used while the light plot is created to keep running tallies of the number and placement of instruments, dimmers, and circuits used in the plot. The **shop order** lists additional equipment that may need to be rented, while a **perishable list** itemizes the consumable supplies necessary for the plot. **Manuals** and **cut sheets** are reference documents

that provide information about the use and configuration of different electrical devices and components of the lighting package.

THE LIGHT PLOT

The **light plot** is a map showing all of the lighting instruments and electrical devices, their control assignment, and their relative hanging locations in the performance space. The main purpose of a light plot is to graphically communicate the number, location, and types of lighting instruments that will be used in the production. It may also furnish information about the color, circuitry, and focus of each lighting instrument. Though it doesn't need to be as detailed as the scenic designer's groundplan, the light plot often displays spatial information about the architecture, the masking, the scenery in the air, where (and when) important scenery or properties are located on the stage, and the number and type of backdrops.

As the document's creator, the lighting designer has a choice about the amount of information that is shown in the light plot. The map can provide as much or as little information as he or she desires. The amount of information included in the plot is often relative to the number of basic questions that may need to be answered during the load-in.

Figure 4.1 shows an overall view of the light plot for the production of *Hokey: A Musical Myth.* For purposes of clarity, alphabetic letters contained in

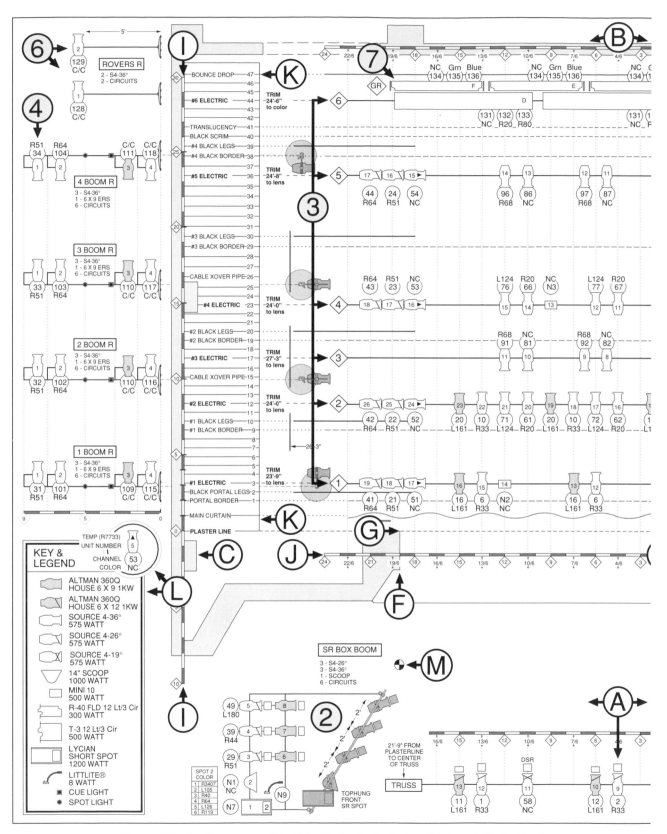

Figure 4.1 The Components of the Light Plot for the Production of *Hokey: A Musical Myth*

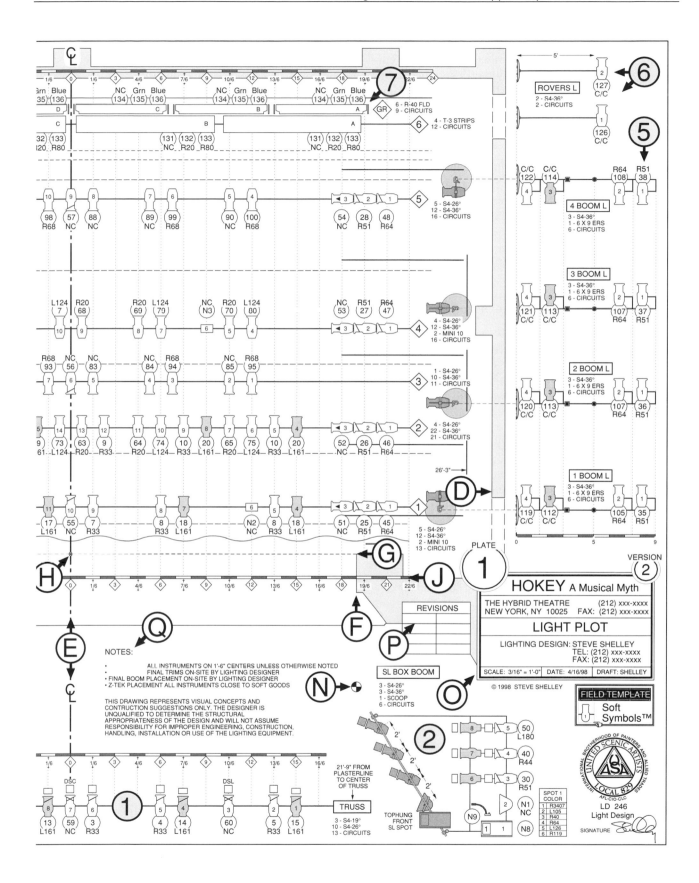

large white circles identify elements of the drawing and the architectural space, while large numbers contained in shaded circles identify the different hanging positions. A clean version of this light plot, without identifying circles, can be found on pages xviii–xix.

An Examination of the *Hokey* Light Plot

Figure 4.1 shows the *Hokey* light plot, drawn like most light plots from a perspective above the theatre while facing the stage. This groundplan view is often the same viewpoint used by the scenic designer to show the spatial locations of the scenery. From this perspective, the **front of house** hanging positions (above the audience) are at the bottom of the plot (A), while the back wall of the theatre is at the top (B). This implies that stage right is on the left side of the map (C), and stage left is on the right-hand side (D). Due to spatial constraints, this version of the plot has been reduced, but light plots are typically drawn in either a 1/2″ = 1′-0″ or 1/4″ = 1′-0″ scale. The scale chosen is often determined after considering the size of the architectural space, the overall size of the document, the number of individual instruments and their numeric attributes that must be seen, and the scale used by most plastic lighting drafting templates.

There are two basic "road markers" in a light plot: The **centerline** (E) bisects the distance between the walls of the proscenium (F), while the **plaster line** (G) defines the upstage edge of the proscenium arch. The point where these two lines intersect is often referred to as the **groundplan zero point** (H). All left, right, or depth measurements are taken from this point.

Two scales on the *Hokey* light plot provide distance information from the groundplan zero point. The **up and downstage scale** (I), positioned on the stage right wall, shows the distance between the plaster line and the electrics, the masking, or any flying scenic pieces. The **left and right scale** (J) on the apron of the stage shows distances from either side of centerline, and can be used extensively when the instruments are being hung. The plot can be accordion-folded so that the left and right scale can be positioned adjacent to each electric while measurements are made on the battens to establish each instrument's hanging location during the hang.

The area of the light plot identifying all of the objects hung in the air is called the **lineset schedule** (K), shown on the stage right wall. In proscenium theatres, the lineset schedule identifies the number and contents of all of the battens in the fly system. In fixed-grid theatres, the lineset schedule may only be a name, listing elements and their relative distance from a common starting point. The trim heights of the electrics are often shown adjacent to the lineset schedule.

In this light plot, the lineset schedule is shown on stage right, the same side of the stage as the locking rail of the fly system in the theatre. Standard practice is to show the true scaled distance of the battens from plaster line and each other in the lineset schedule. Although not all peripheral goods may be drawn on the light plot (soft goods storage, unused movie screens, etc.), the lineset schedule lists all the goods hung on each batten so that the relationship between the electrics and other flying elements can be known. In the *Hokey* plot, the lineset schedule lists all of the masking and backdrops that will be used for the piece. Solid lines indicate where the masking will land on the stage, while dashed lines indicate the position of goods trimmed in the air.

The **key and legend** (L) identifies the type, beam angle, wattage, and anything unique about each kind of lighting symbol used in the plot. It also translates the unit and channel numbers, along with any accessories associated with each lighting symbol. In the *Hokey* light plot, the channel assignment is located inside the circle adjacent to the instrument, and the color is noted immediately underneath the channel.

The **sightline points** (M and N) are points drawn in the audience to indicate the position of the most extreme seats in the house. They're the visual barometers used to confirm that the masking is adequate. If the occupants sitting at these points can't see the side backstage walls, any rigging hardware above the stage, or any other areas that are intended to be out of sight, then the masking is considered a success.

The **title block** (O) provides the basic overall information about the light plot. It communicates the title of the show, the name of the theatre, the plate number of the drawing, and informs the viewer of the document's function. It may also list the identities and contact information for the director and the designers. The title block informs the viewer of the scale being used, the date that the light plot was published (released for public consumption), and the name of the person who created the document. When a paperwork package is sent ahead to either a remote theatre or a lighting rental shop, the light plot may be the only document that filters down to the people who need further information. The title block is one location to list contact information, providing a conduit for questions. Simple answers provided prior to a hang can eliminate assumptions, hours of miscommunication, and lost stage time.

The **revision area** (P), adjacent to the title block, is important because it indicates that changes have been made. It is very confusing to view two different versions of the same light plot and not know which version is more current. The portion of the light plot containing information best communicated as text is referred to as the **notes area** (Q). This is the area of the plot that explains anything out of the ordinary, specifies standards required, and can include disclaimers, safety indemnity clauses, or language regarding intellectual property rights.

An Examination of the *Hokey* Lighting Systems

The *Hokey* light plot shows three front of house lighting positions. The **truss** (1) contains two straight **frontlight** washes consisting of five instruments each, and three specials. The warm wash, channels 1 > 5, is colored in Roscolux 33, while the cool wash, channels 11 > 15, is colored in Lee 161. The five beams of light in each wash will create a downstage zone of straight frontlight in two colors. Additional zones of straight frontlight, provided by instruments hung in the overhead electrics, will complete the two color straight frontlight system. On the stage left side of the truss, the instrument inventory and the number of circuits that will be required are listed. These facts are shown for each position, and are often referred to before and during the hang.

On either side of the truss are the two **box boom** positions (2). Each position contains three color washes in Lee 180, Roscolux 44, and Roscolux 51, along with a worklight, a followspot, and a running light. The stage right washes are assigned to channels 29, 39, and 49, while the stage left washes are assigned to channels 30, 40, and 50.

Upstage of the plaster line, the light plot shows six **overhead electrics** (3), or **electrics,** which in this case refers to battens hanging above the stage. (Any batten that has at least one instrument or electrical device hung from it can be considered an electric.) The first electric has five pairs of instruments equipped with the same color as the frontlights on the truss, Roscolux 33 and Lee 161. They will be focused as the midstage zones of the straight frontlight systems. The warm frontlights are located in channels 6 > 8, while the cool frontlights are assigned to channels 16 > 18. The cen-

ter pair of instruments have been nudged aside to provide room for unit 10, assigned to channel 55. This unit will be focused as a frontlight special to center center. The second electric has a duplication of 10 instruments in the same relationship to centerline, providing the upstage and final zone of frontlight coverage. Also colored in Roscolux 33 and Lee 161, the warm frontlights are assigned to channels 9 and 10, while the cool frontlights are assigned to channels 19 and 20.

The second electric and the fourth electric contain two **downlight** systems, which will each consist of two zones. Again, each zone consists of five pairs of instruments on each electric. The warm downlights are colored in Roscolux 20 and assigned to channels 61 > 70. The cool downlights are colored in L124 and assigned to channels 71 > 80. Since the second electric also contains the upstage zone of the frontlight system, it is not an easy task to recognize the downlights among the rest of the instruments on the electric. The pairs are easier to see on the fourth electric.

The third and fifth electrics contain the two **backlight** systems that will also consist of two zones. The warm backlight is uncolored (NC means "no color") and assigned to channels 81 > 90, while the cool backlight is colored in Roscolux 68 and assigned to channels 91 > 100. Again, the center pair of instruments is nudged aside to make room for specials focused to center.

The first, second, fourth, and fifth electrics have two instruments at each end of the battens that comprise the four zone **pipe end** systems. The warm system is assigned to channels 21 > 28 and colored in Roscolux 51. The cool system is assigned to channels 41 > 48 and colored in Roscolux 64. There's a single instrument containing a template adjacent to each of the pair of pipe end washes. All eight of these instruments, assigned to channels 51 > 54, comprise the **pipe end template** system, which will cover the entire stage in a leafy breakup pattern. The sixth electric contains **striplights**, assigned to channels 131 >133, that will light the back of the translucency. The sixth electric is placed between the translucency and the bounce drop.

In the *Hokey* plot, a note adjacent to the stage right side of each electric states the vertical **trim height** that will be required from the stage to each overhead electric. This distance will be graphically shown in the lighting section. Adjacent to the electrics on the opposite end of the pipe is the list of instruments and the number of circuits that will be required for that particular position.

Upstage of the proscenium, on either side of the stage, the light plot shows four **sidelight booms** (4 and 5). Though the detailed components of each boom are drawn offstage of the side walls, dashed lines connect the individual positions to their actual location in the groundplan. The instruments on the booms combine to create four sidelight washes. Usually, the system of instruments mounted above eye level is called **head highs.** The instruments closest to the deck are referred to as **shinbusters,** while the instruments above them are called **mids.** Upstage of the booms, on either side of the stage, pairs of **rovers** (6) are mounted on adjustable stands. Usually, enough cable is assembled with each of these units so that they can be placed anywhere on their respective sides of the stage. This allows the instruments to act like specials, which can move, recolor, or refocus for each act.

Finally, the light plot shows a row of striplights close to the back wall, "above" the sixth electric. Instead of a horizontal line drawn between each instrument (a batten), a small vertical line on either side of each striplight indicates that the units will actually sit on the deck. These instruments are collectively called the **groundrow** (7). Located between the translucency and the bounce drop, this system will combine with the sixth electric to light the back of the translucency.

THE LIGHTING SECTION

The **lighting section** is the second primary graphic document in the paperwork package, showing a side view of the performance space and the audience seating area. This sectional view allows the designer to accurately define hanging positions, select and place types of instrumentation in each hanging position, and thus define the focus of lighting systems. It also shows the full range of focus motion possible from each hanging position, so that instruments can be assigned to the appropriate location that will best illuminate the desired focus point. Finally, the section allows the lighting designer to define the relationship of the hanging positions to the surrounding technical elements of the production, the performance space, and the audience. Most lighting designers believe that the section must be constructed prior to the light plot, so that the correct type of instrument with the proper beam spread will be selected to create the systems and specials.

The general orientation of the lighting section is almost always absolute; the stage is drawn at the bottom of the document, while anything above the stage is located toward the top of the document. The point of view (looking towards stage left or stage right) is a choice often determined by the side of the stage containing more scenery or more changes in height. Sometimes it is necessary to draft two sections, one for each side. The lighting section has several purposes:

- Show the accurate height, depth, and location of each batten or hanging point in the performance facility.
- Show the accurate location of all hanging positions in the performance facility.
- Show accurate dimensions of the masking, scenery, and other relevant production elements.
- Show the relationships between the hanging positions and the architecture, masking, scenery, and the sightlines.
- Illustrate the typical appearance of the stage to the audience; are the overhead electrics to be exposed or concealed from the audience's view?
- Show the focus coverage of the different lighting systems and selected specials.

Figure 4.2 shows an overall view of the lighting section drawn for the production of *Hokey: A Musical Myth.* For purposes of clarity, alphabetic letters contained in large white circles identify elements of the drawing and the architectural space, while numbers contained in large shaded circles identify the different hanging positions. A clean version of this section, without identifying circles, can be found on pages xx–xxi.

An Examination of the *Hokey* Lighting Section

Figure 4.2 shows the *Hokey* section, which is drawn looking from centerline to stage left. The back wall of the theatre (A) is drawn on the left-hand side of the paper, defining the architectural depth of the performance space, and the audience is drawn on the right. In a case of clarity winning the battle against accuracy, the full fly system of the Hybrid Theatre isn't shown to allow the text in the drawing to be readable.

There are two basic "road markers" in a section. The **plaster line** (B), the upstage side of the proscenium, defines the horizontal axis, while the **stage** or **deck** (C) defines the vertical axis. The point where the plaster line touches the stage is the **section zero point** (D). All depth and height measurements refer to this point.

Some visual elements are duplicated between the light plot and the section. These include the **proscenium** (E), which is "cut in half" to illustrate the height of the proscenium opening. Since the battens are hung from the grid, the **lineset schedule** (F) has moved to the top of the document. The distance between the contents of the lineset schedule and the plaster line in the lighting section should match their counterparts in the groundplan view. It is common practice to place a section sideways to a light plot for the same production to confirm the distance accuracy of the lineset schedules between the two documents.

The **up and downstage scale,** providing depth distance, is duplicated both above (G) and below (H) the stage. The **vertical scales** (I and J), and their dashed lines in between, demarcate the vertical space. The lowest line drawn in the vertical scales is the **head height line** (K) drawn at 5'-9" above the stage. This arbitrary measurement indicates an "average" height, which is used to define the vertical placement of focus points.

Another carryover from the groundplan is the side view of a single **sightline** (L), representing the eyes of the selected member of the audience. While the pair of sightlines in the groundplan view defined the parameters of the side masking, this singular point may be located at a different distance from plaster line, and is used to define the relative trim heights of any scenery, masking borders, and overhead electrics. The imaginary lines drawn from the **sightline point** (M) into the area over the stage show the limits of vertical visibility, which may define the height to which much of the scenery and electrics are trimmed.

One element not included in this shortened section is the **grid,** the structure above the stage, which supports all of the rigging for the battens. The **battens, pipes,** or **linesets** (N), drawn as lines in the groundplan view, are drawn in the section as small circles under dotted lines to represent the end view of pipe hanging from system cables. In most productions attempting to "mask" the stage, the battens and their system cables are concealed. The drawn location of the battens indicates their vertical distance above the stage, or the trim height of each pipe. Battens not currently used in the production may be drafted in their "gridded" po-

sition, the uppermost limit to which the batten can be raised. The distance from the stage to this highest "out" position is also known as the "total pipe travel" for the batten. The pipe travel distance of a batten can be an important measurement. If the distance is "short" or scenic units are too tall, the bottom of gridded scenic units trying to fly out and disappear may remain exposed to the sightline under the borders.

The **masking legs** and **borders** (O and P), shown as dotted and shaded lines in the groundplan, are presented in this view as solid lines. Being drawn as thicker lines makes it possible to easily see the distance between each leg (or the depth of each leg opening), while the borders determine the limits of vertical visibility.

The **title block** (Q) is often a copy-and-paste of the title block from the light plot. The only difference is the plate number and the title informing the viewer of the document's function.

An Examination of the *Hokey* Lighting Systems in Section

In this section, the front of house hanging positions, include the **truss** (1) and the stage left **box boom** position (2). The **overhead electrics** (3) are shown as instruments hung from battens, with a diamond indicating the numeric name assigned to each electric. This section also shows the four stage left **sidelight booms** (4) sitting on the stage. They too are labeled with small diamonds, their numbering relative to plaster line. The final lighting position in this section is the **groundrow** (5), positioned on the deck upstage between the translucency and the bounce.

To ensure a blend of the different system washes throughout the depth of the stage, the section is constructed so that the middle of one beam marks the beginning of the next beam continuing the system upstage. This ensures that there will be adequate overlap at head height between each zone of coverage.

Figure 4.3 shows the hanging positions and the unshuttered beam edges of the instruments that will provide the two color-three zone **frontlight** washes (channels 1 > 20). The truss position is not shown, only the resulting beam edges. The beam overlap ensures even coverage from plaster line to the middle of the fourth opening.

The two overhead electrics (1 and 2) are close to the same trim, meaning that beam spread and inten-

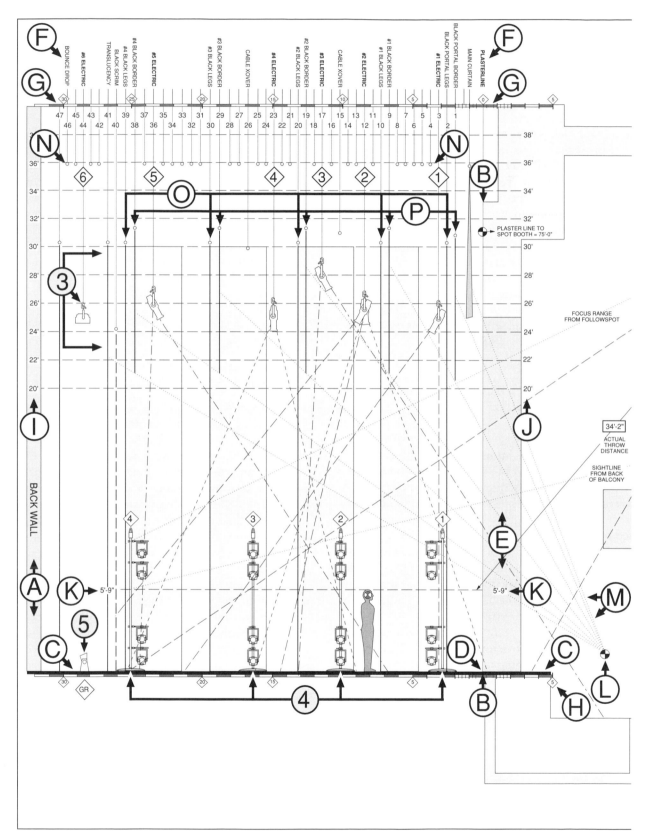

Figure 4.2 The Components of the Lighting Section for the Production of *Hokey: A Musical Myth*

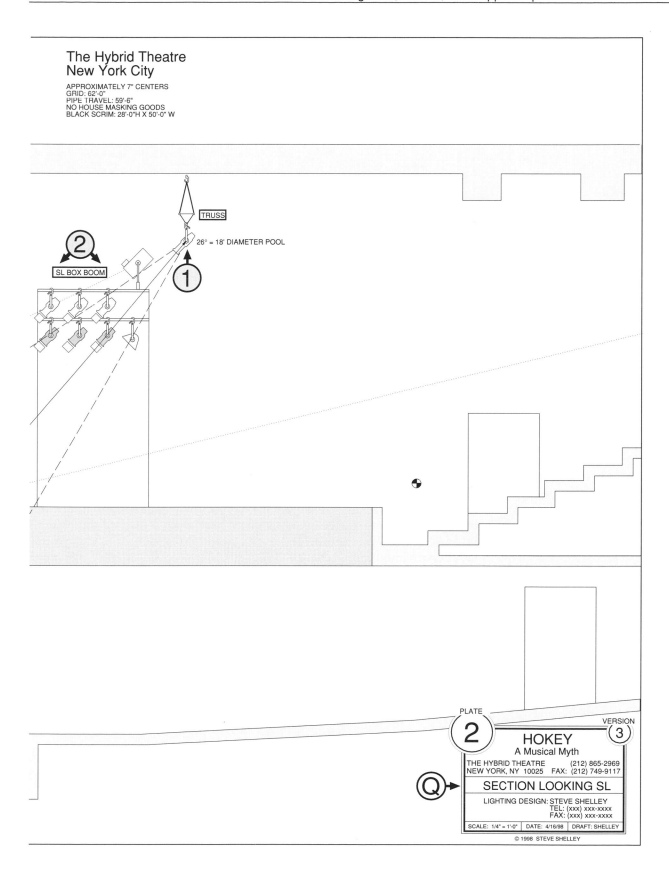

The Hybrid Theatre
New York City

APPROXIMATELY 7" CENTERS
GRID: 62'-0"
PIPE TRAVEL: 59'-6"
NO HOUSE MASKING GOODS
BLACK SCRIM: 28'-0"H X 50'-0" W

TRUSS

26° = 18' DIAMETER POOL

SL BOX BOOM

PLATE

2

VERSION

3

HOKEY
A Musical Myth

THE HYBRID THEATRE   (212) 865-2969
NEW YORK, NY 10025   FAX: (212) 749-9117

SECTION LOOKING SL

LIGHTING DESIGN: STEVE SHELLEY
TEL: (xxx) xxx-xxxx
FAX: (xxx) xxx-xxxx

SCALE: 1/4" = 1'-0" | DATE: 4/16/98 | DRAFT: SHELLEY

© 1998 STEVE SHELLEY

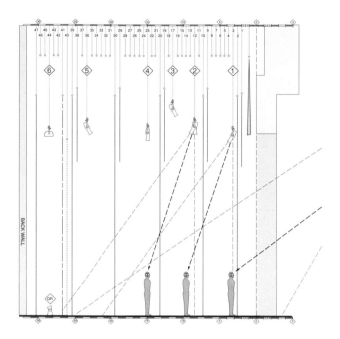

Figure 4.3 The Frontlight Section

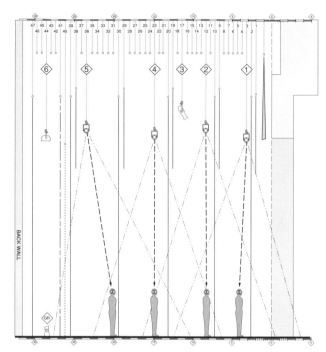

Figure 4.4 The Pipe End Sidelight Section

sity is equal between the two upstage zones. The three small figures indicate the focus point location for each zone. The dashed lines indicate the hot spot for each beam.

From this section its apparent that the top edge of the truss frontlight zone may require a shutter cut, so the stage isn't illuminated with frontlight far upstage during moments of downstage isolation. The frontlight on the second electric will also require a top shutter cut to eliminate light that would otherwise hit the face of the scenic stack, the black scrim.

Although the box booms are shown in the lighting section, drafting their lighting beams or the beams of any other instruments not targeted straight into the stage requires separate beam sections. The focus of box boom systems will be tailored and adapted on site to the architecture and scenery, so box boom lighting sections are often not drafted except for special focus situations. Their presence in the lighting section is to provide the viewer with their relative location to section zero.

Figure 4.4 shows the hanging positions and the unshuttered beam edges of the instruments that will provide the two color-four zone pipe end sidelight washes (channels 21 > 28 and 41 > 48). The beam overlap ensures an even blend in sidelight coverage over the depth of the entire stage. All four overhead electrics are at approximately the same trim, meaning that

beam spread and intensity are equal through the four zones. From this section, it is apparent that the sidelight on the fifth electric will require an upstage cut to eliminate the light hitting the scenic stack.

Figure 4.5 shows the hanging positions and the beam edges of the instruments that will be used to provide the two color-two zone downlight washes (channels 61 > 80). The beams overlap to ensure an even blend of downlight over the depth of the entire stage. For this plot, note that the coverage is intended for floor coverage more than performer coverage. There's no head high coverage downstage of plaster line or upstage in the fourth opening. Since both electrics are at approximately the same trim, beam spread and intensity are equal between the two zones.

Figure 4.6 shows the hanging positions and the beam edges of the instruments that will be used to provide the two color-two zone backlight washes (channels 81 > 100). Again, the beams overlap, ensuring an even blend of backlight over the depth of the entire stage.

Although the downstage electric is at a higher trim, the beam spread and intensity level will be close between the two zones. The downstage zone on the third electric may require a top shutter cut to keep light out of the audience's eyes.

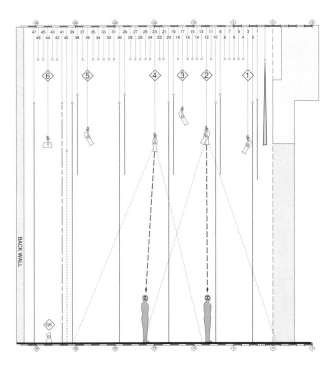

Figure 4.5 The Downlight Section

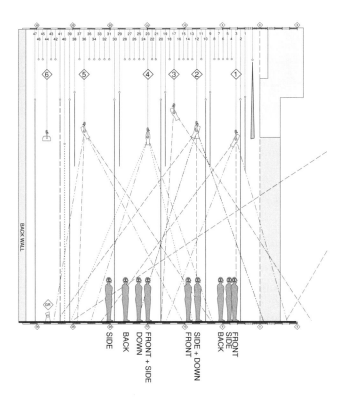

Figure 4.7 The Combined Lighting Systems Section

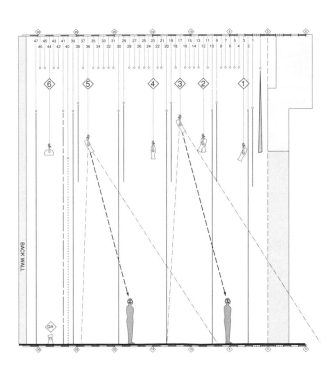

Figure 4.6 The Backlight Section

Combining the beam edges for all of the systems into a single document can be confusing, but seeing all of the systems simultaneously represented in a single section can be important during the load-in process. If the electrics change trim height or batten location, the lighting designer can see what effect that movement will have on the focus range of all affected systems.

To provide visual clarity, the beam edges of the different systems are drawn with different dashes. Figure 4.7 shows the combined lighting section for *Hokey*. Long dashed lines represent the beam edges of the frontlight, while the beam edges of the four side-light systems are shown as dash-with-two-dot lines. The beam edges of the downlight systems are drawn as short dashed lines, and the beam edges of the back-light systems are shown as dash-and-one-dot lines.

THE SUPPORT PAPERWORK

Although a lot of information is displayed on a light plot, the graphic map often doesn't visually present all of the information about every lighting instrument. Each instrument has its own **electrical path,** which can

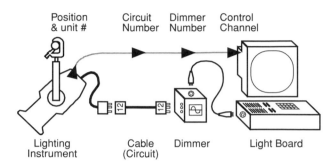

Figure 4.8 The Electrical Path in a Computer Lighting System

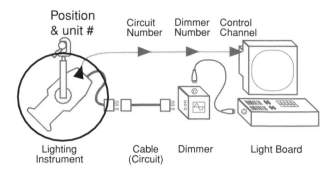

Figure 4.9 The Electrical Path Highlighting the Instrument's Position

be traced from the instrument to the handle or channel that controls its intensity.

Figure 4.8 traces the electrical path for a computer lighting system, showing the four intersections, or fields of information:

- The position and unit number of the instrument
- The circuit number (the identity of the cable connecting the instrument to the dimmer)
- The dimmer number (into which the circuit is plugged)
- The channel number (assigned to control the dimmer)

All of this information is part of the **lighting database,** a collection of facts about each of the instruments or electrical devices in a light plot. The lighting database can be sorted by the four different fields in the electrical path and viewed in different forms. Although each form contains the same information, it's sorted by different criteria.

The Instrument Schedule

The **instrument schedule** sorts the lighting database by the hanging position and unit number, mirroring the arrangement of the instruments and electrical devices drawn on the light plot (Figure 4.10).

Figure 4.9 highlights the instrument's location in the electrical path. If the unit's position is known, the instrument schedule is the document searched to gain additional information. Additionally, visual searches for blank spaces in this paperwork can reveal instruments that have not been assigned a purpose or focus, and may be available for use as a new special.

The formula used to sort the hanging positions in the instrument schedule use a combination of four general rules; they are sorted from the perspective of the lighting designer sitting in the audience, by their relation to plaster line, by their relative height above the stage (with the highest positions appearing first), and finally by their position relative to centerline. The combination of these rules means that the overhead front of house positions are sorted "backwards" so that the FOH position farthest from plaster line and highest above the stage appears first, followed by the next closest FOH position, and so on. Once the overhead FOH position closest to plaster line has been listed, the box boom positions are next. When there are matching positions on either side of centerline, the question often arises as to which side to list first. Because the starting point for numbering units on the electrics begins on stage left, standard practice is to list the stage left side of matching positions first. The box boom farthest from plaster line would be listed first, and the stage right box boom closest to plaster line listed last. Footlights downstage of the proscenium, being the lowest position closest to the plaster line, would be the final FOH position listed.

After the front of house positions, the overhead electrics are usually listed next, starting with the position closest to plaster line, the first electric. After the electric closest to the back wall is listed, the next highest positions are addressed. Often this consists of the galleries and the ladders. Again, the stage left position closest to the plaster line would be listed first, concluding with the farthest upstage right position listed last. The final hanging positions are those that sit on the deck, which usually include the booms and the groundrow. The boom closest to plaster line on stage left would be listed first, the boom farthest upstage

Position	#	Cir	Dim	Chan	Type	Watt	Purpose	Color	Notes
Truss	1	A-1	175	15	Source 4 20°	575w	Cool Area 5	L101	Tophat
Truss	2	A-2	174	5	Source 4-26°	575w	Warm Area 5	R33	Tophat
Truss	3	A-3	173	60	Source 4-19°	575w	DL Special	NC	Tophat
Truss	4	A-4	172	14	Source 4-26°	575w	Cool Area 4	L161	Tophat
Truss	5	A-5	171	4	Source 4-26°	575w	Warm Area 4	R33	Tophat
Truss	6	B-1	170	3	Source 4-26°	575w	Warm Area 3	R33	Tophat
Truss	7	B-2	169	59	Source 4-19°	575w	DC Special	NC	Tophat
Truss	8	B-3	168	13	Source 4-26°	575w	Cool Area 3	L161	Tophat
Truss	9	B-4	167	2	Source 4-26°	575w	Warm Area 2	R33	Tophat
Truss	10	B-5	166	12	Source 4-26°	575w	Cool Area 2	L161	Tophat
Truss	11	C-1	165	58	Source 4-19°	575w	DR Special	NC	Tophat
Truss	12	C-2	164	1	Source 4-26°	575w	Warm Area 1	R33	Tophat
Truss	13	C-3	163	11	Source 4-26°	575w	Cool Area 1	L161	Tophat
SL Bx Boom	1	BBL-1	19	N8	Starklight	1200w	SL Box Boom Followspot		See plot for color
SL Bx Boom	1A	BBL-2	20	N9	Littlite®	8w	SL Box Boom Run light	NC	For music stand
SL Bx Boom	2	BBL-3		N1	14" Scoop	1kw	House Left Work	NC	
SL Bx Boom	3	BBL-4	22	30	Source 4-26°	575w	SL Box Boom Lav Far	R51	Tophat
SL Bx Boom	4	BBL-5	23	40	Source 4-26°	575w	SL Box Boom Rose Far	R44	Tophat
SL Bx Boom	5	BBL-6	24	50	Source 4-26°	575w	SL Box Boom Dk Lav Far	L180	Tophat
SL Bx Boom	6	BBL-7	22	30	Source 4-36°	575w	SL Box Boom Lav Near	R51	Tophat
SL Bx Boom	7	BBL-8	23	40	Source 4-36°	575w	SL Box Boom Rose Near	R44	Tophat
SL Bx Boom	8	BBL-9	24	50	Source 4-36°	575w	SL Box Boom Dk Lav Near	L180	Tophat
		BBL-10					Spare		
		BBL-11					Spare		
SR Bx Boom	1	BBR-1	25	N7	Starklight	1200w	SR Box Boom Followspot		See plot for color
SR Bx Boom	1A	BBR-2	26	N9	Littlite®	8w	SR Box Boom Run light	NC	For music stand
SR Bx Boom	2	BBR-3		N1	14" Scoop	1kw	House Right Work	NC	
SR Bx Boom	3	BBR-4	27	29	Source 4 26°	575w	SR Box Boom Lav Far	R51	Tophat
SR Bx Boom	4	BBR-5	28	39	Source 4-26°	575w	SR Box Boom Rose Far	R44	Tophat
SR Bx Boom	5	BBR-6	29	49	Source 4-26°	575w	SR Box Boom Dk Lav Far	L180	Tophat
SR Bx Boom	6	BBR-7	27	29	Source 4-36°	575w	SR Box Boom Lav Near	R51	Tophat
SR Bx Boom	7	BBR-8	28	39	Source 4-36°	575w	SR Box Boom Rose Near	R44	Tophat
SR Bx Boom	8	BBR-9	29	49	Source 4-36°	575w	SR Box Boom Dk Lav Near	L180	Tophat
		BBR-10					Spare		
		BBR-11					Spare		

Figure 4.10 A Partial Instrument Schedule Showing the First Three Hanging Positions of the *Hokey* Light Plot

right would be listed last, and the instrument schedule would conclude with the groundrow.

The standard practice is to arrange the instrument schedule so that only one position appears on a single page. Not only does this visually separate positions within the document, but a single page can be removed while hanging the plot while the rest of the light plot's information is retained. When adjacent hanging positions contain relatively few instruments, however, the two positions are sometimes combined onto a single page with spaces in between. Ideally, some amount of white space is left on each page where added instruments or notes specific to the hanging position can be written.

Figure 4.10 shows a combination of the first three hanging positions of the *Hokey* light plot. Columns containing the position and unit number are listed first in bold type, to confirm the sort order and the identity of the document. The next three columns are sorted in a logical progression, following the electrical path of each instrument to its control channel. The instrument is plugged into a circuit, which is then plugged into a dimmer, which is then softpatched to a channel. When the columns follow the electrical path, visually comparing two pieces of relevant information is simplified. In this case, the male connector from truss unit #1 is plugged into a female connector of a cable marked "A-1." The male plug on the other end of that cable is plugged into dimmer 175. In the patch screen of the light board, dimmer 175 is then softpatched into channel 15.

The rest of the columns provide other information about truss unit # 1. The instrument type is identified, along with the wattage of the lamp. The purpose or focus of the instrument is followed by the color it will receive. The final column lists any notes. In this case, the instrument is earmarked to receive a tophat.

While the instruments are being hung and circuited, the instrument schedule is often the document on which circuitry or dimmer information is recorded. It can also be used to double-check other attributes of the instrument, such as color or accessories. Finally, the instrument schedule is the document used while circuits are plugged into dimmers, and when dimmers are softpatched to channels.

The Channel Hookup

The second form sorts the lighting database by its "handle" or control channel. This list is called the **channel hookup,** which displays this sort in the same numerical order as the handles on the manual light board or the channels displayed on a computer lighting monitor (Figure 4.12).

Figure 4.11 highlights the control channel's location in the electrical path. The first row of a channel hookup for a light plot using computer control lists the softpatched contents of the first channel (usually channel 1), while the final row in the document lists the contents of the highest channel number used in the plot. When questions arise about the contents of a channel, the channel hookup is the form that is used to search for information.

Note that the channel numbers for the *Hokey* light plot are assigned so that systems of focused instruments are numbered from stage right to stage left. This convention is based on the fact that English text runs left to right on the printed page. This implies that the natural inclination of the English eye is to view the left side of a document first. In this same manner, when the lighting designer views the stage from the audience, it can be said that his or her eye looks at the left side of the stage picture first, so the numbering of the channels are assigned in this manner. Numbering the channels in the opposite direction is a preference of the lighting designer, but whatever side of the stage is chosen to begin the numbering of each system, that "starting point" should be retained in the channel numbering of the entire plot.

The rows in an instrument schedule can be single spaced; an added instrument can be noted at the bottom of that position's page. Attempting to insert an additional instrument to a hookup, however, can introduce the need for paper surgery involving scissors and tape. For that reason, the hookup is often produced with blank rows between each channel number. Not only does this visually separate the channel numbers on the document from one another, it also provides space for newly-softpatched instruments.

Figure 4.12 shows the hookup for the first 10 channels of the *Hokey* light plot. The control channel number in the left-hand column is listed in bold text to confirm the sort order and the identity of the document. The next three columns continue the electrical path, but in reverse order from the instrument schedule. This is because the electrical path is also reversed. The channel is controlling a dimmer, which has a circuit or cable plugged into it. The other end of the cable is plugged into an instrument at a remote lighting position. The arrangements of the columns provide a logical method to visually compare the intersections in the electrical path. Presuming the light plot has been

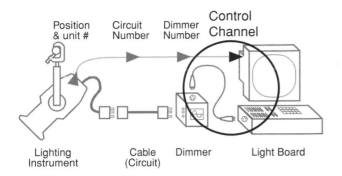

Position & unit # Circuit Number Dimmer Number Control Channel

Lighting Instrument Cable (Circuit) Dimmer Light Board

Figure 4.11 The Electrical Path Highlighting the Control Channel

properly soft and hardpatched, the patch screen of the computer light board will confirm that channel 1 controls dimmer 164. An inspection of the input for dimmer 164 will confirm that a cable with a male plug marked C-2 is plugged into it. Tracing the cable to the truss, the female end of the cable will terminate with a plug marked C-2, which is plugged to truss unit #12.

The rest of the columns reiterate the same information as the instrument schedule, identifying the type, wattage, and purpose of truss unit #12. Finally, the notes column will state the fact that the instrument should receive a tophat. After the light plot has been assembled, the hookup is the document used while performing a channel check.

Hybrid Theatre 1998   *Hokey* **Channel Hookup**   Date: 4/30/98

Chan	Dim	Cir	Position	#	Type	Watt	Purpose	Color	Notes
1	164	C-2	Truss	12	Source 4-26°	575w	Warm Area 1	R33	Tophat
2	167	B-4	Truss	9	Source 4-26°	575w	Warm Area 2	R33	Tophat
3	170	B-1	Truss	6	Source 4-26°	575w	Warm Area 3	R33	Tophat
4	171	A-5	Truss	5	Source 4-26°	575w	Warm Area 4	R33	Tophat
5	174	A-2	Truss	2	Source 4-26°	575w	Warm Area 5	R33	Tophat
6	7	7	1 Electric	15	Source 4-36°	575w	Warm Area 6	R33	
6	7	7	1 Electric	12	Source 4-36°	575w	Warm Area 7	R33	
7	4	4	1 Electric	9	Source 4-36°	575w	Warm Area 8	R33	
8	3	3	1 Electric	8	Source 4-36°	575w	Warm Area 9	R33	
8	3	3	1 Electric	5	Source 4-36°	575w	Warm Area 10	R33	
9	84	E-4	2 Electric	12	Source 4-36°	575w	Warm Area 13	R33	
10	94	F-5	2 Electric	22	Source 4-36°	575w	Warm Area 11	R33	
10	90	F-5	2 Electric	18	Source 4-36°	575w	Warm Area 12	R33	
10	81	D-5	2 Electric	9	Source 4-36°	575w	Warm Area 14	R33	
10	77	D-5	2 Electric	5	Source 4-36°	575w	Warm Area 15	R33	

Expression 1; 150 chan, 174 dim   Lighting design by Steve Shelley   Page 1 of 13

Figure 4.12 A Hookup Showing the First 10 Control Channels of the *Hokey* Light Plot

The Circuit Schedule

The third form uses an intermediate intersection in the electrical path to sort the same lighting information. This list is called the **circuit schedule** (Figure 4.14). The information is displayed in the numerical order of the circuitry used to connect the instruments to the dimmers. To prevent confusion, every circuit has a unique label.

Figure 4.13 highlights the circuit number's location in the electrical path. The circuit schedule usually lists every available circuit in the house electrical infrastructure, along with every circuit added for that particular show. Usually, there are many open (or unused) circuits. When it is necessary to find alternative or additional paths from a hanging position to the dimmers, the circuit schedule is the form consulted to search for possibilities.

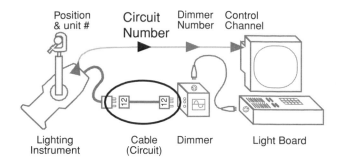

Figure 4.13 The Electrical Path Highlighting the Circuit

Figure 4.14 shows the circuitry schedule for the first 10 circuits of the *Hokey* light plot. It shows that circuit 1 is currently unused, and that two instruments are plugged into circuit 2, implying that the units are two-fered into the circuit. It is possible to see that cir-

Hybrid Theatre 1998   *Hokey* Circuit Schedule   Date: 4/30/98

Cir	Dim	Chan	Position	#	Type	Watt	Purpose	Color	Notes
1									
2	2	18	1 Electric	4	Source 4-36°	575w	Cool Area 10	L161	
2	2	18	1 Electric	7	Source 4-36°	575w	Cool Area 9	L161	
3	3	8	1 Electric	5	Source 4-36°	575w	Warm Area 10	R33	
3	3	8	1 Electric	8	Source 4-36°	575w	Warm Area 9	R33	
4	4	7	1 Electric	9	Source 4-36°	575w	Warm Area 8	R33	
5	5	55	1 Electric	10	Source 4-26°	575w	CC Front Special	NC	
6	6	17	1 Electric	11	Source 4-36°	575w	Cool Area 8	L161	
7	7	6	1 Electric	12	Source 4-36°	575w	Warm Area 7	R33	
7	7	6	1 Electric	15	Source 4-36°	575w	Warm Area 6	R33	
8	8	16	1 Electric	13	Source 4-36°	575w	Cool Area 7	L161	
8	8	16	1 Electric	16	Source 4-36°	575w	Cool Area 6	L161	
9	9	51	1 Electric	3	Source 4-36°	575w	Temp DS Center	NC	T: R7733
9	9	51	1 Electric	17	Source 4-36°	575w	Temp DS Center	NC	T: R7733
10	10	21	1 Electric	18	Source 4-26°	575w	in 1 SL Far 1/4 Lav	R51	

Expression 1; 150 chan, 174 dim   Lighting design by Steve Shelley   Page 1 of 15

Figure 4.14 The Circuit Schedule Showing the First 10 Circuits of the *Hockey* Light Plot

cuit 3 is connected to 1 electric #5 and 8 (again a two-fer situation), but it is necessary to visually "skip over" the dimmer and channel column to reach that conclusion. Aside from that, the columns are again logically arranged to follow the electrical path. Circuit 3 is plugged into dimmer 3, which is then softpatched to channel 8. The rest of the columns reiterate the rest of the information regarding the instruments plugged into circuit 3. The instrument type, wattage, and purpose of the instrument is identified, along with a column for additional notes.

During the load-in circuits are often swapped or exchanged to facilitate the installation of the instruments. A final version of the circuitry schedule may not be attainable until after the entire lighting package has been mounted, hot tested, and deemed operational. For this reason, producing the circuit schedule document is often delayed until after the focus session has concluded.

If the number of circuits in an existing lighting package are finite, or if adding circuitry is not an option, the number of circuits may become a parameter. If a show with added circuitry has an extended run, plug burnouts or wire breaks within cable may be more likely to occur over time. These are three scenarios in which the circuit schedule may become the reference document used to find alternate electrical routes from the instruments to the dimmers.

The Dimmer Schedule

The fourth form uses the final intersection in the electrical path to sort the same lighting information. This list is called the **dimmer schedule** (Figure 4.16). The information is displayed in the same numerical order as the patch display in most computer light boards. To prevent electronic confusion, every dimmer has a unique number.

Figure 4.15 highlights the dimmer's location in the electrical path. The dimmer schedule usually lists all of the dimmers that exist in a lighting package. The first rows of a dimmer schedule list all of the circuits that are hardpatched into dimmer 1, along with the identity number of any assigned control. The final dimmer entry is the highest dimmer number in the lighting system. When questions arise about the contents of a given dimmer, this document should be consulted for answers. This form is also often produced with blank rows between each different number, allowing for handwritten circuitry additions to any dimmer.

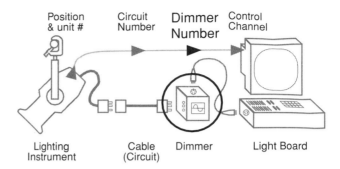

Figure 4.15 The Electrical Path Highlighting the Dimmer

Figure 4.16 shows the dimmer schedule for the first 10 dimmers of the *Hokey* light plot. This form is often produced with the dimmers listed in bold type in the left-hand column to confirm the sort order and the identity of the document. The next two columns again present the rest of the electrical path, but since the dimmer is an intermediate intersection in the path, it is necessary to visually "skip" over columns to confirm relationships that exist for each row.

The dimmer schedule for *Hokey* shows that dimmer 1 is "open" at this time, or available for use. Since the dimmer number matches the circuit number, it's possible to infer that dimmer 2 is "hardwired" to circuit 2. To check the channel assignment, however, it is necessary to visually skip over the circuit column to see that dimmer 2 is assigned to channel 18. Likewise, determining the position and unit number at the other end of the circuit, requires visually "skipping" over the channel column. To the right of the position and unit columns are the rest of the logistical information: the type, wattage, purpose, color, and notes about each instrument.

The primary function of the dimmer schedule is to identify the circuits that are hardpatched into the dimmer, then to identify the control channel to which the dimmer has been assigned. This form is consulted when a search for additional control to the lighting system is taking place. A visual gap in the list may indicate an open or unassigned dimmer that can receive a circuit.

In many cases, the circuitry and the specific dimmers are unknown until the hang is finished and the installation of the lighting package is complete. The dimmer schedule often isn't produced until that time, which may not be until the focus session is concluded.

Hybrid Theatre 1998   *Hokey* Dimmer Schedule   Date: 4/30/98

Cir	Dim	Chan	Position	#	Type	Watt	Purpose	Color	Notes
1									
2	2	18	1 Electric	4	Source 4-36°	575w	Cool Area 10	L161	
2	2	18	1 Electric	7	Source 4-36°	575w	Cool Area 9	L161	
3	3	8	1 Electric	5	Source 4-36°	575w	Warm Area 10	R33	
3	3	8	1 Electric	8	Source 4-36°	575w	Warm Area 9	R33	
4	4	7	1 Electric	9	Source 4-36°	575w	Warm Area 8	R33	
5	5	55	1 Electric	10	Source 4-26°	575w	CC Front Special	NC	
6	6	17	1 Electric	11	Source 4-36°	575w	Cool Area 8	L161	
7	7	6	1 Electric	12	Source 4-36°	575w	Warm Area 7	R33	
7	7	6	1 Electric	15	Source 4-36°	575w	Warm Area 6	R33	
8	8	16	1 Electric	13	Source 4-36°	575w	Cool Area 7	L161	
8	8	16	1 Electric	16	Source 4-36°	575w	Cool Area 6	L161	
9	9	51	1 Electric	3	Source 4-36°	575w	Temp DS Center	NC	T: R7733
9	9	51	1 Electric	17	Source 4-36°	575w	Temp DS Center	NC	T: R7733
10	10	21	1 Electric	18	Source 4-26°	575w	in 1 SL Far 1/4 Lav	R51	

Expression 1; 150 chan, 174 dim   Lighting design by Steve Shelley   Page 1 of 14

Figure 4.16 A Dimmer Schedule Showing the First 10 Dimmers for the *Hokey* Light Plot

Color Cards and Floor Cards

One area of a light plot that often changes during the progression of a performance is equipment that is accessible from the deck. This often translates to focus or color changes in the sidelight booms, along with any rovers or practicals specific to an act. **Color cards** and **floor cards** are reference documents created to reflect changes in color or circuitry that occur in one portion of a light plot during the course of a performance. When sidelight is concerned, this often results in two color cards—one for each side of the stage. The floor card provides focus information for instruments on both sides of the stage, and lists any other information specific to a particular act.

In addition to what may be indicated on the light plot, the color and floor cards clarify the amount of color and templates that the lighting designer intends to use in the sidelight booms. Before load-in, these documents give the production electrician a preliminary idea of the amount of electrical work that will take place on stage during the performance.

The Color Cards

Color cards are documents showing changes in the instruments of a hanging position over the course of a multiscene performance. In most cases, this means that the documents show the color and accessories that will be required for each of the boom sidelight units for each act of a show. Prior to each act, the deck electrician refers to a color card to complete three actions. First, change the colors in the sidelights. Second, preset the position, circuit, and color of any additional

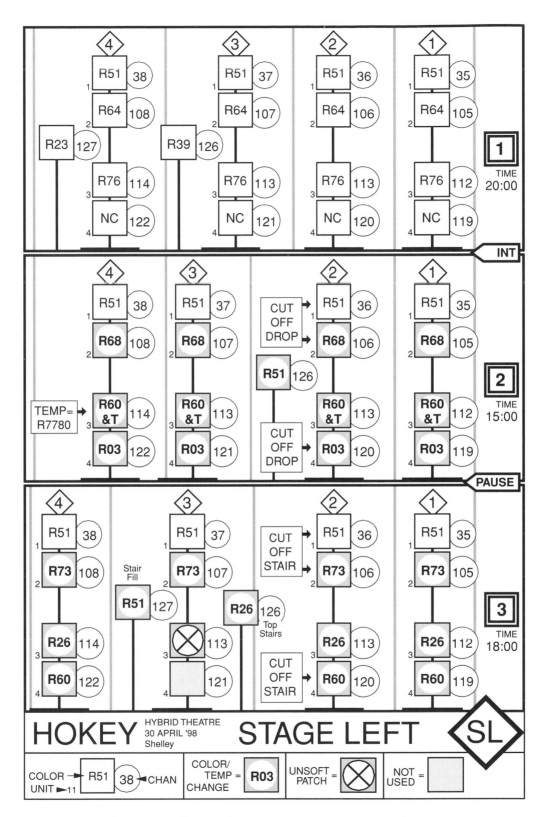

Figure 4.17 The Stage Left Color Card for *Hokey*, Showing All Three Acts

instruments on floor stands. Finally, plug any special practicals, effects, or other sources into the circuitry on that side of the stage. When the changes are complete, the status of the physical color, circuitry, and instrumentation for that side of the stage should match the card. Ideally, the color card shows all of the changes on one side of the stage for an entire performance, allowing the production electrician to see the total amount of color and accessories that will be required for that entire area in a single document. From a different perspective, it allows the lighting designer to trace the usage of a single instrument or an entire system through the course of a performance. For example, if the shinbusters have not been used in a scene for their original intent, the designer may change their color and use them in another scene for a completely different purpose. Sometimes, however, the number of changes between acts in the sidelight position is so extensive that a separate color card is required for each act. While this increases the number of documents, color cards quickly answer any questions about color media or the use of any sidelight instrument through the course of a show.

Enough copies of the color cards are distributed so that all electricians assigned to work on stage (or **deck electricians**) can complete their tasks with a minimum of direction. One approach is to attach a card to each sidelight boom, while a second approach may be to supply one card to each deck electrician. The method of distribution should be defined, since the possibility always exists that the cards will need to be revised. If the distribution method isn't clearly defined, deck electricians may unknowingly use outdated versions to perform incorrect actions.

Figure 4.17 shows the stage left color card for the production of *Hokey*. The card is divided into two main areas: The **footer** includes the title block information and the legend, while the **boom area** shows the channel and color for each instrument, for each act. The title block information in the footer includes the name of the show, the theatre, the version (the date), the lighting designer, and the side of the stage being presented. The legend under the title block explains how to read the symbols on the card.

The boom area of this color card is drawn from the perspective of a person standing on centerline and looking into the lenses of the instruments on stage left. The numbered diamonds above each of the four booms on the card matches the identity of the four booms on the stage. Boom 1 Left, for example, is drawn on the right-hand side of the card. When viewed from the proper perspective on centerline, Boom 1 Left is farthest downstage, the farthest boom "to the right." By arranging the card to match the actual configuration on stage, information can be easily compared from the physical instruments to the drawn information on the card.

The boom area is divided into three sections. Each section represents the status of the same instruments during each act of the show. The name and length of the act are listed adjacent to the first boom in each section. Tall lines represent vertical pipe supporting the booms, while squares represent the lighting instruments. The shaded lines represent the masking legs, to assist general orientation and rover placement. Each channel is listed in a circle adjacent to each instrument, providing the channel hookup information for that side of the stage. This means anyone using the card can activate any channel and check its circuitry or color without referring to an additional document.

The Floor Card

The companion to the color card is the **floor card,** which is a miniature groundplan of the stage. It graphically shows any special instrument focus and any preset checklists to be performed before each act. It is the document used for the second portion of presetting the deck. One technique involves inserting a color card and a floor card together into a plastic page protector, with the color card on one side and the floor card on the other. The combination of the two documents shows all of the information that the deck electrician will need to preset that act.

Prior to each act, the deck electrician refers to the floor card to complete four actions. First, to change any focus in the system sidelights. Second, to focus any additional floor stands or special units. Third, to check the focus and function of any crucial overhead specials required for that act of the show. Finally, the card is used to perform any preset checklists prior to each act. When the change is complete, the focus and function of the equipment on the stage should match the card. If there's room available on the document, it can be a repository for other information regarding the act, including memory numbers, the length of scenes or acts, or the timing of any deck cues.

Figure 4.18 shows the floor card for *Hokey*, Act 1. The document is divided into three components: The **footer** displays the title block and legend information, the **notes** are located above the footer, and the **groundplan** of the stage occupies the rest of the document. The title block information includes the name and act

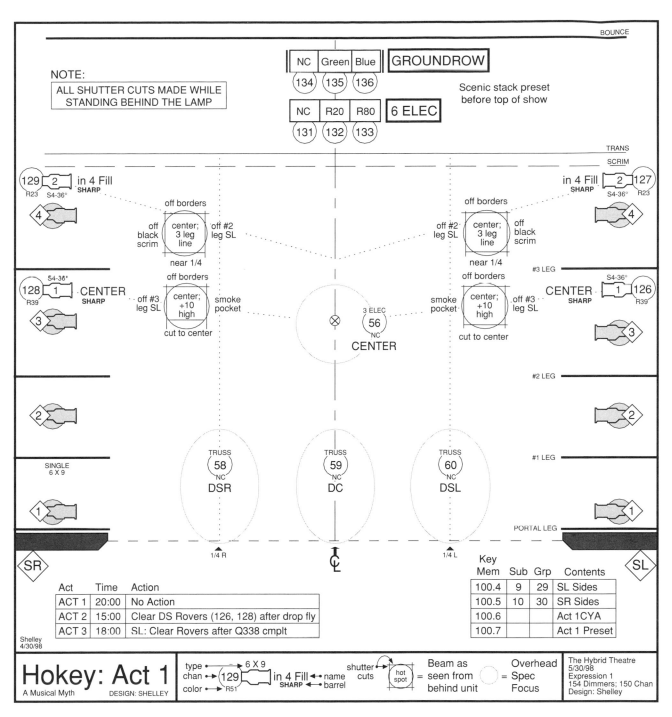

Figure 4.18 The Floor Card for *Hokey*, Act 1

of the show, the length of time for the act, along with the version (the date) of the document. The legend in the middle of the footer shows how to read the symbols, while the right-hand side lists other archival information.

The notes area on the *Hokey* floor card indicates memory preset numbers, along with times for each act. The rest of the card is the groundplan, showing the information about each additional unit, and indicating any special scenery involved in the act. The top of the page shows the channels and colors for the lights contained in the scenic stack. This information isn't necessary unless something about that area changes for that act. If the color in the instruments or the scenic backing changes, the channels should be checked for color consistency or to be certain that no light is leaking under the bottom of the drop. Overhead specials specific to the act are shown as dashed pools so that they can be included in the pre-act check as well. The rovers are shown on the sides of the color card in their relative position to the sidelight booms. The card reiterates any special circuitry that needs to be plugged, reducing the need to flip the page protector and check information from the color card. The text in front of the instrument identifies the focus point and barrel focus of the instrument.

The presumption is made that the electrician will stand behind the instrument or look away from the light while performing the focus. Based on that, the focus details are shown from the perspective of standing behind the beam of the instrument, rather than looking into it.

Figure 4.19 shows a close-up of the focus chart used to locate the focus point and indicate any shutter cuts. The circle indicates the beam pool. The text inside the circle indicates the location of the focus point. Each line crossing through the circle indicates a shutter cut. The adjacent text gives a written description of the cut. This written focus format will be used throughout the rest of this text to indicate the focus for all instruments.

Figure 4.19 A Close-Up of a Focus Chart

The Combined Color and Floor Card

Depending on the complexity of the show or the preference of the production electrician, the color card and floor card may be combined into a single document. If all of the information can be included in this format, combining the two documents into one means one less piece of paper to update. Figure 4.20 shows the same information as the previous floor and color card for *Hokey*, Act 1, produced in a different layout. The color and focus information is combined into a single document. In this layout, the rovers are located upstage of the booms, but each rover has its own groundplan showing the placement of the unit. A rectangle above each rover identifies its name. The groundplan under the rectangle shows the placement and groundplan focus for the instrument. The front view underneath shows the height placement of the instrument and the focus point, along with the top and bottom shutter cuts. Although this version is more compact, it doesn't include any additional channels or preset checklist information.

The Analysis Spreadsheets and Shop Order

While the light plot is being created, the house inventory should be kept close at hand. In situations without a rental budget, the house inventory may be the parameter that defines the boundaries of the lighting design. Other situations may financially allow additional equipment to be brought into the space to complete the lighting package.

On the other hand, productions often occur in a **four-wall theatre,** a term implying that the only thing the theatre contains is "four walls." In this situation, the entire lighting package and anything else the electrics department might require to mount the lighting package will have to be obtained from other sources. That may range from every instrument and component of the light plot, to every focusing ladder, to any workboxes, tools, the production table, down to a paper cutter for the gel.

In our example, the Hybrid Theatre owns a focusing lift for the stage, and ladders to access hanging positions in the house. The technical representative of the theatre has confirmed the house inventory, which includes some instruments, dimmers, and cable. As the light plot is constructed, a method can be employed to keep track of the placement of the house inventory

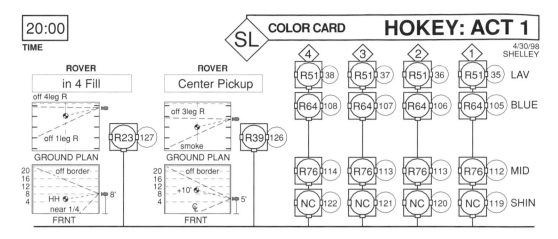

Figure 4.20 A Combined Color and Floor Card for *Hokey*, Act 1

while maintaining an accurate count of additional equipment.

Forms can be used to track this dispersal of equipment and control. The **instrument spreadsheet** can be used to keep a running tally of the instrument distributed to each hanging position, while a **circuitry and dimmer spreadsheet** can be used to keep track of those elements required to control each of the instruments. While these running lists of the "nuts and bolts" allows the lighting designer keep track of a house inventory, they're even more important when the light plot involves rental equipment.

Presumably, the lighting designer has analyzed the budget, the house inventory, and the existing circuit and dimmer layout within the facility prior to creating the light plot. Once the light plot has been completed, a **shop order** can be constructed that lists all of the additional equipment that will be necessary to create the lighting package. Initially, the document enables lighting rental shops to produce rental bids. After a shop has been selected, the document is used as a "shopping list," to assemble the equipment for the load-in.

The Instrument Spreadsheet

The **instrument spreadsheet** shows the distribution of each type of instrument within all of the different hanging positions. Construction of this document begins by confirming the wattage and type of each functioning instrument in the house inventory. Once the total for each instrument category is listed in the document, the lighting designer can then "juggle" existing

and rented equipment, and make informed choices while constructing the light plot.

Figure 4.21 shows the completed instrument spreadsheet for *Hokey*. The document is laid out so that the positions label each row, while the instrument types identify each of the columns. In this case, the house instrumentation is separated from the rental units by a "shaded split" column, and listed in three columns on the left-hand side. The rest of the columns indicate the type of instruments that will be included in the shop order. The farthest right-hand column is a formula that produces a total for each position.

The three rows at the bottom of the spreadsheet serve two functions. The top row on the left-hand side of the shaded split shows the total number of house instruments used in the plot. The second row lists the available instruments available in the inventory. The bottom row is a formula that subtracts the total number used from the existing stock. These cells show the number of instruments remaining, which will be used as spare instrumentation. On the other side of the shaded split, the bottom three rows contain slightly different information. The top row totals each type of rented instrumentation, the second row adds spare instrumentation, and the bottom row is formulated to add the two cells above it together, resulting in a sum of equipment that will be included on the shop order.

Note that the bottom right-hand cell (188) is the total sum of the rest of the row immediately to its left, that is, the total for all of the types of instruments. The cell immediately above it (also 188) is the sum of the rest of the cells above it, totaling all of the positions.

Hybrid Theatre 1998   *Hokey* **Instrument Spreadsheet**   Date: 4/16/98

	House 1kw X12	750 X9	House Total	Source Four 575w 19°	26°	36°	14" 1kw Scp	Mini 500w 10	T-3 500w 3 Cir	R-40 300w 3 Cir	Stark 1200w Spot	Total	
Truss	5		5	3	5							13	Truss
SL Box	3	3	6				1				1	8	SL Box
SR Box	3	3	6				1				1	8	SR Box
1 Elec		5	5		5	7		2				19	1 Elec
2 Elec		5	5		4	17						26	2 Elec
3 Elec			0		1	10						11	3 Elec
4 Elec			0		4	12		2				18	4 Elec
5 Elec			0		5	12						17	5 Elec
6 Elec			0						4			4	6 Elec
1 Bm L		1	1			4						5	1 Bm L
1 Bm L		1	1			4						5	1 Bm L
3 Bm L		1	1			4						5	3 Bm L
4 Bm L		1	1			4						5	4 Bm L
Rovers L			0			2						2	Rovers L
1 Bm R		1	1			4						5	1 Bm R
2 Bm R		1	1			4						5	2 Bm R
3 Bm R		1	1			4						5	3 Bm R
4 Bm R		1	1			4						5	4 Bm R
Rovers R			0			2						2	Rovers R
Groundrow			0			2				6		8	Groundrow
Total Used	11	24	35	3	24	96	2	4	4	6	2	176	**Subtotal**
Existing Stock	15	30	**45**	1	3	6	1	1	0	0	0	12	**Spares**
												188	
Remaining	4	6	10	4	27	102	3	5	4	6	2	**188**	**Total**

Expression 1; 150 chan, 174 dim   Lighting design by Steve Shelley

Figure 4.21 The Instrument Spreadsheet for the *Hokey* Light Plot

Any discrepancy between these two cells alerts the user to any anomalies that may occur when rows or columns are inserted without formula information.

The Circuitry and Dimmer Spreadsheet

Another document used during the plotting process is the **circuitry and dimmer spreadsheet,** which illustrates how the preinstalled circuits and dimmers will be utilized. It also shows the location and number of additional circuits and dimmers that will be added. Initial construction of this document begins by a detailed analysis of the location and capacities of the preinstalled circuits and dimmers in the performance space. After a study of the house drawings and other information from the technical specifications, each circuit and dimmer is determined and listed by location. As the lighting design takes shape in the plotting process, seeing the amount and location of circuitry and the number of dimmers used allows the lighting designer to make informed choices.

Hybrid Theatre 1998   *Hokey* **Circuitry and Dimmer Spreadsheet**   Date: 4/30/98

POSITION	Circuits in light plot					Circuits		Exist Dim 30 24		Added Dim 48 24 48			NOTES	POSITION
	575	1K	1.15K	2K	TOTAL	exist	add	2.4K	4K	2.4K	1.2K	4KW		
Truss	13				13		13			5		8	Home run	Truss
SL Bx Bm		1	3		4	6		4					Pros L: 19 > 24	SL Bx Bm
SR Bx Bm		1	3		4	6			4				Pros R: 25 > 30	SR Bx Bm
1 Electric	7	1	5		13	12	3	12	3				1 Elec: 1 > 12	1 Electric
2 Electric	18		5		23		23			23			Home run to rack	2 Electric
3 Electric	11				11	12			11				SL Flr Pockets	3 Electric
4 Electric	14	1	1		16		16			18			Home run to rack	4 Electric
5 Electric	15		1		16		16					16	Home run to rack	5 Electric
6 Elec			12		12	15						6	3 Elec: 31 > 45	6 Elec
1 Bm L	4				4	4					4		Run to rack DL	1 Bm L
2 Bm L	4				4	4					4		Run to rack DL	2 Bm L
3 Bm L	4				4	4					4		Run to rack DL	3 Bm L
4 Bm L	4				4	6			4				UL Pocket: 43 >48	4 Bm L
1 Bm R	4				4	4		4					Home run house	1 Bm R
2 Bm R	4				4	4					4		Run to rack DL	2 Bm R
3 Bm R	4				4	4					4		Run to rack DL	3 Bm R
4 Bm R	4				4	6					4		Run to rack DL	4 Bm R
Rover	2				2	4		4					UL/UR Pock: 49	Rover
Groundrow	9				9	9						9	US Pockets	Groundrow

Total circuits required by plot: **155**
Total number of existing circuits used: **76**
Total circuits added: **95**
Total existing dimmers used: **24** | **22**
Total added dimmers used: **46** | **24** | **39**

Company switch is DSL.
House dimmers are DSR.

	2.4K	1.2K	4KW
Total need to add	46	24	39
Total 48 x 2.4KW	48		
Total 24 x 2.4KW		30	
Total 32 x 4KW			48
Extra dimmers	2	6	9

Note: All 1kw circuits are works;
run to SM switchbox

Expression 1; 150 chan, 174 dim   Lighting design by Steve Shelley

Figure 4.22 The Circuitry and Dimmer Spreadsheet for the *Hokey* Light Plot

Once the light plot is complete, the added circuits and dimmers in the document are included in the shop order. Seeing the amount and location of circuitry and dimming equipment that will be used in the show helps gauge the amount of time and labor that will be necessary to install the lighting package.

Figure 4.22 shows the circuitry and dimmer spreadsheet for *Hokey*. Like the instrument spreadsheet, the positions are shown on each row. In this case, however, there are five vertical sections to the document. On the left side, five columns analyze the circuitry for the production, listing the number, wattage size, and the total number of circuits required for each hanging position.

The next two columns examine the circuitry that will be required for the light plot. The left-hand column of the pair shows hanging positions where circuits currently exist. When the totals from the "existing circuits" column are subtracted from the "total circuits in the light plot" column, the result is the number of additional circuits required at each hanging position in the "added circuits" column. The notes column on the right-hand side of the page identifies the house circuits that will be used, or indicates the path for added cable.

The remaining five columns analyze how the circuits in the light plot will be assigned to the house and road dimmers. The left-hand pair show circuits assigned to the 30-2.4kw and 24-4kw dimmers that exist in the theatre, while the following three columns show the assignment of remaining circuits to the added road dimmers. By having the combined electrical paths displayed on a single document, the lighting designer can see where and how much additional cable will be required, and if any replugging will be needed to retain the amount of control desired. It also allows the designer to make certain that the proper adapters are included to hardpatch house circuits to road dimmers, or added circuits to house dimmers.

The Shop Order

The **shop order** is the list of equipment that will be added to create the lighting package. Since the amount of equipment required to produce a lighting design is unknown until the lighting design is completed, the shop order is often one of the last documents created in this packet. Once created and checked, the shop order is usually sent to various lighting rental companies for a **bid,** the term describing the rental price for the shop order. After the bids have been submitted a lighting rental shop is selected.

If a theatre owns any equipment, the combination of the house inventory and any shop order rental should result in more equipment than required by the lighting plot. If it's a four-wall theatre, the shop order will list every piece of equipment that will be needed to produce the light plot. Sometimes the design of the plot may not be complete by the time the shop order is needed, in which case every attempt is made to provide the most calculated guesstimate. The package may slightly change or be tweaked while being processed, but once the price for the rental has been determined, radically altering the amount of equipment can cause renegotiation, loss of confidence, and wasted time. It's important to remember that the shop order becomes a portion of the binding contract that is made between a lighting rental shop and the production, so anything specific that is needed should be included in this document. If items aren't included in the shop order, their later inclusion may change the rental price.

Usually the shop order begins with a **title page,** which provides the basic information and equipment summaries for the production. The title page should include the following schedule, contact, and note information:

- The name of the show, and the name and address of the theatre. If the shop has installed other lighting systems in the space, they may know about problems, work-arounds, or additional equipment that may be required.
- A version number on every page, usually the date the shop order was created. If there's more than one published version of the shop order, the version number or date confirms that everyone's working with the same document.
- Schedule information, including the date and time that the package loads out of the shop, or loads into the theatre, or both.
- The anticipated date that the package will return to the shop. The dates are important because the length of time the lighting package is out of the shop, coupled with the size of the package, determines the rental price that will be presented to the employer, usually the general manager.
- A sentence saying whether or not the lighting rental shop will be responsible for delivering and picking up the lighting package. Some shops include the delivery and pickup of the equipment in the rental price. Others add it as an additional cost after the final price has been determined.
- The amount of labor, if any, supplied by the production to assemble the package in the shop. If no one from the show is present to oversee the assemblage of the rental order, some shops charge additional monies for their personnel to perform in that capacity.
- Contact information for the designer, the production electrician, and the employer (including street addresses, telephone, fax, and e-mail). When questions arise, the shops know whom to contact and how to get in touch with them.
- A summary of the requested instrumentation, control, dimming equipment, cable, hardware, special effects, and any specially built devices constructed by the shop. These numbers are what the lighting shops analyze, along with the length of the rental period, to determine the weekly or total rental cost.
- A summary of the requested perishables (if it should be prepared with the lighting package).

Sometimes perishables aren't included in the shop order, and they may be purchased from a separate vendor. If the color isn't included with the shop order, however, it won't be cut and framed with the rest of the order, and may then require time for preparation during the load-in.

- Any general notes or requests. These usually include broad topics, giving the lighting shops an idea of the standards that the show will accept. Examples include "all instruments painted black" (or whatever color if they're to be exposed), "no substitutions of equipment without written consent of designer" (sometimes they do), "all instruments equipped with lamp, c-clamp, and safety cable," or "each instrument type to have spare lamps" to name a few.

One important statement that should be included can be interpreted as insulting, since it's stating a basic fact that should be assumed. However, assumptions can become the cause for harsh feelings. The note often reads: "The entire lighting package is to be made ready by the supplier and is to include all components, including hardware, connectors, cables, controls, frames, etc., so as to comprise a complete working system." This basically states that whatever the lighting shop eventually produces in the form of the lighting package will indeed all plug together to make the complete working light plot. After receiving an incomplete package, hearing the resulting telephone explanation of "but it wasn't on the order" can be very disappointing. Not only is it incredibly irritating, this situation can also delay the schedule and waste time.

Although the designer's basic instinct may be to include every backup and contingency on the shop order, moderation has to be taken into consideration. Granted, if the shop is not in the city where the production will be produced, some overage needs to be included. On the other hand, it's a bit unreasonable to request massive numbers of spare instruments, duplicate consoles, or backup dimmer racks. One method that's used to determine the number of spare instruments is to add 10% of each type of instrument to the shop order.

It's worth noting that if the shop order isn't specific about the exact needs for the show, the shop can supply the show with whatever is available to them at that time. If the backstage space in the theatre available for rental dimmers is constrained, for example, list the specific dimmer rack that will fit in that area. Otherwise, the shop may substitute the generic re-

quest with another rack, which may not fit into the space.

Following the title page, the rest of the shop order lists the basic components of equipment for the show, typically sorted by these categories:

- Lighting instruments (Group the units by type, usually starting with ellipsoidals. Include wattages and beam spreads where applicable.)
- Cable (multicable or bundle, number and length of individual jumpers, two-fers, three-fers, breakouts)
- Hardware (mounting or accessory items including truss, pipe, base plates, sidearms, c-clamps, pipe stiffeners, scenery bumpers, tophats, barndoors, and template holders)
- Control (type of light board, software format if applicable, number and length of control cables to connect the light board to the dimmers; also may include number of monitors for the board, number of monitors for the production table, length of monitor cable, compatible printer and printer cable, voltage regulators, and any additional control converters or opto-isolators)
- Dimmers (Specify number, wattage, and rack configuration, along with feeder cable. Feeder cable length and proper wire gauge size should be indicated, along with the type of power that will be used.)
- Specialty items (including color scrollers, gobo rotators, and any accompanying control or power cables)
- Special effects (including fog machines, hazers, strobe lights, mirrorballs, confetti cannons, and so on)
- Perishables (including color, templates, tieline, tape, marking utensils, and so forth).

The format of the shop order may be adapted to the particular lighting rental shop that will be supplying the equipment. Their choice of format will reflect the way that they process the order. Some shops enter the elements of the shop order into their computer system, so they can keep track of their inventories. A copy of that document should be checked for accuracy before the lighting package gets loaded into the road boxes.

Other shops process orders using copies of the submitted shop order. They prefer that the document be laid out as a **departmental shop order,** listing each equipment category on a separate page. That way each separate page can be distributed to the applicable department within their facility. Using this shop order format is acceptable when there's ample room on site to open many road boxes at once, since equipment will be loaded into the crates solely by type or size with no attention paid to position. It's highly likely that the 6 × 16 ellipsoidals for the box booms will be in the same road box as the 6 × 16 ellipsoidals for the fifth electric. If the shop order is processed using this system, areas on the paperwork should be assigned to note checkpoints in the process, including the number of the road box and the date the equipment is packed. On large orders, a groundplan showing the load order of the road boxes in the truck (the **truck pack**) may be necessary as well.

Even if the road box has labels indicating its contents, there's no certainty that everything will be listed. Without a detailed list tracing each movement of equipment out of the shop, claims can be made that equipment was packaged, while the equipment in question can't be found on site. This can result in money being paid for equipment that was never received.

Regardless of the format used when preparing the shop order, a second document is often created to provide clarity in the assembly of the equipment. The **position breakdown** is a reiteration of the shop order, but instead of total numbers for the entire package, the document lists every piece of equipment that will be used in each hanging position. The position breakdown allows the production electrician and the personnel assembling the package to see the distribution of the equipment when the lighting package is installed in the performance facility. Not only does this document answer questions about the shop order, the position breakdown allows road boxes to be loaded by hanging position. This can be a tactical advantage when the amount of space on stage is limited, or the lighting package is being transported to the facility in several trucks.

Figure 4.23 shows a compressed departmental shop order for *Hokey*. Each item is listed separately, and rectangles are included on the right-hand side of the page to note the date when equipment is pulled from stock, where it is packed, and the truck number that it will be loaded into when departing the lighting rental shop.

Manuals and Cut Sheets

The possibility always exists that equipment used in a light plot won't perform properly. Following Mur-

phy's law, if there is any chance that equipment will fail, it will. If unknown or untested equipment can behave in an unexpected manner, it will. With that in mind, the amount of information needed for any piece of equipment is determined on a case-by-case basis. The newer or less familiar the equipment, the farther from a point of service, or the less troubleshooting time allowed in the schedule, then the greater the need to acquire as much contact, assembly, and troubleshooting information possible. Any equipment provided to the lighting designer that includes the phrase "beta-test" should set off alarm bells, signaling the amount of caution with which it should be approached.

For these reasons, it's wise to have manufacturer's cut sheets and a manual for every device whose complexity or failure might become a time-consuming problem. A **cut sheet** is typically a single page of paper providing information about a piece of equipment. Ideally, neither of these documents will be needed, but they may hold the solution in moments of urgency. If nothing else, they may include a phone number, a fax number, a web page address, or an e-mail address to establish direct communication with the manufacturer.

If a manual exists for an unfamiliar electrical device, you should consider having a copy of that manual on site where the electrical device is going to be used. When the board operator isn't intimately familiar with the console, a manual should be acquired with the light board. Discovering that no one knows how to program the suddenly-needed software function at 2 A.M. can test friendships, since it may result in waking up a comrade to determine the programming sequence. If the shop is kind enough to supply a manual for the console, the document is typically returned at the end of the rental. Keeping a stock of manuals on hand can quickly become an expensive and time-consuming proposition, so shops are often justified when the cost of a missing manual is added to the final rental settlement.

If it's a new light board, gather whatever preliminary manuals, notes, or data you can find from any source available. Ask for phone numbers of anyone representing the new board and anyone who will admit to having used the console. If the production is utilizing a new kind of atmospheric generator, such as fog, smoke, or haze, the material safety data sheet may need to be given to the management of the theatre, the performer's representative, or the fire marshal.

The case can be made that gathering this information is the domain and responsibility of the pro-

Hybrid Theatre 1998   *Hokey* **Shop Order**   Date: 5/1/98

INSTRUMENTS

	Qty		Item	Watt	Pull Date	Road Box	Truck #
	4	-	Source Four 19 degree	575w			
	27	-	Source Four 26 degree	575w			
	102	-	Source Four 36 degree	575w			
	3	-	14" Scoop	1kw Clear			
	5	-	Mini Ten	500w Clear			
	4	-	T-3--3 circuit/12 Lt striplights	500w Clear			
	6	-	R40--3 Circuit/12 Lt striplights	300w Flood			
	2	-	Starlight short throw followspots	1200w			

HARDWARE

	Qty		Item	Pull Date	Road Box	Truck #
	135		C-Clamps			
	40	-	18" Single Tee side arms			
	6	-	24" Double Tee side arms			
	5	-	5'-0" adjustable stands			
	15	-	36" Pipe Stiffeners			
	6	-	Scenery bumpers			
	25	-	Source Four tophats			
	15	-	Altman 360Q tophats			
	175	-	Source Four color frames			
	8	-	T-3 hanging irons (matching)			
	12	-	R-40 groundrow floor trunions (matching)			
	12	-	10'-0" long 1 1/2" steel pipe (threads one end)			
	12	-	50 Lb. Base plates			
	5	-	Adjustable stand floor plates			
	30	-	Source Four template holders ("A" size)			
	8	-	Altman 360Q template holders			
	30	-	Source Four Donuts			
	2	-	Starlight yokes & color boomerangs (no stands)			
		-	50' Z-tec Painted Black per Production Electrician			
	170	-	Safeties			

Expression 1; 150 chan, 174 dim   Lighting design by Steve Shelley   Page 1 of 4

Figure 4.23 A Partial Shop Order for the *Hokey* Light Plot

duction electrician. If the production electrician's time is being consumed getting the light package out of the rental shop, however, someone else had best get the information. Blamestorming at 11 P.M. on a Friday night in front of the newly-dead dimmer rack does no one any good, and the lack of foresight and documentation may delay and ultimately jeopardize the lighting for the production.

The lighting designer bears ultimate responsibility for the lighting of the show, and that may include providing leadership in times of crisis. Knowledge is the key that will ultimately allow the designer the ability to make the best decision for the production in times of human or equipment failure.

SUMMARY

Once the light plot, section, and support paperwork packet is created, attention can now turn to the packet of paperwork that will provide additional information, beginning with the load-in and concluding with the completion of the focus session.

5

The Load-In and Focus Packet

The load-in and focus packet includes documents used to install, program, and focus a light plot as rapidly as possible. A **hang plot** details the relationship of the masking and the scenery to the overhead hanging positions. A **headset layout diagram** can be used to graphically define the communication that will be used. **Focus cues, infrastructure cues, submasters,** and **groups** programmed into the computer lighting console can accelerate light board activity. **Spike groundplans** and **focus documents** can be used to expedite the focus session, while **focus charts** can be used to record or regenerate the focus.

THE HANG PLOT

The **hang plot** is a more detailed view of the goods listed in the lineset schedule, which was seen in both the light plot and the section. Although the lineset schedule labels the equipment on each batten, the hang plot provides a more complete picture of the fly system for that production. Ideally, it is the result of coordination between the scenic and lighting elements of the show. If nothing else, the hang plot shows the specific overhead hanging positions that will be used for the electrical equipment.

Figure 5.1 shows the *Hokey* hang plot, which is separated into two series of columns, the lineset schedule and the spot line schedule. The **lineset schedule** details the relevant information about each batten: label number, distance from plaster line, and the name and

trim height of the goods or electrics. In some cases, the notes column indicates the distance from centerline where the legs or scenic pieces will be hung. It can also list any other special notes. The **spot line schedule** refers to any hanging points or additions in the air other than the counterweight system. This may range from rope running through single sheaves that are "spotted" at specific points in the grid, to aircraft cable attached directly to the grid. A column may also be included indicating the estimated weight of each lineset or added spot line.

The hang plot can be used as a common reference document for many departments and is often one of the first documents that is used during the load-in. The production electrician may use the information supplied on the hang plot to calculate lengths of additional cable, while the props department might refer to it to see where the sidelight booms will be located relative to the performance surface. The carpentry staff can use the hang plot, along with other scenic drawings, to install the scenery.

THE HEADSET LAYOUT DIAGRAM

The production table (or "tech table") is usually placed in the center of the house during load-in. During the technical rehearsals, it is occupied by the lighting designer, the director, the stage manager, and other members of the staff. The table's optimal placement is at the most centralized viewing perspective in the

Hybrid Theatre 1998   *Hokey* **Hang Plot**   Date: 4/30/98

LINE	DIST.	GOODS	TRIM	DIST. CL	NOTES	DIST.	DIST. CL	SPOT LINES
	0'-0"	Plaster line						Plasterline
	1'-0"	House Curtain						
1	2'-0"	Portal Border	20'-6"		2'-6" extensions each end (10'H X 50'W)			
2	2'-7"	Portal Legs		18'-0"	3'-6" extensions each end (30'H X 7'W)		18'-0"	
	3'-0"					3'-0"	24'-6"	#1 Boom L & R
3	3'-2"	1 Electric	23'-9"		19-S 4's, house circ: trim to lens			
4	3'-9"							
5	4'-4"							
6	4'-11"							
7	5'-6"							
8	6'-1"							
9	6'-8"	#1 Black Border	21'-0"		2'-6" extensions each end (10'H X 50'W)			
10	7'-3"	#1 Black Legs		18'-0"	3'-6" extensions each end (30'H X 7'W)		18'-0"	
11	7'-10"							
12	8'-5"	2 Electric	24'-0"		26-S 4's, bundles to SL side; trim to lens			
13	9'-0"							
14	9'-7"							
	10'-0"					10'-0"	25'-7"	#2 Boom L & R
15	10'-2"	Cable Xover			5 circuit bundle; 2 Boom R to SL dim			
16	10'-9"							
17	11'-5"	3 Electric	27'-3"		11-S 4's, bundles to SL floor; trim to lens			
18	12'-0"							
19	12'-7"	#2 Black Border	21'-0"		2'-6" extensions each end (10'H X 50'W)			
20	13'-2"	#2 Black Legs		18'-0"	3'-6" extensions each end (30'H X 7'W)		18'-0"	
21	13'-9"							
22	14'-4"							
23	14'-11"	4 Electric	24'-0"		18-S 4's, bundles to SL; trim to lens			
24	15'-6"							
25	16'-1"							
	16'-3"			25'7"		16'-3"	25'-7"	#3 Boom L & R
26	16'-9"	Cable Xover			5 circuit bundle; 3 Boom R to SL dim			
27	17'-5"							
28	18'-1"							
29	18'-9"	#3 Black Border	21'-0"		2'-6" extensions each end (10'H X 50'W)			
30	19'-5"	#3 Black Legs		18'-0"	3'-6" extensions each end (30'H X 7'W)			
31	20'-1"							
32	20'-9"							
33	21'-5"							
34	22'-1"							
35	22'-9"							
36	23'-5"	5 Electric	24'-8"		17-Source 4's, bundles to SL; trim to lens			
37	24'-1"							
38	24'-9"	#4 Black Border	21'-0"		2'-6" extensions each end (10'H X 50'W)			
	24'-10"			25'7"		24'-10"	25'-7"	#4 Boom L & R
39	25'-5"	#4 Black Legs		18'-0"	3'-6" extensions each end (30'H X 7'W)			
40	26'-1"	Black Scrim			24'-0" tall X 48'-0" wide			
41	26'-9"	Translucency			30'-0" tall X 48'-0" wide			
42	27'-4"							
43	27'-11"							Groundrow
44	28'-6"	5 Electric	24'-6"		4-T-3 strips, bundles to SL; trim to color			Groundrow
45	29'-1"							
46	29'-8"							
47	30'-3"	Bounce Drop			30'-0" tall X 48'-0" wide			

Grid: 68'-0"; Pipe travel: 59'-6"   Lighting design by Steve Shelley

Figure 5.1 The *Hokey* Hang Plot

house, the most "typical" audience view. From that location, almost all directorial and design choices are made. In thrust or arena theatres, it's not uncommon for the production table to be moved to different locations during the technical rehearsal period, allowing the design elements of the show to be created and viewed from several visual perspectives.

For the lighting designer, the production table becomes his or her office from the beginning of the cue level setting session through the end of the final rehearsal. Trying to simultaneously see the stage, the monitors, and the paperwork while communicating on headset during rehearsals often means that the lighting designer is essentially "tied" to the production table. If the stage manager and light board operator aren't present at the production table throughout the entire rehearsal process, the most essential item that must be present at the table is a headset. If followspots are involved, the need is even greater.

Being able to communicate to the correct personnel, while not having to listen to other departments, is one reason to construct a **headset layout diagram**. Headset systems are often equipped with more than one channel or line of communication. The headset layout diagram attempts to provide the sound department with the lighting designer's desires and his or her preferences as to who should be on which channel. Typically, the lighting designer needs to communicate with the stage manager (to listen and discuss cue placement and timings), the board operator (to make cue adjustments), and any assistants (giving direction and listening for information). The followspots are often assigned to a different channel when they are coordinated by an assistant or the stage manager.

Figure 5.2 shows the preliminary headset layout diagram for *Hokey*, detailing the location and channel assignments for the different headset positions. Channel A is often designated as the general channel for communication with the stage manager; other channels are assigned by the amount of communication activity. Other departments on headset usually don't want to listen to the numerous changes made in each light cue being given to the board operator. On the other hand, in the midst of a complex technical rehearsal, the lighting designer can't be concerned with discussion over headset about the sound levels or the movement of the set. The diagram may also show the location for all cue lights, providing the production electrician with information about the circuitry that will be required for that system.

COMPUTER LIGHT BOARD INFORMATION

It is often heard that there's no reason to program anything into the light board until the focus is complete. That statement may very well be accurate if the board used for the show is a manual light board. If the light board for the show is a computer lighting console, however, it can be used as a timesaving tool for many tasks.

Every computer light board has memory components, including the memories that are used to play back light cues. A system that partitions blocks of memory for additional tasks will be examined in the section discussing the **disk master chart**. Many current lighting consoles can label memories using alphanumeric keyboards, but if the keyboards are absent or nonfunctional, the memory's number may be the sole means of providing identification. Systems can be employed that allow memories and entire disks of cues to be more readily identified, which will be examined in the section discussing **cue information and identification**. Utilizing memories for more tasks than playing back memories for a show will be discussed in the section on **infrastructure cues**. Programming memories onto physical and electronic handles makes them simpler and easier to use. Using the physical handles on a lighting console will be discussed in the **submaster** section, while the programming of electronic handles will be examined in the section discussing **groups**.

The nature and design of a computer light board allows it to be much more than just a channel activator. Prior thought about the contents of the light board can help expedite the entire technical process by speeding the load-in, facilitating the focus, expediting cue construction, and rapidly performing preshow checks. The lighting designer must understand how computer light board memory works to be able to make optimal use of its features.

Memory Review

The main purpose of most computer lighting consoles is to record memories that will be played back during the show. Since almost all computer consoles automatically play back memories in numerical succession, cues are usually recorded in sequence. "Running the show" is then reduced to pressing the GO button every time the stage manager gives the command to

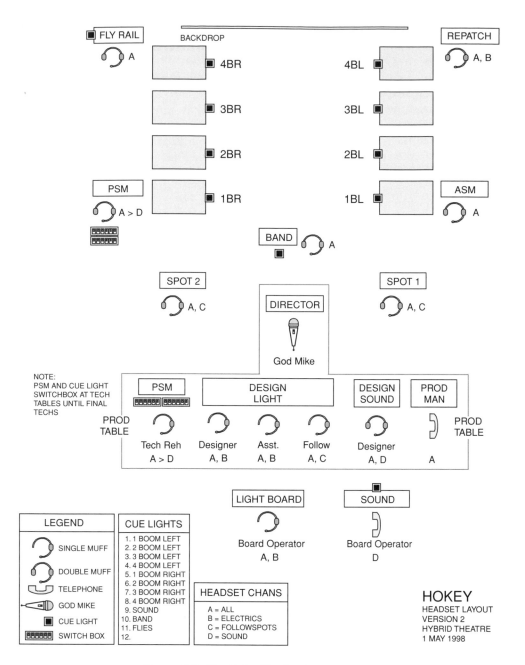

Figure 5.2 The *Hokey* Headset Layout Diagram

do so. Since any "look" can be recorded in any memory, memories could be randomly recorded with no attention paid to their purpose or identity. Obviously, that scenario could easily spell disaster. If the first act of a show takes place in moonlight while the second act takes place during a sunrise, for example, how might those memories be recorded to identify each

cue? An examination of light board memory will answer this question.

Most current computer lighting consoles have the capability to record memories labeled with whole numbers (1, 2, 3, and so on) numbered up to 999, along with nine "point" memories in between each whole number (1.1, 1.2, and so on). This means that the highest possible memory number is 999.9. Since any lighting "look" can be recorded to any memory, establishing a structure to identify sections of cues can be helpful, if not a necessity.

If point cues are temporarily set aside, a total of 999 whole numbers remain that can be assigned to different memories. To reduce that sea of numbers into something manageable, visualize a large roll of film that's been removed from a camera. Instead of 24 exposures, this roll of film has 999 pictures. After the film is developed, the frame numbers start with 1 and end with 999. Imagine cutting the film into 10 lengths. Each of the 10 filmstrips consists of 100 pictures (except the last strip, which only has 99). Set 9 of the strips aside, and consider only the first strip.

In Figure 5.3, the first strip of 100 pictures includes pictures taken at night. The first picture in Figure 5.3 is an obscured view of the moon at night; the moon's outline can barely be seen because of the cloud. Label that picture number 101, since it's the first picture on the first strip of film. The center picture, taken with the moon clearly in view, is labeled number 102. The third picture has been taken after a bank of clouds has obscured the moon, and is labeled number 103. The rest of the pictures on the strip of

film weren't used, so they're black. Set the first strip aside, and examine the second strip of film (Figure 5.4).

The second strip of 100 pictures was taken at dawn. The first picture in this strip of film, shown in Figure 5.4, is on a beach, just before sunrise. Label that picture as number 201. The second picture shows the sunrise, and is labeled number 202. The third picture shows the sunrise after a bank of clouds has obscured the sun. That picture is labeled number 203. The remaining 97 pictures on the second strip are also black. The two strips of film will now be edited and combined. After cutting away the unused excess, the exposed pictures are taped together. Their numerical sequence is now 101, 102, 103, 201, 202, and 203.

Each of those strips of film is the same as 100 whole-numbered memories. Each picture is the equivalent of a recorded memory. The first picture (101) is the equivalent of the preset for the first act; it was obscured, as if the curtain was closed and the full image couldn't be seen. The second picture of the moon (102) is the equivalent of the curtain opening to be viewed by the audience. The third picture was again obscured (103) like the image left on stage after the curtain has been closed. Although the remaining 97 pictures or

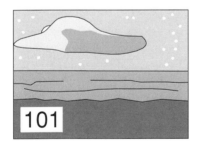 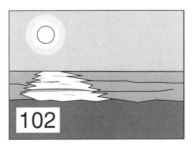 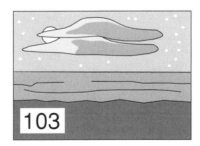

Figure 5.3 The Moonlight Pictures

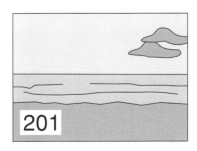 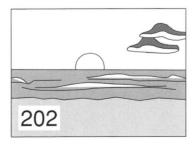 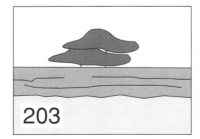

Figure 5.4 The Dawn Pictures

memories could be created, they were black (or unused). In computer light board memory, if the memories aren't created, then no label numbers for the individual memories exist. Those nonexistent numbers are "skipped over" to the next recorded memory. The next sequential number after memory 103 is memory 201, the first picture (or memory) for the second act. A list of all of those pictures together, seen on a computer monitor display, might look like this:

Cue	Time
101	3
102	10
103	5
201	3
202	10
203	5

Each memory or cue number has a unit of time assigned to it. This means that when the GO button is pressed on the computer, it will take 3 seconds for the 101 "picture" or memory to be "developed" or loaded into an active fader, allowing it to be seen on stage. When the same button is pressed again, 10 seconds will elapse while memory 102 is loaded into an active fader, replacing memory 101. Time of almost any duration can be assigned to most memories, including tenths of a second.

In the first strip of film, picture 102 showed the moon without clouds, while picture 103 was the analogy used "when the curtain closed." In the course of rehearsal, however, a stage action is added. Someone lights a torch. A new "picture" needs to be added and inserted between two existing pictures. One way to create this would be to relabel (or re-record) memory 103 to become memory 104. Then the torch cue could be created, and labeled (recorded) with the old label, memory 103. The memories would then remain in sequence. Instead of reprogramming, however, most computer light boards allow nine **insertion memories,** or **point cues** (.1, .2, .3, and so on), that can be created between each whole-numbered memory. The torch cue could be recorded anywhere from cue 102.1 to 102.9 and, when recorded, still be in sequence between memories 102 and 103. Memory 103 could remain untouched.

Understanding memory numbers is like imagining a long roll of pictures. "Developed" pictures have a recorded memory number. Black portions (or unrecorded numbers) are skipped over to the next sequential memory number. Memories can be inserted in sequence between other memories.

Numerical Mnemonics

In the picture analogy, the pictures for Act 1 were numbered in the 100's, while Act 2's pictures were numbered in the 200's. When recording memories into computer lighting consoles, many lighting designers use this same numbering scheme. Knowing the memory number allows the lighting designer, the board operator, and the stage manager to be aware of their current location within the context of the show. This is an example of **numerical mnemonics.** The phrase means that the numerical digit assigned to the memory is assisting the brain to remember something else. In this case, if the memory number is a 100, then it's a cue for Act 1. If a memory is a 200, it's a cue for Act 2.

The concept of numerical mnemonics can be used to structure the RAM of the lighting console. Specific numbers can be assigned to cues and other board functions, which will inform the lighting designer of the memory unit's identity, location, or function. Since there are typically 999 whole memory numbers contained in the RAM of a computer light board, partitioning the acts into 100's means that any other memories not associated with cues for the show can be recorded using numbers other than 100 or 200. This means that memory 1 > 99 and memories 300 > 999 are available for other tasks. Partitioning the cues into acts is the first step towards designing a disk master chart.

Disk Master Chart

Blocks of memories not used as light cues can be partitioned as locations to expedite a focus, store other "looks," or speed preshow checks. Functions can be assigned to blocks of memory using a **disk master chart,** which can be constructed once the identity and parameters of the console are determined. The information includes the following:

- The name of the manufacturer, the name of the lighting console, and the software version number
- The storage medium of the console; floppy disk, hard drive, etc.
- The total number of memories that can be stored at any one time in RAM
- The highest number that can be assigned to a memory

Hybrid Theatre 1998   *Hokey* **Disk Master Chart**   Date: 4/30/98

	FUNCTION	BLOCK	PRE	TIME	DELAY	NOTES
0	Focus Cues		0.7			Can be deleted after focus
100	Hokey Act 1	100	101			
200	Hokey Act 2	200	201			
300	Hokey Act 2 continued					No blocker; cues track from 200's
400	Hokey Act 3	400	401			
500	Library Act 1	500	501			
600	Library Act 2	600	601			
700	Library Act 2 continued					No blocker; cues track from 600's
800	Library Act 3	800	800			
900	Light Check; Position	900	901	5	20	Filament warmer
950	Light Checks; System	950	951	5	20	Filament warmer

Expression 1; 999 memories   Lighting design by Steve Shelley

Figure 5.5 The *Hokey* Disk Master Chart

• Confirmation that the console can record point cues

After the parameters of the lighting console are known, a disk master can be constructed.

Figure 5.5 shows the disk master for *Hokey*, which partitions the memory into blocks of 100's and 50's. The function column identifies the assignment for each block of memory. The first memory of each block is a "blocker" cue, stopping all tracking information from previous memories. The "PRE" or Preset column shows what memory number will contain the preset or first memory for each act or block.

Focus Cue Block

The first 100 cues in the *Hokey* disk will contain channel information that will be used during the focus session. Most light plots are comprised of several systems. Although the instruments in those systems may be located in different hanging positions, the focus points or beam edges will be focused in relationship to one another. Some systems will be focused so that their beams all land the same distance from centerline (sidelight), while other systems will be focused so that their beams are matching distances from plaster line (frontlight). After the first channel in a system is focused, it may be reactivated with the next channel in the same system, so that an aspect of the focus from the previous instrument can be matched while focusing the next unit. The first light beam becomes a point of reference while focusing the second unit.

Focus cues can be preprogrammed to achieve the same effect. Instead of activating two channels, the only button that is used is the GO button. Program-

ming these cues also defines the choreography of the focus, since the cues activate channels in a specific sequence "across" a hanging position. In this case, the disk master shows that the focus cues will be allocated to the zero block, so the focus cues begin with cue 1.

Figure 5.6 shows a partial focus cue list for the *Hokey* plot. To keep the focus in sequence with the cues, unit 1 on the first electric will be the first instrument activated. The focus would proceed towards stage right. Each memory brings up the next instrument to be focused.

When 1 electric #9 is focused, cue 8 activates both channels 7 and 8. Channel 8 has already been focused in cue 5, so unit #9 can be matched to the beam edge of unit #5. When 2 electric unit #26 is focused (channel 42), cue 18 will activate it and 1 electric #19 (channel 41). Since channel 41 has been focused, the beam edge of 2 electric #26 can be matched to channel 41.

Focus cues can minimize time spent waiting for matching pairs of channels to be determined or activated. Only the GO button is required to progress through the focus. Many productions traveling with their own lighting console create a focus disk that contains more sophisticated focus cues. Additional memories can be programmed that activate entire color systems, rather than just pairs of instruments.

Act Cue Blocks

The disk master for *Hokey* indicates that Act 1 will occupy less than 100 whole numbered memories, so it will be assigned to the 100's block. It's anticipated that the second act, however, may require more than 100 whole-numbered memories, so both the 200's and

CUE	Position & Unit	CHAN		CUE	Position & Unit	CHAN	
1	1P1	45		21	2P23	16	20
2	1P2	25		22	2P22	6	10
3	1P3	51		23	2P21	71	
4	1P4	18		24	2P20	61	
5	1P5	8		25	2P19	20	
6	1P7	18		26	2P18	10	
7	1P8	8		27	2P17	71	72
8	1P9	7	8	28	2P16	61	62
9	1P10	55		29	2P15	19	20
10	1P11	17	18	30	2P14	72	73
11	1P12	6	7	31	2P13	62	63
12	1P13	16	17	32	2P12	9	10
13	1P15	6		33	2P11	63	64
14	1P16	16		34	2P10	73	74
15	1P17	51		35	2P9	9	10
16	1P18	21	25	36	2P8	19	20
17	1P19	41	45	37	2P7	64	65
18	2P26	41	42	38	2P6	74	75
19	2P25	21	22	39	2P5	10	
20	2P24	51	52	40	2P4	20	

Figure 5.6 The Partial Focus Cue List for *Hokey*

300's will be allocated to the Act 2 cues. Although this means that Act 3 will begin in the 400s, this numerical identity shouldn't become a source of confusion.

Allocating blocks of cues doesn't have to be limited to acts; each block of 100's can be subpartitioned and assigned to individual scenes. For example, the first act of *Hokey*, allocated to the 100's block, will have three scenes. It's anticipated that the first scene will have some amount of light cues, those cues may be assigned to memories 101 > 124. The second scene might be allocated to memories 130 > 155, while the third scene may be allocated to memories 160 > 192. As long as the lighting designer remembers the cue block structure, he or she can identify memory 142 as a cue in the second scene of the first act.

Having to communicate in three-digit numbers throughout the course of a show can become exhausting for everyone involved. One work-around is to initially establish the memory number loaded into the console, and then truncate the rest of the memory numbers for that act. As an example, as the show is about to begin, the stage manager confirms the complete preset memory number: "Jim, we're in memory 100.7 for the top of the show, correct?" Once Jim confirms that the memory loaded into the active fader is 100.7, the stage manager then calls the rest of the

Act 1 cue numbers eliminating the "100" digit, asking only for the remaining two integers. Rather than "cue 101," the next cue is "cue 1." As Act 2 is about to begin, the stage manager again confirms the complete preset number: "Jim, we're now in cue 200.7 for Act 2, correct?" Once confirmed, the rest of the cues for Act 2 will be called starting with cue 1 as well.

Once the full memory number is confirmed prior to the beginning of a sequence, truncating memory numbers usually creates no problems. Since the memory numbers are sequentially recorded, this reduces the amount of speech on headset, and allows the stage manager to concentrate on other matters.

Library Blocks

During the course of technical rehearsals, entire cue sequences may change in one rehearsal, only to be restored in the next. If the rehearsal process seems to suggest that kind of liquidity, then it is wise to set aside someplace within the RAM and the disk to archive old lighting memories.

In the midst of a technical rehearsal, for example, the transition sequence from Scene 1 to Scene 2 may be completely changed. Memories 127, 128, and 129 may no longer have application to the show. The lighting designer's first instinct might be to delete these now-obsolete memories and record new looks labeled with those same memory numbers. The stage manager wouldn't need to change any numbers in the call book. At this point, however, it may be prudent to consider the larger picture. If this is a new production, there's no telling if the new transition sequence will be the final version. It's never been done before. Indeed, the lighting designer could delete the old memories, create a new sequence, tech the new sequence, and then be told that "the first way really was the best; let's go back and try that again now."

If there's a printout of the original transition cues, then restoring them won't take much time. The old sequence, once discarded, can now be quickly read back into the old memory numbers. If there's no written record and the original cues have been deleted, however, time will be spent while the lighting designer tries to quickly reconstruct the old sequence. Worse yet, if the transition in question is still not settled in the mind of the director, it may be necessary to tech each version of the sequence several times until the final version is determined.

One way to preserve several versions of sequences or store currently unused light cues is to allocate blocks of memory to act as storage areas. The cues still exist, but are "hidden" from active show use until called for. **Library blocks** refer to areas of the RAM used to store this dormant cue information. The disk master for *Hokey* has allocated enough 100's so that a library block is dedicated to each act. The 500 block will contain stored cues for Act 1, and so on. Allocating enough room in the RAM so that the size of the library block matches the same amount of space allocated to each act's cue block means that the memory numbers can be easily transferred.

In the example, memory 127 would be recorded as memory 527 (which can be written as M127=> M527). The other two memories would also be transferred: M128 => M528, and M129 => M529. Then the original 127 > 129 memories could be deleted, and fresh programming could take place. If the two cue sequences were to be run alternately so that the creative staff could make their choice between the two versions, the new cues could be seen in the 120's sequence, while the old cues could still be used, stored in the 520's. Once the final version was chosen, the chosen memories would be recorded as memories 127 > 129.

Cue Information and Identification

Ideally, labeling each memory used in the show with an alphanumeric name makes it simpler for the lighting designer to rapidly scan a cue list printout for information. When it's not possible to "name" each memory on the disk, though, several systems can be used to identify different types of cues.

Act Preset Check Cues

If changes are made to the lighting package before an act (sidelight color change, rover refocus, and so on), preset checks performed behind the main curtain can confirm that the lighting package is correctly colored, focused, and functional. The intent of a preset checklist is to eliminate unnoticed and incorrect details being seen after the curtain goes out. **Preset check cues** are a systematic method used to see the instrument that is no longer correctly focused, a unit that's received the wrong color, or a lamp that has burned out.

The key to constructing an expedient preset check is to define the largest number of channels that can be turned on at one time without losing the ability to see the beam edges of the individual instruments. Rather than a time-consuming check of individual channels, a sequence of recorded preset cues can confirm the ready status of the lighting package used in that act. A typical preset sequence might consist of the following:

- All of the stage left sidelights and deck specials that are used only in the act, brought up to 50%

so they can be seen. (Instruments activated in other acts aren't applicable and can be confusing.)
- All of the stage right sidelights and deck specials that are used only in the act, brought up to 50% so they can be seen.
- A combination of all of the cues for the entire act (upstage of the curtain) combined into a single cue. This "super cue" contains the highest recorded level for each channel used in that act.

In almost all cases, the light cues will be different for each act. The set of preset check cues will be performed before the show and repeated during each intermission, but the contents of the memories will be different in each sequence. To identify these sets of cues, while keeping them in sequence with the rest of the memories used in the production, the preset check memories can be recorded as point cues. Since the 100's in the act cue blocks are designated to be blockers (stopping all tracking), the preset check cues can be recorded between them and the first cues for each act. One way to identify the preset check cues at the beginning of an act is to consistently record them in this sequence:

- 100's cues = stopper cues (containing all hard zeros, stopping any channels tracking from the previous act)
- .4 cues = stage left sidelights and deck specials
- .5 cues = stage right sidelights and deck specials
- .6 cues = the highest recorded level for every channel used in the cues for that particular act, the super cue
- .7 cues = preset cue for that act
- Cue "1" = the first cue called after the curtain has gone out.

To further distinguish the preset check cues from the "body" of the act cues, unique times can be assigned to the cues. Using the structure of a preset check sequence, a cue list monitor display might look like this:

Cue	Time	(Function)
400	2.5	(Fade final Act 2 memory to black)
400.4	2.5	(Stage left sides and deck specials)
400.5	2.5	(Stage right sides and deck specials)
400.6	2.5	(Super cue)
400.7	7	(Preset for Act 3)
401	5	(First cue called after curtain out)

Regardless of the act or the series of 100's, seeing that sequence of cues and times on the monitor display will inform the lighting designer of the identity and function of the cue. The final preset cue for the act could be a point 9 memory (400.9). If a second preset cue is required to initiate an effect memory, however, there will be no numeric location to place the effect without violating the preset structure.

Autofollows

Autofollow memories are linked to other cues. They begin without a separate press of the GO button. On manual light boards, autofollow cues are typically initiated without a separate spoken command from the stage manager. As soon as the prior light cue is complete, the autofollow cue is immediately taken. Since autofollow cues aren't called, they can be identified by being labeled with an odd-numbered point cue. When the lighting designer looks at the cue list monitor screen and sees a separate point 5 (.5) memory in the middle of other whole-numbered memories, then it can be discerned that the memory in question is an autofollow cue. For this system to retain accuracy, added cues that are called by the stage manager are then often given an even point number (.2, .4, etc.).

Ghost Channels

Channels without assigned dimmers can be viewed as spare control or as unwanted clutter on the monitor display. If there's a chance that the channels will never be assigned, however, they can still have a purpose as **ghost channels** and provide the lighting designer with information. Most computer printouts detailing the contents of a production show no indication of any dates whatsoever. If a date is indicated, the time clock chip inside the computer usually notes the moment when the printout was requested, not the last time the memories were altered. Although it's certainly valuable to know when the printout was produced, it may not be enough. Knowing the date that the cues were last altered may also be the needed piece to complete a puzzle.

Time Stamp Channels   Three unassigned channels adjacent to each other can be assigned as **time stamp** channels, providing a "version number" for that printout and the memories in the computer. By assigning the first channel as the day, the second channel as the month, and the third channel as the year, the time stamp channels will always show the last alteration date of the cues. Of course, the channels have to be constantly updated every time the cues are altered or the system has no value. When the system is kept intact, the time stamp channels will clearly show when the memories were last altered.

If there are several different disks of different versions of the same cues, the time stamp channels will show which version was last altered in the RAM of the light board. In *Hokey*'s hookup, the time stamp channels are assigned to the final three channels on the first monitor screen. Channel 123 is the month, channel 124 the day, and channel 125 is the year. Care should be taken on a tracking light board not to assign any hard commands to the channels in any internal cues. If the channels are kept "clean," the change in date can be made in the first memory and given the command to track, resulting in every cue reflecting the date change.

Blackout Cues   Some light boards don't automatically display a cue list on the monitor. If a cue contains no channel intensity information, it may take moments to determine if the cue is a blackout, or if errant programming has taken place and channel intensity information lost.

One work-around for this dilemma is to designate a block of unassigned channels as **ghost blackout channels** to identify an "empty cue." In the *Hokey* hookup, channels 137 > 140, containing no dimmer assignments, have been designated as ghost blackout channels. They are activated to a unique level only in cues that are black on stage. In the *Hokey* memories, if channels 137 > 140 are displayed at an intensity of 11% (a unique level), then that memory is a blackout cue. Any channel intensities other than time stamp channels are suspect, and should be checked.

Key Memory Numbers

This is every lighting designer's nightmare scenario: The cues for a production are contained on several disks. A disk containing memories for some portion of the show is loaded into the computer light board's RAM, the disk is removed, and then the board operator disappears. The lighting designer is left staring at the computer monitor. Which act is loaded into the board? Is this the right version of the act? Which disk was loaded into the board?

Every lighting designer has been there. Preprogramming disks with **key memory numbers,** however, can provide a structure that allows a designer to identify which memories are currently loaded into the light board. The memories "carry" a unique identity by numerical sequences in their ghost channels.

David K. H. Elliott, at that time the resident lighting designer at American Ballet Theatre, introduced me to the concept of disk management when I began my tenure at that company. At that time, ABT produced an active repertory of 20 different ballets and 5 full-length ballets that would change on a yearly basis. Although the company traveled with its own lighting package and a computer console addressing 72 dimmers, the local house light board was also used to control front of house instruments and striplights.

Not only was it impossible for all of the memories to fit onto a single computer disk, the size of the repertory was so large that disks were changed at each intermission. At any time, though, it was still possible to view the monitor of either light board to confirm that the correct memories were loaded for the correct ballet. This was accomplished by using ghost channels to label the memory numbers.

Each repertory ballet or act of a full-length ballet typically had no more than 100 cues. Based on that assumption, the cues had been allocated into blocks of 100's. Each ballet started with a different series of 100's, so a disk contained nine sets of cues for nine different ballets. The 100 series of cues were for the ballet titled *Murder,* the 200 series of cues were for the ballet called *Requiem,* and so on. There were a total of eight show disks in the ABT repertory ballet library, which, multiplied by the nine ballets on each disk, resulted in a total of 72 ballets.

That being the case, although every ballet had its own block of cues on its own disk, by looking at the computer screen alone, it would still be impossible to tell which disk had been loaded. Granted, the screen might display light cues starting in the 100's, but unless the board operator was present to confirm which disk had been loaded, it might be *Murder,* or it might be the 100 series of cues from another disk.

To eliminate that confusion, David had created a labeling system which assigned a unique four-digit number to each ballet or full-length act. This four-digit **key memory number** was split between the first digit and the final three digits. The first digit was the ghost label channel identifying the number of the disk, and the next three digits identified the block of 100's cues on that disk. The key memory number for *Murder* was 7100, meaning that on Repertory Disk 7, all of the cues that were in the 100's belonged to *Murder.*

At that point, the highest channel number used in the ABT hookup was 72. Since the screen displayed 100 channels, channel 100 was assigned as the ghost channel that labeled the number of the disk. The

floppy disk containing the last nine ballets was labeled Disk Seven. When that disk was loaded into the light board, channel 100 had a recorded intensity of 07%. Therefore, if the computer monitor showed that memory 101 was the next cue and that channel 100 was at 07%, the combination of the numbers identified the memory and the disk that had been loaded into RAM. The board had to be loaded for *Murder.*

System Size

When most computer light boards are turned on so that no information is contained in their memory, the system size is reset to default values. The **system size** refers to the number of dimmers that the board will recognize and the number of channels that appear on the monitor screen. On modern consoles, the number of dimmers is more than 500 while the number of channels may be more than 1000.

Most lighting consoles display 100 or 125 channels per page. If the screen shows channels 1 > 100 and the designer needs to see the level of channel 150, the page button is pressed, and the second page of numbers is shown on the display. You can't usually page "back." If the second page is showing on the monitor screen, and the number of channels remains set at 1000, it is necessary to press the page button eight more times to jump through the rest of the screens and eventually show the first page of channels. Likewise, the default number of dimmers is usually much more than the average situation will warrant. Since most lighting consoles address every dimmer in every memory regardless of channel assignment, a cue-intensive disk can slow the reaction time of some light boards to a crawl.

Because of these awkward limitations, one of the first operations performed when programming a disk from scratch is to change the system size to a more "user-friendly" configuration. Most light boards allow this modification. The number of dimmers is reduced to a size reflecting the actual number of dimmers that will be controlled, while the number of channels is reduced to reflect a number slightly higher than the number of channels indicated in the hookup. If the highest channel number in the hookup is 180, for example, the number of channels in the system might be reduced to 200. This allows 20 channels that may be assigned to additional dimmers or ghost channels, and the page button will only need to be pressed once to show the alternate screen of channels.

The reason to be aware of this limitation is dependent on the lighting console. On some older computer light boards, the system size is an absolute given.

Once memories have been recorded, the system size can no longer be altered. If the number of dimmers or channels is altered, all information regarding memories will be erased from the RAM of the console.

Because of that fact, a cue-intensive production scheduled for a tour that doesn't carry its own lighting console should be viewed with particular attention. The identity of each house light board should be ascertained as soon as possible before any other decisions are made. If a console with these kind of limitations is in any of the venues, defining the manufacturer, software version, and house dimmer configuration for that particular facility should be used to define the system size of the lighting package. Doing so will retain compatibility in the system size and the channel hookup throughout the length of the production, and will make certain that the same memory information can be used in all theatres possessing the same lighting console.

Infrastructure Cues

Although the computer lighting console has many advanced functions, the fundamental method used to turn on lights often requires a series of keystrokes. Repeatedly activating system washes during the cueing process can also become time consuming. In addition to that, the computer lighting console may be the single electronic device controlling running lights, spotting lights, special effects, color scrollers, or triggering numerous other devices. Preprogramming handles that reduce the number of keystrokes or activate these devices can save time during the cue construction process.

Aside from the perspective of time management, the lighting console is often the only device controlling light on the stage. When safety is considered, it's wise to consider ways to rapidly get light on the stage in extreme situations. Moments may occur when worklight is immediately needed on stage and no one will be near the worklight switchbox. Regardless of the memory loaded into the faders, instruments controlled by the console may be the only alternative to get light on the stage. Systems should be in place to be able to rapidly react, provide basic illumination, and avoid moments of crisis.

Memories and other functions programmed in the "background" can be used to expedite all these situations. Generically referred to as **infrastructure cues,** this programming is often completed before the console is used for any scheduled task. The purpose of infrastructure cues is to provide alternative handles that activate several channels using relatively few keystrokes.

There are two main types of infrastructure cues. One series of memories activates entire **system washes,** while the second series activates all of the instruments at each **hanging position.** These two series of memories can be converted to handles and manipulate the channels in a light plot in two distinct ways.

System Wash Memories

System wash memories are collections of channels that, when loaded into a fader, turn on entire washes of light. After they are programmed they can be converted to other functions within the lighting console and used as building blocks in the creation of light cues, as preshow checks, or as worklight.

Figure 5.7 shows the system wash memory list for *Hokey*. Each row shows the memory number, time fade (or count, shortened to "Cnt"), channel intensity, and the channels involved. For example, memory 951 is the third memory shown for the *Hokey* light plot, which contains channels 1 > 10 at Full. The rest of the memories are collections of channels arranged by color wash and following the same sequence as the channel hookup: frontlight, overhead sidelight, downlight, backlight, and boom sidelight. The time assignments and delays will be examined when preshow light checks are discussed in Chapter 11.

Hanging Position Memories

Hanging position memories are collections of channels that, when loaded into a fader, turn on all of the instruments at a single hanging position. After they are programmed they can be converted to other functions within the lighting console and used as handles during load-in, as preshow checks, or as general illumination.

Figure 5.8 shows the hanging position memories for *Hokey*. Each row shows the memory number, the time fade, the channel intensity, and the channels involved. The delays will be examined when preshow light checks are discussed in Chapter 11.

Submasters

Autotransformer light boards are equipped with a grand master handle that can control the rest of the dimmers in that rack. Rotating the handle of each dimmer allows it to "click in" mechanically and be controlled by the grand master. In this way, moving

Hybrid Theatre 1998   *Hokey* **System Wash Memories**   Date: 4/30/98

Cue	Cnt	Dly	Lvl	System	CHANNELS
950	3		0	Blocker	1 > 122 @ 0
950.7	10	30	30	Warmup	1 > 122 @ 30
951	5	20	Full	R33 Front	1 > 10
952	5	20	Full	L161 Front	11 > 20
953	5	20	Full	R51 Bx Bm	29 30
954	5	20	Full	R44 Bx Bm	39 40
955	5	20	Full	L180 Bx Bm	49 50
956	5	20	Full	SR R51>>	21 > 24
957	5	20	Full	SL R51<<	25 > 28
958	5	20	Full	SR R64>>	41 > 44
959	5	20	Full	SL R64<<	45 > 48
960	5	20	Full	R20 Down	61 > 70
961	5	20	Full	L124 Down	71 > 80
962	5	20	Full	NC Back	81 > 90
963	5	20	Full	R68 Back	91 > 100
964	5	20	Full	Lav Boom	31 > 38
965	5	20	Full	Blue Boom	101 > 108
966	5	20	Full	Mids	109 > 114
967	5	20	Full	Shins	115 > 122
968	5	20	Full	Templates	51 > 54
969	5	20	Full	Specials	55 > 60
970	5	20	Full	All Cyc	130 > 135
971	5	30	50	Foh INHIB	1 > 5 11 > 15 29 30 39 40 49 50 58 59 60
972	5	60	50	US INHIB	6 > 10 16 > 20 21 > 28 31 > 38
					41 > 48 51 > 57 61 > 122 126 > 135
973	3		0	Blocker	1 > 122 126 > 136 @ 0

Expression 1; 150 chan, 174 dim   Lighting design by Steve Shelley

Figure 5.7 The System Wash Memories for *Hokey*

the single grand master handle can move all of the dimmers. This function has been built into most manual light boards using scene or independent masters physically manipulated by small handles or sliders.

This same function has also been built into computer consoles. The physical handles are also often sliders and are called submasters, or **subs.** Rather than physical handles mechanically controlling individual dimmers, channels are usually assigned to submasters by a series of keystroke commands. Some computer light boards allow a channel to be controlled by only one submaster at a time, whereas others provide subs that can control only a single channel. Most lighting consoles, however, are equipped with submasters that can contain numerous combinations of channels, and

usually have three different "personalities" or attributes: inhibitive, pile-on, or timed.

Comprehending submaster attributes allows the lighting designer to take advantage of their features. To understand submasters, imagine a manual light board that has one grand master and three sliders.

Each slider controls one dimmer and one lighting instrument. The grand master is a common concept; it overrides all of the other sliders. An **inhibitive submaster** acts just like the grand master. Often the difference is that the grand master on a manual light board is "fixed," or nonchangeable. It will always control all of the sliders. The inhibitive submaster on most computer lighting consoles can be programmed to control any number of channels.

Hybrid Theatre 1998 *Hokey* **Hanging Position Memories** Date: 4/30/98

Cue	Cnt	Dly	Lvl	System	CHANNELS																
900	3		0	Blocker	1	>	122	@	0												
900.7	10	30	30	Warmup	1	>	122	@	30												
901	5	20	30	Truss	1	>	5		11	>	15		58	59	60						
902	5	20	30	SL Bx Bm	30	40	50														
903	5	20	30	SR Bx Bm	29	39	49														
904	5	20	30	1 Elec	6	7	8	16	17	18	21	25	41	45	51	55					
905	5	20	30	2 Elec	9	10	19	20	22	26	42	46	52		61	>	65		71	>	75
906	5	20	30	3 Elec	81	>	85		91	>	95										
907	5	20	30	4 Elec	23	27	43	47	53		66	>	70		76	>	80				
908	5	20	30	5 Elec	24	28	44	48	54	57	86	>	90		96	>	100				
909	5	20	30	6 E/Grndrw	130	>	135														
910	5	20	30	SL Sides	35	>	38		105	>	108		112	>	114		119	>	122		
911	5	20	30	SR Sides	31	>	34		101	>	104		109	>	111		115	>	118		
912	5	30	50	All Foh INHIB	1	>	5		11	>	15		29	30	39	40	49	50	58	59	60
913	5	60	50	All US INHIB	6	>	10		16		20		21	>			31	>	38		
					41	>	48		51	>	57		61	>	122		126	>	135		
920	3		0	Blocker	1	>	122	@	0												

Expression 1; 150 chan, 174 dim Lighting design by Steve Shelley Page 1 of 11

Figure 5.8 The Hanging Position Memories for *Hokey*

Figure 5.9 shows the grand master (GM) on the left at 100% (or Full). Above each slider is a front view of each instrument, showing the lens and the light coming out of the unit. The three sliders are at zero, so each of the three lighting instruments is dark. No light is coming out of the lens of the instruments.

Figure 5.10A shows that while the grand master remains at full, the three sliders have been brought up to different levels. Dimmer 1 is at 30%, dimmer 2 is at 70%, and dimmer 3 is at 50%. The light from the three instruments reflects the levels of their respective sliders.

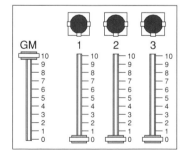

Figure 5.9 A Manual Light Board with a Grand Master and Three Dimmer Sliders

Figure 5.10B shows the sliders unchanged from their settings, but the grand master has been reduced to 50%. The grand master has "overridden" the individual sliders. Although the sliders haven't been touched, dimmer 1 is now reading at 15%, dimmer 2 is at 35%, and dimmer 3 is at 25%, half of their slider intensity.

The third illustration, Figure 5.10C, shows the sliders unchanged from their settings, but the grand master has been taken to zero. Again, the grand master has "overridden" the individual sliders. Although the sliders haven't been touched, no light is coming out of the instruments.

No matter what level sliders 1 > 3 are placed at, the grand master will override their levels, and the instruments will remain at zero. For any of the sliders and their instruments to be able to function, the grand master must be brought up above a level of zero. The grand master is inhibiting the other three sliders. Now imagine if the grand master only controlled sliders 1 and 3.

Figure 5.10D shows the three sliders unchanged from their settings, with the grand master still at zero. Since slider 2 is not controlled by the inhibitive action of the grand master, the light from the second

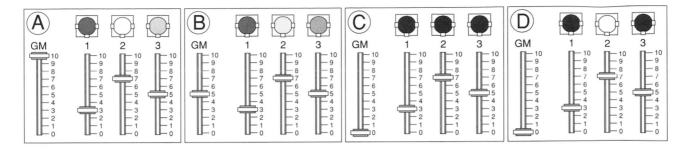

Figure 5.10 Illustration of Inhibitive Submasters

instrument is reading at 70%. If an inhibitive submaster doesn't control a dimmer, it will function regardless of the submaster's intensity.

A **pile-on submaster** overrides the sliders in the opposite manner. Any slider assigned to the submaster can have its own individual level at any time without the submaster being activated. When the submaster is brought to full, however, all of the lights will also come up to full, regardless of their slider position. Imagine the same manual light board as in Figure 5.10, except the grand master has been replaced with a pile-on submaster.

Figure 5.11A shows the three sliders unchanged from their previous settings, with the pile-on submaster at zero. Since the pile-on submaster is dormant, the intensities of light from the three instruments match the level of their respective sliders.

In Figure 5.11B, the three sliders are unchanged from their previous settings, but the pile-on submaster has been brought up to 50%. Although slider 1 remained unchanged at 30%, the pile-on submaster has overridden its level, and the light from instrument 1 is at 50%.

In the next illustration (Figure 5.11C), the three sliders are unchanged from their previous settings, but

the pile-on submaster has been brought up to Full. The pile-on submaster has overridden all three sliders. The light from all three instruments is reading at Full.

In the final illustration (Figure 5.11D), the three sliders remain unchanged. The pile-on submaster has been taken down to zero. The pile-on submaster no longer has any control over the three instruments. The light from all three instruments has returned to their original intensities, matching the levels of their respective sliders.

Figure 5.12 shows the three sliders taken down to zero. The pile-on submaster, though, has been taken to full. The light from all three instruments is at Full. The pile-on submaster has overridden the level of the sliders.

Any channels assigned to a pile-on submaster can have their own individual levels at any time. When the pile-on submaster is taken to a level higher than the level of the slider, the level of the submaster will override the level of the slider.

The last usual personality is that of a **timed submaster**, which acts like a pile-on submaster, but adds three time elements to the sub: up, duration, and down. Imagine the manual light board. Both the pile-on sub and the grand master have been eliminated. Imagine

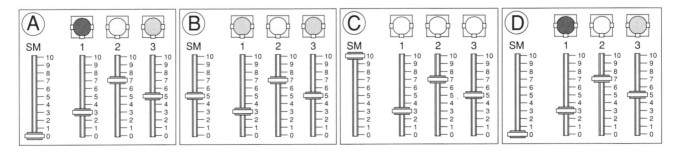

Figure 5.11 Illustration of Pile-On Submasters

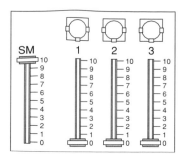

Figure 5.12 The Final Pile-On Submaster Position

that a light cue is required that activates all three sliders from zero to different levels in 5 seconds, waits for 10 seconds, and then fades all three sliders back down to zero in 7 seconds.

- To accomplish the two fades, Figure 5.13A shows the sliders preset at zero. No light is coming out of the instruments.
- In Figure 5.13B, the sliders have faded up to their respective levels in 5 seconds.
- After 10 seconds have passed, Figure 5.13C shows that the three sliders have faded back down to zero in 7 counts.

Channels recorded to a timed submaster can be used in any other memory or cue. When the timed submaster is activated, however, the submaster is programmed to fade the assigned channels up to their respective levels in a length of time, wait for a time duration, and then fade the channels back down to their previous levels in an assigned time.

Inhibitive and pile-on attributes will be assigned to the submasters programmed for *Hokey*. For this production, however, timed submasters will not be used.

The Submaster List

There are 24 submasters on the lighting console, and *Hokey* will use all of them. On this lighting console, the submasters are laid out in two rows of 12 submasters each. Figure 5.14 is the **submaster list,** which uses a combination of the two types of infrastructure cues. When these contents are programmed, the physical handles may be used to activate channels while creating cues, performing preshow checks, or rapidly supplying illumination for worklight. Since submasters have a physical handle, any electrician can be called upon to operate them.

Submasters 12 and 24 have been assigned as inhibitive submasters. Submaster 12 controls every instrument upstage of the main curtain, while Submaster 24 controls every instrument downstage of the curtain. If a blackout check must be performed behind the main curtain after the audience has entered the theatre, Submaster 12 can be pulled down without affecting any channels being used as curtain warmers. When the main curtain has to close quickly, Submaster 24 can be pulled down, eliminating any light from the front of house (FOH) that might otherwise splash onto the curtain. Unless they are needed, however, both handles will remain at Full through the entire show.

If the light plot includes channels containing houselights, curtain warmers, page bow lights, or conductor specials, those channels should not be included in the FOH inhibitive sub (Submaster 24) since it's possible those channels may be needed while the submaster is pulled down. This will be examined more closely in Chapter 11. For the same reason, channels controlling running lights, spotting lights, or other devices that should remain constant shouldn't be included in the upstage inhibitive sub (Submaster 12).

Note that if music stand lights don't need to be dimmed, the lighting console should not control them.

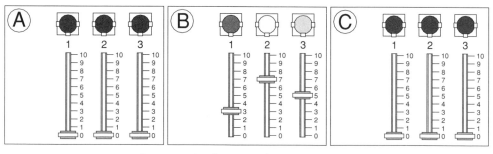

Figure 5.13 Illustration of a Timed Submaster

Hybrid Theatre 1998   *Hokey* Submaster List   Date: 4/30/98

Sub	Lvl	System	CHANNELS																	
1	Full	Truss	1	>	5		11	>	15		58	59	60							
2	Full	SL Bx Brn	30	40	50															
3	Full	SR Bx Bm	29	39	49															
4	Full	1 Elec	6	7	8	16	17	18	21	25	41	45	51	55						
5	Full	2 Elec	9	10	19	20	22	26	42	46	52		61	>	65		71	>	75	
6	Full	3 Elec	81	>	85		91	>	95											
7	Full	4 Elec	23	27	43	47	53		66	>	70		76	>	80					
8	Full	5 Elec	24	28	44	48	54	57	86	>	90		96	>	100					
9	Full	6 E/Grndrw	130	>	135															
10	Full	SL Sides	35	>	38		105	>	108		112	>	114		119	>	122			
11	Full	SR Sides	31	>	34		101	>	104		109	>	111		115	>	118			
12	Full	US INHIB	6	>	10		16	>	20		21	>	28		31	>	38			
12	Full		41	>	48		51	>	57		61	>	122		126	>	136			
13	Full	R33 Front	1	>	10															
14	Full	L161 Front	11	>	20															
15	Full	SR R51>>	21	>	24															
15	Full	SL R51<<	25	>	28															
16	Full	SR R64>>	41	>	44															
16	Full	SL R64<<	45	>	48															
17	Full	R20 Down	61	>	70															
18	Full	L124 Down	71	>	80															
19	Full	NC Back	81	>	90															
20	Full	R68 Back	91	>	100															
21	Full	Lav Boom	31	>	38															
22	Full	Blue Boom	101	>	108															
23	Full	Templates	51	>	54															
24	Full	Foh INHIB	1	>	5		11	>	15		29	30	39	40	49	50	58	59	60	

Expression 1; 150 chan, 174 dim   Lighting design by Steve Shelley

Figure 5.14 The Submaster List for *Hokey*

When the light board crashes, the music stand lights will turn off, and the orchestra will stop playing music. Although the show may still be performed with worklight on stage, it won't matter if the musicians can't see their music. The show may be lost.

Submaster Notes

In addition to controlling systems or positions, submasters can be used for other functions as well. Here's a short list of other functions that submasters can perform:

- If atmospheric effects and fans are assigned to submasters, consider assigning the control of the sources and the control of the fans onto two separate submasters. Often this will provide more overall control. If enough submasters are available, consider splitting the sources to separate subs to provide even more atmospheric control.

- If the light plot has scrollers or other devices, consider assigning all of the scroller or device channels to one submaster, and all of the instruments to an adjacent submaster. This speeds preshow checks of all the devices.

- Strobe lights can often require several channels of control. These channels can be assigned to separate submasters and adjusted manually to determine levels of control, which can then be programmed into the appropriate memory.

- Moving light fixtures have numerous attributes, which require several channels of control. Attributes that will often be universal, such as color, may be assigned to submasters to manually adjust the color of all of the fixtures at one time.
- Consider assigning any series of channels that operate together and require an extensive series of keystrokes to be activated.
- Any channel or device that needs to activate like a switch may seem prudent to assign to a submaster, including worklights, systems that can be used like worklights, or emergency lights.
- Consider assigning channels that may always need to be active, but may be forgotten in the cue construction process: spotting lights, running lights, or cue lights.
- Some consoles allow effect memories to be assigned to them, which often affect the intensity of the units involved. The lighting console should be carefully studied before adopting this plan.

Groups

While submasters refer to actual physical handles, **groups** refer to a function or a button that's a software handle. On most computer lighting consoles, each group can contain any number of channels at different levels, and a single channel can be controlled by more than one group. Most current lighting consoles provide at least 100 groups.

One reason to consider the group function is that a group can eliminate repetitive keystroking of the same channels by the board operator. Although constructing a group can be time consuming, once the group exists, it's a handle that can access numerous channels with a minimum of keystrokes.

Another reason to consider group use is that while a submaster can be assigned as either pile-on or inhibitive, the channels included in the sub can't be controlled both ways. The contents of a group, on the other hand, can be activated and override any recorded information in either direction. A group can bring entire collections of channels to full or take the same collection of channels to zero.

Most computer lighting consoles don't allow memories to be used as handles within other memories. Since groups can be activated within cues, they can be used in that function as a cue storage device. For example, if the combination of channels has been balanced to create the perfect sunset in the midst of an

otherwise complex cue, the channels involved in creating the sunset can be activated and recorded into a group. The sunrise cue in another scene can be constructed more rapidly by activating that group and piling it onto any other memory in the show.

Groups can be programmed that copy the system wash memories. These groups can then be used as building blocks to activate entire systems while creating cues. When groups are used in this way, however, close attention should be paid to the recording process. Errant channels recorded in the wrong group may then be incorrectly recorded into memories. For example, an errant channel, accidentally assigned to the cool backlight group, may not be seen when the cool backlight is activated on top of other systems. Unfortunately, every time the cool backlight group is activated, the errant channel will then be accidentally programmed into every memory. Not only can it confuse the lighting designer to no end until the discovery is made, but since the errant channel has been recorded in several cues, eliminating the error will waste precious board time.

Groups can be built that duplicate the hanging position memories (position groups). Sometimes the flexibility to turn an entire electric on or off can be useful. When an overhead electric is flying out to trim, for example, turning on every instrument on the entire electric with one set of keystrokes allows all of the lenses to be seen from the sightline point. Not only does the position group expedite the trimming process; it confirms that the border conceals all of the lenses on that electric.

Position groups are also useful as a means of eliminating the contents of an entire hanging position. For example, when a midstage drop flies in during a cueing session, light from overhead instruments may splash onto the face of the drop. Time can be wasted while the errant instruments are located and turned off. On the other hand, position groups can be used to deactivate all relevant overhead electrics to zero. Individual channels can then be activated to build the cue, and errant channels can immediately be seen.

Figure 5.15 is a portion of the **group list** for *Hokey*, showing the programmed contents for groups 1 > 31. This series of groups includes both system wash and hanging position memories.

Note that the channels in the *Hokey* groups are all recorded at Full. The contents of a group must be recorded at a level above 00% for the group to function as a software pile-on submaster. If channels 1 > 10 @ 00% are recorded as group 1, activating that

Hybrid Theatre 1998 · · · *Hokey* Group List · · · Date: 4/30/98

Grp	Lvl	System	CHANNELS
1	Full	R33 Front	1 > 10
2	Full	L161 Front	11 > 20
3	Full	SR R51>>	21 > 24
4	Full	SL R51<<	25 > 28
5	Full	SR R64>>	41 > 44
6	Full	SL R64<<	45 > 48
7	Full	R20 Down	61 > 70
8	Full	L124 Down	71 > 80
9	Full	NC Back	81 > 90
10	Full	R68 Back	91 > 100
11	Full	Lav Boom	31 > 38
12	Full	Blue Boom	101 > 108
13	Full	Mids	109 > 114
14	Full	Shins	115 > 122
15	Full	Templates	51 > 54
16	Full	Specials	55 > 60
17	Full	All Cyc	130 > 135
18	Full	All FOH	1 > 5 11 > 15 29 30 39 40 49 50 58 59 60
19	Full	All US	6 > 10 16 > 20 21 > 28 31 > 38
			41 > 48 51 > 57 61 > 122 126 > 135
20	30	Warmup	1 > 122 @ 30
21	Full	Truss	1 > 5 11 > 15 58 59 60
22	Full	SL Bx Bm	30 40 50
23	Full	SR Bx Bm	29 39 49
24	Full	1 Elec	6 7 8 16 17 18 21 25 41 45 51 55
25	Full	2 Elec	9 10 19 20 22 26 42 46 52 61 > 65 71 > 75
26	Full	3 Elec	81 > 85 91 > 95
27	Full	4 Elec	23 27 43 47 53 66 > 70 76 > 80
28	Full	5 Elec	24 28 44 48 54 57 86 > 90 96 > 100
29	Full	6 E/Grndrw	130 > 135
30	Full	SL Sides	35 > 38 105 > 108 112 > 114 119 > 122
31	Full	SR Sides	31 > 34 101 > 104 109 > 111 115 > 118

Expression 1; 150 chan, 174 dim · · · Lighting design by Steve Shelley

Figure 5.15 A Partial Group List for *Hokey*

group to any percentage (Group 1 @ Full) will still result in the channels reading at zero. Since the groups for *Hokey* are all recorded at Full, each group can be activated to its entire intensity range. Group 1 can either be used as an inhibitive submaster (Group 1 @ 00%) or as a pile-on submaster (Group 1 @ Full).

FOCUS INFORMATION

A focus session is the period of time when the lighting designer instructs an electrician where to point and how to shape the beam of each instrument in the light plot. Each instrument is turned on one at a time, so

that the beam can be seen. The instrument is targeted to a designated focus point and immobilized (or "locked off"). The beam is then sized, softened or sharpened, and the edge of the light may be shaped with shutters or barndoors.

In an ideal world, each instrument in a system would be pointed to its individual focus point, after which all of the instruments in that system would be activated and visually checked for symmetry. Though it makes perfect sense to focus using this idealized process, it's often too time consuming. Moving ladders to different hanging positions can often take more time than actually focusing the instruments, so focus sessions are normally choreographed to reduce the amount of ladder movement between each hanging position. After all of the instruments in one position have been focused, the ladder is moved to the next hanging position. The need to return to a hanging position a second time can be seen as a waste of time.

Conducting a focus session based on hanging position means that completed systems can't be viewed until every hanging position involved in that particular system has been focused. Using this method, once a position is accessed, each instrument is rapidly focused one after another. As an example, focusing a sequential series of instruments on an overhead electric may result in focusing a downlight, followed by a backlight, then a frontlight, then a special, and so on. Since each instrument is focused "out of context," decisions about the focus, and the shaping of each instrument in a system has to be predetermined before the focus begins. Consider the process that occurs to focus a single instrument:

1. The unit number (position identity) of the instrument is determined.
2. That unit number is referenced with the instrument schedule and the corresponding channel number is identified and communicated to the board operator.
3. The channel number is activated, and the instrument turned on.
4. The assigned purpose of the instrument is communicated to the lighting designer.
5. The lighting designer compares the assigned purpose of the light beam to the reality of the situation and determines any adaptation that must occur to produce the overall desired result.
6. The lighting designer then directs the focusing electrician as to where to point and how to shape the light from the instrument.
7. When the light is focused to the designer's satisfaction, the unit number of the next instrument to be focused is determined.

Since the amount of time to physically point and shape each instrument will vary for each unit, expediting a focus session may start by looking at the other variables. All methods should be considered that will reduce the time between the first instrument being finished and the next instrument being touched by the focusing electrician. To achieve that goal, methods need to be in place that rapidly define and communicate each instrument's channel and focus point to the lighting designer. If needed, a written system needs to be in place to notate the finished focus of each instrument.

Since most focuses are performed in sequential hanging position order, the format of an instrument schedule is most often used to conduct the sessions. That format also allows the channel numbers for adjacent instruments to be rapidly identified. Although an indication of focus may be listed (in the case of the *Hokey* instrument schedule) in the "purpose" column, defining the actual focus point for each instrument speeds the process.

When the *Hokey* light plot was created, the section was used to define the up and downstage coverage between the zones for the different systems. Beam sections drawn as front elevations determined side-to-side coverage and hanging placement between instruments in each zone. The up and downstage placement of the focus points can be measured from the section, while the left and right focus points can be measured from the beam sections drawn as front elevations.

To identify those focus points on the stage, the deck is often divided into a grid. One line of reference is made on centerline to define the depth of the playing area, while another line of reference is made from either side of centerline. Both lines typically start from groundplan zero. These lines of reference are often measuring tapes attached to the stage, or strips of jute webbing with distances marked in large numerals. The successes of these systems depend on translating each set of focus point coordinates into simple to read documents.

Another technique used to define focus points on stage is a series of **spike mark groundplans.** Using these documents is another way to establish a reference framework.

Spike Groundplans

Spike groundplans reflect measurements that will be made as reference marks on the performance surface. These marks combine to establish a gridwork that can be used to define the playing area and focus points for systems of light. Groundplans will be used to explain the placement of the reference marks. When on stage, the marks will become individual pieces of tape, called **spike marks.** Spike marks can also be used to locate the scenery or show the placement of a specific point on stage. Productions involving multiple scenes often employ a multicolored spike mark system to eliminate confusion as to the identity or purpose of any given mark.

Figure 5.16 shows the boundaries and the width of the performance area that will be initially defined. Determining the width of the performance area starts

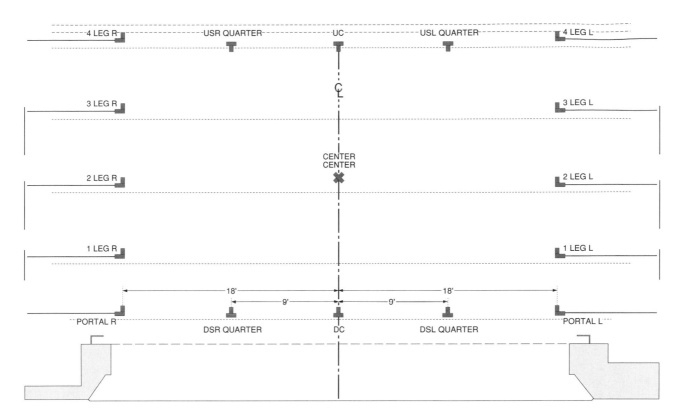

Figure 5.16 Spike Marks Defining the Width and Depth of the Playing Area for *Hokey*

at centerline. The distance between centerline and the black legs on either side of the stage is divided in half. Since the black legs for *Hokey* will be placed 18′-0″ on either side of centerline, these "quarter lines" will be located 9′-0″ from either side of centerline. To keep the amount of spike tape to a minimum, these spike marks are placed at the up and downstage edge of the lighting boundaries, the light lines. To avoid confusion, these spike marks are often constructed like the letter T. The downstage light line is defined by the T's labeled DSR quarter, DC, and DSL quarter. The upstage light line is defined by the T's labeled USR quarter, UC, and USL quarter.

The distance from the downstage light line to the upstage light line is measured on centerline and divided by 2. That point is spiked as center center with an "X," the middle point of the performance area. The locations on the stage denoting the onstage edge of each black masking leg is also spiked with pieces of tape.

Now that the performance area has been segmented into a grid, the rest of the spike marks will be used to define focus points. During a focus, the lighting designer may be standing on a focus spike mark,

but the hot spot of the instrument's beam is actually pointed to the designer's head. If the show being focused involves a cast of tall performers, the short lighting designer may need to stand on tiptoe, or even a box, to achieve accurate focus points.

The first set of focus spike marks will be for the frontlight system. In the *Hokey* light plot, the two frontlight systems each consist of three zones. The section shows that the focus points for the three zones will be located at 3′-0″, 10′-0″, and 16′-0″ upstage of plaster line. After checking the frontlight beam section, the width of the leg opening is divided by the number of instruments plotted at the hanging position. The focus points will be placed 7′-0″ apart.

Figure 5.17 shows the frontlight spike marks on the groundplan. Each "cross" shows where the lighting designer will stand to establish a hot spot location, or focus point. The numbers in the circles represent the channel numbers of the instruments assigned to the Roscolux 33 frontlight system. The text above each circle shows the hanging location for each instrument. These spike marks will also be used as the focus points for the Lee 161 frontlight system.

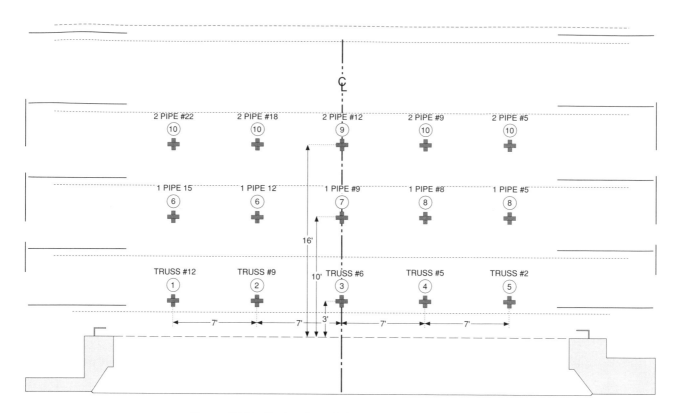

Figure 5.17 The Initial Frontlight System Spike Marks for *Hokey*

The groundplan of Figure 5.17 shows a total of 15 spike marks. Since the focus points for other systems will need to be defined in different locations on the stage, spiking each focus point in each system will result in too many marks. Even a multicolored system of spike marks could be confusing during the haste of a focus call. To reduce the possibility of confusion, the number of spike marks on the stage needs to be kept to a minimum.

Upon review, the 15 spike marks are based on five 7'-0" wide measurements, which are duplicated three times (for each of the three zones). Instead of the 15 marks, five pieces of tape can be used to establish the width measurements, while three pieces of tape can be used to establish the zone measurements. The focus points are then determined by triangulating between those *X* and *Y* coordinates. Although this system requires more thought, it reduces the amount of tape on the performance surface and the amount of time required to place the marks.

Figure 5.18 shows the focus points for the same frontlight system, but the spike marks have been reduced to eight pieces of tape. Five long strips on the

apron indicate the 7'-0" distance between each focus point, and three small pieces of tape on centerline define the depth location for each zone. During focus, the lighting designer triangulates between the strips of tape on the apron, or apron strips, and the centerline pieces to stand at each focus point. The apron strips are larger to make it easier to see while standing upstage. The apron strips will also be used for other lighting systems, and their larger size will speed recognition of the distances for both the designer and the focusing electrician.

Figure 5.19 shows the triangulated spike groundplan for the Roscolux 51 lavender pipe end system assigned to channels 21 > 28. The instruments will focus across centerline to the quarter line mark on the opposite side of the stage. Another way to say this is that the overhead sidelights will all focus to the "far" quarter line. To define the depth placement, the focus points are triangulated between the far quarter line spike marks and the black masking legs. Because it is a visual triangulation, there's no need for additional spike marks. These are the same focus points that will be used to focus the Roscolux 64 blue pipe end system assigned to channels 41 > 48.

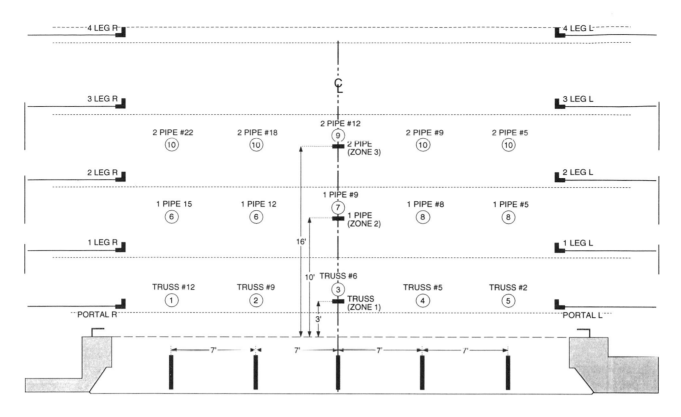

Figure 5.18 The Adjusted Frontlight System Spike Marks for *Hokey*

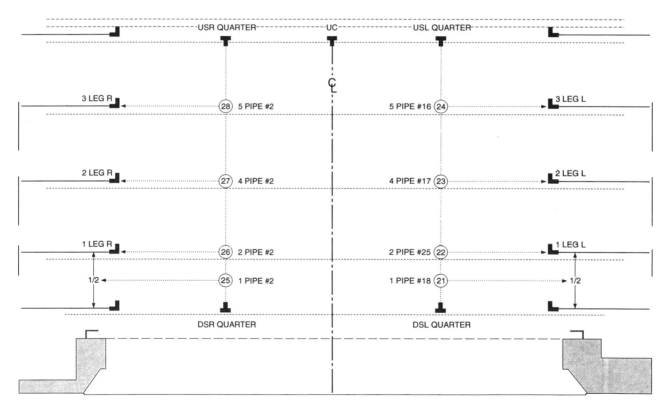

Figure 5.19 The Pipe End Sidelight System Spike Marks for *Hokey*

Figure 5.20 is the focus groundplan for the no color template system, assigned to channels 51 > 54. Eight instruments (four on each side) have been plotted that, when focused, will create a full stage template wash. The quarter lines and the masking legs define the offstage focus points. Rather than focus directly at center, the near focus points "overlap" to achieve a blend with the offstage beams.

Figure 5.21 is the focus groundplan for the Roscolux 20 amber downlight system, assigned to channels 61 > 70. The section has shown that the focus points for the two zones will be located at 8'-6" and 16'-0" upstage of plaster line, so two pieces of spike tape will be placed at those points on centerline. Since there are five instruments equidistantly spaced in each zone, the left-and-right distances can be determined by the apron strip spike marks that were originally used for the frontlight system. These same focus points will also be used for the Lee 124 downlight system assigned to channels 71 > 80.

Figure 5.22 is the focus groundplan for the no color backlight system, assigned to channels 81 > 90. The section has shown that the focus points for these two zones will be located at 5'-6" and 18'-0" upstage of plaster line, so two pieces of spike tape will be placed at those points on centerline. Again, since there are five instruments equidistantly spaced in each zone, the left and right distances are determined by the frontlight apron strip spike marks. These focus points will also be used for the Roscolux 68 backlight system assigned to channels 91 > 100.

Figure 5.23 is the focus groundplan for one side of the Roscolux 51 sidelight system, assigned to channels 35 > 38. The focus points are triangulated between the "near" quarter line (the quarter line closest to the instrument), and the "opposite" black masking legs (on the opposite side of the stage). Since this is a visual triangulation, there's no need for additional spike marks. The preliminary plan is to use these focus points for each system of boom sidelight.

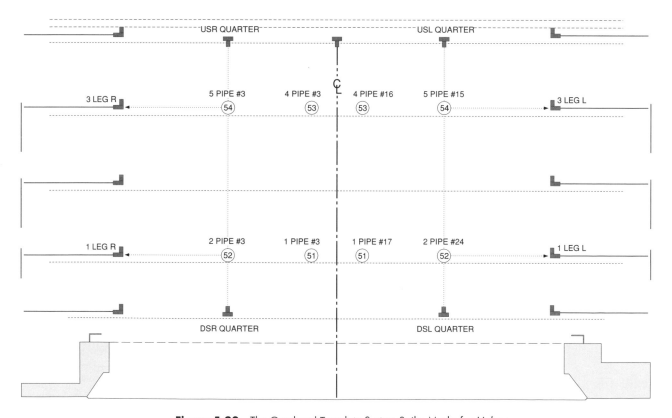

Figure 5.20 The Overhead Template System Spike Marks for *Hokey*

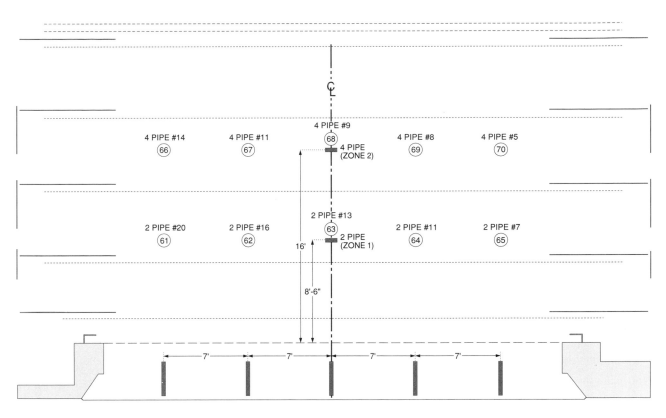

Figure 5.21 The Downlight System Spike Marks for *Hokey*

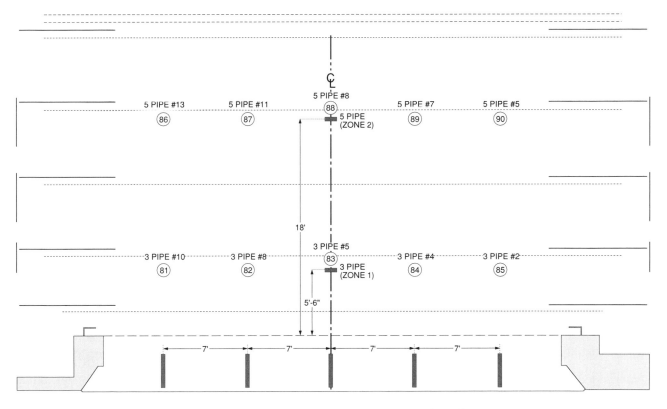

Figure 5.22 The Backlight System Spike Marks for *Hokey*

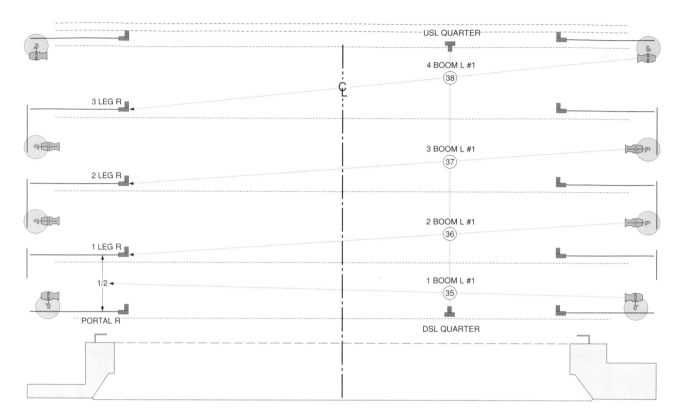

Figure 5.23 The Sidelight Boom Spike Marks for *Hokey*

Figure 5.24 is the combination of all the focus groundplans into a single document. This master system spike groundplan will be the document used during load-in to rapidly spike the stage for the focus session.

Focus Tools

Once the reference gridwork of spike groundplans is established, it becomes a communication framework that defines the location of any light beam focused within its boundaries. The focus points can then be written on a reference document that will provide this information to the lighting designer during the focus session. This document may be altered versions of other paperwork, or it may be a unique document the lighting designer has in hand while the instruments are being focused. Since the lighting designer typically moves about the stage to establish the focus points, the focus document is designed to be a compact set of paperwork that will provide complete focusing information.

Since the focus session typically proceeds sequentially through each hanging position, some designers merely use a copy of the **instrument schedule**. This is often the focus document used if the designer can easily determine the location of the focus point by translating the written indication in the "purpose" column (or its equivalent).

If the lighting designer is more comfortable with a graphical layout, the focus document used may be the **light plot.** Some designers prefer the light plot because it's visually simpler to compare the focus between two instruments from the same system in different zones. If the lighting designer's familiar with the plot and has the focus firmly in mind, he or she may merely make shorthand notes for specials. If the focus involves extensive scenery or numerous scenes, every note necessary to point and shape each light may be indicated on the map. Doing so attempts to eliminate any need to

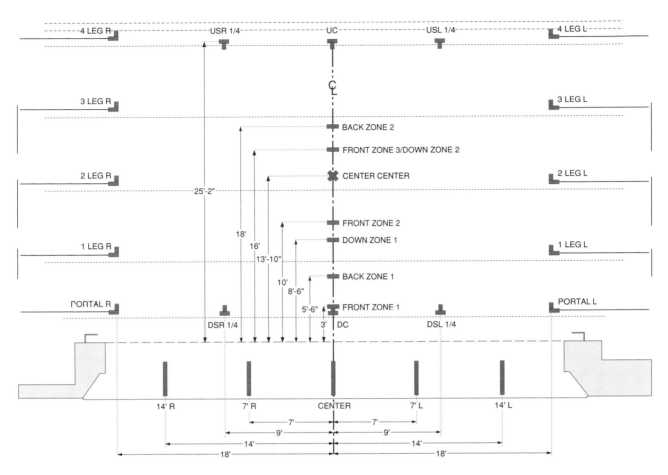

Figure 5.24 The Master System Spike Mark Groundplan for *Hokey*

refer to other paperwork. Dependent on the complexity and size of the drawing, however, it may be difficult to handwrite all of the information so that it can easily be seen.

Figure 5.25 is half of the truss from the *Hokey* light plot with focus notes indicated above each instrument. Using the light plot graphically shows the designer the focus, color, and channel number. Presenting it in this arrangement attempts to speed the time between the activation of each channel and the physical pointing of the instrument.

If it's known in advance that the light plot will be the focus document, the drawing can be created with that in mind. The axis of each unit on the drafting can indicate not only the prehung direction of an instrument; it can also show the designer to which system the lighting instrument belongs. If the lens of the icon is pointed upstage, it often indicates that the instru-

ment will be focused as straight frontlight. Instruments drawn at a 45° angle toward the top of the document can represent area or diagonal frontlight. Lenses drawn toward the bottom of the document often represent backlight or downlight, while instruments drawn at a 45° angle toward the bottom of the page can represent diagonal backlight. Instruments with special focus can have separate icons near the instrument to indicate their purpose and visually separate them from the systems.

Some lighting designers find a graphical presentation of the focus confusing. When that's the case, an adaptation of the instrument schedule can be employed, presenting the same focus information in a spreadsheet layout known as a **focus schedule.**

Figure 5.26 is the focus for the same instruments in the truss position of *Hokey* presented in a focus schedule format. The advantage of the focus schedule

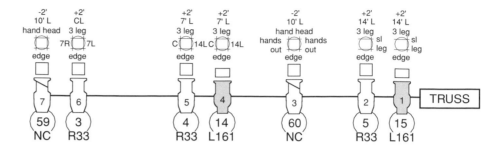

Figure 5.25 The *Hokey* Truss with Focus Notes

is that in addition to the focus information, all of the lighting database information is also included. The document is separated into three groups of information: the database information (position, unit number, circuit, dimmer, channel), the instrument information (purpose or focus, unit type, wattage, color, notes), and the focus information. The *X* axis of each focus point is listed in the "U/D" (upstage/downstage) column, while the *Y* axis is shown in the "L/R" (left/right) column. The "Lens" column tells the designer the sharpness of the beam edge, while the remaining four columns list the position of any shutters or barndoors.

Although methods have been discussed that define the focus points, and different forms have been examined to speed communication, the focus will undoubtedly change in the performance space. As a matter of fact, on-site conditions may force extensive alteration to the focus of every instrument. There may not be time or room to keep track of those changes on the focus document. In those situations, a separate written journal may be required to record the focus information for each instrument or electrical device.

Focus Charts

Focus charts are a written "snapshot" of the direction, beam edge, and shape of each lighting instrument in the light plot. Preparing and utilizing these documents can require some amount of time and effort. Before focus charts are produced, the need for their existence should be carefully judged.

The question to be asked is this: Will this production (or any facet of it) ever have another life? If the production is a fund-raising benefit, for example, it may consist of pieces taken out of context and adapted to this singular performance. If the pieces already have a lighting design, the need to produce detailed focus charts may be unnecessary. If the benefit consists of pieces that have never existed before, however, there may be a possibility that one of the pieces may be performed again based on these light cues and this focus. In that case, the need for focus charts should be reconsidered.

In another scenario, if an entire production has never existed before, the possibility of a future incarnation of any portion of the show must be determined.

Hybrid Theatre 1998   *Hokey* Focus Schedule   Date: 4/30/98

Pos	#	Cir	Dim	Chan	Purpose	Type	Watt	Color	Notes	U/D	L/R	Lens	Top	Bot	Left	Right
Truss	1	A-1	175	15	Cool Area 5	Alt 6 x 12	1kw	L161	Tophat	+2'	14'L	Med	3 Leg	Edge	7'L	SL Leg
Truss	2	A-2	174	5	Warm Area 5	Source 4-26°	575w	R33	Tophat	+2'	14'L	Med	3 Leg	Edge	7'L	SL Leg
Truss	3	A-3	173	60	DL Special	Source 4-19°	575w	NC	Tophat	-2'	10'L	Soft				
Truss	4	A-4	172	14	Cool Area 4	Alt 6 x 12	1kw	L161	Tophat	+2'	7'L	Med	3 Leg	Edge	C	14'L
Truss	5	A-5	171	4	Warm Area 4	Source 4-26°	575w	R33	Tophat	+2'	7'L	Med	3 Leg	Edge	C	14'L
Truss	6	B-1	170	3	Warm Area 3	Source 4-26°	575w	R33	Tophat	+2'	C	Med	3 Leg	Edge	7'R	7'L
Truss	7	B-2	169	59	DC Special	Source 4-19°	575w	NC	Tophat	-2'	C	Soft				
Truss	8	B-3	168	13	Cool Area 3	Alt 6 x 12	1kw	L161	Tophat	+2'	C	Med	3 Leg	Edge	7'R	7'L
Truss	9	B-4	167	2	Warm Area 2	Source 4-26°	575w	R33	Tophat	+2'	7'R	Med	3 Leg	Edge	C	14'R
Truss	10	B-5	166	12	Cool Area 2	Alt 6 x 12	1kw	L161	Tophat	+2'	7'R	Med	3 Leg	Edge	C	14'R
Truss	11	C-1	165	58	DR Special	Source 4-19°	575w	NC	Tophat	-2'	10'R	Soft				
Truss	12	C-2	164	1	Warm Area 1	Source 4-26°	575w	R33	Tophat	+2'	14'R	Med	3 Leg	Edge	7'R	SR Leg
Truss	13	C-3	163	11	Cool Area 1	Alt 6 x 12	1kw	L161	Tophat	+2'	14'R	Med	3 Leg	Edge	7'R	SR Leg

Figure 5.26 The *Hokey* Truss Focus Schedule

Having focus charts from the prior incarnation of a production allows for accurate archival analysis of individual light cues. If there is no doubt that this production has a short shelf life, then the focus can be approached as a once in a lifetime opportunity. On the other hand, experienced lighting designers can rattle off numerous "it will never be seen again" productions that have resurfaced. That being said, making the choice not to construct focus charts is a questionable one. If the personnel or time is available to record an original focus, it should be pursued.

The geographical location of the production may also define the need for focus charts. If the theatre is located near a source of vibration such as a highway, a subway, a bridge, or an earthquake zone, the chance for instruments to drop out of focus is much greater. Audience reaction, such as stamping feet or clapping hands, may also cause vibration. If the show is performed outside, the additional element of weather strongly suggests the need for focus charts.

Other elements within the production may require the need for focus charts. If the possibility exists that scenery, costumes, properties, or performers may run into instruments during a performance, the charts will be needed to check the focus of those instruments prior to each performance. The extended run of a production usually demands focus charts because they are the reference document used when instruments drop focus, get hit by scenery, need to be replaced, or need to have the "focus broken" to replace burnouts. The focus charts should become part of the archival packet after the show has opened. For all of these reasons, some form of focus charts have value. They should be constructed, filled out, and maintained.

All of the written information about the focus of each instrument usually won't fit onto a light plot, nor can it easily be recorded onto the instrument schedule. A separate focus chart format is strongly suggested to be certain that every action taken to each lighting instrument is accurately documented. Focus charts are usually sorted like an instrument schedule, grouping the units by hanging position, sequentially listing the numbered units, and listing all lighting database information. This allows the document to be used for troubleshooting without having to refer to a separate document.

Unlike an instrument schedule, however, the layout of focus charts often requires much more paper. In addition to including the lighting database information for each instrument, there needs to be enough room to manually fill out the form as the focus occurs.

As each instrument or electrical device is focused, a scribe simultaneously details each action applied to every unit. Often, focus charts utilize the reference gridwork to locate the focus point, and include places to note any movement of the barrel, lamp carriage, or shaping of the light beam.

As a focus proceeds, the channel-caller tells the board operator which channels to activate, while the scribe writes the actions taken to each instrument. At the completion of the call, these written "snapshots" of each instrument provide a description of the location of each light beam and how it was shaped. If time or lack of personnel doesn't permit the charts to be recorded during the focus, additional time may be necessary to perform the same function.

In addition to defining a structure in the choreography of the focus session, the scenic design may have a major impact on the appearance of focus charts. Multiple settings in a production may introduce the need for additional fields to inform the lighting designer of which scenery should be present when each instrument is focused.

One thing that must be included with a finished set of focus charts is a "key," explaining any focusing shorthand that was used while the focus was being recorded. Too often, old focus charts are brought out from the caverns for a revival only to find that they contain no information about the shorthand system that was used to record the focus.

Focus Chart Layout

Figure 5.27 is the first page of a focus chart for the same instruments in the truss position for *Hokey*. The document is broken into two sections. The top of the document includes the header, listing the name of the show, the position, and the title block information.

Each large rectangle in Figure 5.27 represents a single instrument. Each rectangle is divided into three sections. The left side contains all of the lighting database information under the unit number. The right side shows a groundplan of the stage for any handwritten notes or for a drawing of the light beam's location. It also has space under the groundplan to indicate the X and Y coordinates of the focus point. The top of the middle section is the purpose or focus name of the instrument. Under that are boxes to check indicating the lens position (Soft, Medium, or Sharp). Under that a circle represents the beam of the instrument. Notes on the four sides indicate any shaping cuts anticipated with shutters or barndoors, usually

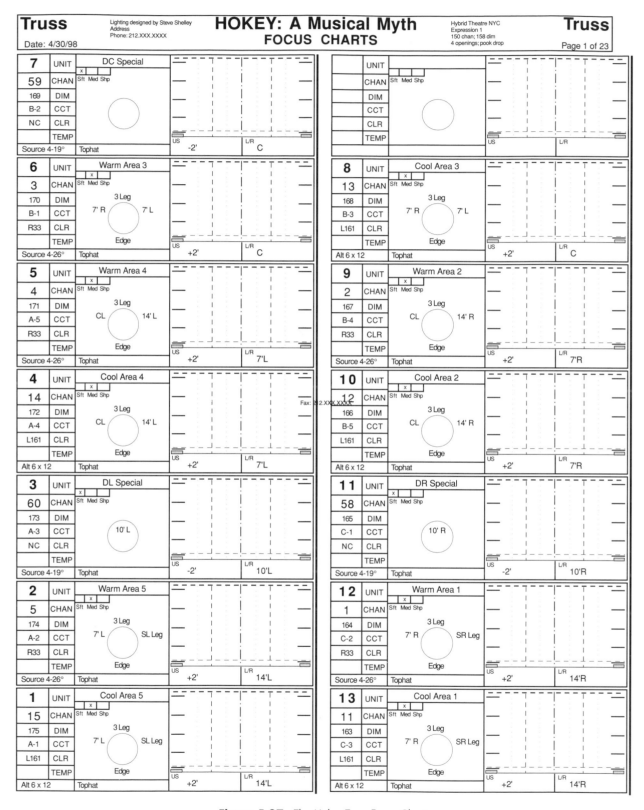

Figure 5.27 The *Hokey* Truss Focus Charts

drawn from the point of view of "behind" the instrument. During the focus session, lines will be drawn on the edges of the circle to indicate the true shaping of the beam.

The unit numbers on the left-hand side of the page increase from bottom to top, and then continue to increase on the right-hand side of the page top to bottom. This is because unit 7 is on centerline, and the focus of the instruments often mirror each other. One side of the paper is the reverse of the other, in some cases allowing the focus of the instruments to match. When questions arise about the focus of the matching instrument on the opposite side of the hanging position, the eye can easily move across the page to retrieve the information.

SUMMARY

Once the load-in and focus paperwork packet have been created, attention can turn to the packet of information that will be used to create and document the light cues for the production.

6

The Cue Construction Packet

Once the lighting package is focused it becomes a functional lighting system. The next paperwork packet facilitates and documents the creation of the lighting cues. The **magic sheet** is a map that acts as a graphic representation of the lighting systems and specials, while the **cheat sheet** identifies the instruments in their dimmer or channel order. The **cue master** is a list that shows the purpose of each light cue and the progression of light changes for the show.

Board operator sheets, followspot cue sheets, and **repatch sheets** record the tasks assigned to other members of the electrics department. A set of forms may be used to monitor the status of the light cues and the lighting package as the design evolves, which include **light cue sheets, cue track sheets,** and **work note sheets.** Altogether, this packet of tools assists in the creation, implementation, and documentation of the lighting cues for the production.

The purpose of each of these documents is to be quick-glance or quick-fill-in reference tools. Their design should allow them to be easily read and simple to understand, allowing the designer's eyes to spend as much time looking at the stage and the cue, not at the paper. Since the typical production table is inevitably cramped, the paperwork is also designed to be as compact as possible, allowing all necessary documents to be viewed simultaneously. The designer's eyes can refer to whatever document is necessary without having to scan visually for other information.

THE MAGIC SHEET

The **magic sheet** is the graphic tool that compresses the entire lighting package into a single graphic map of focus locations, showing the focus, color, and control channel for every lighting instrument or electrical device involved in the lighting package. From an artistic point of view, the magic sheet is the lighting designer's palette, showing the designer all of the components available to paint each stage picture. While an artist uses a palette to mix colors for the canvas, the lighting designer consults the magic sheet to identify channels of colored light that can be mixed on the stage. The successful magic sheet is laid out so that the designer can easily scan the document to find the necessary channel number. There are as many ways to construct a magic sheet as there are to design lights. Since one of the purposes of the document is to pinpoint a single number in the least amount of time, many lighting designers construct their own magic sheet, rather than assign the task to an assistant.

From a mechanical point of view, the magic sheet is the repository of all pertinent information required to create the light cues, along with any other information pertinent to the cueing process. Operator's names, scene lists, and programming language are examples of handwritten notes that may be added to the sheet during the cueing process.

The Magic Sheet Layout

Figure 6.1 is the *Hokey* magic sheet, which is made up of three main areas. The top two-thirds of the page is devoted to all channel and device information. The bottom left-hand side of the page contains the submaster assignments, and the bottom right-hand portion of the page lists all of the group information.

Since the channel information will be referred to most often, it's listed on the top of the page. White

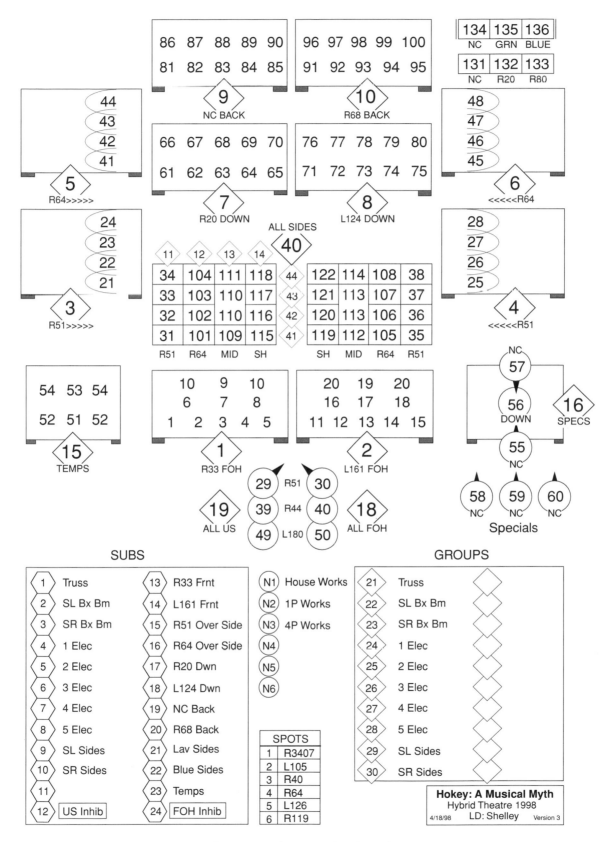

Figure 6.1 The Magic Sheet for *Hokey*

areas on the document can be used for reference notes. Notes used while creating or altering light cues are added to this document, reducing the need to refer to other documents. The submaster and group areas list the current state of their contents. Additional diamonds appear in the group area for new combinations of channels.

The channel information area is made up of small copies of the show's groundplan. The channel numbers on each groundplan refer to the focus points of instruments focused at those locations. The diamond under each groundplan is the group number assigned to that entire system. The phrase under the diamond identifies the name and color of that group and system in the *Hokey* light plot.

The layout of *Hokey*'s magic sheet arranges the different systems of light in the same relationship as their location on the light plot. Using this layout means the eye is visually scanning the same relative area on the page as the light plot or the stage. The top of the page shown in Figure 6.1 shows the two backlight systems in No Color and in Roscolux 68 (channels 81 > 90 and 90 > 100). Under the backlight systems are groundplans for the downlight systems, which are colored in Roscolux 20 and Lee 124 (channels 61 > 70 and channels 71 > 80). The two multi-rectangle boxes under the downlight are the channel numbers for the sidelight boom units. The bottom row of rectangles belongs to the first boom stage right (channels 31, 101, 109, and 115) and the first boom stage left (channels 35, 105, 112, and 119). Moving upward, each higher row identifies the channel numbers for each successive boom on either side of the stage.

All of the boom sidelight is assigned to group 40, shown by the large diamond between the two rectangles. All of the instruments on the first booms on both sides of the stage are combined into group 41. On the other hand, all of the top instruments on both sides of the stage, colored in Roscolux 51, are loaded into group 11, reducing the number of keystrokes required to turn on these collections of units. Activating groups 11 > 14 will control each system of sidelight, while groups 41 > 44 control each opening of sidelight.

Below the multi-rectangle sidelight boxes are two groundplans showing the two frontlight systems in Roscolux 33 and Lee 161 (channels 1 > 10 and 11 > 20). While group 1 will activate all of the Roscolux 33 frontlight, group 2 will activate the Lee 161 frontlight. Under the frontlight groundplans are a series of small circles with arrows. These refer to the box boom in-

struments (channels 29, 30, 39, 40, 49, and 50) listing their three respective colors.

On the top right hand side, the two sets of rectangles are the channel numbers controlling the lighting behind the translucency. The top threesome with a vertical line on either side are essentially the same symbol as the groundrow striplights (channels 134 > 136), while the threesome underneath indicate the T-3's hung on the 6th overhead electric (channels 131 > 133). The color is listed under each channel to prevent confusion. The two groundplans underneath the striplight rectangles contain a series of curves, which reverse and repeat on the opposite side of the page. These all refer to the pipe and systems (channels 21 > 28 and 41 > 48). The curves show the approximate location of each channel's beam edge once the instruments are focused.

Underneath the pipe end groundplans on the right side of the page is a groundplan containing circles and arrows. This groundplan shows the approximate focus and location for all of the specials included in the light plot. For example, channel 57 will be focused as a No Color backlight to center center, channel 56 will be focused as a downlight to the same area, while channel 55 will illuminate that area of the stage from a frontlight position. Finally, the groundplan on the opposite side of the page shows the approximate focus for the overhead template system (channels 51 > 54).

The Cheat Sheet

The **cheat sheet** is the companion road map to the magic sheet. While the magic sheet sorts the dimmers or channels into graphic focus locations, the cheat sheet presents the same information as a compressed hook-up. The cheat sheet's purpose is to identify the contents and attributes of every handle or control channel in the same order as the dimmer sliders or channels on the monitor display. Notes above each channel number identify the channel's focus, hang location, color, and purpose.

On most American computer light boards, channel numbers and intensity information are displayed in rows. To facilitate channel recognition, the successful cheat sheet mirrors the layout of the computer monitor. Not only is the document arranged in rows to match the horizontal layout of the computer display, each row of the cheat sheet contains the same number of channels as each row of the display. The designer's eye searches the same area of the paper as the screen to speed the scan for information. Duplicating the monitor layout explains why the questions asked during the initial gathering of information ("How many channels are displayed in one row on the monitor screen?" and "How many rows appear on one monitor screen?") can be so important.

Figure 6.2 is the cheat sheet for *Hokey*. It mirrors the computer monitor, displaying 25 channels per row. The text above each channel number indicates the channel's focus location on the stage. The text above the focus location indicates the channel's hanging location in the light plot. The letters at the top of each section of channels identifies the color and system name for the group of channels. As an example, channel 1 is focused down right (DR), is hung on the front of house (FOH) position, and is a portion of the Roscolux 33 frontlight system (R33 Front). In the case of sidelight, the "<" and ">" symbols are used to indicate the instrument's direction of origin. Double "<<" symbols are used to differentiate overhead sidelight.

THE CUE MASTER

The third document required to create light cues is the tool that eventually provides the lighting designer with a record of the placement, speed, and purpose of each memory. This document is called a **cue master**. Initially, a cue master can be used during production meetings and design conferences to track the progression of the show when concepts, scene progressions, transitions, and specific moments are discussed. During this process the purpose and number of cues can change radically, and several versions of this document may be produced.

The cue master can also be used to communicate preliminary cue placement to the stage manager. In most cases, the stage manager needs to have this information recorded in the call book prior to the first technical rehearsal. Otherwise, more time may be spent in that first tech placing the cues than figuring

---

Hybrid Theatre 1998   *Hokey* Cheat Sheet   Date: 4/30/98

R33 Front										L161 Front										R51>> Far 1/4				
FOH					1E			2E		FOH					1E			2E		1E	2E	4E	5E	1E
DR	DRC	DC	DLC	DL	MR	CC	ML	UC	Sd	DR	DRC	DC	DLC	DL	MR	CC	ML	UC	Sd	in1>	in2>	in3>	in4>	<in1
1	2	3	4	5	6	7	8	9	10	11	12	13	14	15	16	17	18	19	20	21	22	23	24	25

Far 1/4 <<R51					R51 Bx		R51 Bm Near 1/4			Near 1/4 Bm R51			R44 Bx		R64>> Far 1/4					Far 1/4 <<R64				L180 Bx
2E	4E	5E													1E	2E	4E	5E		1E	2E	4E	5E	
<in2	<in3	<in4	>SR	SL<	in1>	in2>	in3>	in4>	<in1	<in2	<in3	<in4	>SR	SL<	in1>	in2>	in3>	in4>	<in1	<in2	<in3	<in4	>SR	SL<
26	27	28	29	30	31	32	33	34	35	36	37	38	39	40	41	42	43	44	45	46	47	48	49	50

Templates				NC Cen Pools			NC Tr Spec			R20 Downs										L124 Downs DS				
1E	2E	4E	5E									2E				4E					2E			
DC	Sd	UC	Sd	1P	3P	5P	SR	C	SL	DR	DRC	DC	DLC	DL	UR	URC	UC	ULC	UL	DR	DRC	DC	DLC	DL
51	52	53	54	55	56	57	58	59	60	61	62	63	64	65	66	67	68	69	70	71	72	73	74	75

L124 Downs US					NC Backs										R68 Backs									
		4E					3E					5E					3E					5E		
UR	URC	UC	ULC	UL	DR	DRC	DC	DLC	DL	UR	URC	UC	ULC	UL	DR	DRC	DC	DLC	DL	UR	URC	UC	ULC	UL
76	77	78	79	80	81	82	83	84	85	86	87	88	89	90	91	92	93	94	95	96	97	98	99	100

R64 Bm Near 1/4				Near 1/4 Bm R64				Mids SR			Mids SL			Shins SR				Shins SL				Time Stamp		
in1>	in2>	in3>	in4>	<in1	<in2	<in3	<in4	in1>	2|3>	in4>	<in1	<2|3	in4>	in1>	in2>	in3>	in4>	<in1	<in2	<in3	<in4	Mon	Date	Year
101	102	103	104	105	106	107	108	109	110	111	112	113	114	115	116	117	118	119	120	121	122	123	124	125

Rovers				T-3				Groundrow		Blackout Check														
DSL	USL	DSR	USR	NC	R20	R80	NC	Grn	Blue															
126	127	128	129	130	131	132	133	134	135	136	137	138	139	140	141	142	143	144	145	146	147	148	149	150

Expression 1; 150 chan, 174 dim   Lighting design by Steve Shelley

Figure 6.2 The Cheat Sheet for *Hokey*

out how to make them run smoothly. Presuming the lighting designer and the stage manager are two different people, the appearance or structure of the cue master may need to be coordinated. Time constraints may be such that a meeting between the two prior to the first tech to discuss cue placement may not be possible. If the cue placement is recorded by the lighting designer in some format that can be passed on to the stage manager, the cues can be placed into the call book without the lighting designer's direct participation. Coordinating the format of the cue master can reduce the amount of discussion necessary between the pair to transfer the information. For the most part, the cue placement will be known by both, reducing concern if a discussion about that aspect of the show can't take place until the technical rehearsals begin.

If the medium is music, the placement information may be Post-its™ or small flags pasted into the score, allowing cue placement to be easily shifted. If the medium is spoken word, placing the cues may be a matter of copying the light cues from the designer's script into the stage manager's call book. Cues based on movement, however, can be more challenging. Communicating cue placement may become dependent on movement vocabulary and pictograms.

A cue master can facilitate cue level setting sessions by identifying the change and timing required for each cue. The document shows the total number of cues involved in the show, and can indicate repeated looks. Updating the document through the session and the technical rehearsals allows the lighting designer to keep track of the cues that have been constructed, updated, and stored.

During technical rehearsals, the cue master continues to be a communication tool between the lighting designer and the stage manager, used to define cue placement and timing. An up-to-date cue master matching the cue list contained in the lighting console provides a basis for communication and analysis when the monitor display is not available for reference. Regardless of the form, the cue master or its equivalent is an important tool.

The Spreadsheet Cue Master

Figure 6.3 is the **spreadsheet cue master** for the opening scene of *Hokey*. Each cue is listed on a single row. For multiscene productions, the first column allows the eye to easily identify the particular section of the piece being viewed. The second column is the memory number of the light cue or the number the stage

manager calls to arrive at each particular lighting state. The "on" column indicates the moment at which the stage manager says, "Go." The "for" column gives the reason why the cue is occurring in the first place. The "action" column gives a brief description of what lights actually move in each cue. The form is double spaced, providing space to write changes or additional cues. It is often wise to triple space the cue master during initial light cue level setting sessions and technical rehearsals when productions are particularly volatile.

The final five columns of this form include information about the followspot cues. Though not as detailed as a followspot cue sheet, the form shows pickup assignment, color, and live actions that the followspots need to accomplish. Depending on the complexity of the show, separate followspot cue sheets may be required.

The Movement Cue Master

A second method used to record cue placement information without a script or score is a format called a **movement cue master** or a **movement track sheet**. Figure 6.4 illustrates the same opening moments of *Hokey* in a movement cue master, constructed during rehearsals. It shows a more complete picture of the movement of the show, allowing the cue placement to be anticipated.

The document is read from top to bottom. The header includes the pertinent information, including a space to include the date and the page number. A single column on both the left- and right-hand sides can be used for time notations. The simple groundplans repeat vertically down the page, so that the movements can be "tracked." The open area to the right of the groundplans is provided for written notes that clarify or reiterate the movement pictograms made in the groundplans. The written boxes show the placement of the cues, while the small attached circles indicate the time durations.

When a production involves a script, a **script cue master** can be constructed as a variation of a movement cue master. If the pages of the script are in a small format, they are often enlarged with a photocopy machine onto a single side of each page, making the text easier to read and allowing more room for notes. Miniature versions of the groundplan are then photocopied to the back of each page of the copied script, and the cue master script is assembled into a three-ring binder. Blocking notes can then be marked on the

Hybrid Theatre 1998   *Hokey* Cue Master   Date: 4/30/98

SEC	CUE	CNT	ON	FOR	ACTION	SP1	SP2	SP3	SP4	SPOT NOTES
Open	100	3			Blocker					
	100.7	3		Preset	Pool in 4 L; blue bk					
			Curt complt; music	Judy		Judy	Judy			SP3 pickup in wing
	101	5|10	Judy arm back	Move to center	Center up					
	102	7	2nd spin	1/2 group enter	Lav side/R20 back	Ø		Ø		Lag out
	103	10	End music phrase	Rest group enter	Bright; add NC back					
Pook	104	7	Judy start X DL	Judy speech	DL Spec up					
	>>		Judy X SL 1/4	Judy		Judy		Judy		Color change
	105	5	Judy finish speak		DL Spec down	Ø		Ø		
Pine	106	7	Lorraine X DR	Lorraine speech	DR Spec up		Lor		Lor	
	107	5	Lorraine speech		DR Spec down		Ø		Ø	
Tee-boo	108	7	Mitch X DC		DC Spec up	Mitch		Mitch		
Storm	109	5	Mitch finish speak		DC Spec down					Odds open for trio
	>>		End trio dance		spots out	Ø		Ø		
	110	7|10	End 2nd circle		Cooler					
	111	10	All start to center		Darker; green	Judy	Judy	Grp	Grp	Judy salsa
	112	7|10	All start leave cent	Judy @ center	Center up			Judy	Judy	Swap + color roll
	113	2|3	Judy X SR		DSR up; lose rest	Ø	Ø	Ø	Ø	

Expression 1; 150 chan, 174 dim   Lighting design by Steve Shelley

Figure 6.3 The Spreadsheet Cue Master for the Beginning of *Hokey*, Act 1

miniature groundplans on one page, which correlate to the enlarged script on the opposite page. When a production is based on movement and text, placement can be indicated in either the groundplans or the script.

FORMS

The next portion of the packet monitors the cues and actions taken by members of the lighting department during the course of the production.

Light Board Operator Sheets

During a live theatrical presentation, several actions must be coordinated for the lighting design to succeed. If the action taken for each light cue doesn't occur in the proper sequence, the lighting can be destroyed. Although the stage manager gives commands to initiate actions, the particular action that must occur for each command must be clearly understood by the light board operator. One of the lighting designer's responsibilities is to insure that the command and action for

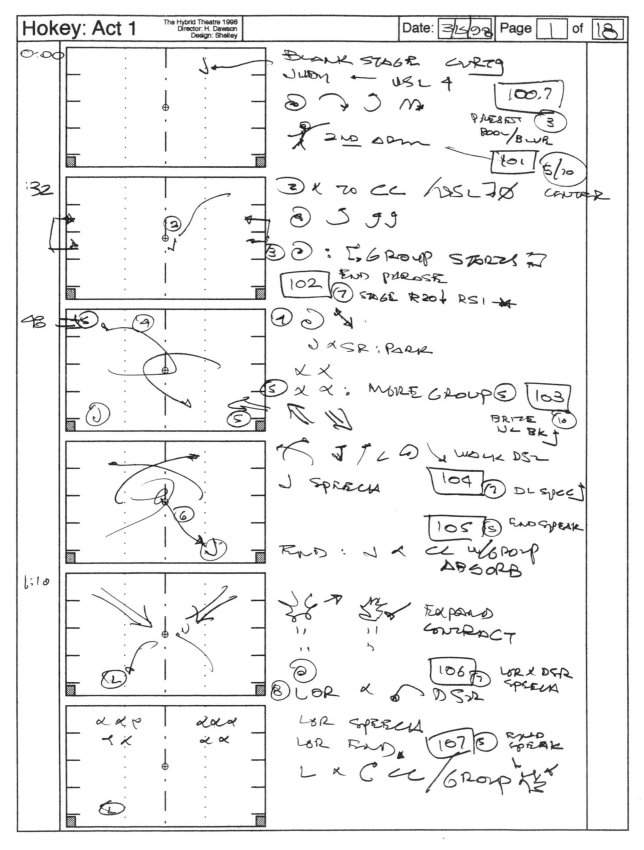

Figure 6.4 The Movement Cue Master for the Beginning of *Hokey*, Act 1

every lighting cue is clearly understood by the light board operator.

In a relaxed production, the light board operator's actions may only involve pressing the GO button on the computer lighting console and operating the house lights. A complex production, on the other hand, may require the board operator to initiate additional actions during cues. This may include operating sub-masters, activating special effects, or presetting fader banks. The **light board operator sheet** is a form that, when filled out, provides the light board operator with step-by-step written instructions describing what actions to perform for each light cue. The form is laid out so that the cues are arranged in sequential rows that read from the top to the bottom of the page. The height of each row (or cue) is vertically compact to allow the greatest number of possible cues to be viewed on each page. During rapid multi-cue sequences, less time spent flipping through cue sheets means more time spent making the actions properly happen. If a single cue requires extensive vertical space, it may be prudent to photocopy the final version of the cue sheets onto either side of each copied page. This can then be assembled in a three-ring binder, and given to the board operator. During the performance, it will then be possible for the board operator to turn one page and see the next two pages of cue sheets.

Manual Light Board Operator Sheets

A manual light board operator sheet is laid out so that consistent areas are provided to inform the operator of the action required for each cue, as well as any actions that must be performed prior to or after every cue. Some manual light boards require more than one board operator in which case two sets of board operator sheets may be required. Preset light boards often necessitate separate board operator sheets; one form is for the electrician operating the cross-fader and other masters, while a second form shows the contents of each preset.

When a single electrician operates a manual light board, the layout of the cue sheet is designed to mirror the spatial layout of the console. Every handle, function, or option present on the light board is represented in the diagram, reducing the amount of writing required to record the action of any cue. Mirroring the layout of the light board to the document, makes it simpler for the board operator to spatially match the information between one area of the paper and the same area of the light board.

Figure 6.5 shows the manual light board operator sheet for a LMI two-scene preset light board that was used during the workshop production of *Hokey*. The tall rectangles on the left side of the diagram reflect the same arrangement of the faders on the light board. The blackout switch (BLKOUT) is above the grand master (GM). The *X* and *Y* cross-faders (X and Y) are adjacent to the independent master (IND). The sliders (numbered 1 > 18) have tall rectangles below them to write preset intensities and large arrows to indicate cues that involve slider movement. The rectangle above each dimmer represents the independent/master switch, located on the board in the same position above each slider.

The area above the switches includes a space for the cue name, the time, the preset scene, and the actual action required to execute that particular cue. The

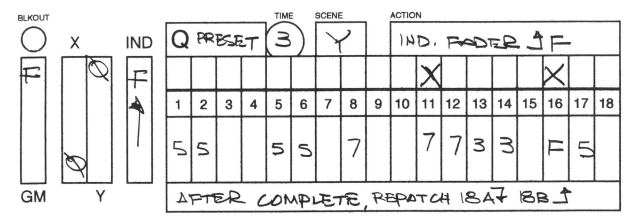

Figure 6.5 A Manual Light Board Operator Sheet

horizontal rectangle under the sliders is a space to write actions taken after each cue. In this example, the action of the cue is to fade the independent fader up to full in 3 seconds. (The contents of the independent fader are sliders 11 and 16, denoted by the "X" above each number.) After the cue is complete, the board operator is instructed to repatch dimmer 18.

Computer Light Board Operator Sheets

The computer board operator sheet also reflects the spatial layout of the console used for that production, showing the timed cross-faders, submasters, and other functions of the console. The header of the document, includes the identity of the console, the show, the disk, and the page number of the cue sheet.

Figure 6.6 shows the same preset cue for *Hokey* that was previously run on the LMI preset light board. This particular light board has two split cross-faders and 24 submasters. The cue block on the left-hand side of the page includes the memory number (100.7) and its time duration. The rest of the row shows any cross-fade information and any notes that must occur prior to or after each light cue. The circled "go" under the "A/B" boxes indicates to the operator that memory 100.7 should be loaded into the A/B cross-fader.

Followspot Cue Sheets

The three main attributes of a followspot (or a **spot**) are the size of the light beam, the color of the light beam, and the speed in which the light beam fades up or dims down.

The need for followspot cue sheets depends on the complexity of their usage, the number of spots involved, and possible archival necessity. If there are only two or three followspots, for example, the cues may be written in the margin of a script or score. If the performance involves movement, the cues may be written on a movement track sheet. For any number of reasons, however, separate cue sheets may be required. If the show will have numerous performances, substitute followspot operators may be involved. The show may be complex enough to warrant a spot director to choreograph and initially call the followspots. When that's the case, part of the spot director's responsibility will be to produce accurate cue sheets that can be read by someone else once the show has opened and the spot director is no longer on salary.

Four Spot Cue Sheets

Figure 6.7 shows a followspot cue sheet for four followspots at the beginning of *Hokey*. While copies of these cue sheets may be distributed to the operators during the technical rehearsals for the show, the spot director will be the person making updates and creating the final version. Since the followspot operators may be attempting to read these cue sheets while operating their instruments, the layout and fonts used in this document are larger than usual. Not only does this enlarged format make the document easier to scan

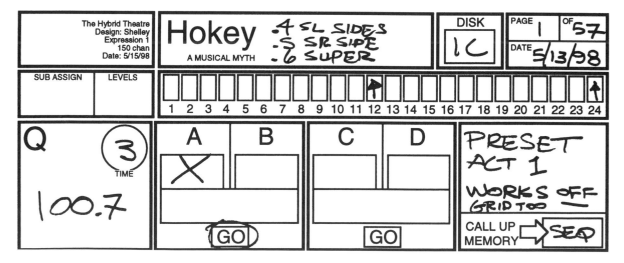

Figure 6.6 A Computer Light Board Operator Sheet

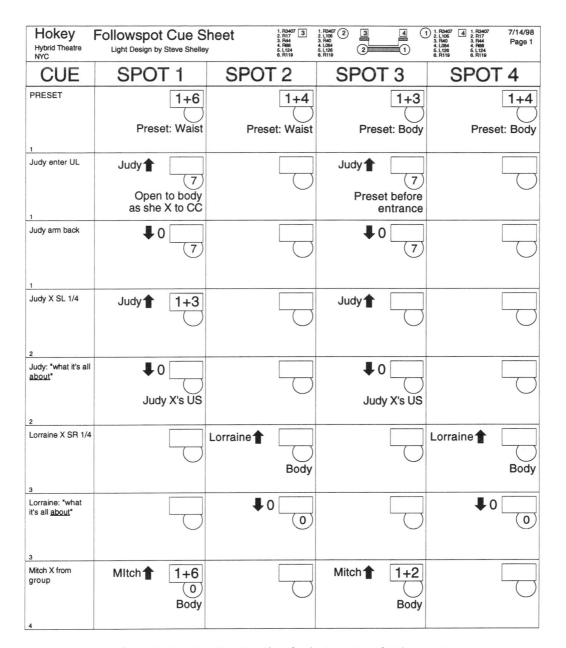

Figure 6.7 A Four Spot Cue Sheet for the Beginning of *Hokey*, Act 1

and read, enough white space remains so that written notes can be made directly onto the applicable cue.

The cue sheet is made up of two sections. The header lists the pertinent production information and provides a miniature magic sheet, identifying the location and the color for each of the four followspots. The body of the document consists of five columns. The left-hand column indicates the cue placement for each followspot action, while each of the remaining columns is assigned to a specific spot. Each row is a separate cue, so that the actions of one followspot relative to another can be "tracked."

The spot director has defined "defaults" for each spot, so that the cue sheets list only actions outside of the "norm." Less effort is spent maintaining the cue sheets, and the spot operators have less to mentally process before each action. The first row indicates the preset iris size and color for the beginning of the first Act of *Hokey*. Spot 1 will begin the show colored in frames 1 + 6 (noted in the color rectangle), with a waist-sized iris, while Spot 3 will be preset in frames 1 + 3 with a body-sized iris. The next row shows that both Spot 1 and 3 will fade up (or pickup) Judy on her entrance upstage left in 7 counts (noted in the time circle). Additional notes are indicated under the time circle.

Initially, the preliminary version of this document will be double spaced. The open row between each cue provides space to add cues or write notes. After the followspot cues are more finalized, later versions of the document will be single spaced. The final page layout is designed to be vertically compact, so that as many cues as possible can fit onto a single page. This will reduce the number of times pages have to be turned during the show.

Repatch Sheets

Situations arise when there are more instruments that need separate control than dimmers available to contain them. This can be seen as an inconvenience, but it does not always need to be viewed as a constraint. Although many instruments and their dimmers may be used throughout the course of a production, some dimmers will control specials or systems that are infrequently activated. When one of those instruments is dormant, its dimmer may be utilized to control a different instrument. The circuit to the original instrument is unplugged or switched off, while an alternate instrument's circuit is plugged or switched on in the same dimmer. This action is known as **repatching**. Keeping track of what circuit is active in which dimmer at what point in the show often requires a **repatch sheet**. The design and management of a repatch system is often viewed as a skill, and not an activity to be entered into lightly. Many lighting designers avoid the exercise altogether, since it often means that a "repatch electrician" must be added for the show. Other designers consider the potential hazards of circuits accidentally getting "lost" or unplugged not worth the risk. On the other hand, repatching may be the only available solution to acquire the amount of control necessary for a lighting package.

Repatch Work Sheet

The first step taken to design a repatch system is defining which dimmers will be dormant when an alternate

instrument needs to be controlled. Figure 6.8 is a **repatch work sheet** that was used for a workshop production of *Hokey*. All of the systems and specials that wouldn't be used in every scene were listed in each row, while the different scenes of moments of the show were identified in each column. An "X" showed when each system or special would be active in the show. By visually comparing the presence or absence of the X's, it was then possible to determine two items that didn't appear in the same or adjacent scenes. Hypothetically, those two items could share the same dimmer.

Figure 6.9 shows the sorted repatch work sheet from the workshop production of *Hokey*. The arrows show four instances where two circuits were used that didn't conflict with each other. These eight items were paired into four dimmers. Their dimmer identities were then defined by their physical accessibility within the dimmer rack setup. In the Quantum Theatre, dimmers 9 through 12 were the most accessible locations in the racks, meaning they had the smallest chance of knocking adjacent plugs out of their dimmers. When there are more circuits than dimmer inputs, the circuits have to be physically plugged and unplugged into the dimmer. To prevent confusion, the plugs are usually relabeled and identified by their respective dimmer number and a letter. Four circuits that would be repatched into dimmer 9 would be relabeled: 9A, 9B, 9C, and so on.

Figure 6.10 is the final repatch sheet used for the workshop production of *Hokey*. The left-hand column lists the cue that was used to initiate the repatch. The following columns show the repatch action, the circuits, the affected instrument's focus, and the scenes in which the circuit was used. The scene columns aren't necessary from the electrician's point of view, but they're a visual aid for the lighting designer to track the path of the patch's components.

The inclusion of "buffer cues" for repatch actions reduces the chance of a "live" repatch being performed. This can occur if a repatch is performed when a dimmer is active, resulting in unwanted instruments popping on at inappropriate moments. For *Hokey*, the sheet shows that the repatch in dimmer 11 occurred after light cue 27 was complete. Dimmer 11 actually faded out in light cue 26, but the repatch action was assigned one cue after the fadeout occurred. If the repatch had been cued during light cue 25 (while dimmer 11 was still active), the 5 Electric backlight would have snapped off, and the downstage right rover would have popped on. Building in the additional buffer cue

Quantum Theatre 1994   *Hokey* Repatch Work Sheet   Date: 8/21/94

System	Act One				Act Two			Act Three		
	Intro	Storm	Lovers	Tear	Forest	Dream	Rock	Party	Duel	Finale
1E Front		X	X							X
3E Down	X				X		X			
5E Back			X	X					X	X
DSL Spec	X			X		X				
DC Spec						X			X	X
DSR Spec	X			X		X				
L180 Bx Bm		X		X		X			X	X
L124 Down		X	X	X	X	X			X	
Temps		X				X		X		
DSL Rover	X					X		X	X	
USL Rover		X							X	
DSR Rover	X					X				
USR Rover		X						X	X	
Fire							X			
Lanterns								X	X	
Railing									X	X

LMI 2 scene; 18 dimmers   Lighting design by Steve Shelley

Figure 6.8 The Initial Repatch Work Sheet for *Hokey*

ensured that unwanted changes did not occur while dimmer 11 was possibly active.

Light Cue Sheets, Work Note Sheets, and Cue Track Sheets

Forms may be used that monitor the status of the light cues or the lighting package as the production evolves. While the looks for the show are being created, **light cue sheets** may be necessary to document the channel intensities of each lighting state. **Work note sheets** can save time and energy during work calls, and provide a diary of any problems concerning the lighting package.

One document that should be generated is a **light board printout**. After the show is frozen, there is no substitute for a complete printout containing all of the light board information. If the board doesn't have a functioning printer, off-line editing programs may be

System	Act One				Act Two			Act Three		
	Intro	Storm	Lovers	Tear	Forest	Dream	Tribe	Party	Duel	Finale
1E Front		X	X							X
Fire							X			
3E Down	X				X		X			
Lanterns								X	X	
5E Back			X	X					X	X
DSR Rover	X					X				
DSL Spec	X			X		X				
Railing									X	X

Figure 6.9 The Sorted Repatch Work Sheet for *Hokey* Showing Systems That Are Mutually Exclusive

Quantum Theatre 1994   *Hokey* Repatch Sheet   Date: 8/21/94

CUE	PATCH			CIR	System	Act One				Act Two			Act Three		
						In	St	Lov	Tr	F	Dr	Tr	P	D	Fin
Preset	9A	↑	ON	1P12	1E Front	X	X								X
	9B	↓	OFF	SR2	Fire							X			
	10A	↑	ON	3P7	3E Down	X				X		X			
	10B	↓	OFF	SL 1	Lanterns								X	X	
	11A	↓	OFF	5P8	5E Back			X	X					X	X
	11B	↑	ON	SR1	DSR Rover	X					X				
	12A	↑	ON		DSL Spec	X			X		X				
	12B	↓	OFF		Railing									X	X
AFTER Q 27 Complete	11A	↑	ON	5P8	5E Back	X				X		X			
	11B	↓	OFF	SR1	DSR Rover								X	X	
1st Int.	9A	↓	OFF	1P12	1E Front	X	X								X
	9B	↑	ON	SR2	Fire							X			
	11A	↓	OFF	5P8	5E Back			X	X					X	X
	11B	↑	ON	SR1	DSR Rover	X					X				

LMI 2 scene; 18 dimmers   Lighting design by Steve Shelley

Figure 6.10 The Final Repatch Sheet Used for *Hokey*

an alternative solution, and don't have to be printed at the theatre. The printed cue sheets and cue lists clarify any mysteries regarding the contents or timing of any light cues. The patch printout gives absolute confirmation regarding the channel assignment of any dimmer. The group printout identifies all of the building blocks, while the submaster printout may identify altered handles used for the show. All printouts should be labeled with the basic show information, including the name of the show, the date of the printout, the dimmer configuration, the theatre location, and the type of light board.

Other documents may be created that will aid in the analysis of the show for future productions. **Track sheets,** spreadsheet combinations of several light cues, are indispensable for analyzing the show or reproducing the lighting in future incarnations. During the rehearsal process, however, the core records that need to be documented revolve around the contents and timing of each light cue.

Light Cue Sheets

The main purpose of **light cue sheets** is to provide a moment-by-moment snapshot of each light cue. Ideally, each light cue sheet should reflect the channel intensities of its respective cue. During the level setting session, an assistant transcribes the directions given by the lighting designer to the board operator to create each cue. As each channel is activated, the assistant records its intensity level. Listening, writing, and sorting through the cue sheets is a skill known as "tracking the cues." Sometimes cues are tracked to keep an up-to-the-moment record of each cue. If the show goes through major lighting changes, cue sheets can be "cut"; that is, they're dated, taken out of the sequenced stack, and stored at the end of the pile of cue sheets. Just as simply, cue sheets can be "restored"; that is, taken out of the pile in the back and reinserted into the sequenced stack. Though requiring another person at the production table to create and maintain the sheets, there are conditions that can warrant the time and effort to have a hard copy of the light cues.

One practical reason to track cues comes when the computer lighting consoles crashes, losing all unrecorded memory. If no printout exists, the light cue sheets are the only records of the lost information. Refeeding cues back into the console is much faster than reconstruction.

When there is no monitor at the production table, the cue sheet assumes that role. Constantly updated through the cueing process, the form becomes the "display screen," allowing the lighting designer to see the current state of the dimmers in any given look. When a multiscene preset console is being used, the light cue sheet may be used to perform double duty. While the assistant records the presets during the level setting session, the preset operators concentrate solely on adjusting the dimmers. Once the session has concluded, the light cue sheets are photocopied, and a copy is then given to the preset operators. During the rehearsal process, the assistant updates the changes in the cue sheets. After each rehearsal, the updated light cue sheets are cleaned, photocopied, and can then be distributed to the preset operators for the next rehearsal.

Sometimes it's not possible to preprogram light cues into the console prior to the load-in. In addition to that, there may be not time available to look at the light cues prior to the technical rehearsal. In that situation, loading prewritten cues into the console during the load-in might solve the dilemma. This process requires the lighting designer to pre-think and pre-write each light cue without seeing the lights. Although this takes time and some imagination, the exercise can clarify the movement and necessity for each cue. When the console is available during the load-in, the light cue

sheets can be used to program the cues without the lighting designer's involvement.

Cue Sheet Layout   Regardless of the layout of the document, only one light cue should occupy one page. That way, when a new cue is created between two existing cues, the new track sheet is merely inserted between the other two, and the cues remain in sequence. Likewise, no matter how large the piece of paper, all of the channels involved in a single cue sheet should fit onto a single piece of paper. Otherwise, there's every chance that two or three pieces may get separated. A light cue sheet is often laid out to provide as much information as possible on the page, so that the fewest pencil or pen marks are needed to fill in the information about a single light cue.

Figure 6.11 shows a cue sheet for *Hokey*. It's divided into two sections, the header and the channel information area. The left-hand side of the header labels the cue and the memory if they're not the same. Adjacent to that is information about the timing of the cue (up, down, wait, or delay). Two blank areas are provided to name the cue or identify the moment. Next to that a space indicates whether the cue is a base cue for a restore (copy 2 Q). A space for traffic information is provided next, indicating if the next action is out of sequence (Goto Q). Any movement of the individual faders is listed on the right, next to the title block, which is tucked on the right-hand side out of the way.

The channel information area is a compressed version of the hookup. In fact, this cue sheet for *Hokey* is a modified version of the cheat sheet. By showing much of the same information as the cheat sheet, the lighting designer can analyze the cue without referring to other documents. When the cheat sheet was discussed, it was suggested that the number of channels per row on the cheat sheet should equal the same number of channels on the monitor. In the case of a cue sheet, matching the numeric numbering on the monitor display is even more strongly suggested. Matching the layout of the monitor display simplifies the task of visually transcribing the channel intensities from the screen to the paper cue sheet. The need for this visual match may not be apparent until faced with a rapid light cue level setting session.

During level setting sessions, the lighting designer's concentration is aimed solely at the primary paperwork and the stage. The assistant is performing two tasks at once: recording every level change on the light cue sheet as it is requested, and simultaneously watching the monitor display to visually confirm that

CUE	MEM	TIME				ACT 1 SC 1	COPY 2Q	GOTO Q	FADERS				HOKEY
		UP	DN	WT	DLY				A	B	C	D	Expression 1
1	101	5	10			POOKIE → LL			X				Hybrid '98
													LD: Shelley

R33 Front										L161 Front										R51>> Far 1/4				
DR	DRC	DC	DLC	DL	MR	CC	ML	UC	Sd	DR	DRC	DC	DLC	DL	MR	CC	ML	UC	Sd	in1>	in2>	in3>	in4>	<in1
1	2	3	4	5	6	7	8	9	10	11	12	13	14	15	16	17	18	19	20	21	22	23	24	25
																							0	
																							5	

Far 1/4 <<R51			R51 Bx		R51 Bm Near 1/4				Near 1/4 Bm R51				R44 Bx		R64>> Far 1/4				Far 1/4 <<R64				L180 Bx	
<in2	<in3	<in4	>SR	SL<	in1>	in2>	in3>	in4>	<in1	<in2	<in3	<in4	>SR	SL<	in1>	in2>	in3>	in4>	<in1	<in2	<in3	<in4	>SR	SL<
26	27	28	29	30	31	32	33	34	35	36	37	38	39	40	41	42	43	44	45	46	47	48	49	50

Templates				NC Cen Pools			NC Tr Spec			R20 Downs										L124 Downs DS				
DC	Sd	UC	Sd	1P	3P	5P	SR	C	SL	DR	DRC	DC	DLC	DL	UR	URC	UC	ULC	UL	DR	DRC	DC	DLC	DL
51	52	53	54	55	56	57	58	59	60	61	62	63	64	65	66	67	68	69	70	71	72	73	74	75
						5																		

L124 Downs US					NC Backs										R68 Backs									
UR	URC	UC	ULC	UL	DR	DRC	DC	DLC	DL	UR	URC	UC	ULC	UL	DR	DRC	DC	DLC	DL	UR	URC	UC	ULC	UL
76	77	78	79	80	81	82	83	84	85	86	87	88	89	90	91	92	93	94	95	96	97	98	99	100
															7	7	7	7	7	7	7	7	7	7
															5	5	5	5	5	5	5	5	5	5

R64 Bm Near 1/4				Near 1/4 Bm R64				Mids SR			Mids SL			Shins SR				Shins SL				Time Stamp		
in1>	in2>	in3>	in4>	<in1	<in2	<in3	<in4	in1>	2l3>	in4>	<in1	<2l3	<in4	in1>	in2>	in3>	in4>	<in1	<in2	<in3	<in4	Mon	Date	Year
101	102	103	104	105	106	107	108	109	110	111	112	113	114	115	116	117	118	119	120	121	122	123	124	125
															5	5			5	5	0			
																				3				

Rovers					T-3			Groundrow			Blackout													
DSL	USL	DSR	USR		NC	R20	R80	NC	Red	Blue	Ghost Channels													
126	127	128	129	130	131	132	133	134	135	136	137	138	139	140	141	142	143	144	145	146	147	148	149	150
							3			5														
										3														

Figure 6.11 The Cue Sheet for *Hokey*, Light Cue 1

the request has been correctly executed. Since the assistant's eyes have to be in three different places at once, using light cue sheets whose layout doesn't match the channel positions on the monitor display can be a critical mistake. Preset board cue sheets that will be used by the operators demand that the rows of dimmers match the spatial arrangement of the banks of dimmers. Otherwise, rapid presetting can become difficult, if not impossible.

Each row of channel numbers has the cheat sheet area above them, and two rectangles below them. The two rectangles under the channel numbers are filled in with two sets of numbers: The upper row of rectangles show the channel intensities that have moved to achieve this lighting look, while the lower row of rectangles reflect the channel intensities from the preceding cue.

Cue Sheet Example As the preset light cue (memory 100.7) is being created, the levels are written in the top row of rectangles, under the channel numbers. When the lighting designer gives the direction to record the completed state as memory 100.7, a blank cue sheet is then placed to the side of the just-recorded cue. All of the channel intensities of memory 100.7 are then copied onto the lower row of rectangles of the new cue sheet that will become cue 1. Once the copying is complete, the channel intensities of the documents match, except that the new cue sheet has the channel intensities written in the lower row of rectangles.

As the designer begins to build cue 1 from the preset cue, the assistant records the changes in the upper row of rectangles. If the channel doesn't change, then the channel intensity shown in the lower rectangle is duplicated in the upper rectangle. Figure 6.11 reflects this point in the cueing process. All of the lower rectangles reflect the channel intensities copied from memory 100.7; channels 24 + 91 > 100 @ 50%, and channels 122 + 136 @ 30%. When light cue 1 was created, the following changes occurred: channel 24 @ 00%, channel 57 @ 50%, channels 91 > 100 @ 70%, channels 116 + 117 +120 + 121 + 136 @ 50%, channel 122 @ 00%, and channel 133 @ 30%.

Once the designer has instructed the board operator to record the new state as light cue 1, the assistant visually combines the readings for both rows of rectangles, and copies those levels to the bottom row of rectangles on the next blank page that will become light cue 2.

After becoming familiar with the cue sheet, the lighting designer can "read" the two cues on one page,

seeing the previous cue in the lower row of rectangles, and the changes made to create the current light cue in the upper row of rectangles.

Work Notes Sheet

After the load-in begins, work notes are taken about problems to fix or adjustments to be made. At the end of each rehearsal period, the production electrician may need to know the work notes that will need to be addressed, so that he or she can determine the amount of labor that will be required and prioritize the schedule. Unfortunately, the work notes regarding physical labor may be buried in a legal pad, surrounded by notes ranging from light cue changes to concept alterations for an entire section of the show. A list specifically detailing the amount of electrics work, generated by the end of the rehearsal, may be a necessity.

The **work notes sheet** is a form used to produce that list. The document is a single written location to centrally notate all work activities. At the end of each rehearsal period, the production electrician can scan this list to gauge the amount of work and the size of the crew that will be required for the next work call.

The layout of the form provides a method to speed corrections and coordinate efforts between technical departments. Figure 6.12 is the work notes sheet constructed specifically for the *Hokey* light plot. The document is laid out in an instrument schedule format, so that as the notes are written, they are sorted by hanging position. Once the document is scanned, personnel can be deployed to remote hanging positions, and areas of the stage can be kept clear to retain ladder access. The notes can specify other objects that may be required for focus notes, so that the proper departments can be informed of their need in advance.

Using a fresh form each day allows the dated documents to be kept as a diary of the lighting package. As work calls progress, the notes are crossed off, but the dated form is retained in a notebook. These "equipment track sheets" can be reviewed to see when specific problems became apparent. They can document patterns of equipment failure and provide a history of when and how problems were addressed. This information may be vital in negotiating any additional costs that may result from on-site emergency repair calls.

Cue Track Sheets

If the production is going to have a future incarnation, there will undoubtedly be changes. A change in venue, a change in dimmer size, or a change in control, to

Hybrid Theatre 1998   *Hokey* Work Notes Sheet   Date: 5/30/98

TRUSS	#	Chan	NOTE

1 Bm L	#	Chan	NOTE

BX L	#	Chan	NOTE
	2	29	DROPPED

2 Bm L	#	Chan	NOTE
	2	107	SWAP UNIT

BX R	#	Chan	NOTE
	7	50	BOTTOM CUT

3 Bm L	#	Chan	NOTE

1 Elec	#	Chan	NOTE
	18	21	SHUTTER
	10	55	FOCUS TO STAIR?

4 Bm L	#	Chan	NOTE
	3	111	ALL OVER SCRIM

2 Elec	#	Chan	NOTE

1 Bm R	#	Chan	NOTE
	1	31	BURNOUT?

3 Elec	#	Chan	NOTE

2 Bm R	#	Chan	NOTE

4 Elec	#	Chan	NOTE
	13	113	SR WORK BO?
	15A	136	ADD 36° - STAIR

3 Bm R	#	Chan	NOTE

5 Elec	#	Chan	NOTE
	11	89	SOFTEN EDGE

4 Bm R	#	Chan	NOTE

STUFF	MOVE HAZER TO SR

Expression 1; 150 chan, 174 dim   Lighting design by Steve Shelley

Figure 6.12 The Work Notes Sheet for *Hokey*

name a few. This may be the opportunity to expand on the original concepts of the show. On the other hand, financial constraints may force the lighting designer to cut, change, or reconfigure the light plot.

To make informed decisions, one of the first things the lighting designer needs to know is how much and when each instrument was used in the first incarnation of the light plot. Upon analysis, it may be discovered that specials or channels within systems were sparingly used, if at all. It is entirely possible that other specials focused to the same area were utilized instead, and some instruments may never have come up. If the visual result was satisfactory, the unused units might be reassigned to a new purpose or simply eliminated from the plot.

Attempting to determine the number of times that any given instrument was used through the course of a production is often only possible by comparing individual cue sheets to another. This cue comparison is also often the only systematic method available to accurately determine the need for separation of control between channels in any given system. Comparing cue sheets can take hours, and the results may still not be accurate. Without this level of analysis, decisions to eliminate instruments or combine units into a single channel must be made based on instinct, rather than knowledge. It may not be realized until too late, in the middle of the single dress rehearsal, that these instinctual decisions were errors in judgment.

In other scenarios, the show may be moving to a performance facility with a completely different lighting console, requiring a time-consuming refeed of the light cues. It may be necessary to reconfigure the channel hookup or incorporate a repatch system. For that matter, the need for a repatch system may not become apparent until the middle of the load-in, when the true count of functioning dimmers is determined to be less than initially claimed.

The **cue track sheet** is the document that can be used to address all of these situations. Not only does it show a spreadsheet format of channels and cues like the track screens found on some console displays, the cue track sheet adds elements of the cheat sheet and the cue master to create a single compact tool. Regardless of the size of the assembled document, the track sheet shows everything about the light cues for a production. It shows the moving and tracking channels in each cue, and the progression of intensities for each channel. When a cue doesn't work, it's possible to analyze the problem on paper, rather than spending time at the light board viewing the monitor display.

Cue Track Sheet Layout Figure 6.13 shows a partial cue track sheet for *Hokey*. It's comprised of four basic components. The **title information** is in the upper left-hand corner. Underneath the title are the **memory and cue information** columns. The **channel numbers** and **cheat sheet** run across the top of the page, while the channel intensities (or **cue content**) makes up the rest of the document.

The title area lists the show, the portion of the show presented, and the key memory number. The header and footer can display additional information, including board type, dimmer configuration, the original creation date, and the version number of this particular document. Other data may include the name of the lighting designer, the name of the document creator, and the page number of the document.

The memory and cue information area begins with the cue or memory number in the left-hand column. The next column shows the time assignment for each cue, which can include any waits or delays. As an example, light cue 109 has a delay of 4 seconds attributed to its time. This implies that memory 109.5 is an autofollow. Tracing a cue across the sheet will explain what is actually moving in that particular cue, so the "For" column from the cue master has been removed, leaving the "On" and "Action" columns.

The information above the channel numbers is copied from the cheat sheet. To eliminate confusion, the nomenclature from the cheat sheet is matched to the cue track sheet. The channel numbers are duplicated below the cue content area, making it easier to vertically scan and trace the path of a single channel.

The cue content area consists of a grid; following the path of a single row across shows the total contents of a single light cue, while the vertical columns show the progression of each channel's movement. The information in the cue content area is formatted. The numbers that are bold and centered in a cell are receiving a "hard command" to move in that cue. Non-bold numbers aligned to the right side of the cell aren't moving; they're "tracking through" the cue. The highlighted hard commands make it easier to scan across the track sheet and see what channels are moving for any cue. Although a channel's intensity may read "70" on the monitor display, all zeros are typically truncated from the cue track sheet, making the level contents of each cell easier to read. The corresponding cell in the track sheet lists the intensity only as a "7."

By vertically scanning and comparing columns, it's easy to gauge the overall use of any channel. It's

Hybrid Theatre 1998   *Hokey* Cue Track Sheet   Date: 5/30/98

Hokey: A Musical Myth — Hybrid Theatre; Expression 1   Key:

MEM	CNT	ON	ACTION	dr (1)	drc (2)	dc (3)	dlc (4)	dl (5)	mr (6)	cc (7)	ml (8)	uc (9)	Sd (10)	dr (11)	drc (12)
100	3		Blocker												
100.7	3		Preset												
101	5|10	Judy arm back	Center up												
102	7	2nd spin	Full stage	5	5	5	5	5	5	5	5	5	5		
103	10	End music phrase	Brighter	7	7	7	7	7	7	7	7	7	7	3	3
104	7	Judy start X DL	DL Spec up	7	7	7	7	7	3	3	3	3	3	3	3
105	5	Judy finish speak	DL Spec down	7	7	7	7	7	7	7	7	7	7	3	3
106	7	Lorraine X DR	DR Spec up	7	7	7	7	7	3	3	3	0	0	3	3
107	5	Lorrain finish speak	DR Spec down	7	7	7	7	7	7	7	7	7	7	3	3
108	7	Mitch X DC	DC Spec up	3	3	3	3	3	0	0	0	0	0	3	3
109	5 D4	Mitch finish speak	DC Spec down	7	7	7	7	7	7	7	7	7	7	3	3
109.5	10	Auto	Lose sides	5	5	5	5	5	5	5	5	5	5	3	3
110	7|10	End 2nd circle	Cooler	3	3	3	3	3	3	3	3	3	3	7	7
111	10	All start to center	Darker; green	0	0	0	0	0	0	0	0	0	0	5	5
112	7|10	All start leave cent	Center up											5	5
113	2|3	Judy X SR	DSR up; rest Ø											7	0
MEM	**CNT**	**ON**	**ACTION**	1	2	3	4	5	6	7	8	9	10	11	12

Expression 1; 150 chan, 174 dim   Lighting design by Steve Shelley

Figure 6.13 The Initial Cue Track Sheet for *Hokey*

also possible to see the use and movement of different systems. If the channels in a particular system are arranged in adjacent channels, it's possible to scan down adjoining columns and compare the level information between the channels in the system. Figure 6.13 shows that channels 1 > 5 all move together. This is also true for channels 6 > 8, and channels 9 + 10. Since those collections of channels have matching intensities through the entire example, then the channel numbers can be combined into a series of single columns.

Figure 6.14 shows the result of this cell compression. Columns of duplicate intensities have been eliminated. This reduces the width of the document, making it more compact and easier to read. Channel separation in the hookup may be retained, however, to make the plot simpler to focus and use.

Since the hard commands for each cue are highlighted, it's also possible to make judgments while making changes in a cue. After consulting the cue track sheet, it can be quickly determined if the changes made in the cue should be re-recorded tracking or cue only.

MEM	R33 Front DS (1>5)	MS (6>8)	US (9>10)
100			
100.7			
101			
102	5	5	5
103	7	7	7
104	7	3	3
105	7	7	7
106	7	3	0
107	7	7	7
108	3	0	0
109	7	7	7
109.5	5	5	5
110	3	3	3
111	0	0	0
112			
113			
MEM	**1>5**	**6>8**	**9>10**

Figure 6.14 The Condensed Cue Track Sheet for *Hokey*

After analysis of the cue track sheet, group and submaster lists may be adapted so that newly identified collections of channels can be more rapidly manipulated.

Cue Track Sheets: Programming The conventional method of programming memories into a lighting console (or "**feeding the cues**") is to program the level changes for a memory, and then record that memory. When memories are fed into the lighting console using a cue track sheet, the bold formatting makes it simpler to see which channels are moving from the previous cue. This formatting can reduce the amount of effort and time spent feeding several cues into the console. To compare the movement between nonadjacent channels, the cue track sheet can be accordion-folded, hiding intermediate columns. After folding the cue track sheet, it is easy to compare the intensity levels between channels 1 and 100.

Often examining the progression of intensity changes for a single channel requires the viewer to look at each memory, one at a time. Some advanced lighting consoles, on the other hand, can view the cue content like a spreadsheet. The memories are displayed as rows while the channels are shown as columns, like the cue track sheet. Some consoles allow intensity information for a single channel to be altered in more than one memory while viewing that screen. Instead of programming cues "horizontally," the cue track sheet makes it possible to utilize this display, and program level changes in a "vertical" direction. Initially, all of the memories are recorded without cue content, creating an empty grid. Since the path of the channels can be seen, the "vertical" movement of each channel can then be programmed. Depending on the number of channels or the number of intensity changes, this may reduce the number of keystrokes, and reduce the amount of programming time.

Cue Track Sheets: Repatch If a repatch system must be designed within an existing light plot, the cue track sheet can be used to show channels that might be combined, allowing a repatch to take place and reducing the need for a dimmer. The first step taken is to determine the total number of dimmers that are available for use, or the total number of dimmers that must be eliminated from the present channel hookup. In this example, two channels (and their respective dimmers) must be eliminated to fit within the new dimmer configuration.

Scan the partial cue track sheet on the left-hand side of Figure 6.15 for columns that have few entries. In this case, a scan of the columns shows that channels 51 > 54, plus 56 and 57 are fairly active. Since the cells are centered and highlighted, the channels are moving quite a bit. Scanning the columns a second time shows some relatively open columns. Channels 55, 58, 59, and 60 each appear briefly.

The right-hand side of Figure 6.15 isolates those four channels, showing that while channels 58 > 60 all move within one cue of each other, channel 55 is dormant until cue 111. One dimmer will be gained by repatching any of the 58 > 60 sequence with the contents of channel 55, since all of them will be at zero when channel 55 comes up. The effort to gain a second dimmer, though, is a bit more complex. Channel 60 shouldn't attempt a repatch with 58. They're both moving within one cue of each other and there's no buffer cue between the channel movements. The same situation exists for channels 58 and 59. Channel 60 fades out in cue 105, two cues before channel 59 is activated to Full in cue 108. Checking the "On" and "Action" columns on the left-hand side of the cue track sheet shows that there is some amount of time between cues 105 and 108.

The left-hand side of Figure 6.16 illustrates the solution. Channels 55 and 58 can repatch with each other, and channels 59 and 60 can repatch with each other. That means there will be two repatch cues. After cue 105 is complete, the contents of what is now channel 60 will be switched off, and the contents of what is now channel 59 will be switched on. After cue 107 is complete, the contents of what is now channel 58 will be switched off, and the contents of what is now channel 55 will be switched on. Analysis of the track sheet has shown one possible way to eliminate two dimmers. The contents of channel 58 are now hardpatched into the same dimmer controlled by channel 55, while the contents of channel 60 are hardpatched into channel 59.

The right-hand side of Figure 6.16 shows the reprogramming required for the repatch to succeed. Channels 55 and 59 have had the additional channel movements programmed to reflect the movements that used to be made by channels 58 and 60. The added movements have been italicized. A bullet has been added after the channel has gone to zero to help illuminate the moment when the repatch can occur. The four channels have been combined and programmed into two channels.

Figure 6.15 (Left — A Partial Cue Track Sheet)

MEM	1E DC 51	2E Sd 52	4E UC 53	5E Sd 54	1P 55	3P 56	5P 57	SR 58	C 59	SL 60
	Templates				NC Cen Pools			NC Tr Spec		
100										
100.7										
101						5	7			
102							5	7		
103	5	5	5	5		5	5			
104	5	5	3	3		3	3			F
105	7	5	7	5		5	5			0
106	3	3	3	3		3	3	F		
107	5	5	5	5		5	5	0		
108	0	0	3	0		0	0		F	
109	5	5	5	5		3	3		0	
109.5	F	7	F	7		5	5			
110	7	7	7	7		5	5			
111	0	0	0	0	7	0	5			
112						F	F			
113						0	0			
MEM	51	52	53	54	55	56	57	58	59	60

Figure 6.15 (Right — the Same Track Sheet Showing Isolated Channels)

MEM	1E DC 51	2E Sd 52	4E UC 53	5E Sd 54	1P 55	3P 56	5P 57	SR 58	C 59	SL 60
	Templates				NC Cen Pools			NC Tr Spec		
100										
100.7										
101						5	7			
102							5	7		
103	5	5	5	5		5	5			
104	5	5	3	3		3	3			F
105	7	5	7	5		5	5			0
106	3	3	3	3		3	3	F		
107	5	5	5	5		5	5	0		
108	0	0	3	0		0	0		F	
109	5	5	5	5		3	3		0	
109.5	F	7	F	7		5	5			
110	7	7	7	7		5	5			
111	0	0	0	0	7	0	5			
112						F	F			
113						0	0			
MEM	51	52	53	54	55	56	57	58	59	60

Figure 6.15 A Partial Cue Track Sheet on the Left; the Same Track Sheet Showing Isolated Channels on the Right

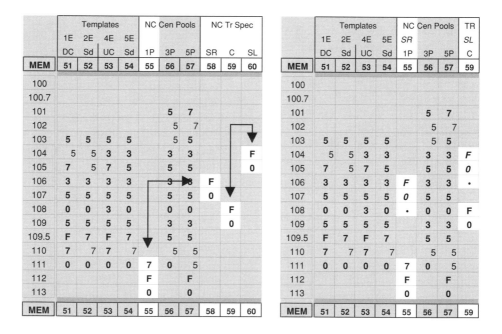

Figure 6.16 A Partial Cue Track Sheet Showing Channel Combinations on the Left; After Reprogramming on the Right

There's no question that the cue track sheet can be time consuming to compile. Once completed, however, the cue track sheet is one of the best tools in any designer's arsenal to analyze or reproduce lighting. The final document eliminates pounds of printouts, expedites cue analysis, and, considering the reduced number of pages, can be easily sent as a fax. It can reduce delays and overnight delivery service charges.

Other Paperwork

Other paperwork is necessary to coordinate all of the efforts between departments. A copy of the production schedule will state when activities occur or when the lighting designer can work on stage. A contact sheet is an absolute must—without being able to communicate, the lighting designer is dead in the water. Knowing the route to the stage door on the first day of load-in can also be helpful.

SUMMARY

Once the cue construction paperwork has been completed, the preparation of the paperwork packets for the production is complete. Although many documents may be required for communication or reference, these initial packets can be distributed to show relationships, provide information, and determine conflicts with other production elements prior to the load-in.

7

Prior to Load-In

This chapter examines some of the events that take place prior to the load-in. This is the period of time when the lighting and other design elements, combined with the performance facility information, are reviewed, analyzed, and discussed. Reexamination may show that the electrical infrastructure of the performing facility is not as extensive as was originally understood. Additional architectural information may reveal obstructions on the stage or in the fly system. Components of the lighting package may require substitution to conform to up-to-date inventories. Peripheral tasks may increase the complexity of the production schedule. Regardless of the number of these unforeseen parameters, extensive production meetings often take place to examine the impact of any new information to the production schedule, and to consider every option.

THE PRODUCTION SCHEDULE

The production schedule is the plan that identifies the time line for an entire show. Although it may encompass weeks or months, its most critical portion begins with the load-in. At that point, it lists in detail the beginning and completion times for every task that takes place during each portion of the day.

A Typical Production Schedule

Although the typical sequence of activities was mentioned when the parameters were discussed, it's valuable to review them again. At the beginning of the load-in, the show equipment is unloaded, and any flying scenic goods and overhead electrical equipment

are hung. The performance surface (if there is one) is installed. Additional scenery, along with properties and wardrobe, are assembled, prepared, and stored. Infrastructure information is loaded into the lighting console. The scenic and electrical trims for the show are set, the onstage positions of deck scenery are spiked, after which the lighting instruments are focused. Light cue level setting sessions define each look, while sound cue levels are established and recorded.

The show is ready for a technical rehearsal when the performance surface has been safely installed, the backstage is clean and clear, and the scenic goods are placed and prepared. The instruments have been focused, the peripheral lighting (spotting, worklights, and cue lights) is set, and cues are in the board. The headsets and monitors are operational, the production table is set, and the wardrobe has been prepared.

The technical rehearsals allow all departments to add their elements to the performancs and complete the stage picture. After the technical and dress rehearsals are completed, the house is cleared. Final preshow checks are made, and the show is performed. After the show, notes are given for the next performance, or everything is dismantled, packed, and loaded out.

Constructing a Production Schedule

In a broad sense, manipulating the tasks that comprise a production schedule can be compared to fitting together individual pieces to create a finished jigsaw puzzle. Some pieces fit with each other; other pieces don't. Some pieces can only fit in one direction; other pieces can be attached to one another in a variety of combinations. Reflecting the needs of each show, a length of time and an objective are assigned to each separate activity, creating a puzzle piece. After analysis, the task's objective and time duration may be split into two separate units, creating two smaller pieces. Though additional pieces can be seen as creating more confusion, it can also be viewed as introducing more flexibility. More pieces mean more possible combinations. After all of the activities have been divided to their individual time-defined components, the total number of puzzle pieces is known. The process then becomes one of comparing the pieces to one another, in search of a "fit," when two or more activities can simultaneously occur. Finding the proper fit to construct a complex production schedule is a time-consuming task that should be discussed, analyzed, and discussed again.

One method used to initially determine the production schedule involves thinking backwards, so that the time line begins with the first performance. A list is created that catalogues all of the activities that will be required to mount a specific production. Once durations of time are assigned to each task, the tasks are then listed in reverse order, beginning with the first performance. For the first performance to smoothly occur, dress rehearsals and technical rehearsals need to take place. Since the technical rehearsals must begin at a specific point prior to the opening of the show, all work preparing for the initial rehearsal needs to be completed prior to that time. This process continues backwards to the date of the load-in.

Once the load-in begins, the schedule will be reshaped through the course of each day. At the end of the day, informal production meetings are often held to define and prioritize the objectives of the following day's schedule. Successful execution of a production schedule depends on communication and coordination, and the ability to recognize and anticipate potential problems. If everyone involved in the production is aware of the goals, all departments can work together to accomplish those goals.

Refining a Production Schedule for the Electrics Department

Variables in or outside of the electrics department may alter or shift the amount of time required for each electrical task:

- What work will be accomplished prior to the arrival of the company? Does the technical agreement state that lighting instruments will be hung prior to the company's arrival? Will masking goods be installed prior to the load-in?

- How many hours of time exist prior to the first performance? If the call is departmentalized, how many people are allocated per department?

- Is there time allocated for the basic lighting tasks: a hang session, a hot test session, a focus session, a cue level setting session, a technical rehearsal, and a dress rehearsal? What tasks can be combined?

- How much lighting equipment is being supplied by the show? How are the road instruments packaged to speed the hang?

- Is the show carrying its own lighting console? Is it possible to prewrite any cues prior to load-in, either in the shop, on another console, or using off-line editing software?

Adjusting to the Scenic Design

Often, the intricacies of the budget and the amount of labor available are more fully understood by employers and production managers. Understanding the components of the scenic design, however, allows the lighting designer to add his or her perspective, and help refine the production schedule. Staggering departmental tasks or altering installation sequences may speed the overall production schedule.

If the scenic design is a non-modular enclosed box set, its configuration may demand that the load-in schedule become departmentalized. In many cases, the overhead electrics may have to be hung and flown out prior to the installation of the scenery. If the installation of the overhead lighting package is delayed until after the scenic components are assembled, the amount of time spent hanging instruments in the air may hinder the rest of the schedule. Scenic beams, walls, ceilings, and platforms may impose time-consuming traffic maneuvers for an A-frame ladder during the focus session. Anticipating this situation may suggest the acquisition of a focusing ladder that occupies less square footage on the deck (also known as a smaller "footprint"), which can then more rapidly navigate around the scenery during the focus session. If the same box set contains no openings large enough to allow the focusing ladder access onstage once the scenery has been installed, a scenic wall may require a technical redesign prior to the load-in. If the wall is connected to the rest of the set with lash cleats or pin-hinges, for example, it can be simply and rapidly removed during work calls, allowing the ladder access to the onstage scenery and the overhead electrics.

The speed of a focus session can often be linked to the number of objects on stage that require additional movement out of the path of the focusing ladder. Consider scheduling the focus session after important props are placed, approved, spiked, and then removed. This scheduling technique may also be applied to platforms or stairs. Modular construction may allow the scenic units to be removed during the initial focus, reducing the amount of time consumed by additional ladder movement. These considerations should be addressed during preliminary production meetings.

Special attention should be paid if the scenic design includes a raked stage. Although small platform pieces can be constructed allowing the focusing ladder to be level while sitting on the stage (counter-rake), shuffling the pieces can increase the amount of time required to complete the focus session. Alternate methods of hanging and plotting should be considered to retain a constrained production schedule. This may include the use of **triangle truss** or **box truss,** which are support devices typically constructed of lengths of tubing with diagonal bracing to provide structural support. Truss is manufactured in a variety of sizes and lengths, and when properly suspended, can support not only lighting instruments but also the personnel who will focus them. Another method involves hanging high-grade traveler track adjacent to overhead electric positions and equipping it with a **focus chair** that can slide on the track. Electricians can access the chairs from ladders or positions offstage of the rake, eliminating the need to move a ladder onto the slanted surface.

Shelley's Notes: Confirm Paperwork Distribution

If paperwork is sent to an out-of-town theatre, call and confirm that the theatre has received and distributed the paperwork to the proper parties. Do not assume that silence implies acceptance of the lighting package. It's not impossible that the package containing the information has been lost, misplaced, or misinterpreted.

As an example, I once produced an extensive lighting paperwork package and sent it off to the theatre barely meeting the contractual schedule defined by the producer. I heard nothing from the production electrician for weeks and presumed that everything had been received and approved. One week prior to load-in, I called him and discovered he had never received any paperwork from his production office. I immediately called the production office, since duplicating the paperwork package at this late date would involve some amount of time and effort.

When I asked about the package in question, the receptionist in the production office immediately knew what I was talking about. "Oh yes," she said, "we received that package for Mr. Shelley weeks ago. And we're holding it here safe and secure until his arrival."

"That's very kind," I responded, "but this is Mr. Shelley. And I sent that package so that your staff would open it, study it, and respond to it a month ago. Please, don't wait for me. It's not a package that was sent to me, it was sent from me. Open the box and give the information to the house staff. There are no doubt issues that should be discussed now, not then."

INITIAL PAPERWORK AND TOOLS

One decision the lighting designer needs to make prior to the load-in is the amount of information to have on hand when first walking in the door. The phrase "that paperwork's on the electrics truck" takes on a whole new meaning when the electrics truck isn't the first to get unloaded, or when its axle breaks prior to reaching the dock, or when it's missing in the blizzard on the other side of the Continental Divide.

As the distinguished lighting designer Ms. Jennifer Tipton once said, "If you have a choice between taking your paperwork or your underwear, take the paperwork. You can light a show without undies, but you can't do much lighting with underwear." Many lighting designers walk into theatres with that point of view, expecting delays in the arrival of equipment. They begin the day with enough paperwork to perform all work ignoring the contents of the truck, thereby avoiding any possible waste of stage time. Paperwork may include a copy of the light plot, the section, focus spike groundplans, preliminary paperwork, infrastructure programming information, the magic sheet, and the cheat sheet. The focus document may also be included, so that any changes made during the hang may be directly noted onto the paper that will be used during the focus session.

Since the amount of paperwork and equipment can quickly become cumbersome, many lighting designers coordinate their baggage with the production electrician. The road crew may also arrive with everything needed to accomplish every facet of work possible without the equipment packed in the electrics truck. This may include tape measures, scale rules, marking devices such as chalk or spike tape, and any hanging information. A set of show disks will often travel separately from the electrics truck. If the disks contain any preprogramming, they may be loaded into the house lighting console and the process of softpatching dimmer information can begin. Even if the disks contain no information whatsoever, their presence may allow preprogramming to occur.

If house equipment is being used for the front of house positions, consider bringing precut or sheet color for those positions. If the overhead electrics are going to consist of house equipment, consider bringing the reference information needed to hang those positions as well.

THE NIGHT BEFORE THE LOAD-IN

The night before a load-in a lighting designer's emotions can range from a relaxed feeling of confidence to a feeling of paranoia and dread. The "night before" can often feel like the final period of time before the clock regulating stage time starts ticking. It's the last time that tasks can be approached in a leisurely manner. When nerves and anxiety try to take hold, regain your mental equilibrium by reviewing the load-in.

Remind yourself of the goals to be accomplished the next day, and imagine the steps required to complete each task. Are there enough copies of the paperwork available for additional last minute distribution? Is all of the paperwork prepared, allowing all questions to be rapidly answered? This may be the point when the designer discovers the need for another list.

✓ Before the Lighting Designer Walks into the Theatre:

- Make certain that the plot is updated and that all distances from centerline are known.
- Check the section for all trim heights and focus point locations. Make any notes required.
- Make certain that the master system spike groundplan is updated and ready for use.
- Make certain that the focusing documents are updated, and consider rehearsing the focus at home the night before the focus session. Some lighting designers quiz themselves by flipping to random instruments in the focus document. They see if every fact that may possibly be needed during the focus is present on the reference document.
- Determine which documents will be needed, and where to place them so that they are rapidly available. Don't store the light plot in the bottom of the carry-on bag.

A moment should be taken to remember other tools that the lighting designer possesses. The ability to prioritize, troubleshoot, problem solve, and communicate are all skills that will be called on throughout the production process. Superceding those talents, however, are the lighting designer's practical judgment; common sense and a sense of safety.

SUMMARY

Once the paperwork and equipment have been packed for transport to the theatre, and a mental review of the next day's production schedule has been reviewed, the lighting designer is prepared for the load-in.

part three

Using the Tools

8

Load-In and Setup

This chapter examines events that occur at the beginning of stage time, between the start of load-in and the focus session.

When the load-in for a production begins, it's often greeted with an emotion bordering on relief. A great deal of time has been spent analyzing, discussing, and preparing every aspect and contingency of the activities for the production. Although a lot of time has already been dedicated to the production, the execution of that effort has always been referred to in the future tense. Finally, the activities will begin to happen—now.

From a distance, the first day of load-in can be viewed as a quick-paced, exciting, terrific learning experience. If the process hasn't been thoroughly analyzed and preparation hasn't been done, however, the load-in can be an exhausting, overwhelming exercise in backpedaling. It seems that before one unexpected question is resolved, a second unexpected question is posed. When this situation occurs, and the questions can't be immediately answered, the best initial response is to define how soon an answer is needed. Then find the personnel or documents that will provide an answer to the question.

In the best of times, it's a joy to be able to see the often-discussed plans fit smoothly into place. At other times, it's irritating to see minor misunderstandings cost stage time. The worst of times is when problems continually crop up. At that point, disappointment can easily turn into the act of assigning blame. Conflict can rapidly surface. There may be conflicts between members of the crew, conflicts between members of the staff, or possibly conflicts between the crew and the lighting designer. Since each of these situations has the potential to affect the schedule, the lighting designer should be aware of these issues. If the choice is

made to remain oblivious to developing conflicts, that inaction may contribute to the possibility of an emotional outburst, which, feelings aside, will inevitably cost stage time.

The lighting designer, along with the rest of the department heads (both road and house), is responsible for more than just making the show happen. Although they need to make certain that everyone's time in the theatre is safe, they also need to monitor the relationships that can develop, so that the speed of the load-in doesn't become affected by bad feelings.

BEFORE THE WORK BEGINS

The lighting designer can do nothing but help his or her cause by arriving at the theatre early on the load-in day. By arriving prior to the beginning of the call, the lighting designer will have the opportunity to see the performance space.

Prior to the beginning of the call, the contact sheet should be reviewed to memorize the names of the crew heads. Calling individuals by their names shows a measure of respect, and it also reduces the miscommunication that can occur when someone doesn't know that he or she is being addressed. If there's a production staff (road crew) in addition to the staff of the facility (house crew), all of the lighting designer's requests will be directed to them. If the staff of the show is reduced, however, memorizing the names of the house crew heads will enable the lighting designer to establish a better working relationship.

Ideally, this is not the lighting designer's initial view of this stage. Previous visits have clarified all of the observations, measurements, and questions about the performance space. The technical representatives or the crew heads have been introduced during preliminary meetings and discussions. On the other hand, if the combination of a distant location and a lack of financial funds have resulted in all information being transferred long distance, this may be the designer's first opportunity to view the space, and make initial face-to-face contact with the house crew.

If this is the first contact with the performance space, it's wise to check the spatial relationships that exist in the theatre. The primary document that is often used is the section, which should be consulted to confirm that the drawn document matches the reality of what's in the air above the stage. Next, the section and the light plot should be consulted to confirm that the drawn location and number of front of house positions really agree with the actual architecture.

A measuring tape can be used to check the sightline for accuracy. If the distance from the plaster line to the sightline is greater than originally thought, it may provide some amount of "cushion" in the vertical height of the masking and the electrics. If the distance is less, this is the best time to consider other options. This distance will be examined in more detail when setting the trims is discussed. The distance of the sightline from centerline should also be compared to what's drawn on the groundplans. The groundplan sent to the lighting designer may not have indicated an entire section of seats extending further offstage than the drawn sightline point. In that situation, it may be necessary to reconsider the width of the portal leg opening, and possibly the rest of the masking as well. If any changes are considered necessary, the production manager or technical director should be consulted immediately. Any alteration is then mutually agreed upon and communication between the proper parties takes place before the beginning of the call.

Union Considerations

Most productions employ stagehands that are paid by the production. They may or may not belong to the International Association of Theatrical Stage Employees (**IA**). The stagehands that work for the show (the **road crew**, or the production crew), along with the lighting designer and other technical managers, supervise the installation of the production into the performance facility. The technical staff of the performance facility (the **house heads**) supervise additional stagehands that are hired to perform the tasks necessary to mount the production.

Many professional stagehands are IA members and belong to local chapters of the union. The professional union for lighting designers is the United Scenic Artists (**USA**). IA stagehands have a structured agreement that defines the work hours that can take place in a single 24-hour period, with appropriate compensation for each one of those hours. This hourly structure can be unique in each union situation. USA designers, on the other hand, have no hourly theatrical rate in the present contract. Although the USA lighting designer is paid by the week or by a fee, he or she must be aware of the clock. Along with the rest of the technical staffs working on the show, the lighting designer strives to make certain that the work is being completed in the budgeted amount of time, and that the stagehands are receiving the breaks required by their contract.

Regardless of union affiliation, the unspoken understanding that often exists between lighting designers and stagehands is that the lighting designer provides the direction for the tasks (the light plot, the other paperwork, the objectives), while the stagehands provide the methods and the labor to achieve those objectives. In practice, this means that the lighting designer's responsibility is to watch the load-in without being distracted by performing physical labor. Or, simply put, when the lighting designer is working in a union house, he or she should not be required (nor allowed) to touch any equipment. Instead of expending effort on tasks that are assigned to others, the lighting designer should be concentrating on the accuracy of the work being performed. With the production electrician, the lighting designer must consider the most time-efficient sequence that may be applied to the tasks necessary to produce the show. Every union house has its own set of rules defining when coffee and meal breaks are required. If you observe them and are polite, considerate, and respectful, a positive working relationship with the crew can be developed. Always be aware of the fact that you are a guest. Just as it's impolite to move furniture in your host's home, moving equipment in someone else's theatre without asking is impolite. For example, asking permission to move a road box so that your work measuring the stage can continue, is a good idea, and you may be allowed to do so. Sometimes there are many ways to accomplish the end means necessary to produce the show.

Regardless of the size or affiliation of the crew, knowing who is in charge and being aware of the local rules will reduce the number and severity of misunderstandings. The more union or house rules the lighting designer knows, the better equipped he or she can be to contribute to time-management decisions. In many cases, the leader of the road crew (the technical manager or the production manager) may already have the local rules memorized. Often these rules have been examined in other conversations when the options for the production schedule were considered. Here are some of the questions that assist informed decisions to be made:

- Who is the house union steward? This position may be separate from the house heads. It is often the position responsible for the payroll and checking everyone's contracts. In fact, the house steward is probably the person who will know the accurate answers to the rest of these questions.
- Is the crew departmentalized?
- How long can work proceed before a coffee break has to be taken? How long should the coffee break last?
- How long can work proceed before a meal break has to be taken?
- Does the crew have to all break at the same time for meals? Can there be a "split" between crews? (This is discussed later in more depth.)
- How long, prior to the end of a work call, does "wash-up" occur? (The point when the crew stops work to "wash their hands" prior to a meal break.)
- How late can the work call extend without going into overtime?
- Does the entire union load-in crew need to be retained throughout the entire focus?

Two other basic questions should be addressed that may have a direct effect on a union call. If the production schedule has been altered or is unclear, the questions are worthy of consideration, since they will have a direct effect on the lighting designer's internal time clock:

- At what time is the focus session scheduled to begin?
- At what time is the focus session scheduled to end?

Information Distribution Check

After the initial introductions are made, casually inquire and confirm that everyone has the correct matching information. Presumably, the road crew has had the relevant paperwork for some time, so this double-check is hopefully limited to the house crew. The house master electrician should have the plot, the section, and the support paperwork. The house head fly-person should have some form of the hang plot and the section. The head carpenter should have the ground-plans, the section, and the hang plot. If the paperwork has been misplaced, or never got to the house heads in the first place, this is the moment where having extra copies may save time. Otherwise, the lighting designer may start the day by determining the location of the theatre's photocopy machine and the amount of time required for it to warm up.

Being certain that everyone has the same information reduces misunderstandings. If the transferal of this information is not confirmed, those misunderstandings, which may not be discovered until much later in the load-in process, may result in hours of duplicated effort.

The First Misunderstanding

The beginning of the load-in can easily be thrown into confusion when the house heads provide the lighting designer with accurate, but new, information. Basic assumptions made by the lighting designer, based on inaccurate information may be discovered to be incorrect. This information may be pointed out in casual statements like "The battens are really 10'-0" shorter than the drawing shows," or "They keep saying in the tech packet that our borders are 15'-0" tall. Heck, we don't have any borders taller than 8'-0" at the most."

Thankfully, a member of the house staff has informed you of the discrepancy. If the ramifications of that correct piece of information drastically alters the shape or plan of the lighting design, it's unfortunate, but it happens. Don't waste time assigning blame. The house crew works with the physical objects on a daily basis, not the representational drawings. They rarely refer to the tech specs because they work with the equipment, not the lists. Without attending every production meeting for the show, it's impossible for them to understand the physical interrelationships between the technical elements and the light plot. Hopefully, this correct information will be received before the load-in begins. This time can be used to analyze the situation with a bare stage, drawings, and the appropriate personnel without the surrounding distractions of a load-in.

First, thank the individual for providing the information. Next, confirm the accuracy of the information. If the new data is true, the leader of the road crew should be informed. If the impact of the information could affect the production schedule, the proper parties should be made aware of the situation. A course of action may be chosen that allows the crew to continue work, while avoiding any tasks related to the potential problem. By temporarily avoiding the situation, alterations to the plan won't delay or duplicate any efforts. Take the time to specifically identify the problem and its potential affect on the production. Consult the members of the production crew who might be affected by any change. When the solution is determined, the change should be communicated to all affected parties, and the paperwork should be updated to reflect the change.

THE LOAD-IN BEGINS

The beginning of a load-in can often be seen as controlled bedlam. Trucks are unloaded, equipment is moved into the space and distributed onto the stage, components of the house inventory are brought out of storage for use, and questions are being answered everywhere. Crates, boxes, racks of costumes, rolls of vinyl, pipe, scenery, soft goods, and numerous other components are all brought into the space.

During the load-in, the playing area can be extended offstage to any area on the stage that is underneath any batten that will come to the deck during the load-in. This expanded area can be called the **hot zone**. Since it is the primary workspace used to perform most initial tasks, accessing the hot zone can often turn into a test of wills. Scheduling activities in this area often requires combining the skills of a New York City traffic cop and the diplomacy of the State Department.

In constrained spaces, preserving the hot zone may result in equipment covering the seats of the house, filling the aisles, the concession areas, and even the lobby of the theatre. Everyone has a purpose, and is trying to get a jump on the day. The overall goal is to assemble and install all of the lighting, scenery, properties, and sound equipment into predesignated positions within the time allowed.

While unloading equipment into a space can be seen as an exercise to "just get the gear in the door," the mechanics of a load-in are often approached from a different perspective. To avoid clogging the hot zone, much of the equipment must be placed in temporary storage locations. Those locations are often carefully considered before the load-in begins. Random dispersal of the gear may result in additional time and effort spent retrieving the equipment back to the playing area when it's needed. Worse yet, it may end up "buried" in such a remote location that it might not be found again until the load-out. The people directing the equipment's distribution attempt to assign convenient temporary storage locations, and reduce the number of movements required by the equipment.

Before the load-in begins, the production manager, the road heads, and the house heads construct a general plan of equipment distribution. Initially, equipment is usually divided into two categories: Things on wheels that can be placed almost anywhere, since moving them a second time doesn't require extensive time or effort. Other things without wheels should be placed in out-of-the-way locations that won't have to be moved again until used. This plan attempts to allocate storage areas to each department so that the equipment is only moved twice. First, it is moved into the space so that when the trucks are empty, the hot zone is clear and ready for use. Its arrangement is also planned so that when the time comes, the equipment can be moved into the hot zone for assembly in a manner requiring the least amount of time and effort.

Usually, the production electrician or an assistant directs the lighting equipment to its locations. Equipment that will be installed in the front of house positions are often initially directed to an area adjacent to the front of house access, which may be the steps in the lobby. Additional dimmers brought in for the show (road racks) are often placed in the location that will become their home, so that they can be installed at any time. The instruments for the overhead electrics and any accompanying cable are stored on the sides of the stage, or nearby in the audience so that they'll be close at hand when it's time for the electrics to be hung.

The lighting designer's designated role during this time is to be an observer and a source of information. Although some requests for information may be questions regarding "when" ("How soon before you're going to want to start the focus?"), most of the questions directed to the lighting designer will be asking for definitions of "where." This may range from locating points ("Where do you want the production table?"), to confirming points of boundaries ("Where's the onstage edge of the legs?"), to establishing relationships between objects ("Before we hang the legs, where do you want the sidelight booms?"). In some cases, a defined "guesstimate" may be acceptable to allow work to continue in a constant direction. In other cases, a concrete response may be required. Being able to provide comprehensible, accurate answers requires prior analysis, comprehension, and preparation for each aspect of the overall design.

The ability to provide a concrete response to the "where" questions is directly related to the lighting designer's ability to quickly define the performance space into spatial points of reference. Defining the space is often achieved by placing spike marks on the stage.

 ### Shelley's Soapbox: Keep the Hot Zone Clear During Load-In

I think of a load-in like drafting. When I've got a light plot on the drafting table, I try not to clutter up the workspace by placing books, paper, and other debris on top of the plot. When I let the clutter accumulate, the first thing that needs to occur before resuming work on the plot is the task of unearthing of the document.

During the initial load-in, all cases, boxes, or equipment should ideally be placed somewhere else other than the hot zone. Anything placed or temporarily stored under a batten used by the show will have to be cleared from that area before any work involving that batten can begin. If the choice must be made, things in the way that are castered are good. Things in the way that are not castered, requiring some amount of time to move again, are bad.

Key tip-off phrases include "Hey, Bert, let's just drag this pile of jumpers out to the center of the stage" or "Just dump all of the gel frames under the first electric. We'll sort out what we need." Find the production electrician and have him or her delicately intervene. Perhaps the pile could be located somewhere else. If it really has to be there, perhaps it could it be placed on something with wheels when it makes its debut onto the stage. Hopefully, those same wheels will allow it to rapidly disappear when the time comes.

 ### Shelley's Soapbox: Establish Your Base of Operations

During the first hours of a load-in, I've found it critical to define an area as my "base of operations." I want my information and tools close to me. I don't want the base to be moved, yet I want it secure and accessible. The first key word is accessible. If the answer to the

question is in your bag, which is safely stowed in the production office on the third floor, everything can potentially come to a grinding halt, while you scramble to the third floor to retrieve the answer. If your bag, which was offstage safely out of the way, suddenly got in the way, you may spend some time quizzing the entire crew to determine the new storage location of your bag.

During the initial load-in, I attempt to locate my base of operations down center. Usually, I find that down center is out of everyone's way. Not only can I perform any work that's necessary, I can also monitor the entire stage. If there's enough room downstage of plaster line, I'll establish a base of operations on the edge of the apron. If there's no apron, I'll establish a base in the first row of seats. If there's an orchestra pit, I'll move to a side area of the apron so that my bag stays on stage.

When there's enough room, this base can also be an ideal load-in location for the electric workbox, the color distribution box, or a table from which to work. If possible, I'll use an empty scenery hamper for the table of my "office." When I need to clear the area, or move the "office" to a different part of the stage, I can easily wheel the hamper to the location of my choosing.

Shelley's Notes: Paperwork Changes

Changes occur as soon as the load-in of a light plot begins. A change has three points in its lifetime. Initially, it is born when the decision is made to do something different than was originally planned. Secondly, it receives an identity when it's recorded onto a document that uses it as a point of reference. Finally, it ceases to be a change when it is absorbed into an updated generation of documents, turning it into a known fact.

When the production electrician is informed of a change, he or she must write down the information into the appropriate paperwork, decide its significance, and choose whether or not to inform the lighting designer of the change. Likewise, when the lighting designer is informed of a change, he or she must record the change into the applicable documents, decide its significance, and choose whether or not to inform the production electrician of the change. These choices are based on the judgment of both individuals, which is why the communication between the lighting designer and the production electrician must be clear.

The point when revised documents are published vary by designer. For many designers, that time is after the focus session has been completed, and the lighting package has "settled down." The changes from all of the various documents used through the load-in are then updated into the lighting database and all other relevant paperwork. Once published, obsolete paperwork should be clearly marked as such. Although some lighting designers want reprinted plots, magic sheets, and cheat sheets before the light cue level setting session, others are more comfortable retaining their original version of these documents containing the handwritten changes.

 Shelley's Notes: Keeping Paper and Keeping Track

Throughout the course of the load-in, consider keeping copies of the important paperwork at your fingertips. I've found that most initial questions can be answered by carrying a copy of the light plot, the section, the magic sheet, and the cheat sheet. There's no telling where or when a question may be asked, and if the paperwork isn't with me, time can be wasted searching for the answer. By keeping these pieces of paperwork with me at all times, changes can be updated, regardless of my location. I've also found it useful to keep the paperwork in my pockets, not carried in my hands. Once it's set down on a crate, the crate may be moved while my back is turned and then the paperwork is gone.

When changes are made, the support paperwork will eventually need to be updated to include them. For the most part, though, I've found it simpler to record the changes on the documents that will be used when creating the light cues (magic sheet and cheat sheet) or on the base documents showing the overall design (plot and section). In addition to the typical changes of circuitry, color, and channel information, there may be additional or altered groups or submasters. When possible, I attempt to design the layout of the magic sheet to include extra white space for the purpose of recording additional groups or subs. Typically, I'll be looking at that document when I'm searching for a handle. I've found that those handles can be seen as tools, but if they're not identified, they may as well be forgotten tools in the cellar.

To maintain communication and not introduce out-of-date data to the situation, a single location must be defined during the load-in as the repository of all current information. Common wisdom states that after the support paperwork leaves the hands of the lighting designer, the most current data regarding the lighting package is the version possessed by the production electrician. If told of any changes in circuitry after the load-in begins, I immediately take those changes to the production electrician and they're recorded into his or her support paperwork. Changes in purpose or focus, on the other hand, may not need to be immediately transferred to the lighting database since they don't affect the installation of the light plot.

Being able to quickly scan a page and see those changes, though, reduces the time spent updating information. I usually mark the changes in the appropriate document with a red pen. When changes are updated or communicated, I can find them. If the changes are made in a neutral color, they're easier to miss, and obsolete information may be distributed. During updating sessions, consider using a highlighter to mark on top of the red pen changes, reflecting the fact that the change has been applied to the updated material. At the conclusion of an updating session, scanning each page for highlighter will confirm that all the changes have been made.

The need to assign additional channels of control to devices may not become apparent until the middle of a load-in. In that situation, the lighting designer should determine the additional channel assignment. If the device is assigned to a channel without informing the lighting designer, he or she may unknowingly assign an additional instrument to the same channel. The channel will be constantly changed to control the intensity of the instrument, while simultaneously altering the amount of voltage being fed to the device. If the device requires a constant voltage, this action may damage it. The lack of communication will cause improper programming to occur as the memories are constructed, and the location of the unlisted device may remain unknown until crisis results due to its absence. Peripheral devices are peripheral only until they can't be found. Then they become a priority.

 Shelley's Notes: Delays during Load-In

Whenever a lighting package travels some amount of distance to a theatre, the possibility always exists that the transport may not arrive at the facility at the scheduled time. If the trucks don't show up at the beginning of the load-in, there may be a crew standing around with nothing to do. If the house equipment to be used includes instruments in the overhead electrics, the house electrician may be resistant to clogging up the hot zone with those units. This makes sense, since there's always the possibility that when the first electric is being hung, the truck will arrive, causing interruption and chaos.

If the front of house color, accessories, and board information is on site, however, work can still be accomplished. The house console can be programmed, while the front of house instruments can be prepared for focus. If the trucks are still absent by the time the programming has been completed and the instruments are prepared, consider focusing the front of house instruments without the rest of the light plot or any scenery. If the spike groundplans are accurate, the performance space can be spiked, and a limited focus can occur without clogging the stage.

Certainly, it's preferable to focus the entire light plot in a single session. Having the lighting and scenic package in performance positions ("the stage is set") means that the scenery doesn't have to be imagined, and the focus between systems and hanging positions can be accurate. On the other hand, since the focus will have to take place anyway, it may be prudent to take your best guess and focus what's available while the stage is otherwise dormant. When the trucks finally arrive, all concentration will be directed to the load-in and the entire schedule will be compressed. Waiting until the stage is set before focusing any front of house instruments will translate into that many more mean instruments which have to be focused in even less time.

Spiking the Deck

The beginning of the load-in is often the last time the deck is available to measure any points or boundaries. Placing a measuring tape undisturbed on the stage may not be possible until the equipment is installed, assembled, and the peripheral items removed. Since the moment when the stage will again be clear may very well coincide with the beginning of the focus session, the amount of time available to make any spike marks on the stage is brief, and it had best be completed with precision and speed. Failure to accomplish this goal promptly can easily result in delays caused by equipment in the way or even the inability to place the spike marks at all.

If no time is available at the beginning of the load-in to accomplish this activity, two scheduled periods of time may be available to complete the task. There may be a short period of time taken for a crew break in the middle of the morning call (coffee break), or the lunch break may allow the task to be completed if the stage is left unoccupied. If for some reason the time to make spike marks on centerline runs short, measuring the up and downstage placements can still be completed with relatively few interruptions on the side of the stage receiving the least amount of traffic, usually the side of the stage opposite the loading door.

To place any spike marks based on measurements, a measuring tape is strongly suggested. After the tape is positioned, the marks can be accurately made. Since the goal is to rapidly complete this activity, some thought should be given to determine the minimal number of measuring tape positions required to produce the maximum number of spike marks. The initial mark that will define all measurements left and right is the centerline. Since the centerline is defined as the equidistant point bisecting the width of the proscenium opening, the simplest way to accurately determine that point is to measure the width of the proscenium and divide by 2. Any other method involving multiple measuring tapes is comparably haphazard, and the flawed information can indirectly lead to calamitous setbacks to the schedule.

Once the centerline is defined (creating the algebraic X axis), the Y axis must be determined. This second axis is often the plaster line, but the lineset for the main curtain, or the upstage side of the steel guides containing the fire curtain (the **smoke pocket**), are also used as an alternate line of reference. Although a case can be made in defense of each location's use as a demarcation, the choice of reference rarely affects the success of the show. What's vital is that all personnel who use the demarcation to define the location of anything on the stage must mutually agree on the line of reference.

That reference line affects the location of everything from the location of added linesets, to the depth of an added built apron, to the location of spike marks for the Act 2 chair. Everyone connected to the production must agree on what is being used for the line of reference. Choosing a singular alternative can have dramatic impact on a show. Consider a scenario created when the built show deck, containing thousands of dollars of machinery, doesn't fit onto a stage. The resulting waste of time, effort, and money can be directly traced to the one individual who chose to use the main curtain as the line of reference, instead of the otherwise mutually agreed-on plaster line.

In this case, the plaster line will be used as the *Y* axis to locate the focus spike marks for *Hokey*. If there is no mark on centerline to define this line, one is often created using a carpenter's snap line stretched between the proscenium arches. For some productions, this line of reference is all that's required in the opening moments of a load-in. The first installation activity of many productions is to install the performance surface, based upon these *X* and *Y* coordinates. When that's the case, the remaining spike marks can be made directly on the performance surface. If a performance surface is installed later in the load-in, however, it may be necessary to spike the deck a second time prior to the focus. Until that time, however, the first set of spike marks can act as the reference points during the scenic and electrical hang, and may be used during the focus session as well.

Now that the *X* and *Y* coordinates have been established, measurements can be made to create the

spike marks, which will define the focus points, boundaries, and reference points within the performance space. The document that will be used as the template to create these points is the master system spike groundplan that was created in the load-in and setup packet of information.

Figure 8.1 shows the master system spike groundplan, indicating all of the distances involved. At the intersection of the centerline and the plaster line (or the zero zero point), a taped cross is placed to visually provide a temporary reference point. After the taped cross is made, a measurement is made directly upstage to match the distance from plaster line to the system pipe that will contain the black portal legs (2'-7"). At this point, a T is placed, marking the down center light line. Often, one of the first inquiries is in regards to the location of the leg line, so the initial marks are made to either stage left or stage right. The measuring tape, attached to this T, is laid out to either side, parallel to

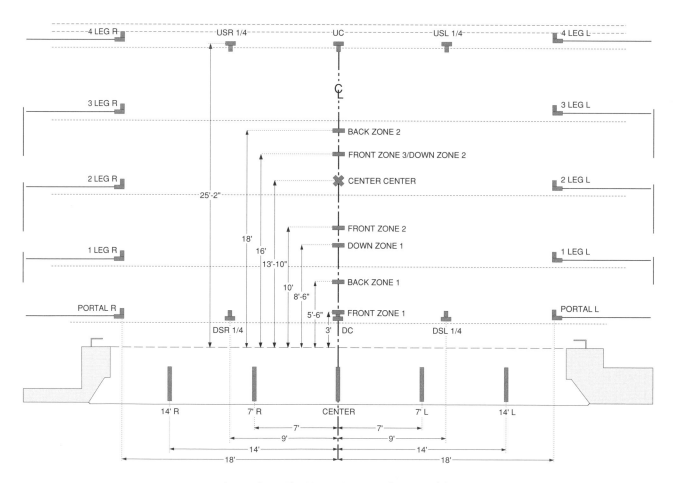

Figure 8.1 The Master System Spike Groundplan

the snap line chalk of the plaster line, offstage into the wings. After being tightened, the measuring tape is then used as the basis for the downstage quarter line light lines (9'-0"), the portal leg lines (18'-0"), the frontlight focus strips (7'-0" and 14'-0"), and the center of the sidelight boom bases (28'-0").

In many theatres, a mark denoting centerline has been made adjacent to the back wall. When this is not the case, it may be necessary to employ a second tape measure to determine a centerline point upstage. Each tape is attached to a matching point on each side of the proscenium arch, typically at the corners of the proscenium. They're then laid out diagonally, so that the two spools of the measuring tapes meet upstage. After the tapes are tightened, the distances on the two tapes are adjusted, until the measurement of both tapes meet at the same distance. Presuming that both tapes are equal, the matching distance must be on the centerline. After this upstage centerline point is marked, a second snap line is often applied to define the entire length of the centerline.

Once the snap line has been removed, one measuring tape is then reattached to the downstage taped reference cross, and laid out running straight upstage on the snap line. Since the master system groundplan has been drawn indicating distances from plaster line, the taped cross will be used as the downstage reference point. Once the measuring tape has been laid out and tightened, the centerline marks made on the master system groundplan will be duplicated onto the stage. For visual clarity, the three different zone marks are often made in different colors. The frontlight zones may be marked first (3'-0", 10'-0", and 16'-0"), followed by the downlight zones (8'-6" and 16'-0"), and finishing with the backlight zones (5'-6" and 18'-0"). The center center "X" (13'-10") is placed as an intermediate point of reference. Finally, the upstage light line "T" (25'-2") is spiked.

The measuring tape can then be attached to the upstage center T, and laid out to stage left or right, again parallel to the plaster line. After being tightened, the upstage quarter line light line T's can be spiked (9'-0"), along with the onstage edge of the #4 leg (18'-0"), and the center of the sidelight boom bases (28'-0"). The onstage edge of the intermediate black masking legs lines may be spiked by measuring up from the intersection cross to match the distance from plaster line to each of their system pipes (7'-3", 13'-2", and 19'-5"). After these marks are made, measurements are made offstage from centerline to each side of the stage (18'-0"). Later in the load-in process, carpenters

may spike the onstage edge of the intermediate black masking legs. If the lighting designer doesn't anticipate the need for these marks during the load-in, the general location of the spike marks may be determined by standing at the black portal leg, and "sighting" upstage to the #4 leg. The decision not to spike the intermediate black legs will reduce the amount of time required for the overall spiking process.

 ### Shelley's Soapbox: Provide Your Own Measuring Tape

Years ago I purchased a lightweight, compact 50'-0" fiberglass measuring tape that lives in my carry-on bag. It accompanies me to every load-in. Why carry a tape measure? If I combined the amount of time wasted watching a carpenter try to find his crate, or watching the stage manager check his crates, or watching the production electrician empty his tool bag, I could have finished the spike marks. Besides, why should I place the responsibility on any of them to having a tool that I need at every stop? Having my own tool allows me to perform my work at any time without dependence on others. I can make measurements anytime I want, without spending time requesting assistance.

Why carry-on? When the luggage gets lost, measurements can still be made at any time. Presuming I arrive early at the performance facility with the tape in my bag, measurements can be made prior to the arrival of any show cargo. Why 50 feet? I've rarely trimmed a batten higher than 50 feet. I've never needed to locate a light boom further than 50 feet from centerline. I've never had to contend with more than 50 feet of stage depth. Certainly, determining the centerline in some theatres has required a measuring tape longer than 50 feet, but that single measurement has typically been the sole distance requiring a longer length of tape.

Why fiberglass? I could circle the globe with the shards of metal tapes that have been broken by ladders or crates wheeling over them, or people tripping over them. As a final thought, by not carrying a metal tape, the number of times my bag has been dissected by airport security looking for that "dangerous-looking round thing" has been drastically reduced.

 ### Shelley's Soapbox: Spike Marks

Spike marks may have multiple uses in addition to being reference points for the lighting designer. If the carpenters do not place spike marks, the lighting designer's spikes may be utilized during the scenic hang to locate the center of each batten. They may also be used to determine the onstage edge of all of the masking and scenic legs. They may be referred to throughout the entire load-in process until the performance surface is installed.

Defining the space and providing reference points can be significant, and in my experience, I've found that I should place them myself. Allowing anyone other than myself to make the spike marks can introduce an element of uncertainty. Regardless of who makes the marks, at some point during the load-in, their validity may be questioned. If I've performed the procedure myself, I don't need to be concerned with that uncertainty. I'll know that the mark has been correctly placed.

Tales from the Road: Spike Marks without a Performance Surface

We were loading into the theatre on schedule. The light plot contained two zones of backlight, four zones of sidelight, and three zones of frontlight. Since the focus points were three distinct sets of distances from plaster line, I had placed the spike marks for the zones on centerline in three different colors of tape, along with apron stripes along the downstage edge. If the decision was made to focus the plot before the vinyl surface was installed, I was completely ready. If the choice was made to install the vinyl surface first, all I needed was a short amount of time once the vinyl was taped down to place another set of spike marks.

Suddenly both of those scenarios were thrown into doubt. The props head refused to lay the vinyl panels to create the performance surface until the focusing lift was off the stage. He had a point. Upon inspection, the focusing lift appeared to weigh about a ton, and the edges of the wheels looked like they could cut slits in the vinyl like a knife through warm butter. A review of the production schedule, however, showed that we were running out of time; the vinyl panels would need to be installed as the ladder moved upstage. Once the ladder completed each electric and moved upstage, the vinyl would immediately be installed in the freshly abandoned area.

Although I agreed in principle to this method of installation, I was still uncertain how to accurately complete the focus session. Since the initial installation of the vinyl was to begin at the downstage edge of the stage, no apron stripes would remain uncovered. As each panel of vinyl was installed, another series of reference marks would be permanently obscured. Since I had no assistance, there was no one available who could replace the spike marks onto the vinyl as they were being covered. There was no time to interrupt the focus session while I wildly ran about with a measuring tape. How could focus be accurately performed without spike marks on the deck of the stage?

After some amount of thought, I devised a plan. Since the focus points on the stage required triangulation anyway, I decided to extend the distance between the spike marks and the focus points. I went into the first row of the house, and sighted the locations of the apron stripes and the quarter lines to their matching locations in the first row of seats. At each location, I placed large strips of colored marking tape on the backs of the seats facing the stage. Presumably I'd be able to see these marks while standing upstage during the focus session. I then went to a location offstage of the planned edge of the vinyl floor. After laying out the measuring tape from plaster line running straight upstage, I duplicated the spike marks that had initially been placed on centerline, placing a second set of marks offstage in the wings. Since there were a variety of focus points for the different systems, I attached matching pieces of the colored tape on the light plot, so that while focusing, I would know which color referred to what zone. Finally, I focused a rover offstage onto the new spike marks, so that they could be seen in the darkness during the focus.

The "offstage" spike marks functioned splendidly, and the focus session proceeded without hesitation or confusion on my part. The only hitch in the proceedings was when the props man observed that someone had stuck a bunch of colored tape on the audience seating, and began tearing the tape off before the focus was complete.

Tales from the Road: Spike Marks without Walls

We were loading in the electrics for the show. The scenery truck containing the walls and ground cloth had not yet appeared. After some time, phone calls were made to find the scenery truck. It soon became clear that no one, including the dispatcher, had any clue as to the whereabouts of the scenery truck. Without a set, how could the focus be performed? We threw our hands in the air, proclaimed nothing could be focused (since it would all have to be redone once the scenery was in place), and proceeded to wait. And wait. As time wore on without the scenery truck's arrival, we started becoming concerned, since it was becoming apparent that whenever the set did arrive, there would be little time between the assembly of the set and the technical rehearsal. As the clock continued to tick, our concern grew to dread. The technical rehearsal was now in doubt. When (or if) the scenery showed up, there would barely be time to set it up and allow the performers to see the layout prior to the performance, much less focus the lighting. In an act of self-preservation, a plan was devised.

Together with the carpentry department, the set's location on the stage was defined. A groundplan was used to tape out the locations of the walls on the stage. Since the stage would (eventually) be covered by the show's ground cloth, there was no concern about spiking the stage with small discrete pieces of tape; the wall became an entire strip of tape. While this process was being completed, gallows humor suggested that, if nothing else, the performers could enact their blocking within the confines of the spike tape. The true test of their mime training, we decided, would be "walking up the stairs" stage right. After the tape on the stage traced the location of the walls in the groundplan, the points where tape crossed (the intersection of walls) were labeled with a large number, and the groundplan of the stage was ready for focus.

While the stage was being taped, four pieces of 1 × 4 were located, all of which measured taller than the highest wall. These were broadly marked in 1-foot increments on both sides of the wood. Once these "walls" had been taped, the focus session began: Four stagehands, each carrying one of the spiked pieces of wood, were assigned the roles of "wall intersections." They were directed to one of the large numbers marked on the stage (where two walls would meet) or other various locations to become "walls," "windows," or "doors." After they were directed to the proper location, the proper instrument would be turned on, pointed to the appropriate focus point, and the focusing electrician could accurately execute all of the required shutter cuts on the "walls." The number of directions required to position the "walls" during this time made the focus session sound like an extended square dance: "Jerry, you move to wall point 3, Sab-

rina, swing around behind him to wall point 5." Although it took a little longer, in time the focus was complete. A spare A-frame ladder was cast in the role of the stairs so that the instruments could be focused to that area of the stage as well.

The set truck finally arrived, an hour before curtain. After the ground cloth was placed, rapid measurements were taken so that the walls of the set would be placed on the same points where the strips of tape had marked their location on the bare stage. The set pieces were assembled and the performance started a bit late, but the focus looked better than it had in some time.

HANGING THE LIGHT PLOT

Once all of the equipment has been brought into the facility, attention turns to the installation of equipment over the stage. Battens are lowered to chest height ("working height") so that equipment can be attached to them. Typically, while the carpenters tie scenic goods to upstage battens, the electrics department starts mounting instruments onto battens downstage. The two departments attempt to complete their tasks while staying out of each other's way. The objective at this point is threefold: One, install the equipment and clear the stage as rapidly as possible so the performance surface can be installed. Two, safely install the equipment in such a manner that whatever flies up in the air stays there. Safety concerns aside, any overhead electric that has to later return to the deck will often result in a delay and cost stage time. Finally, the third objective is to mount the equipment and install it correctly so that it works the first time.

Before the Light Plot Is Hung

When the light plot is created on paper, the lighting designer makes choices that define the location of each instrument. When the physical lighting instruments are actually hung, lack of attention may easily compromise the symmetry of the beams or the ability of the instruments to focus properly around scenic elements. The effect of this carelessness may affect the overall speed in which a lighting package is readied and ultimately have an impact on the integrity of the lighting design.

If the coordinates of centerline and a Y axis (plaster line) are determined prior to the hang, duplicating the positions indicated on the drawing can be performed with a minimum of effort. Typically, defining the distance of each instrument from a single reference point on paper is the first step taken to ensure accuracy of the eventual hanging position. Using an overhead electric as an example, the reference point often used is the centerline. Flexible hanging positions like sidelight booms can be defined by measurements taken from both centerline and plaster line. Prior definition of the location of each c-clamp or mounting device ensures no delays will occur during the hang while waiting for the locations to be determined.

Three methods are commonly used to define and communicate the hanging locations to the electricians. The first method transforms the distances shown in scale on the light plot into marks made on full-scale reference strips, ranging from rolls of adding machine paper to jute webbing. During the load-in these **hanging tapes** or **webbings** are then usually taped or tied onto the hanging position while the units are mounted. Once the instruments have been attached, they are checked for function and accuracy, after which the reference strips are often removed. Although it is possible to mark different hanging positions on either side of a single reference strip, this technique is not encouraged. The order in which hanging positions are addressed can easily change during the course of a load-in. A situation can easily develop where one reference strip may be suddenly needed at two different hanging positions at the same time.

The second method uses a copy of the light plot, which is cut into individual hanging positions. The pieces are then pasted onto a series of stiff mounting surfaces, resulting in **hanging cardboards**. Hanging cardboards are often used because all of the necessary information can be dispensed with the single graphical document. Usually, circuitry information is written directly onto the cardboards as the instruments are plugged. In many cases, each cardboard displays each instrument's unit, dimmer, color, and channel number, along with a copy of the legend to explain its type, wattage, and any additional accessories.

The third method utilizes the **instrument schedule**, with an additional column indicating the hanging location measurements. The measurements are then verbally called out while the distances are marked directly onto the hanging position. The use of this method means that the one person handling the document must also verbally communicate all of the information regarding any attributes of the instruments.

Since all of these different methods use different formats to present the information, discussion between the lighting designer and the electrician (road or house) should take place prior to the load-in to agree upon the method that will be employed. By doing so, the lighting designer will produce paperwork that the electrician will actually use. If the two don't mutually decide on the method employed for the hang, the paperwork produced by the lighting designer may be an unused duplication of effort, and have no value to the electrician or to the hang. For example, the lighting designer may produce an instrument schedule which includes a column of measurements from centerline. This may later be seen as a waste of time, when it's discovered that the hanging method employed by the electrician utilizes hanging cardboards. In another example, if the scale requested by the electrician for the hanging cardboards is different than that used for the light plot, photocopiers can be used to reduce or enlarge drawings to the desired size. As an overall observation, the electrician is in charge during the hang. No matter how foreign the format may seem to the lighting designer, any paperwork generated for that purpose should be tailored to the electrician's preferences.

Some situations allow the production electrician to preassign all of the components in the electrical path of the lighting package. In these cases, the instruments, circuitry, and dimmers are preassigned prior to the hanging activity. Although this technique is often used in productions that install a lighting package with little dependence on preexisting circuitry, it is also employed when some portion of an existing lighting package could potentially become a constraint. By defining the electrical destination of each instrument, a rough guesstimate of the amount of additional cable that will be needed can be calculated. These situations amplify the need for paperwork created by the lighting designer that will save the electrician preparation time, not require a duplication of effort. Prior communication will allow the right paperwork to be created the first time.

Preparations to Speed the Hang

Although the stated intent of the following checklist is to accelerate the hang, it could also be subtitled as methods employed to not delay the hang. In general, come to the hang prepared. Make certain that the prepared paperwork will be used. Check the paperwork for inaccuracies. Don't presume that a facility is a general store; "common" tools may not be easily and quickly found at the facility. Time spent looking for things you should have brought with you is time not spent completing a task.

☑ Basic Checklist for Reducing the Amount of Time Required to Hang the Instruments:

- Arrive with the reference tools used during the hang: a copy of the light plot, a measuring tape, and a scale rule.
- Arrive prepared with hanging tapes, cardboards, or distances written on the instrument schedule. Bring the tools to mark the hanging positions, including chalk and spike tape.
- Arrive with the color preframed and sorted in the unit order of each hanging position. Electricians will be able to work on the hang, not preparing the color. If color may have to be cut on-site, bring the tools to perform that task: a paper cutter or a matte knife, brads (for metal gel frames) or a stapler (for paper frames).
- Arrive with the templates pretrimmed and inserted in the correct orientation into template holders. On multivenue productions, consider carrying one set of templates prepackaged in holders, one set trimmed and loose, and one set fresh (for unique template slot sizes). Bring a tool that can trim the fresh templates, eliminating time spent acquiring the tool on-site.
- Arrive with any iris components ready and prepared to be inserted into instruments. If iris instruments are required in the light plot, be certain that those are set aside or easily identified, to eliminate delay.
- Clearly mark any equipment being added to the existing house inventory to prevent confusion of ownership during load-out.

Hanging Procedures

In an ideal world, the lighting designer should not need to be actively involved in the hang. This activity often occurs prior to the lighting designer's arrival at the performance facility. Presuming that the paperwork package that has been sent ahead is accurate, the lighting designer may arrive on-site after the instruments have been hung, accessorized, circuited, tested, and ready for focus. In the real world, however, people make mistakes, assumptions, errors in judgment,

or the lighting designer may have unknowingly not provided a critical piece of information to allow the hang to be correctly completed. Hours of stage time can be lost duplicating effort either prior to or during a focus session. Whenever the situation presents itself, the lighting designer should consider being present at the hang or having an assistant on-site to make decisions. If nothing else, the lighting designer should be reachable by telephone, curtailing erroneous on-site decisions made based on incomplete information.

When the lighting package is hung, several procedures must occur. The instrument will be mounted, circuited, accessorized, prepared for testing, and possibly prefocused. Initially, the correct type of instrument with the right lamp is mounted in each location denoted on the light plot. The type and size of mounting hardware are typically defined by the hanging position. Since the typical mounting position is made of steel pipe, c-clamps or sidearms are the typical mounting hardware that is used. Securing the mounting hardware of the unit to the hanging location and locking any other moving parts ensures that the position of the instrument won't change, preventing the unit from having an adverse impact on the safety of the situation. It also means that the beam of the instrument will be positioned accurately and precisely, reducing the number of delays incurred during and after the focus session.

Once securely attached to each hanging position, circuitry is supplied to the plug of the instrument. Either the plug is connected to a preinstalled circuit built into the facility, or connected to a length of cable that spans the gap. The name assigned to the circuit, whether it is a label on the cable's plug or the circuit number of the permanent electrical installation, is then recorded on the support paperwork. Accurate identification of the circuitry will prevent loss of time if any problems result from a disruption in the electrical path of any particular instrument.

Two basic rules are used during the hanging process. The first rule is to make certain that the finished installation of the unit conforms to safety standards. Once the instrument is tightly attached to the hanging position, a **safety cable** is often added to each instrument to prevent the possibility of instruments falling from any position due to failure of mounting hardware. The second rule is to complete any preparation to the instrument prior to focus while the unit is close at hand. Preparation of each instrument should include the installation of any accessories, which may be added to each unit to control the shape or color the beam. These accessories include gel frames with color, barndoors, tophats, or color scrollers, to name a few. Sometimes the seemingly simple task of adding these accessories can take a considerable amount of time. Adding these items during the hang (as opposed to the focus) allows the total size, weight, and center of balance for each instrument to be known. This may affect the amount of force required to secure the instrument to the hanging position, or the final performance location of the entire hanging position to prevent the audience from viewing the accessories during the performance.

Color (according to the design) placed in front of the lens of each instrument aids in the instrument's identification. Coloring or installing accessories in front of the instrument's lens may draw attention to the fact that the unit has a broken color frame holder. This may require replacement of the barrel or the entire instrument—an action quickly taken on the deck that could take several minutes in the air. Coloring the lens of the instrument may also point out the fact that the color was prepared in an incorrect size. Some lighting designers insist on waiting until the focus session to color each instrument. The delay caused by that choice, however, could cost 10 to 20 seconds per instrument. On a 300-instrument show, that time can add up. If the instruments are precolored prior to focus, the focusing electrician's time isn't spent on top of a ladder sorting through several pieces of color. Instead, his or her attention is solely directed to executing the lighting designer's requests.

Other accessories added to the instrument that affect or shape the beam include templates or template devices, such as gobo rotators, placed inside the instrument. Since manufacturers produce instruments with varying sizes of template slots, matching the correct size of template holder or device to an instrument can be a comedy of errors during the hang, but can quickly become serious business when causing delays during the focus session. Discovering that the size of template holders or devices traveling with the show doesn't fit into the template slots of the house ellipsoidals is an activity that should take place when the instruments are close to the stage, not in the air.

When this process is complete, the unit is then prepared for testing, which includes the removal of all shutters or barndoors from the path of the beam, allowing the light generated by the lamp to be seen when the instrument is turned on. Failure to clear this path may slow down confirmation that the instrument actually works. If the lamp inside the instrument is allowed to remain activated for an extended amount of time, heat generated by the lamp may create enough temperature to damage the shutters, the lens, the internal wiring of the instrument, or start a fire inside the instrument.

The instrument may also be pointed and locked in a specific predetermined direction (prefocus). One basic choice made by the lighting designer is whether to prefocus the instrument in the direction of the eventual focus, or to avoid the focus point altogether. Prefocusing the unit in the direction of its assigned purpose may reduce the length of time required to achieve the final placement of the instrument during the focus session. Prefocusing to avoid the focus point is a technique used when several instruments are assigned to a single channel of control. When all of the instruments are activated during the focus, each instrument, in turn, is aimed to the focus point, allowing the lighting designer to see the addition of each beam one at a time.

If PAR cans are included in the light plot, consider prefocusing the axis of their elliptical lamps. Most PAR cans are designed so that the lamp is held in place with a metal retaining ring. By loosening the ring, the lamp can be twisted to the proper axis position. Accessing the ring and performing this operation, however, can be difficult and time consuming. Presetting the PAR lamp to the axis direction drawn on the plot, while the instrument is accessible on the deck, may avoid delays during the focus session.

The use of instruments with variable beam spreads introduces another element that may affect the speed of the focus. Presetting the lens positions of zoom ellipsoidals or the beam size of Fresnels can be considered while the instruments are being hung. Typically, this technique is employed when variable beam spread instruments are plotted for use as entire systems of light. Defining the approximate beam spread for these instruments requires preparation on the part of the lighting designer. Beam sectional drawings determine the actual throw distance of each instrument from each hanging position. If the variable beam instruments are plotted for several different systems, several actual throw distances will be defined and recorded prior to the load-in. While the hang is taking place, this distance can be duplicated to match the eventual actual throw distance of the instrument in question by measuring the distance from a non-mounted instrument to an unobscured wall. After the diameter of the desired pool size is measured on the wall, the focus knobs of the instrument are adjusted to match that diameter. The placement of the knobs or the number of rotations is recorded for each actual throw distance, and is then applied to each instrument in each system.

After this series of procedures have been completed on every instrument, the hang is complete and the instruments are ready to be tested.

Positioning the Booms

Defining the final location of sidelight booms often involves a complex set of decisions. Oftentimes each boom's final location will be determined by a combination of several different factors specific to that position and gut instinct. The ideal system is created when all of the positions are located equidistant from centerline, safely secured and hidden from the audience, and each system on the combined booms provide an even blend of light, covering the entire depth of the performance space.

Ideally, the booms are placed the same distance from centerline so that the matching instruments in a system will be of equal intensity. This matching distance is defined by a measurement from centerline, which may be determined by the size of the light beams produced by instruments focused to the near side of the stage. Usually, the beam spread of those units is large enough so that light from the "near focus" instruments splashes on the near masking legs. Often this means the lenses of the instruments are placed between 8 and 12 feet offstage of the onstage edge of the legs.

After that initial placement, however, the elements of the surrounding environment have to be considered. One element that may alter this location is the sightlines from the audience. Common practice dictates that the lenses of the instruments should not be visible to the audience, and booms may need to move further offstage to be concealed from view.

The length of the overhead battens can also affect the distance. When sidelight booms are located under overhead electrics, they're often positioned offstage of the end of the batten pipe, so that the electric can still be lowered to the deck without hitting the sidelights. Often, however, the battens extend too far offstage. If the booms are moved far enough offstage to clear the battens, they may become ineffective. One choice often made is to place the boom directly underneath the overhead electric in that opening. This is based on the assumption that the chance of the electric batten having to be lowered to the deck is less likely than any adjacent battens, which may be equipped with scenery.

Shifting the position offstage may then involve consideration of the width of the masking leg. A boom placed "too far" offstage may encourage performers to walk onstage of the instruments, though hidden from the audience. The performer's movement through the light will produce a visual "flicker" on the stage and the opposite legs, which can distract from the performance. This can be solved with spike marks restricting offstage traffic paths, movement of the booms onstage, or occasionally, a piercing glare.

The on and offstage location of a sidelight boom can also be affected by the shutter cuts of the individual instruments. Although the light from each system ideally fills the entire depth on the near side of an opening, visually preserving the black surround often means that side shutter cuts reduce the coverage of that depth. By eliminating light off the next set of black masking legs upstage of the instrument (legs on the opposite side), the coverage at the near side is reduced. The closer a performer gets to the near legs, the greater the possibility that the performer may pass between these shutter cuts, moving through holes in the sidelight coverage while crossing up or downstage. This visual effect of the bodies running in and out of light near the legs can also result in a visual "flicker." Since the beam spread of the instruments used on sidelight boom is typically fixed, attempting to reduce this visual effect may require the boom to be shifted farther offstage.

The up and downstage location of a sidelight boom is similarly complex. If all the sidelight booms were placed in the downstage side of each opening, the upstage cuts required to keep light off of the backdrop would result in reduced coverage in the upstage side of each near opening. If all of the sidelight booms were placed in the middle of each opening, more even coverage would result. Shuttering the side cuts to keep light off the backdrop and the proscenium, however, would result in a loss of coverage in the near side of the area close to the down and upstage light line. If all of the sidelight booms were placed in the upstage side of each opening, it would be a reversal of the first example. Side shutters cutting light off the proscenium would result in a loss of coverage in the downstage side of each near opening. To cover as far down and upstage as possible, while providing as much possible intermediate coverage, many lighting designers choose to place the first boom close to the downstage light line, the middle booms in the center of their respective openings, and the final boom as close as possible to the upstage light line.

Scenic elements, like scenic legs, midstage drops, or the size of any scenery moving through the opening can modify this choice. Other elements can also add complexity to the decision. These elements can include the point of origin and length of the circuitry supplying power to the boom, peripheral movement offstage of the boom, and equipment surrounding the boom. In addition to that, the focus of any special instruments on the boom, backstage traffic, and the stage manager's backstage calling position may affect the location as well. The final position of the sidelight booms will vary with each production.

When the final location of the sidelight booms is determined on one side of the stage, their positions are often duplicated to place the booms on the opposite side. By mirroring the locations, the performers aren't forced to remember different spatial relationships between the booms and the surrounding elements in each opening to the stage.

PROGRAMMING INFORMATION INTO THE COMPUTER LIGHTING CONSOLE

The infrastructure information that is commonly preprogrammed into the computer lighting console includes the focus memories, the system wash memories, the hanging position memories, the groups, the submaster assignments, and the memories outlined in the disk master chart that were defined in Chapter 5. If written memories used as light cues in a prior incarnation of the production exist, they may also be programmed into the lighting console at this time.

Since it provides the basic information that will be used in almost every other board activity, programming infrastructure information into a lighting console is often considered vital. The time the light board operator spends programming board information during the load-in, though, could be applied to other tasks. Generally, most lighting designers view preprogramming as an activity that must be completed before the instruments are tested. Note also that programming this information often takes longer than anticipated. The construction of a typical production schedule is such that, as soon as the instruments have been positioned and tested, the lighting console will be in constant use. In most cases, any other convenient time to preprogram information ceases to exist. Once the instruments are prepared, the next scheduled activity may well be the focus session. Since the focus

session will presumably involve active channel movement, attempting any remaining infrastructure programming at this time may be counterproductive. As soon as the focus session is complete, the light board may be scheduled to construct the light cues for the production, followed by constant rehearsals, and leading to performances. If a work call is not scheduled immediately following the focus session, and the programming has not been completed during the load-in, that infrastructure information will be missing for the rest of these activities. If the need for extensive console programming is anticipated, any alternative to programming information during the load-in should be investigated, in an effort to eliminate the possibility of running out of programming time.

If a console in a lighting shop or another space is available for preprogramming use prior to load-in, either of those situations should be pursued. Major manufacturers provide sample consoles in their offices, which are often available for preprogramming. A different tactic may be to utilize an off-line editing application for the console, if such an application exists. Often, manufacturers gladly provide the software required to perform this function. If the house board is to be used, consider contacting the performance facility and requesting permission to program the console prior to the load-in. If a rental board is used but unavailable until immediately prior to the load-in, consider transporting the console to your home, preprogramming the console on the kitchen table, and then transport the console directly to the load-in.

Presuming that none of those options is available, then the lighting console should be packed to be one of the first items taken off the truck. The programming can then occur during the load-in while the instruments are initially being hung. The two activities can occur simultaneously until the instruments and circuits need to be tested, requiring dimmers or channels to be activated. If the number of dimmers or channels to be checked on the stage is extensive, efforts to continue preprogramming while being interrupted by constant onstage requests will become frustrating for the board operator, the lighting designer, and the electrician checking the instruments.

Attempting to read information from a piece of paper and then keypunch that information into a console without assistance can require intensive concentration and may consume a lot of time. If possible, an assistant should be assigned to assist the board operator in completing this task. The assistant reads the information out loud, while the board operator physically programs the information into the console. Ideally, the assistant is familiar with the layout of the documents. If he or she has never seen the documents before being assigned the task, unfamiliarity with the layout may slow the process.

Typically, a notebook is assembled that contains current copies of all of the paperwork, a light plot, and disks clearly identified with the name of the show, the date, the type of lighting console, and the system size. By labeling the disk in advance, the lighting designer will always know its contents. Often, spare disks are included, which can then be used without interruption of memory transferal if disk failure is experienced. The notebook should also contain board operator sheets, and may include a preliminary copy of the cue master. Note that the production should not expect the house to provide the disks used for memory storage. By providing the disks that will be used for the console, there will never be an issue of how many copies of the show information can be afforded to the production on departure. By providing a storage location for the disks, there's no chance that any disks will be left on speakers, under soft drinks, or underfoot, resulting in the possibility of lost data.

If there's concern that the size of the cue content of the entire show may be larger than allowed on a single disk, the production can be segmented between acts. Whenever possible, it's advised to refrain from this "splitting" of the show between disks. Although the original infrastructure cues, groups, subs, and patch information can be duplicated on each act disk, any updates to the softpatch or infrastructure information will require careful monitoring so that the changes will be reflected on each of the act disks. Productions involving multiple repertory pieces may not have the luxury of this choice.

Ideally, all of the information regarding the show should fit into the same notebook that will be placed in the care of the board operator. Not only will this make it simpler to store for archival purposes, but many light booths often contain extensive paperwork left over from different productions being presented in the facility. By providing a single repository of information, including plastic sleeve jackets for the computer disks, the possibility of losing paperwork or disks will be reduced. If there are disks from a previous incarnation of the production, those disks can be used to initially load information into the lighting console, but they should then be removed from the booth, to prevent accidental re-recording and loss of archival information.

Although many consoles are now being supplied with hard drives, it is still prudent to save information to a floppy disk at the end of the calls. Like all computers, experience has shown that the possibility of hard drive failure can occur at any time. It's often suggested that each segment of the show information should be saved to three disks each. Various methods are used in the sequence of recording the disks, to avoid loss of data during technical rehearsals. Often, the use of three disks allows one disk to be used for off-line editing, leaving the remaining two as backup for the on-site console.

Presuming that the show is an original production, the first action that is usually taken is to define the system size that will be used for the show. The console is turned on so that all previous information is purged from the memory. This ensures that, during the current production, there will be no confusion with information "left over" from prior usage of the console. Presuming the production will use fewer channel numbers than the default number prescribed by the console, this action may reduce the number of screens. After the number of dimmers is defined, the settings for the system size are now complete. The sequence used to program information into the console may next be initially dictated by the lighting equipment that is permanently controlled by the existing dimmers.

If the permanent worklights or houselights are controlled by the console, those channels or dimmers should be immediately softpatched or "parked" to reestablish worklight on the stage, and allow the load-in to continue. **Park** is a specific command function that supercedes any other command. It's often used to "freeze" a channel or dimmer at a level; neither can be "moved" until the command is given to "unpark." This command is often used to control electrical devices that should remain constant at a level and never change.

Once light on stage and in the house is restored, the console can continue to be programmed. If the dimmer assignments to any channels have been determined, that information can be programmed into the console (the softpatch). The default softpatch setting in many lighting consoles pairs each dimmer to the same-numbered channel, known as a **one-to-one patch**. Dimmer 1 is assigned to channel 1, dimmer 2 is assigned to channel 2, and so on. Experienced designers and board operators will eliminate this default setting and remove all dimmer assignments to any channels, an action known as **clearing the patch**. This makes certain that every dimmer is intentionally softpatched to a channel, and eliminates the chance that a channel will activate a default-assigned dimmer. It also allows the patch screen to be used to confirm any unassigned (or unused) dimmers. The softpatch can be entered at any time, but ideally should be complete before channels are tested to confirm that their contents properly function. Once initial softpatching has taken place, the console can continue to be programmed. Programming infrastructure information implies activating channels, and then recording them into cues, groups, or subs.

Programming active channels while instruments are being plugged is a technique that is typically frowned on. Because typical channel activation occurs in zero seconds, sudden unexpected flashes of light from instruments can quickly cause an outcry on stage. The typical solution in this situation is to perform the programming in the "blind" or "preview" displays, thus avoiding any channel or dimmer activation. Any channels that need to remain constant through the hang can be activated in the "live" or "stage" screens while programming continues in the background. Some consoles don't have the flexibility to program while in "blind" or "preview." When faced with this situation, it may be possible to turn the dimmers off during the hanging process. If the dimmers must remain on while the hang takes place, a solution may be to disconnect the DMX outputs to the dimmers from the console, so that the two activities can occur without inconvenience to either activity.

To expedite the eventual tedium of programming, consider determining the fewest number of keystrokes required to complete each series of channel changes. On some consoles, loading cues in "blind" or "preview" can speed the process. The execution of each channel activation records the command into the cue, eliminating the need to keystroke an entire record sequence. Since the logic and command sequences vary between consoles, familiarity with the console (or having a manual at hand) may answer any questions during the process.

When time runs short, the person reading the information to the board operator must gauge the amount of programming that remains. If the focus session is imminent, the priority may be to program the focus cues. If focus cues won't be used, then providing the handles to check hanging positions may be the next priority. If that doesn't appear to be an immediate concern, the handles that will be used to activate system washes during the light cue level setting session may be the programming that takes precedence. If written cues exist from a prior incarnation of the production, the memories that will be used as light cues during the technical rehearsal may be seen as the priority. When faced with a constrained amount of time, the assistant reading the information may need to consult with the lighting designer to prioritize the information that remains to be programmed.

Although programming infrastructure information can become boring, many lighting designers consider the benefits worth the effort, while others consider it vital. Infrastructure programming provides the lighting console with numerous handles and methods to rapidly access channel information, and can save a lot of time.

Before any information is programmed, the sequence of that programming should be considered. If infrastructure cues will also be recorded as a series of groups, the board's command structure should first be carefully examined. Although many light boards allow groups to be recorded into cues, those same boards may not allow cues to be loaded into groups. When this is the situation, the groups should be created first, and then each group should be activated and recorded to create the infrastructure cues. If the cues are programmed first without examining this one-sided relationship, this error in judgment will result in a costly use of time. To have the same channel information available in the two separate functions, the same channel intensities will need to be keystroked a second time to be recorded as a group. That is the case for this particular console, so the groups for *Hokey* will be programmed first, followed by the submasters, and concluding with the infrastructure cues.

Programming Infrastructure Groups

In many lighting consoles, creating groups in any other display other than the group display is simply not possible. Groups are usually not listed on the monitor display until they are created. If several groups are to be created, the programming time can be reduced if all of the groups are initially created at one time. After the groups exist, it's then possible to view and program the channel intensities of each group by pressing the equivalent of the [next] or [last] keys, rather than individually "call up" each group, requiring more keystrokes on the console. To load the groups for *Hokey*, the group list created in Chapter 5 would be used. After the groups are created, the individual channels are programmed into each group.

If time is short, a decision may need to be made as to which series of groups should be programmed first.

If consultation with the lighting designer is not possible at the time, a review of the group's use may provide the answer. The groups for *Hokey* are divided into two separate functions. Groups 1 > 17 activate each system of light, while groups 21 > 44 activate each position. If the focus session is imminent, the ability to check the blending of system washes may supercede the need to activate all of the instruments in a single position. Activating several groups to confirm that all of the instruments in a single position are functional may require some amount of time, but having to activate numerous channels to check a system wash may take longer. The choice may be to program the system groups before the position groups.

Programming Infrastructure Submasters

Unlike cue or group information, submasters usually actively exist and don't need to be created. Methods for recording channel information into different submasters may vary between consoles. Some consoles require that channel content only be activated while viewing the submaster screen, while other boards allow any activated channels or groups to be recorded into the contents of any sub. Since the recording procedures may vary between models and manufacturers, submaster recording procedures should be reviewed to reduce unnecessary keystroking.

The submasters for *Hokey* will be loaded using the submaster list that was created in Chapter 5. Since many of the submasters are repetitions of the channel intensities programmed into the groups, the amount of time this process will require is reduced. Each submaster can be addressed, and then the proper group can be activated within that sub. The keystroking required to activate individual channels will be bypassed.

When the inhibitive submasters (12 and 24) are programmed, they should be double-checked to make certain that they don't contain any ghost or infrastructure channels, including time stamp, key memory number, worklights, running lights, centering lights, house lights, music stand lights, or any devices that should remain constantly on throughout the performance.

Programming Infrastructure Light Cues

When programming light cues into a computer console, a distinction should be made in the construction process. When written cues exist from a prior incar-

nation of the show, they should be programmed after the infrastructure cues have been recorded. If the production is an original presentation, however, the programming may be limited solely to the infrastructure cues, and provide the structure that will be used as a framework by the lighting designer during the cue level setting session. That tactic will be more closely addressed at the conclusion of this section.

Initially, the first step often employed on tracking computer consoles is to program hard zeros into cues that will fade the stage to black, or be utilized as **blocker cues.** This ensures that any subsequent tracking channel changes will be forced to stop at the intended location, preventing them from tracking through the entire disk. When the hard zeros are programmed, any ghost channels that will be used as time stamp, key memory, or blackout information should be left unaffected. While referring to the disk master chart for *Hokey*, channels 1 > 122, and 126 > 136 will be "activated" to a level of zero (00%) and recorded into memories 100, 200, 400, 500, 600, 800, 900, and 950 to track.

Next, the **time stamp** information will be entered with the current date. In this example, the load-in is beginning on August 21, 1998. That being the case, channel 123 would be activated to 08%, channel 124 activated to 21%, and channel 125 activated to 98%. These levels would be recorded in memory 1 and allowed to track, so that they will appear in every memory.

With the basic blocks of memory now in place, the focus cues (memories 1 > 99), the system wash cues (memories 950 > 973), and the hanging position cues (memories 900 > 920) can be programmed. Since many of these cues consist of channel levels that already exist in the groups and submasters, these functions can be used to activate the channels when the memories are created.

Before beginning that process, however, a moment should be taken to consider methods that might reduce the amount of time required to complete the programming. The natural inclination may be to activate the channel levels, or **cue content** to be contained in each of the memories, along with any fade time information, and then record that singular cue. Programming information in this sequence, however, will require several different keystroke combinations in varying sequences. Performing repetitive keystroke combinations, on the other hand, often expedites the process. Consider programming **shell cues**; initially record all of the memories without channel content or time fade information in a single "pass." Once the "shells" of the cues are created, the second step may be to assign all of the time fades to all of the cues in a second pass. Finally, a third pass can insert the intermittent waits, delays, or links between cues. On the final pass, the cue content for each memory can be programmed.

It is at this point that an important distinction in programming memories for light cues should be made. If the cues that remain to be programmed already exist on paper from a previous incarnation, the same sequence that was just described (shell cues) may be employed to program the cue content for the memories used in the show. If the production is an original presentation, however, and a preliminary cue master has been prepared, hesitation at this point is well advised. The assistant may be tempted to save the lighting designer time and program the preliminary shell of the cue, along with its time fades. This should not be done without consulting the lighting designer to determine his or her preference. Many lighting designers use the lack of a cue number on the monitor display as a signpost to inform them of their progress during the cue level setting session. If all of the preliminary shells appear on the cue list screen, this may cause havoc, since it will no longer be possible for the lighting designer to scan for missing memory numbers to determine which light cues remain to be created.

Programming Light Cues from Prior Incarnations

When written cues exist from prior incarnations of the show, the same methods employed to create the infrastructure memories can be used to speed the entry of the light cues for the show into the console. The shell cues can be created, then assigned fade times and other attributes. After those two passes are complete, the cue content can be sequentially programmed, starting with the first light cue in the show.

The sequence may be altered, however, when time grows short. When the instruments and circuits are ready to be checked, the board may need to shift over to activating dimmers, channels, or programming the softpatch. As noted earlier, attempting to program cue information during that time can be difficult at best.

When time grows short, consider programming only the cue information that will be required to allow transitions between scenes to take place within the technical rehearsal. Though the internal cues within each scene will be missing, the rehearsal will still be able to practice the scene changes under show cond-

itions, and the intermediate cues may be easier to program "on the fly." This may be as simple as programming cue information for the first, last, and any intermediate memories to complete each transition sequence. If time still remains after the transition cues have been programmed, the additional internal cues may be programmed in the same order in which scenes will be addressed during the technical rehearsal. If time runs out prior to completion of the programming, the first scene in the technical rehearsal can still occur without delay. Any time not utilized to alter cue information in the current scene can be used to continue programming internal cue information for scenes not yet encountered.

When time grows even shorter, consider ignoring the transitions, and program only the cue information for the first scene that will be addressed during the technical rehearsal. Though it may be frustrating not to complete the programming of most of the cues, the need to begin the technical rehearsal on time will have been addressed. If any time exists when the board is not required for onstage use, it may be possible to continue programming the cues.

Recording the Contents of Memory

This is a critical moment. If the lighting designer is not familiar with this particular lighting console, he or she should be certain to observe this sequence closely, when the information that has been programmed into the RAM of the console is written onto whatever storage format is used, presumably a disk. After a series of selections one is usually confronted with a choice that looks something like this on the monitor display:

SAVE TO DISK

LOAD TO BOARD

Different manufacturers use different nomenclature, and no matter how experienced the lighting designer may be, the display is often confusing. The two procedures that these statements represent reflect a choice of one of two things:

1. The memory information in the brain of the lighting console is about to be written onto the disk, and replace whatever may have been previously recorded on that disk (save to disk).
2. The memory information that is stored on the disk is about to be loaded into the computer's brain, in

some cases replacing whatever may have been previously contained in the brain (load to board).

The lighting designer should be certain that he or she knows which action needs to be accomplished, and what selection should be chosen to accomplish that action. If the brain of the light board has just been programmed or changed, **do not** choose "load to board." Taking that action will tell the computer to load all of the information stored onto the disk, and (possibly) replace the information in the computer's brain, overwriting (or replacing) the information that was just programmed or changed in the light board. In this case, the correct procedure to choose is: Save to Disk.

Numerous instances have been observed when memory transferal has been committed in the wrong direction without backup. Massive amounts of time have been lost and tempers have flared, because not enough eyes were watching the screen during the critical moment when the memory transferal procedure was chosen. The lighting designer should watch the screen to make certain that he or she doesn't contribute to losing data by being unwilling to pay attention. At that moment, that's why the designer has eyes. The lighting designer is not a passive observer; he or she needs to be an involved participant. Nobody's perfect.

Memory transferal is not limited to the single act of knowing the direction of the information. If the show involves more than one series of disks, care should be taken to confirm that any time computer information is being transferred, the correct memory information is being recorded to (or loaded from) the correct disk. One habit many professional board operators practice is this: As soon as a disk has been involved in a memory transfer, the disk is removed from the disk drive. Why? Consider this scenario: Changes for Act 2 have been programmed into the light board's brain, but the disk for Act 1 in still in the disk drive. If the command "save to disk" is given; the Act 2 information will overwrite all of the information that had previously been stored on the disk for Act 1. This is another good example of why it is important to have multiple copies of each series of disks.

 Golden Rule: Save Early and Often

Anytime the board has received additional programmed information and is temporarily dormant until its next use, write the contents of the light board's brain to a disk. To write the contents of the RAM onto a storage disk, the command typically given to the board operator is "run the disk." The board will crash someday, and no one knows when that will be.

Years ago we were cueing the Kirov Ballet at the Metropolitan Opera House. We had just cued the entire first act, a process that had taken about 4 hours. At that time the Met had a Palette V6E, fully protected with surge suppression and voltage regulation; it had been dependable and error-free for years. So, naturally, *just* before we recorded to disk—that's right—the system crashed, rebooted, and the entire 4-hour session was lost. Ever since then, I've been a little more wary of computers. Although computer lighting consoles may allow lighting designers to create art, the art isn't that much good to anybody when it turns into vaporware.

Checking the Light Console Contents

If there is time available after the infrastructure information has been entered into the console, the groups and submasters should be checked on their respective monitor displays prior to the focus or the light cue level setting session. Ideally, the contents of these functions should be checked live on stage after the lighting package is installed. There's no way to predict, however, if that time will be available later in the schedule. Checking the monitor displays will at least provide some measure of reassurance that no ghastly programming has accidentally taken place.

If the infrastructure information has been recorded from one function to the other (groups > memories, for example), then only one function will require visual confirmation. If it's anticipated that the groups will be used during the focus session to check system blending, the contents of the group system washes should be checked first. If there are inhibitive submasters, carefully check the attributes and contents of those subs, and be certain that the handles on the console are at Full. When inhibitive submasters are accidentally left at zero, they act like grand masters, and any channels assigned to them will not be activated.

CHECKING THE PRODUCTION TABLE

The production table is the lighting designer's "office" in the house, where he or she creates and views the lighting cues for the production. The table is often shared by the lighting designer and the stage manager, and may also be occupied by other members of the design team, along with the director. In later rehearsals, the stage manager often moves to the base of operations where he or she will call the show during the actual performance. The director and the other designers may scatter into different locations in the house to view the show from other perspectives. During initial technical rehearsals, however, everyone is based at this single central viewpoint to discuss the timing and placement of all actions and movement on stage, collectively shaping the stage picture. Face-to-face discussions facilitate communication, and reduces the amount of conversation on headset. The production table is usually a temporary structure that can be quickly installed or removed from the seats. Ideally, the footprint of the table used by the lighting designer is large enough to accommodate the monitor, the active paperwork, and spare room for the rest of the files.

During the load-in, the production table is brought out and set up in the seats. If the table isn't constructed for a specific row, the lighting designer should decide in advance where the table should be located to provide an unobstructed view of the entire stage. The table should be placed so that the bottom of the balcony doesn't obstruct the ability to see the entire height of the stage picture. If possible, the table may be placed in a row that has additional depth, allowing easier passage to and from the table. It's worth noting that any lighting designer wearing shorts can be easily spotted in a crowd by the bruises on his or her legs, created when colliding with unforgiving armrests while trying to move to the production table via a row opening that's too narrow. Whenever possible, the production table should be positioned on centerline. When located in a decentralized location, the lighting designer is unable to see what's visually happening on the near side of the stage. Inevitably, there will be surprises in performance when the other side of the stage is seen for possibly the first time.

Because the lighting designer may spend extensive hours at the production table, it should be made as functional and as comfortable as possible. As a working space, it should be laid out with some amount of ergonomic concern. That concern can hit home once it's remembered that the lighting designer is often tied to the space for at least 12 hours a day. Once the table has been set up, check the ergonomics of the space. Sit behind the table and pretend to write something down. Now pretend that action has been repeated for

12 hours. Often the distance or angle of the table relative to the location of the seat is disproportionate. Sitting on the armrests between the seat often solves this discomfort, but after 12 hours that can leave an aching impression. It's worth asking if a wide strip of wood can be placed to span between the armrests, possibly with some kind of padding, allowing the lighting designer's attention to remain in front of him or her, instead of underneath.

If the light board, the stage manager, or the followspots are in a remote location, the lighting designer must have a functioning headset. Headsets to other locations may be added as the situation demands. Although rock and roll presentations often demand headsets that cover both ears (double muff), most lighting designers prefer to have a headset covering only one ear (single muff). This reduces the need to constantly remove a portion of the headset to hear the performers or anyone adjacent to the production table. During the load-in, confirm that the correct numbers of headsets are at the table, the channel separation is correct, and that the required channels are functioning. If possible, request separate channels for the followspots and the lighting console; the light board operator doesn't care about notes being given to the followspots, and the followspots certainly don't care about any of the numerous changes being made in each light cue.

If a computer lighting console is in a remote location, the production table should have a monitor display, allowing the designer to see the activities of the console. The designer typically needs to see the equivalent of a cue list display, showing a numerical list of the memories (with time and attribute information), and a cue content display, showing as many channels and their intensities on a single screen. If a single monitor doesn't provide both of those views, then a "switcher" is often placed at the table to allow the lighting designer to swap between the screens. In lieu of that, the simpler solution is to provide two monitors. Confirm that the monitor or monitors connected to the computer lighting console are operational, that the proper screens are displayed, and that the contrast is set correctly for ease of viewing. If the monitor is monochrome, it should be as neutral a color as possible, to eliminate any color reaction to the designer's eyes. For the same reason, if the monitor is color, the background should be dark, while the channel colors are muted. Ideally, there is enough room on the table between the monitors and the designer to accommodate the active paperwork so that the designer's head merely has to move up and down to retain concentration on the stage.

The table should have a worklight to provide light on the paperwork. The worklight should have a hood, so that the lighting designer doesn't have to stare around a bare bulb. The lighting designer should be able to point the light where desired, and out of his or her own eyes. Finally, the worklight should be dimmable, so that the designer's eyes don't grow tired adjusting between a dark cue on stage and the reflective intensity of the paperwork.

If the production table is some distance away from the stage, communicating with anyone onstage can be exhausting. In those situations, a microphone routed through the sound system to the monitor speakers (a "god" mike) allows directions from the production table to be heard. This microphone may become an important timesaving tool during rehearsals when staging is completely changed. Sometimes the god mike is preset elsewhere, indicating where the director will sit during the technical rehearsals.

A wastebasket should be placed adjacent to the table, to keep the workspace clear and simplify cleanup. If there's any length to the tech period, attempt to find a wastebasket that's waterproof for all the half-filled soft drinks and coffee cups that will inevitably be left on the production table, next to the electronic equipment and all of the paperwork.

Shelley's Soapbox: BYO Production Table Equipment

Working in different theatres can be exciting, but adapting to different production tables on a daily basis can be frustrating. Although it's rare that much can be done to change the seating or arrangement of the surface provided, the rest of the environment can become an irritating distraction. Time and effort can be wasted adapting or replacing the 100-watt non-dimmed bare bulb cliplight that's been provided as a worklight. Wrestling with an antique headset to merely get the microphone placed near the designer's mouth can cause unnecessary agitation. To eliminate these distractions, many lighting designers carry their own headset and dimmable worklight. Though their carry-on weight is slightly increased, providing their own tools means that they don't have to adapt to the worklight or headset de jour.

Carrying your own tools isn't limited to lights or headsets. Some designers bring their own computers, printers, hole punch, staplers, and other office equip-

ment. Being self-contained translates into that much more time spent on stage doing your job, and less time spent searching the theatre for the same equipment that's sitting in your home.

FOLLOWSPOTS

If followspots will be used for the show, their status should be addressed long before the technical rehearsal begins. Ideally, all of the followspots will already exist in the performing facility, so that time and effort isn't spent on their installation. In most cases, if the facility owns followspots, the type and number of spots will be listed on the technical specifications. Determining their capabilities, however, is often not possible to judge until the load-in. Some facilities maintain the instruments, so that all of the beams have an even field and matching intensity. In many cases, however, the instruments are in need of a tune-up.

Although the actual location, condition, and limitations of the followspots can often be seen by turning them on, taking the time to perform that task in the middle of a load-in is often not a realistic option. Instead, the typical method used to gain information is to talk to an electrician who has recently operated one of them. Acquiring this information may reveal the need to rewrite the followspot cue sheets. If rewriting needs to occur, better to find that out during the load-in, rather than in the midst of a hectic technical rehearsal. Here are some of the questions used to define house followspots:

- How may followspots exist in the facility?
- What is the light source? Manufacturer? (Presumably, they'll all be the same instrument.)
- Where are they located? (Are they all located on centerline? If they are spread out, can the outside spots make pickups on their near sides, or do they hit architectural impediments? If the latter is the case, the spot cues may have to be designed so that the outside spots make "cross-shots," picking up entrances on the opposite side.)
- Do they all produce the same amount of light, and if not, which one is the brightest?
- Do the instruments have matching beam size?
- When was the last time they were serviced?
- How are the followspots identified or "numbered"? If the lighting designer renumbers the spots without asking, he or she may be introducing a guaranteed confusion-creator. Consider

that these spot operators may have been running these instruments, using the same identity number, before you were born. ("Whaddaya mean, I'm Spot 3? I've always been Spot 1.")

- How many color frames are in each followspot's boomerang? What is the frame number closest to the nose (or front) of the instrument? If a frost is planned to diffuse the edge of the beam, is there a typical frame number used for that function? Is there a typical frost that has been used to produce a fuzzy beam edge? This topic will be examined in more detail in Chapter 10.
- Do they all have dousers? (If not, now is the time to be aware of that fact and consider workarounds if needed. One possible solution is to use heat-resistant black foil as one of the "colors," and manually "fading" the light.)

At an appropriate time during the load-in, the pieces of followspot color should be provided to the house electrician, along with a list indicating the colors by frame number. This list should include the relative location of the instrument's nose to the frame numbers, reducing the chance of the color frames being loaded backwards into the boomerang. Discovering this numbering reversal immediately prior to the technical rehearsal may result in either delaying the proceedings while the color is straightened out, or hastily rewriting all of the followspot cue sheets.

HOT TEST THE POSITION

As the instruments are being hung and circuited, the circuit numbers are recorded onto some form of the paperwork. Then the circuits are hardpatched into dimmers and (on a computer console) softpatched into channels. Prior to the electrician leaving the remote hanging position, or the overhead electric flying out, one of the final steps that should occur is to **hot test** the position. This troubleshooting process can also be referred to as "wringing out" (any problems at) the position. Though the phrase implies plugging each circuit directly into a hot wall outlet, the surge in voltage can cause lamps to burn out prematurely. For that reason, the hot test often activates instruments through a dimmer.

The hot test is performed by activating each instrument in sequence to confirm that it functions, that it's in the correct dimmer or channel, and that it's ready to be focused. Using the instrument schedule or the light plot, each channel or dimmer number is sequentially brought up to an intensity to activate the instrument. Presuming that the instrument functions, it's then checked to see that it has the proper color, accessories, and prefocus. In addition to confirming the readiness of each instrument, the activity also allows any problems to be corrected prior to the focus session. Once the overhead electrics have been trimmed, fixing problems will be more difficult and take more time during the focus session.

The hot test is sometimes performed only to confirm that the electrical path between the dimmer to the lamp of the instrument is functional. Once the hot test for the entire plot has been performed, all softpatching occurs at once. This may expedite any troubleshooting that may later be necessary when instruments don't activate in channels. Since the circuit and the dimmer previously functioned, the problem must be confined to the softpatch.

In some situations, no built-in circuitry exists between the hanging position and the dimmers. In those cases, bundles or multicable serve in place of built-in circuitry, following the simplest path between the instrument and the dimmer racks. When bundles are used to connect overhead electrics to dimmer racks, performing a hot test while the electric batten is at working height often means that the bundles can't be plugged into the racks. In those situations, hot testing the position can still occur. An additional cable (the hot test cable) bridges the gap between the dimmer racks and the end of the instrument's cable. After the dimmer is activated, each male plug of the electric's bundle is plugged, one by one, into the hot test cable. This confirms that the circuit number on the male plug of the cable is marked correctly, and that the path from the plug to each lamp is functional.

Once the bundles from the overhead electrics are plugged into the dimmers, there may still be errors. When that's the case, however, the problem has to be confined to the hardpatch or the softpatch, since the hot test showed that each instrument and circuit was in working order.

Although most of the instruments hung on the first electric of *Hokey* have been plugged into a raceway attached to the batten, there are more circuits required by the light plot (14) than exist in the raceway (12). To make up the difference, provide some insurance against circuit failure, and allow for possible instrument additions to the hanging position, a bundle of six cables has been added to the first electric during the hang. The position now contains a total of 18 circuits. The instruments have been plugged so that two circuits on the raceway and two circuits in the bundle remain as **spare circuits**. By splitting the spares between the two types of circuitry, a choice can still be made for the route and dimmers utilized for additions or substitutions.

Since the bundle can't conveniently plug into the road racks until the electric is flown out to trim, a hot test cable has been run from dimmer 31 to test the male plugs of the bundle, and dimmer 31 has been brought up to 50%. The instruments not plugged into the bundle have been plugged into the raceway, circuited to the house racks, and softpatched into their respective channels.

The hot test will begin with instrument 1. Since that instrument is plugged into the circuit marked 1E-1 in the bundle, the male plug at the end of the bundle with the matching label will be plugged directly into the hot test cable. Light comes out of the instrument, the color is correct, and the shutters have been pulled. The hot test is removed from the plug marked 1E-1. Instrument 2 has been plugged into bundle circuit 1E-2. When the labeled plug is found in the bundle, that plug is inserted into the hot test. No light comes out of the instrument. The plug from the instrument to the bundle is disconnected from the other end of 1E-2, and a test light is plugged into the circuit. If the test light turns on, the circuit is good, therefore the lamp or something else in the instrument is nonfunctional. If the test light doesn't turn on, the circuit or the connections in the plug are bad or the labeling is incorrect. Either the plug is mislabeled, or the plug requires rewiring, or one of the spare circuits will have to be used.

While the plugs are being opened to check the wiring, the hot test can continue. Instrument 3 is plugged into circuit 9 on the raceway, which is wired directly to dimmer 9, which has already been softpatched into channel 51. The board operator is asked to activate, or "bring up" channel 51 to 50%. When that's been done, instrument 3 doesn't turn on. When the softpatch is checked, it's discovered that dimmer 9 was assigned to channel 52. When the softpatch is corrected, the light from instrument 3 turns on.

This procedure continues through the entire electric, until the entire first electric has been hot tested and declared functional. The entire position can then be flown out above head height (above 7 or 8 feet), or

to its preliminary show trim. Before being flown out, however, the yoke of each instrument is grabbed and shaken, confirming that all of the hanging connections are tight. The instruments won't be loose during the focus, nor will the instruments fall off the batten. The hot test procedure continues until every instrument in each position is functional or noted. Once all of the electric are hung, circuited, colored, hot tested, and prefocused, the next step is to fly the electrics out (or up) to trim.

Tales from the Road: Get Some Cable-Grow in Switzerland

While trying to quickly load into a theatre in Switzerland, we were faced with battens containing no preinstalled circuitry. Instead, individual cables ran to the end of each overhead electric batten and then pulled over to preinstalled circuits in the gallery. The problem, in short, was the length of the cables. Or to put it another way, the cables weren't long enough. When the batten was lowered to the deck, the cables weren't long enough to plug into the gallery circuits. To make matters worse, the instruments were rented, so the male plugs of the instruments didn't match the female plugs of the cables. An adapter containing a small circuit breaker was placed between each cable and every instrument on every electric.

The production electrician refused to hot test the instruments by plugging each of the cables into a single hot test cable while the batten was on the deck. Instead, the entire hanging position was raised to trim, the cable was swagged over to the gallery, and the cables were plugged into the gallery circuits. After the plugging was complete, the instruments were finally tested. And to no one's surprise, several of the instruments didn't work. That's when we discovered that none of the male ends of the cable, currently plugged into the gallery circuits, had been labeled. So the only way to determine which instruments didn't work was to turn on all of the circuits in the entire electric. That somewhat reduced the workload, since we were able to determine the "good lights." Unfortunately, we still had no idea of the circuitry identity for any of the "bad lights"—and there were a lot of them.

By not taking the time to hot test the entire batten and label the cables, two additional layers of confusion had been added. We had no idea if the lamp inside the instrument, the adapter, the cable, the circuit, or the softpatch was bad. And there was little or no way to troubleshoot around them At that point, the ladder was occupied with carpentry troubles, and we couldn't even get to the electric. With so many variables, finding a base from which to troubleshoot was a challenge. The answer was to conduct an extended cross-plugging screaming match, from the stage to the gallery, and then from the stage to the lighting console. Simultaneously, the carpenters were screaming from the stage to the fly floor and the grid to solve the scenic problems. We wasted a lot of time.

SET THE TRIMS

Once the overhead scenery, masking, electrics, and anything else are hung and ready, the next activity is to establish the performance positions of all of these elements in the air. This activity is known as **setting the trims.** Every piece of goods is raised, often to a measured height above the stage. The position of all of the goods is then adjusted, so that the ideal performance locations are determined. Each defined location is then spiked (a **trim**), so that the height of any goods can be moved and still be restored to its performance location. In a mechanical sense, setting the trims for a show attempts to hide the technical elements (battens, electrics, and so on) from the vertical viewpoint of the audience, and physically realize what was drawn in the section. From the lighting designer's perspective, the activity is also performed to achieve two additional goals. First, to make certain that the vertical height of the hanging positions allows the affected light beams to adequately spread and provide coverage, and second, to make certain that the intended focus range for all of the instruments at each hanging position can physically occur. When the trims are set, the activity usually involves communication between the lighting designer, the technical director or production carpenter, and a flyperson on the rail. Once the activity is complete, most of the audience will be unable to see anything above the stage except masking borders.

The location of the actual sightline can affect the success of a trim session. If the measurement between the plaster line and the sightline (taken at the beginning of load-in) matches the distance drawn in the section, applying the trims from the drawing to the goods on the stage should then achieve the desired result. If that physical distance is substantially less than what was drawn, the sightline seats close to the stage will be able to see "higher" into the fly system. In order to

hide the technical elements of the goods, the entire procedure may require reevaluation. If the physical distance is greater than what was drawn, the sightline seats will not be able to see as "high," which may provide a lighting advantage. This visual "cushion" will allow the electrics to be lowered below their drawn locations, if need be, and still remain concealed.

A successful and rapid trimming session is often based on assumptions that were made when the section was originally drawn, and actions taken when the initial load-in occurred. Presuming that the height of the masking legs accurately reflects what's been drawn on the section, the chance of the border trims being too high (allowing the audience to see the battens on which the legs have been hung) won't occur.

If the physical borders match the height listed on the technical specifications, the chance of "seeing over" a border that's shorter than anticipated is reduced. If the actual distance from the stage to the grid has been accurately measured, then the bottom of scenery intended to disappear while being flown out will truly rise into the air and be hidden by the masking. If the cable running from the electrics to the dimmers is long enough, the electrics can be elevated so that they are concealed behind the masking.

The sequence used to set trims is variable, dependent on the amount and type of scenery, and the overhead electric positions involved. The basic sequence, though, often starts with the masking. The first step typically taken to setting trims is to lower the masking legs and the backdrops to their performance positions, or "playing positions," or "in-trims." Once the legs and backdrops have been lowered so that the bottom of the goods touch the stage, they're locked off. This initial step ensures that none of the final border trims will be higher than the top of the legs or backdrops, visually exposing the battens on which these soft goods are tied.

The second step is to trim the masking borders, which is often seen as the key to setting trims. Once all of the borders are trimmed, they'll define the height of the performance space, and establish the vertical stage picture. If a combination of masking and show borders are involved, the initial goods chosen to establish the vertical height of the overhead electrics may be the borders that will allow the sightline seats to see the "highest" into the fly system. Once concealed, the electrics will not have to be trimmed a second time. On the other hand, the borders chosen to achieve initial electric trims may be the goods that will be seen for a majority of the show. Once removed, the affected electrics may then require a second higher trim, used only when those borders are absent. Whenever possible, however, the attempt is made to trim the electrics to a single performance position. Each time an electric changes height, it runs the risk of striking adjacent battens or goods, which may damage the goods or refocus the instruments. In the case of *Hokey*, there is only the black masking borders that need to be considered.

Initially, the black portal border will be trimmed. It was hung during the load-in onto system pipe (or lineset) 1, counterbalanced with weight, and flown out above head height. The bottom of the border is now lowered (dropped in) to working height so that a carpenter can attach a measuring tape to the bottom of the border. The section and the hang plot show that the bottom of the border should be trimmed to 20'-6" above the stage. The carpenter signals the flyperson when that measurement is reached, the lineset is locked off, and with a jerk, the measuring tape drops from the bottom of the border. This process is repeated until all of the black borders are trimmed to the heights stated in the section or the hang plot.

At this point, the production carpenter or the technical director sits in the sightline seat and looks up. He or she is checking two things; first, that the tops of the legs can't be seen, and second, that it's not possible to see over the tops of the borders. Once it's been determined that the masking is successful and complete, the trim continues with the electrics. Lineset 3 (the first electric) is dropped to working height, and an electrician attaches the end of the measuring tape to the color frame holder on instrument 10, the center instrument on the electric. At this point the area above the stage is rather dark, and all of the masking is black. Since the worklights in the first opening are hung on the first electric, seeing the silhouettes of the instruments (to make certain that they're concealed from the audience) may be difficult. To solve this dilemma, the lighting designer activates group 24, the hanging position group which turns on every instrument hung on the first electric. Once the instruments are activated, the signal is given to the flyperson, who then raises the electric to the designated height. The electrician gives the flyperson a signal, the lineset is locked, and with a jerk, the measuring tape drops to the stage.

Although the electric is now at its designated trim, the carpenter or technical director in the audience can still see the illuminated lenses of the instruments "poking out" under the black portal border. There are now two choices: Either the portal border must be lowered or the electric must be raised for the lenses of the first electric to be hidden from the sightline seats. In an effort to preserve the proportion of the stage opening, the carpenter or technical director ask the lighting designer if the electric can be raised. If the electric is raised too far, focused light from some of the instruments may splash onto the #1 black border (lineset 9), which has already been trimmed. In addition to that, the increase in height may hamper the focus range of any instruments targeted to focus points downstage of the portal border. To provide an accurate response, the lighting designer first consults the light plot, determining the furthest upstage and downstage focus points assigned to the instruments on that electric.

Since the instruments have not yet been focused, the section is also consulted. According to the light plot, the farthest upstage beam edges will be the first electric frontlight system controlled by channels 6 > 8 and 16 > 18. According to the section, those beams will land at 21'-6" upstage of plaster line. That measurement is made on the stage. The lighting designer then crouches so that his or her head is at that location on the deck, and looks up at the first electric. If the lenses on the electric can be clearly seen, then the electric may be raised. If the lenses can't be seen, then either the #1 black border will have to be raised, or the electric will have to be lowered. If the electric is lowered, then the portal black border will have to drop in as well to conceal the first electric. When the lighting designer looks up, the lenses can't be seen. Rather than lower the downstage goods, the #1 border and the first electric are raised, until the lenses disappear behind the black portal border from the sightline seat and the lighting designer can still see the lenses of the first electric crouched at the 21'-6" mark on the stage. Since the #2 and #3 black borders are still at the original trim, the height of the stage picture is preserved. Once the lighting designer checks to confirm that beams from the first electric pipe end instruments will still be able to focus "under" the portal border to any downstage focus points as well, the current status of the battens is declared satisfactory, and the battens are locked off.

This process of negotiation continues upstage until all of the electrics are hidden, the focus of each lighting instrument is retained without being blocked by black borders, and the height of the stage opening mirrors the drawn intent as closely as possible. Once the sixth electric is trimmed so that the T-3 striplights are even with the system pipe of the translucency, the entire stage picture is viewed from the sightline in the audience to confirm that everything is hidden. Once declared that this is the final trim, the flyperson then places spike marks on the operating ropes, marking the performance positions of all of the goods. After all of the spike marks have been placed, the trim session is complete.

Shelley's Notes: Trimming

Although concealing the electrics is often the ideal, in reality that may not be possible. Sometimes the audience seating is so close to the stage that successfully hiding the electrics from the designated sightline seat may result in the electrics touching the grid. When that occurs, the overall intent of the production design will suffer. When faced with this situation, the choice is often made to retain the integrity of the stage picture for the majority of the audience. Although the first or second row will see the lenses of the instruments, a seat in the second or third row is designated as the new on-site sightline seat.

If a midstage drop is involved in a quick transition during the production, its low trim is often established after the trim of the black surround has been completed. This confirms that the top of the drop won't be seen. After the in-trim has been spiked, however, the drop may merely be flown out for storage. This may result in the system batten possibly being taken to the grid. If this isn't noticed, when the cue is given for the drop to fly in during the transition, seconds will be lost before the bottom of the drop is seen under the bottom of the borders. The overall time spent for the transition may be needlessly increased. Once the in-trim for the drop is spiked, the drop should be flown out only until the drop is out of the way of any instrument's focus, and the masking border hides the bottom of the drop. Once hidden, the "out-trim" spike for the drop can be marked.

If the top of the drop (and its batten) is seen when the midstage drop is lowered to its in-trim, the next border immediately downstage of the drop may also have to be lowered to cover the top of the drop. A second spike mark will be placed on the border, and it will move on the same fly cues that lower and raise the midstage drop.

If the show has several pieces of scenery flying in and out during the course of the show, it's wise to establish and check all of the trims before telling the fly crew to spike the trims. Asking folks to do the same task again begins to chafe at their interest factor.

While electrics are being trimmed, the choice can be to attach the measuring tape to the nose of the instrument or to the system pipe. I prefer to attach the measuring tape to the "lowest" nose or thing that will be seen from the audience. Often that will be a 6×16 or a 6×22 ellipsoidal, which have longer barrels than other ellipsoidals. Sometimes it's the barndoors on a 2-kw Fresnel. Using this system, it must be decided prior to attaching the tape which instrument is going to stick down the lowest.

When *Hokey* was trimmed, all of the goods were dropped in, the measuring tape attached, and then flown out to trim. Often, this procedure is performed as the borders and electrics are initially flown out. After each border is hung and counterweighted, the tape is attached, the border is flown out (not above head height, but to trim), and the tape is removed. After each of the electrics is hot tested, the tape is attached to the noses of the instruments and the same process is performed. By setting the trims as the goods fly out, the amount of time consumed for the trim session is reduced.

Tales from the Road: The Shrinking Legs

One good reason to preset the legs at playing trim for focus revolves around the story of the shrinking legs. When I walked into the theatre, I was told that the legs were 24'-0" tall. Without taking the time to lower the legs to their performance positions, I proceeded to trim the borders at 22'-0" above the stage. The prehung electrics were then trimmed so that they were concealed. After the focus was concluded and the performance surface had been installed, the legs were dropped in to playing trim. Imagine my surprise when it was discovered that the legs were really only 18'-0" tall. The bottom of the borders came nowhere close to covering the system battens or the top of the legs.

In that situation, the only available solution was to lower the borders. After all of the borders had been dropped in to hide the leg battens, all of the backlight on the electrics hit the borders. After all of the electrics were lowered to get light off the borders, none of the specials were close to their spike marks. Ah, the learning curve.

Tales from the Road: Trimming the Overhead Electrics without Borders

Late in the morning, as we were preparing to set the trims on a show, we were informed that the masking borders had not yet arrived from the scene shop. Consequently, none of the borders would be hung to meet the schedule. Initially, this raised eyebrows of concern because we were scheduled to focus in two hours. Although all of the legs were hung, how would we know how high to raise the electrics to make certain that they would be hidden? Since it was obvious that we wouldn't have the masking borders before focus began, how would we know that the electrics wouldn't have to be retrimmed later to remain hidden, which could then result in a refocus of the affected electrics?

Since each border was assigned to its own lineset, we dropped each batten in to working height, attached a measuring tape to it, and then trimmed the batten to the same height as the bottom of the eventual masking border. Although there were no soft goods on the pipe, the pipe itself provided the straight horizontal line. While sitting in the sightline seat, the electrics were then raised until they were above the border's batten.

By using the battens as the substitute borders, the electrics were accurately trimmed the first time. Although the electrics could be clearly seen above the border's batten, they were trimmed above the bottom of where the masking borders would eventually hang. During the focus session, instead of cutting light off the borders, cuts were instead taken off the battens.

Two days later, the masking borders arrived on-site, and the carpenters hung them on their assigned battens. After the bottoms of the masking borders were trimmed to the same height that the battens had been trimmed to 2 days before, the trimming was finally complete. There was no need for any refocus, and no stage time was lost.

THE FIRST CHANNEL CHECK

Once the overhead electrics have been trimmed and the sidelight booms have been positioned, some amount of the remaining time should be dedicated to performing an initial channel check of the entire lighting package. A **channel check** (or on manual light boards, a **dimmer check**), involves activating each channel individually, in the sequential hookup order. This confirms that the proper instruments function, that the electrical path for each instrument is accurate, and that the color and accessories for each instrument is correct. The amount of time required for this activity can be reduced if color media has been inserted in the instruments during the hang. During the initial channel check, irregularities are often only noted on the worksheet. After the status of the entire lighting package has been seen once, the troubleshooting process can begin.

If time is available after the channel check has been completed, it can be applied to visually check the infrastructure programming. Regardless of whether the programming has been viewed on the monitor display, seeing the correct instruments turn on truly confirms the accuracy of the programming. Checking the contents within one infrastructure function (cues, groups, or subs) will often confirm the accuracy of the other two. If groups will be used initially during the focus session or the light cue level setting session, they are often the function checked. A moment should be specifically devoted to checking any inhibitive submasters, or submasters used for worklight. This is the time to discover and correct any errors in programming. Detecting mistakes at almost any time in the future may be inopportune and a cause for delay.

SUMMARY

Once the light plot is hung, colored, accessorized, prefocused, hot tested, and positioned, the installation of the lighting package is complete. At the same time, the scenery and the performance surface have been installed. The infrastructure and focusing cues are loaded into the light board, the production table is set, the followspots have been examined, the stage has been spiked, and the overhead goods have been trimmed. Although there may be many other tasks for the other departments to accomplish, the focus session can occur on schedule.

9 The Focus Session

This chapter examines some of the events that occur during a focus session, and techniques that can be employed to expedite the process. Keep in mind that there are many different ways to focus front of house lights, overhead electrics, and boom sidelights. No one method is correct. What will be presented here is one combination to demonstrate different focus techniques.

OVERVIEW

In almost every union situation, the focus concludes the load-in portion of the schedule, which requires the largest number of stagehands. Only after the final instrument is touched can the number of paid personnel be reduced to the smaller crew size, known as the show call. In that situation, it is important that the focus session be organized and directed at a rapid pace to make certain that every lighting instrument is addressed in the allotted amount of time. If the final instrument has not been touched by the end of the allocated number of hours, the entire crew's salary may escalate to a higher overtime rate. Since time is precious, performing any task a second time can be viewed as a waste of time. In many cases, fine-tuning the focus of the instruments ("touch-up focus") is delayed until work note calls are scheduled.

Sometimes the nature of the production requires multiple visits to the same hanging position. If the show is a multiset production, some instruments may be specific for individual scenes. In that case, time management may be even more critical. The scenery for a single scene is assembled and positioned, after which the ladder passes along each electric, focusing only the instruments that will be used within that

scenic arrangement. After every instrument has been focused in that scenic arrangement, the scenery is changed to the next scene. Once the next scene is set, the ladder returns to each applicable hanging position to focus every instrument designated for that scene. Since each set will require some amount of time for assembly, while other sets may be similar in nature, the lighting designer must provide a strong input into the order in which the sets are assembled for the focus. Indeed, multiset productions may be focused completely out of order, defined solely by the speed required to change from one scene to another. Regardless of the order, however, the final scene that is focused is often the first scene that will be addressed in the technical rehearsal.

Since the lighting designer is almost always directly responsible for the success of the focus session, he or she has a vested interest in any relationships between the hanging positions and scenic elements of the show. Just as important, the lighting designer must also view any arrangement on the stage from a point of view of what affect that arrangement may have on accessing each hanging position during a rapid focus session.

Generally speaking, focused light falls into one of two categories. The first category is light intended to illuminate the performers, which is then often shaped to reduce or prevent peripheral light from striking masking or scenery. The second category is light whose primary intent is just the opposite; lighting the scenery, and not the performers.

The sequence of a focus usually begins with the instruments in the front of house hanging positions. The instruments in the overhead electrics are usually focused next, followed by the instruments on the ladders. The booms, set mounts, and groundrows are usually the last hanging positions to be focused, because they are often the units most accessible from the stage.

The focus session may involve other people besides the focusing electrician, the board operator, and the lighting designer. A channel caller may be present to quickly translate to the board operator the channel numbers or system handles requested by the designer. A scribe maybe on hand, transcribing the actions applied to each instrument onto the focus charts. If the focus is a regeneration of a prior design, the scribe may merely need to update the charts as changes take place, keep track of which instruments have been focused, and notate units that will require future attention. If the focus session is for an original production, on the other hand, the scribe may be very busy, writing down the location of the hot spots, the beam edge size or softness, and any shaping required for each instrument. In addition, he or she may also need to read information regarding focused instruments back to the designer, allowing the focus of the instrument at hand to be matched or reversed. When more than one instrument is being simultaneously focused, the two assistants must split their concentration. When these two positions are combined into the responsibility of a single individual, the caller/scribe need not be concerned about being bored. The constant need to record information, provide information, write notes in the proper location, and keep up with the designer while calling the channels over the span of an 8-hour focus session can test the mettle of most assistants.

While the caller and scribe are busy keeping up with their logistical tasks during the focus session, the lighting designer's perspective is a completely different perception. The designer must be constantly thinking three or four steps ahead of the present situation. He or she must anticipate potential problems, and have ideas as to how to correct them before they occur. When difficulties present themselves, the designer must know how to quickly solve the problem, or be able to prioritize the difficulty to a future work call. The designer must know what semantics to use while focusing, so that his or her directions are clearly understood and rapidly accomplished.

In addition to pointing the instruments to their desired locations, the lighting designer needs to remain simultaneously aware of several different factors. He or she needs to be aware of each beam's relationship with the entire surrounding environment, including the masking, architecture, the audience's eyes, and the performer's eyes. In addition to that, the designer also needs to remain aware of each instrument's beam in relation to other lights, so that the beams blend between several different instruments in a system. At the same time, the designer may have to coordinate scene changes, prioritize the tasks, direct the personnel, adapt the schedule, contend with the politics, be polite, and complete the focus call without going into overtime.

FOCUS ANALYSIS

Prior to conducting a focus session, it's worthy to consider different tactics and techniques that are used to focus lighting instruments. Analyzing why an audience sees a focused beam of light in a particular way should be examined, since it can have a direct affect on the methods used to focus that particular instrument.

Audience Angle of Observation

In a typical light plot, instruments are focused onto the stage from many different angles and directions. The beam edges of some instruments are more apparent to the audience than others, which is often determined by the relative angles of each hanging position to the audience's **angle of observation**.

This can initially be explained by examining the **law of specular reflection**, which states that "the angle of incidence equals the angle of reflection." What this statement means is that light striking a flat surface from an angle will bounce off the surface, traveling at the same angle in the opposite direction. Or to put it another way, "the angle coming in is the same angle going out."

Figure 9.1 shows a beam of light as a dotted line. The "incoming light" is approaching at the angle of incidence, striking the mirror at a 45° angle. The "outgoing light" is departing at the angle of reflection, also

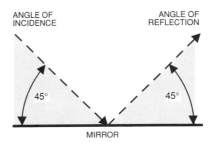

Figure 9.1 Specular Reflection

a 45° angle. This figure is typically used to illustrate the movement of light affected by a reflector, but it can also be viewed as a section view of light bouncing off of a stage.

Light from an instrument at an angle to the stage (angle of incidence), striking a flat surface (the stage), will bounce off in a comparable angle in the opposite direction (angle of reflection). Figure 9.2 shows frontlight, sidelight, and backlight in a proscenium theatre all striking the stage from different angles. As examples, frontlight bounces up towards the backdrop, while backlight bounces out towards the audience. The three angles of light produce individual visual results.

Consider this example: A single ellipsoidal backlight whose barrel sharpness doesn't match the rest of the system is more apparent than a similarly misfocused frontlight or sidelight. This is due to the viewer's angle of observation, the relationship created by the location of the source (the beam's angle of incidence coming from the instrument), bouncing off the stage, and reflecting into the viewer's eyes.

When viewing a light cue from the stage right wings looking onstage, it's difficult to see any beam edges from the stage right sidelights, because those instruments are focused in the same direction as the viewer's line of sight. The line of sight is following the beam's angle of incidence. On the other hand, it is comparatively easy to see the "sharpness" of the beam edges coming from the stage left sidelights, which are reflecting off the stage. From that perspective it is easier to see the beam edges of any lights focused toward stage right: the stage left booms, ladders, or overhead pipe ends. This is because the line of sight is in line with those instruments' angles of reflection. Compared to the stage right sidelight, the beam edges of the frontlight and backlight are also easier to see than the stage right sidelight, since they're only 90° from the viewer's angle of observation.

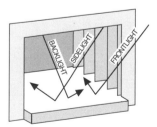

Figure 9.2 Stage Specular Reflection

When more than one system of light strikes the same area of the stage, however, the beam edges that are most readily seen are the ones that are 180° to the viewer's angle of observation. Beam edges from 90° may also be seen, but with difficulty. Beam edges at 0°, or originating from the same direction as the line of sight, are the most difficult to observe. In an uncolored light plot, this suggests three practical implications:

1. A backlight system, consisting of sharp-edged ellipsoidals, should be carefully matched and focused. If one of the backlights is brighter, dimmer, or softer-edged than the rest of the system, chances are greater that the audience will see the anomaly. Backlight or downlight beam edges are the most "exposed" to the audience's angle of observation.

2. When sidelight is combined with systems from other angles, it can often be focused as sharp as necessary to cut the beams off legs or scenery. The beam edges on the floor will not be as readily observed from the audience, since it is 90° to the audience's angle of observation. If light cues are planned that use sidelight as the sole source of illumination, it may be necessary to soften the beam edges of the instruments. If the light cues in question combine backlight with the sidelight, any sharp beam edges from the sidelights will be obscured from the audience's point of view.

3. If the production intends to use relatively bright backlight, the shutter cuts in the frontlights may not need to be matching and precise. The backlight will wash out the irregular beam edges of the frontlight.

Up to this point all attention has been concerned with the angle of reflection. Now consider an example of the angle of incidence. When viewing a light cue from the audience, gaps in focus or irregular blending are most notable in the frontlight. When a performer's face darkens while crossing the stage, it can be noted that he or she is moving through a hole in the coverage between two frontlights. If the focus of a frontlight is too sharp, the sharp beam edge can also be seen on the performer's face while he or she is crossing the stage.

It's much more difficult, however, for the viewer to see sharp beam edges or gaps in coverage from sidelight or backlight without looking at the stage. The lack of smooth blending or sharpness of the beam edges is only obvious to the eye when the angle of observation is the same as the instrument's angle of incidence. From the audience's angle of observation, this implies the following:

1. Frontlight systems need the smoothest coverage. To achieve this, the beam edges are the edges of the beams usually soft, rather than sharp.
2. In most cases, sidelights can be more sharply focused, because only the side sightlines of the audience will be able to see the reflected beam edges from the same angle of observation.

Although these implications are illustrated using a proscenium theatre as an example, they can be applied to other theatre configurations. When the audience views the stage from more than one perspective, like a thrust or arena facility, these observations should be reanalyzed. It's prudent to consider the law of specular reflection and its impact before each focus session.

A Focus Example

The act of focusing a single instrument can be reduced to four basic steps. In most cases, these steps are often made in the same sequence. Since the lighting designer is giving directions, he or she should wait until each direction has been completed before requesting the next action. Likewise, the focusing electrician should communicate to the lighting designer when each requested action has been completed.

1. The lighting designer defines the location of the pool of light ("Hit me hot here" or "Edge of the beam there").
2. The lighting designer is satisfied with the location, and gives a command to immobilize the position of the instrument ("Lock it off"). Whatever immobilizes the "pan" (side-to-side movement) of the instrument is tightened, along with whatever immobilizes the "tilt" (vertical movement) of the instrument. Since the lighting designer may not be able to see when this is accomplished, the focusing electrician should respond when this action is complete.
3. The lighting designer adjusts the size of the pool or the sharpness of the beam ("Flood or spot the beam" or "Run the barrel in or out"), and indicates when the action is satisfactory. If the control for this action requires tightening some portion of the instrument, the focusing electrician also responds when this action is complete.

4. The lighting designer shapes the beam edges ("Put shutter cuts in here" or "Bring in a barndoor to here"). If this action is complex to achieve, the focusing electrician again responds when each action is complete.

FOCUSING TECHNIQUES AND NOTES

In most cases, this process (or a variation of it) must be repeated for each instrument. The more instruments in a light plot, the more often this sequence occurs. If the lighting designer establishes a consistent sequence, the focusing electrician can keep up with, or anticipate the lighting designer's requests. If communication between the two is constant, the amount of time between the completion of actions can be reduced.

Paperwork Techniques

During the focus call, three documents will need to be updated. The focusing document informs the designer of the purpose for every instrument and is marked to reflect the progression of the focus. This may be a copy of the light plot, a focus schedule, or an instrument schedule. The work notes sheet reflects the amount of physical effort that will be required to mechanically correct and complete the lighting system in future work calls. The final document, usually a legal pad, is used to write down concepts, realizations, or any other notes not pertaining to physical labor.

While focusing, instruments fall into three categories. Either the instruments haven't been focused, they have been focused, or they've been "touched." A "touched" instrument has been pointed, but may be only partially focused. It will require additional attention for its focus to be considered complete. Notes must be taken throughout the process that keep track of each instrument's status. Some designers employ different colored highlighters or pens, to indicate the current state of the focus. Other designers make two different kinds of marks on their focusing document next to each instrument: One indicates that the focus is complete, whereas the other shows the units that will require additional work. Often, both the "focus done" and the "more work" marks are made in pencil. In that way, when the "more work" action is completed, the note can be changed. When the page is scanned and no "more work" marks can be found, the entire hanging position can be considered focused. On the other hand, when an error in the focus is discovered, the "focus done" mark can be erased, replaced by the "more work" mark. A final scan of the hanging position displays the units that require a return engagement.

Occasionally, it's necessary to change information about an instrument. Change in purpose, equipment failure, or other elements may require alterations in circuitry, patching, color, or focus. These notes may be made directly on the focusing document but they are all recorded in the support paperwork. The cleaner the support paperwork is kept, the easier it will be to later update the database. Regardless of the system used to denote the changes, they shouldn't obliterate notes or information about the instruments that have been completed. Marking completed focus with a magic marker is not advised. When the information can't be seen, it can't later be used for reference.

Keeping notes on a work notes sheet allows them to be referred to throughout the focus session without the lighting designer. The work notes sheet can be checked and the notes addressed by members of the electrics department throughout the focus without interrupting the designer's concentration.

Positioning the Hot Spot

The first action typically taken to focus an instrument is to position the light beam of the instrument. Once the hot spot has been positioned so that it passes through the focus point, the instrument is locked off. There are many methods used to direct the position of the beam. Typically, the lighting designer stands in a specific location, so that his or her head is at the focus point. Then the beam is positioned so that the middle of the beam passes through the lighting designer's head.

When initially defining the focus point, some designer's choose to look into the beam of light. These "look-at" designers stare into the beam of the instrument to see the filament of the lamp centered in the middle of the reflector. This implies that the hot spot of the instrument is centered on their face. When initially staring into the lamp, some amount of time elapses while the iris of the designer's eye "shutters down." It's an abrupt change for the eye to contend with and occurs numerous times during a single focus session. To reduce the impact of this "wear and tear," some designers hold a piece of saturated gel in front of their eyes while adjusting the hot spot to the focus point.

Other designers "look-away" from the light; they face away from the instrument to position the hot spot. By turning away from the instrument, it is possible to see the hot spot of the light while looking at their shadow and also see where the beam is landing and what the beam is hitting. Subscribers of the "look-away" method are often lighting designers who have been focusing for years. With age, it can take more time for the eye to recover after staring into the beam, which, in turn, means that it takes longer to then read paperwork. They've also realized that, after seeing where the beam lands, it's often necessary to readjust the position of the hot spot a second time. Some designers have refined the "look-away" method, so that they don't even stand at the focus point. They ask for the instrument's beam to be horizontally centered where they stand, and then ask for the beam to be raised or lowered so that the bottom of the beam is touching their foot.

Still other designers direct the positioning of the hot spot from a remote location, standing nowhere near the focus point. The key to their success is their ability to communicate.

Starting the Focus from Center

When focusing multi-instrument straight frontlight, downlight, or backlight systems, the first instrument focused is the unit that will point to centerline. This technique is useful when the beam spread, quality, or condition of the instruments is unknown. By starting the focus of the system with the center instrument, the light beam will require fewer shutter cuts, as opposed to the instruments focused adjacent to the side masking. Seeing the unshuttered center pool first can also simplify defining the location of adjacent focus points to achieve an even wash.

Sometimes the beam spreads of the instruments used in a system are smaller than anticipated. To achieve an even blend, the distance between focus points in the same zone may be reduced to avoid visual "dips" in coverage. If the system focus is started from one side of the stage in this situation, the coverage may "run out" before reaching the opposite side. By starting the focus at center, the focus points in the same zone can be shifted equidistantly from centerline. After the system focus is complete, the coverage may still "run out" before reaching the boundaries of the performance area, but starting the focus from center ensures that the coverage of the system wash will be symmetrical.

Using this technique can also eliminate time spent on repetitive refocusing. As an example, if a straight frontlight system focus begins with the side instruments, a dysfunctional instrument, intended to be focused at center, won't be discovered until midway through the hanging position. One solution to this dilemma is to shift the focus points in that zone closer to center, so that adjacent light beams will provide more "overlap" and ensure coverage. Although this is a viable solution, this tactic will require instruments to be refocused that were already considered complete. On the other hand, if the "middle" instrument focused first to centerline is discovered to be dysfunctional, the remaining focus points on either side of center can be shifted toward the inadequate pool. Using this technique, the rest of the instruments will then be focused once. No time will be lost refocusing any instruments.

Focusing with Ambient Light

Since the beams of the instruments can't be seen as well when worklights also illuminate the stage, the light level in the entire performance space is reduced to a lower intensity. Due to the fact that the schedule is finite, there may still be a need to perform other tasks on the stage, but it's generally understood that the faster the instruments are focused, the sooner full worklight can be restored. Most if not all worklights are turned off during the focus session.

That being said, many designers can count on one hand the number of times they actually focused a show with all of the worklights off. Inevitably, they're presented with a choice of having a dark stage, followed by delays during the cueing process because the scenery's now behind schedule. Or they can contend with some amount of inconvenience and focus with worklights on. Often the latter scenario is chosen, although it may heighten the frustration level trying to communicate over the sound of chain saws or be unable to clearly see a beam of light.

Presuming there are worklights on different overhead electrics, one partial solution to this dilemma is to have the worklights separated into downstage, midstage, and upstage handles. The designer can then keep the portion of the stage being focused relatively dim, while the rest of the stage can still be provided adequate worklight. If that's not an option, it may be possible to use clip lights for the other activities surrounding the focus. Sometimes overhead instruments or rovers can be used to provide visibility for other tasks. At other times, it may be necessary to struggle through a focus session in full worklight as efficiently

as possible. In that situation, time is then set aside when the stage can be darkened, and the focus can actually be seen.

Sometimes contrast between the worklight and the instrument that's being focused can be used. When the beam of light is competing with worklight to be seen, one technique often employed requires the focusing electrician to wave his or her hand through the beam of light, an action commonly referred to as **flagging the unit**. The flicker caused by the electrician's hand interrupting the beam often allows the lighting designer to see the beam edge and determine the accuracy of that unit's focus.

If full worklight must be used during the focus session, consider searching for different locations of the beam edge that may be used as a signpost. As an example, searching for the bottom beam edge during boom sidelight focus can be frustrating. The top edge of the beam, however, may land high on the opposite wall, where the worklight isn't as bright. Consider matching subsequent beams to the top edge, rather than on the difficult-to-see beam edge on the deck.

Focusing with Other Activity

When the stage has to be shared with other departments during a focus session, it's typically due to a constrained schedule. Situations such as these can try the patience of any lighting designer. Frustration can grow high as inconvenience mounts, but this emotion should be tempered with the reminder that the other departments are probably not savoring the experience either. If they had exclusive use of the stage, it wouldn't be as difficult to see, they could make as much noise as they wished, nor would anyone be interrupted by the lighting designer bellowing instructions to the back of the house. Try to keep this in perspective, and attempt to share the working time together peacefully.

If soft goods are being hung upstage during a frontlight focus, the scenery "in the way" may prevent the lighting designer from seeing where the upstage beam edge will land in relation to the upstage light line or the scenery stack. Rather than delay the focus, activate a single channel, focus the hot spot, and then stand on one side of the stage to see the beam "in section." Mentally extend the edge of the beam upstage, gauge where the beam would land, and instruct the top cut accordingly. Afterwards, use the shutter cut of that instrument as a signpost. Retain that channel at a low intensity, and cut the rest of the top shutters in the system to match.

At times, scenery "in the way" can be an advantage. Although battens at working height can obscure the visibility of upstage light lines during frontlight focus, they can also be used as signposts for shutter cuts. Presuming that the battens will remain locked at that height for some amount of time, they can be utilized as signposts for the focusing electricians: "Cut the top shutter into the batten that's getting the black scrim." Consider how inconveniences can become temporary advantages.

When the orchestra rehearsal kicks into high gear in the midst of a focus session, communication can become difficult, if not impossible. If the electrician is familiar with the focus, it may be possible to focus in relative silence. The only speech required may be the channel numbers, which might be provided to the board operator using a headset. An alternative to this method is to determine if a working fire curtain exists. Usually, if it can stop fire, it will at least muffle sound. If readily available, it can be lowered to reduce the sound from the orchestra pit. If this situation occurs as the overhead focus begins, double-check the focus points for any frontlight systems that continue on overhead electrics. If the fire curtain will cover the downstage light line, anticipate the loss of this demarcation. Focus a single overhead sidelight before the curtain is lowered to the deck. After the curtain is in place, the side shutter cut can be used as a signpost for the rest of the instruments. If there's any chance that the focused instrument may get hit by the fire curtain's movement, place spike tape directly on the curtain. Not anticipating the need for this downstage light line signpost can be most embarrassing, since it may then be necessary to raise the fire curtain to establish the first downstage shutter cut.

 Shelley's Notes: General Focus

On the day of focus, I'm much more aware of my wardrobe. By wearing a light-colored shirt I provide the focusing electricians with a higher contrast target to be able to determine the relative location of the hot spot. While focusing, I often wear a baseball cap. Other than the fact that it protects my bald head, the visor can be used like a barndoor. As an example, looking into a boom sidelight to see the beam edge often requires holding a hand in front your face to shade your eyes from the source of the instrument. Using the visor as a "hand," I'll merely tip my head down slightly, so that the visor of the cap blocks the source of the light. Without being blinded, I can see where the scallop of light or the shutter cut is hitting the floor.

When I check a system wash for blending, I don't use my hand. I'll walk between the focus points, and look at the blend of light on white paper attached to a clipboard, or the back of the light plot. I've found that "dips" in intensity are much easier to see on white, rather than on flesh.

If focus cues aren't used, it still makes good sense to reactivate the channel of the last focused instrument in that same system to compare beam edge placement or barrel softness. For example, after the first electric has been focused, activating channels 21 and 22 simultaneously brings up the lavender pipe ends on both the first and the second electric. This allows you to match the softness and location of the beam edge for channel 22 to channel 21 on the stage. This can reduce the task of positioning the hot spot to merely making certain that the second electric's instrument is positioned in the middle of the opening. If the location of the beam edges aren't intended to match, seeing channel 21 will still allow the comparable barrel softness to be checked, along with the upstage/downstage blending between the two instruments.

There are times when using props can expedite a focus and reduce the lighting designer's physical labor. Any inanimate object can be placed as a signpost to define a focus point or a cut line. As an example, when the first frontlight is focused, I'll note where the shadow of my head lands on the stage. While the focus of the first instrument is being completed, I'll place a stool, a bucket, or a roll of tape where each head shadow will land. This eliminates the need to move to each focus point, and I can concentrate on the blending or shaping of the instruments.

Sometimes, there are just not enough props available to temporarily mark the stage. When there's no scenic stack in place, a shoe placed on each upstage quarter line gives the FOH electricians a visual signpost to refer to, and reduces the amount of time I spend standing with my hands above my head screaming "cut the top shutter to my hands." If the theatre doesn't have enough clutter to be used as focus props, I may end up disrobing bit by bit and leaving parts of my clothing around the stage. Although this may reduce the amount of effort on my part, these actions don't go unnoticed by clever carpenters who have screwguns and too much time on their hands. This becomes apparent when you finish the focus, walk to your shoes to put them back on, and discover that they've been screwed to the stage.

 Shelley's Notes: Focusing More Than One Position

Occasionally time constraints are such that it becomes necessary to accelerate the tempo by focusing two lighting instruments, from two different locations, at the same time. If this plan is being considered for an extended amount of time, preparation is required to successfully focus in this fashion. Strongly consider acquiring an assistant to record the focus and keep track of the work notes. If there's no one available for those tasks, you had best prepare the paperwork yourself, since it will be necessary to process the information as rapidly as possible. If you're not the original creator of the paperwork, a complex focus will require study, rehearsal, and possibly regeneration of the focus document into language that you can easily understand.

Instigating an original focus using two electricians can be accomplished by writing the focus directly on the plot. Moving from one position to another is achieved by visually scanning a different area of the same document. Regenerating a focus from charts, however, requires visually flipping between two lighting positions to keep up with the electricians. Index separators or Post-its™ can be used to define the different locations within the paperwork. On other occasions, I've used the instrument schedule, and make shorthand focus notations directly on that document.

During frontlight focus, two electricians can be employed to focus channels that "mirror" each other. One electrician focuses instruments that are pointed on one side of the stage, while a second electrician duplicates the same focus on the matching instrument focused on the opposite side. Box booms can also be focused in this manner, though the angles and size of the beams may overlap on the performance surface. Focusing box booms in this manner requires more careful coordination to avoid confusion.

When presented with the prospect of focusing three positions at once, my first reaction is to check the schedule. Is time so short that it warrants juggling three balls at the same time? In my mind, keeping up with two competent electricians can be an extended exercise in concentration. Directing three electricians in different locations can be daunting, and not something to be entered into lightly. This situation is even more acute if there's no additional person to call out the channel numbers. One constraint that may squash this proposal is the number of available focusing ladders, or the number of available support personnel that will be required to move them.

The key to a successful three-position focus is anticipation, communication, and coordination. The tactical approach to this type of focus is to select nonadjacent hanging positions that won't "compete" with each other, so that the instruments will be pointed to mutually exclusive focus points on the stage. The sequence in which hanging positions are focused may not make conventional sense. Careful location coordination reduces the slowdowns created when the light from one instrument washes out the beam from the second or third instrument. Before the electricians depart the stage, I'll memorize their names. This makes certain that the correct electrician and instrument are being addressed while giving directions, eliminating moments when the correct focus direction is applied to the wrong instrument. Then there are those days when all three electricians are named "Bob."

For this kind of focus to succeed within a constrained schedule, everyone involved must agree that the electrics department has priority over all other departments. Although the rest of the production team can continue work on other tasks, they should be on walkie-talkie. They're then available to be able to respond to any needs or unanticipated problems that the lighting designer no longer has time to address. Often, one of those staff members will stand by to address any situations that may impede the progress of the lighting designer.

A three-position focus implies that the lighting designer will more heavily rely on the talents of good electricians. They'll be much more involved with the shape of the focus. In addition to having excellent focusing skills and an understanding of directions, it's a plus if they also know when to provide me with assistance, reminders, or alerts that they're ready for the next instrument. Since time to check a focus will be limited, I'll involve them much more in the process, asking for their visual judgment and opinions from their perspective.

This kind of focus is the ideal time to utilize additional spike tape, articles of clothing, or anything still not nailed down to indicate hot spots, edges of beams, or shutter cut lines. Having props to indicate locations means I no longer have to stand at a single position, waiting for the hot spot to be focused on my head. After instructing an electrician on the focus of an instrument, I'll leave him or her to follow my instructions, pointing and shaping the light while I attend to another instrument. I'll return to check the finished focus later.

When possible, I'll utilize two of the electricians in a position that includes units which mirror their focus, like the front of house, while the third electrician is assigned to an upstage overhead electric. The instructions for the focus of one frontlight will be reversed-and-repeated for the second frontlight on the opposite side of the stage. Since the frontlight is typically focused downstage, the beams won't overpower the beams of the instruments upstage. Other possible combinations include focusing a boom downstage left, with a boom upstage right, plus an overhead. If there are enough electricians to move the ladders, two nonadjacent overhead positions can be juggled with a single boom.

Before agreeing to a three-position focus, all other options should be considered prior to committing to this course of action. Maintaining the pace, concentration, and speed of a three-position focus is exhausting. The only good thing is that it's not a four-position focus.

Designer Do's and Don'ts

During the focus, the most important task at hand is just that; the focus. Although appearing calm, relaxed, and polite, the lighting designer must constantly be aware of time management throughout the entire session. Here's a list of guidelines to consider during a focus session:

- Take command of the space. This is the only opportunity scheduled to focus the show—and the time is finite. If other departments are behind schedule, negotiate a compromise, so that all facets of work can continue, but if there is a scheduled end to the focus session, the focus is the priority. Establish a pace, and attempt to maintain it.
- Keep your concentration on the job at hand. Return phone calls or schedule meetings during another time. Just as designers can become irritated when crews are absent or dawdling, crews can get just as frustrated waiting for the designer.
- Leave the stage as little as possible.
- Attempt to reduce delays in the process. Anticipate everything possible: channels, ladder movements, the next position to be focused, or scenic requirements. Communicate scenic needs prior

to arriving at the instrument that requires its presence.
- Make certain that all notes are being recorded.
- Attempt to complete the focus for each lighting position to reduce the need for return access.
- Don't get distracted by nonelectrical matters. There are other members of the staff who can address crew call changes, wardrobe difficulties, or other pressing issues. You're the only one who can run the focus.
- Know the names of the people involved in the focus, write them down, and use them. The designer must give directions to many different individuals during a focus. If those instructions are given while turned away from the instrument, the electrician's name may be the only indication that the directions being given relate to the instrument.
- Be polite. When needed, ask for help. Respect your crew, your production team, and your hosts. You may be in charge of the focus, but you are the guest.
- Know when to continue, or when to stop the proceedings. If there's a problem, can it be fixed by someone else? Can it be worked on later? Can it be addressed while you continue somewhere else? Is there a work-around? Circuitry or color mix-ups may need to be reassigned as secondary "distractions" to getting the instruments pointed. On the other hand, there may be a problem that's safety related. Stop your work immediately and bring worklight up on the stage.

FOCUS TIPS

Consider these focus tips:

- Mentally rehearse the focus for the next instrument while the electrician completes the current unit. Consider other elements that may affect the focus. Scenery or additional spike marks may be required.
- Be aware of any other elements adjacent to the beam of the instrument. Stand back and look for beam edges that may be striking architecture, masking goods, or scenery.
- Establish a communication with the focusing electrician. Make certain you both know when the other is waiting for instruction, confirmation, or a response.

- Choreograph each position of the focus. Select the most difficult instrument to reach first. This prevents the first unit that has already been pointed from getting hit by the electrician while trying to focus the second unit.
- If time is limited to record an original focus, consider prewriting the focus on the charts in pencil. Written notes during the focus may be reduced to corrections or changes from the original plan.
- When focusing a system wash from a single hanging position, consider initially skipping other instruments and focusing that entire system. Repeating the same task can be faster. For example, if the electrician has memorized the focus for a system of backlight (the Fresnel is 3/4 flood, is hot on quarter and centerline, and top of the beam drops off the border), then activate those channels, and "run across the pipe," duplicating that focus. A second pass across the electric will allow the rest of the systems or specials to be focused.
- If two electricians are available to focus the front of house lights, consider using them to mirror the instruments on opposite sides.
- Delay any electrical or focus tasks accessible from the deck until last. The relative ease with which equipment in that position can be fixed, changed, and focused will make the end of the focus session go much faster.

 Sneaky Tip: Focusing Ellipsoidals
One reason ellipsoidals are used is their ability to shape the edge of light with the shutters. What some lighting designers constantly deny is the fact that the "fuzziness" or softness of the edge of an unshuttered beam of light will often be different than the beam edge shaped by a shutter cut. When shutters are used, designers often care more about the fuzziness of the shutter cut than the rest of the unshuttered beam.

Many focus sessions have been observed where the designer instructs the electrician to run the barrel to the desired softness while watching the beam edge of an unshuttered ellipsoidal. After the "correct" fuzziness has been achieved, the designer then instructs the electrician to push in a shutter cut. When that's been accomplished, the designer then instructs the electrician to run the barrel again, so that the shuttered edge is now correctly softened. If the amount of time consumed to run the barrel the second time is multiplied by the number of ellipsoidals, the result is time that could have been applied to other endeavors.

If the softness of the shutter cut is important, the first barrel run can be bypassed. Once the instrument has been pointed and locked, push a shutter into the beam of light (ideally one that will be used in the final focus). Run the barrel until the shutter is correctly softened. Then lock the barrel—once. Shape the light and move on.

 Sneaky Tip: Focusing Orphans
Every light plot has an extra lighting instrument here and there that'll be labeled "special." It's been placed there, as the legendary lighting designer Gilbert Hemsley would say, "as a GMOT! A Get Me Out of Trouble special!" Its purpose is vaguely defined, or it may presently have no purpose at all. But it's there just in case there's a need to isolate something, make something brighter, or become that extra special.

Before they have a purpose, however, these specials are orphans without an assigned intent. When possible, assign a dimmer and a channel to the orphans, and focus all of them. If dimmer allocation is tight, keep the circuits separated, but combine them into a single dimmer. If there's been no opportunity to see a rehearsal, check with the stage manager, and focus the orphans to locations that seem like they might become important.

Before skipping the focus of an orphan, remember the amount of preparation and time it took for the electrician to reach that hanging position. Then point that orphan somewhere. Anywhere. Who knows, it might become the missing piece of inspiration.

Though they have no assigned purpose, if your assumptions are correct, an orphan may save the flow of a technical rehearsal. When the request is received to "make that area even brighter," it may be possible to turn *something* on. It may not be the right color, and it may not be the correct focus. But by responding immediately to the request, it may allow the rehearsal to continue. After the rehearsal, or in the next work call, refine the focus and color of the instrument to its new purpose. It's no longer an orphan. It has a home.

 Shelley's Soapbox: Use the Hot Spot of the Light
Occasionally, inexperienced lighting designers can be observed focusing the hot spot of an instrument at a focus point. While shaping the light, they then direct a

shutter or a barndoor to be inserted in a manner that eliminates the hot spot. A typical example of this procedure can be seen in the focus of a pipe end instrument. After focusing an instrument's hot spot in line with a black masking leg, a side shutter cut then inserted to the very same leg. This would appear to be a waste of light.

The question that begs to be asked is "What's the point?" If the beam of light has a purpose, don't defeat that purpose by trying to stick to the rules. Use as much of the light as possible. Focus the hot spot so that, after shaping the light, the hot spot still remains.

The reason to use the hot spot of the beam in the focused instrument is also one of practicality. When the shutter is pushed far into the body of the instrument, the buildup of heat within the reflector can cause severe damage to the instrument. Extended use of the instrument in this position may eventually warp the shutters, making them difficult to utilize in the future. More immediate, however, is the fact that the heat can build up enough to cause the lamp to burn out, or to cause the socket in the instrument to melt down. Ill-focused art can't be seen if the instrument doesn't function.

Golden Rule: Is There a Light Cue Featuring This Instrument by Itself?

Sometimes an instrument is encountered during the focus session that just won't cooperate. After the focusing electrician has unsuccessfully attempted to angle the shutter cut for the third time, or more than three minutes have been spent focusing that instrument, it's time to ask the question: "Will there be a light cue in the show featuring this instrument by itself?"

If the answer is "no," then stop killing yourself and your electrician. There's no reason to focus this instrument absolutely perfectly. A lot of other instruments probably still remain that must be focused. Successfully repairing the cranky instrument that took 45 minutes to fix isn't much of a triumph if only half the plot is focused. On the other hand, if the full plot is focused with one broken instrument, so be it. This single instrument will not make or break the show. Approximate a focus, and move on.

The bottom line is, keep moving. Don't allow a single problem to overwhelm, stall, or freeze you. Let someone else address that problem while you continue with the next position. If there's a problem in the overhead electrics, note the problem and continue through the rest of the focus. If there's time at the end of the focus to return to this nasty instrument, swap it for a different unit. If that can't occur, then the instrument is at least vaguely functional and will not be pointed into the director's eyes. Avoid the moment when the conclusion is made that, after the fact, the instrument wasn't that important anyway. If that time translates into overtime for the crew, you'll be very sorry.

One final note: This rule can be extended to entire systems of light. If the downstage shutter cuts on the frontlights don't exactly match, remember that in most cases there will be backlight on as well. The backlight may very well wash out the uneven shutter cuts in the frontlight from the audience angle of observation.

FOCUS CHECKLISTS

This next section is a series of checklists that warrant consideration prior to the beginning of a focus session. Reviewing these lists can avoid delays.

The Environment

Items that are ideally complete before the focus session begins:

- The electrics are rung out, trimmed, set, and masked. The sidelight booms are immobilized. The sidelight ladders are tied off. The deck rovers are plugged and positioned. There's been a channel check and possible problems have been noted on the instrument schedule or focus schedule.
- The stage performance surface is clear. The area that you and the overhead ladder will occupy has been swept so that the lighting designer doesn't trip, and so the wheels of the ladder don't catch and tip the ladder over.
- All spike marks and/or webbings are set. The designer has already rehearsed much of the focus in his or her head and believes that every spike mark that may be needed has been placed.
- The scenery is preset. Ideally, the performance surface is down. As much of the scenic package as possible is preset into position before the focus begins. Borders and legs are at trim. The downstage backdrop in the scenic stack has been

landed to confirm the upstage light line. If not all of the scenic goods are available, spike marks have been placed to serve as signposts. Obviously, the ideal is to have all the scenery placed prior to the beginning of the focus. Less time is spent mentally pretending where everything is going to be, so that more time can concentrate on the focus.

- The sound check is complete or scheduled for another time. The piano tuning is complete. Any audio that would compete with the lighting designer communicating with the focusing electrician, the board operator, or any assistants is complete.
- Other audio distractions are dispersed. People who need to scream at each other are convinced to take their discussion elsewhere. Projects involving noisy power tools are relocated. Musical instruments requiring tuning or practice are directed to a separate space.
- All extraneous light is reduced. The amount of ambient worklight is reduced or eliminated so that it's possible to see the beam of light and see everything the beam is hitting. The house lights are taken down to half or to a glow. If worklights must be on for work to continue, can only the offstage lights be used?
- The spare equipment and perishables are in accessible locations.
- If there's a scribe, an office position has been created onstage, so that the designer's directions can be heard, and the focus can be recorded. The office position includes a writing surface, a worklight, and enough copies of the forms. The scribe understands how to fill out, report, or update the focus charts.
- The channel caller has a worklight, accurate paperwork, and communication to the board operator. If the channel caller is the lighting designer, do you have a flashlight?
- The board operator knows how to run the console, and can activate and deactivate channels, groups, subs, and can repatch, unpatch, and park dimmers.
- Confirm that the house ladder used for overhead focus has some kind of drop line to facilitate equipment transport to and from the focusing electrician. Otherwise, much time will be spent going up and down, rather than focusing the instruments.

- Consider the installation of a storage area somewhere adjacent to the focusing electrician on the ladder. This may be as complex as an "apron" with pockets, or as simple as a bucket on a drop line. By providing a storage space, the electrician has both hands free to focus, and it reduces the time spent searching or acquiring the proper color or tool.
- If a staff electrician knows the focus, ask permission for him or her to focus the show. After they've seen the focus once, good electricians will begin to memorize the focus, and reduce the amount of time and communication required.
- If a staff electrician knows the show, the console, and the focus methods that are used, ask permission for him or her to run the light board for the focus. Many theatres will permit the "road elec" to run the board. It will often speed the focus session.

The Lighting Designer

A list of items the lighting designer should consider while preparing for the focus:

- Know the constrained vertical boundaries for the production; have a section handy to check the trims of all scenic goods.
- Know the constrained horizontal boundaries for the piece; the spike marks are showing the different onstage edges of the wing and drop scenery, or the location of the not-quite-here-yet walls and doors.
- Know where the downstage and upstage edges of the performance surface are (or will be).
- Know which lights are used in relation to which scenery; make note of individual cuts in the documents referred to while pointing and shaping the lighting instruments.
- The system and special spike groundplans are available to either confirm locations or record additional marks.
- The lighting console is loaded with whatever infrastructure information will be used.
- Worklight control has been assigned; if there are no worklights in the light plot, or if the worklights are in a remote location, a full stage desaturated system wash has been assigned to a

submaster for that additional task. It will always be possible to get light on the stage.

Before the Electrician Departs the Stage

✓ A list to consider before the electrician leaves the stage for a hanging position:

- The channels have been checked for burnouts, color errors, and template accuracy. The electrician is prepared to address problems with a test light, spare lamps, replacement color, frosts, or accessories.
- Though it seems evident, the electrician has a wrench.
- The lighting designer (or the assistant) has accurate paperwork to activate channels. The lighting designer (or the assistant) has focus charts that are readable and easily filled out.
- The electrician knows how to focus each type of instrument at the position.
- The lighting designer knows the mechanics and semantics to properly and rapidly direct the focus for each type of instrument at the position.

FOCUSING THE *HOKEY* LIGHT PLOT

These next sections examine techniques, tactics, and work-arounds used in focusing different systems in the *Hokey* light plot. An actual focus is conducted in an order resembling the instrument schedule; an electrician gains access to a hanging position, and the instruments are focused in order, one unit after another. In contrast to that, these sections will analyze and illustrate the focus of the *Hokey* light plot system by system.

Front of House Positions

The hanging positions that are usually focused first are the front of house instruments (the FOH). From a practical perspective, this is due to the fact that the installation of equipment in those hanging positions is often completed before most of the locations on stage. From a design perspective, the primary reason to focus the FOH first is because they're typically the least flexible locations in the theatre. In most cases, it's difficult, if not impossible, to change their position relative

to the stage. The rest of the hanging locations, along with the scenery and masking, can shift if need be to accommodate architectural or scenic limitations.

Once the FOH focus is complete, the upstage boundaries of the front of house systems will be known. This allows the lighting designer to judge the relative depth of the focus points for the remaining zones in each system. The remaining hanging positions or focus points involved in those systems may need to shift to ensure an even blend of light between the two zones. For example, if there are frontlight systems in the overhead electrics that continue coverage upstage from the FOH positions, the lighting designer had best be certain of the location of all the focus points. Focusing the overhead instruments first, prior to focusing the FOH instruments, may result in a drop in intensity between the two zones of the system. The result may be a second focus for the overhead instruments.

A typical FOH focus begins with the highest location. In the Hybrid Theatre, this means that the truss focus will be the initial starting point. After the truss is completed, the electricians will move to the box booms, and finish the front of house by focusing the instruments on the balcony rail.

✓ A list to consider before focusing the front of house instruments:

- Vertical constraints (onstage edge of black masking legs, or scenic legs, or onstage edges of walls) are placed at playing trim. If the actual goods aren't available, spike marks have been placed to identify the location of the goods. Specific shutter or barndoor cuts relating to these constraints are recorded on the lighting designer's focusing document.
- Horizontal constraints (portal border, main curtain, midstage drops, scrims, and the scenic stack) are at playing trim or are indicated with spike marks. Specific shutter or barndoor cuts relating to the constraints are recorded on the lighting designer's focusing document.
- Any offstage constraints, like an adjustable proscenium or side house speaker stacks, are placed, spiked, or noted.
- Spike marks indicating the eventual center axis of each beam of straight frontlight have been placed along the apron, or on the seating in the house, or webbings have been taped down.

- The downstage edge of the performance surface has been defined. If the performance surface isn't installed before the focus session, spike marks have been placed to indicate the future downstage edge.

Shelley's Notes: Where Is the Downstage Edge?

Sometimes the frontlight will be focused prior to the installation of the performance surface. If the downstage edge of the frontlight will require a cut, the planned location of the downstage edge of the performance surface may become important to the lighting designer.

Why? If the performance surface is black but doesn't cover the light-colored apron, the frontlight may make the exposed apron glow like neon. Or the shadows from the backlight, otherwise undetected, may be seen on the apron, and might steal stage focus from the performers. The typical solution for this situation is to cover the surface of the exposed apron with velour or a fabric matching the color of the performance surface. If the downstage edge of the performance surface ends up nowhere near the location agreed upon, on the other hand, alternate choices may have to be made. In most cases, efforts to mask the exposed apron will be faster and better for the show than changing the focus of the backlight. Better yet, if the location of the downstage edge can be determined prior to the focus, the appropriate cuts can be made, and the additional effort can be avoided altogether.

Whenever possible, avoid situations in which the entire electrics department is on hold, waiting for the downstage edge to be determined by being physically installed. The focusing electricians, after reaching hanging positions, may then be forced to wait in unnatural positions while haggling, that should have taken place long ago, now disrupts the focus session. When this situation occurs, make a conservative estimate based on your best judgment, and stop waiting for the downstage edge.

It's also wise to define the location of the edge of the stage prior to the focus session. Many theatres are equipped with hydraulic pit lifts, which can be lowered to increase the size of the orchestra pit, or raised to increase the size of the apron. If the decision is made to keep the pit lift in the "up" position for the show, then the frontlight can extend downstage onto the apron. This additional light may be useful to illuminate performers who cross downstage of the light line during the bows. If the pit lift's position is lowered after the focus, however, the frontlight focus should be immediately checked. The bottom beam edges may now be splashing onto the front edge of the stage, gaining much more visual attention than desired.

Straight Frontlight Plotting Analysis

The term frontlight is applied to instruments and their light beams that provide facial illumination to the audience. Straight frontlight plots an instrument directly downstage of each focus point, while area frontlight often has a pair of instruments equidistantly spaced on either side of each focus point. Straight frontlight used as the sole source of facial illumination can result in a relatively "flat" appearance from the audience. The performer's face is solely shaped by the shadows that are created relative to the vertical height between the instrument and the performer's head. The successful use of straight frontlight may depend upon supplemental box boom or area frontlight to help provide a more dimensional shape to the performer's face and figure. On the other hand, since straight frontlight is directly downstage of the focus point, this also means that it can often be used more successfully to isolate a performer than most light projected from a front diagonal angle.

The primary goals of frontlight are to provide visibility, allow the audience to see the performer's faces, and to direct the audience's stage focus. Frontlight is often plotted to every anticipated performer location. Coverage may be broken into areas of control, depending on the type of performance, the size of the performance space, and the amount of scenery involved.

A typical frontlight wash consists of an even blend of several instruments into a single zone. Often several zones are plotted, to provide overlapping coverage for the entire depth of stage. If frontlight visibility isn't required upstage, on the other hand, the wash may be reduced to a single downstage zone of frontlight. If a frontlight wash is controlled as a single channel, the need to carefully blend shutter cuts between beams is reduced, since the individual edges won't be isolated. If the frontlight system consists of several channels to provide isolation, however, the beam edges may need to be softer, so that attention isn't drawn to the edges of sharply focused frontlight.

Straight Frontlight Focus

The *Hokey* light plot has two straight frontlight washes on the FOH truss, colored in Roscolux 33 and

Lee 161. The upstage zones of the washes will be provided by instruments hung on the first and second overhead electrics.

Figure 9.3 shows channels 1 > 5, the instruments highlighted inside rectangles on the FOH truss. Colored in Roscolux 33, they'll be focused as the first zone in the pink straight frontlight system for *Hokey*. The apron spike marks, along with the front zone 1 centerline spike mark, provide the triangulation for the focus points. The same focus will be duplicated for channels 11 > 15, the Lee 161 blue frontlight wash. The first instrument that will be focused is unit #6, which will be focused on centerline.

Figure 9.4 is an abbreviated focus chart. The number in the small circle located in the upper left-hand corner indicates the channel number. The text under the circle is the position and the unit number. The

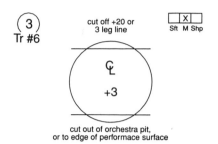

Figure 9.4 Focus Chart for Truss #6

large circle in the middle of the drawing represents the unshaped beam of light (seen as if the viewer were standing behind the instrument). The text inside the circle indicates the *X* and *Y* coordinates of the focus point. Lines running through the circle indicate shut-

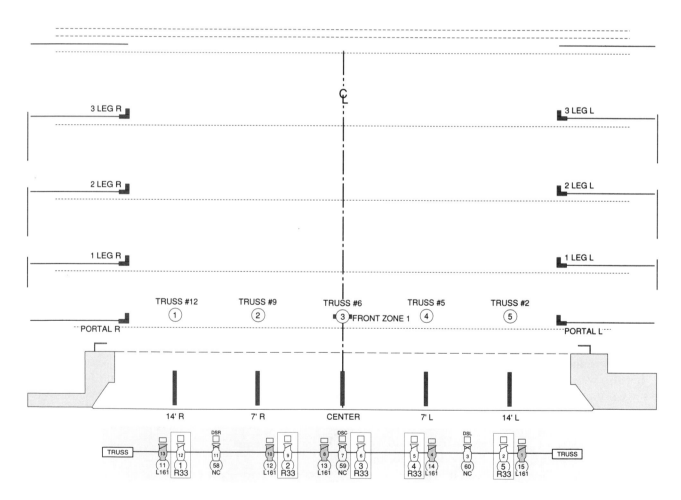

Figure 9.3 The Frontlight Instruments and Their Focus Points

ter or barndoor cuts. The small rectangles on the right side show the barrel softness of the instrument (Soft, Medium, or Sharp).

In this case, truss unit #6 is controlled by channel 3. The focus point is on centerline, 3'-0" upstage of plaster line. The barrel will be moved to provide a medium soft beam edge. The upstage shutter cut will be 20'-0" upstage of plaster line or at the #3 leg line. The downstage cut will be out of the orchestra pit or to the edge of the performance surface.

Figure 9.5 shows channels 1 > 5, after the five instruments have been pointed. Channels 1 and 5 will require side cuts to keep light off the black masking legs. All five channels will require top cuts off of the scenic stack (or the #3 leg line), and bottom cuts to the edge of the performance surface.

Figure 9.6 shows channels 1 > 5 after the shutter cuts have been executed. To achieve side-to-side blending, all of the barrels are medium soft. Though these diagrams show all of the instruments pointed, and then shuttered in two separate steps, each instrument

will be shuttered after it's been pointed during the actual focus. The focus of the first zone of pink straight frontlight is now complete.

Shelley's Notes: Straight Frontlight Tips and Work-Arounds

In many cases, when a theatre owns the frontlight equipment, the instruments have been hung in place for years. Without proper maintenance, there will be dysfunctional units. Since down center is often considered the most important location in most productions, that portion of the stage should be equipped to be brighter than the rest of the frontlight. If the instrument assigned to the down center frontlight is discovered to be dysfunctional, consider "swapping the focus" with another unit in the same system. A good instrument, previously assigned to focus on the quarter line, for example, can exchange focus assignments with the dysfunctional unit. The good instrument can focus to center, while the bad unit takes its place, and

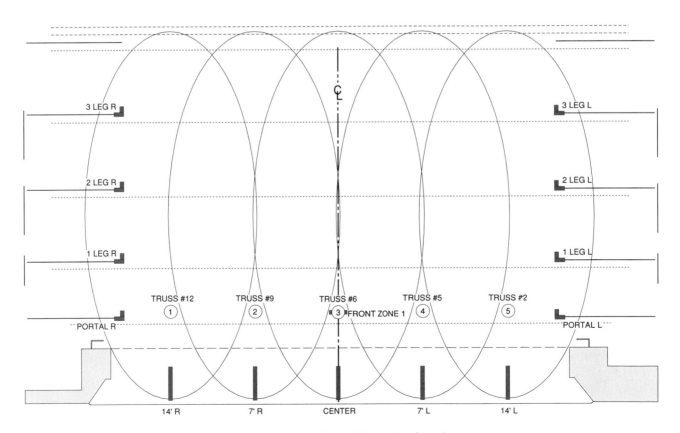

Figure 9.5 The Focused Frontlight Pools Before Shuttering

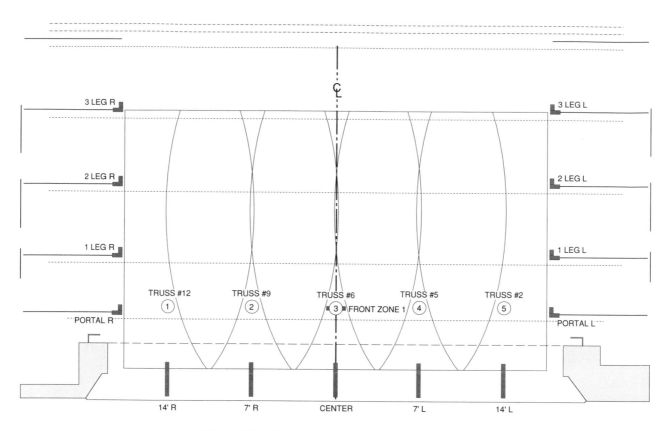

Figure 9.6 The Focused Frontlight Pools After Shuttering

focuses to quarter line. Once focused, the softpatch can be altered so that the channel assignments are also exchanged.

Often, two zones of frontlight may be mounted above and below the same FOH hanging position. To retain the focus angle, the sectional view would imply that the bottom hung instruments focus to the downstage zone, while the tophung instruments focus to the upstage zone. If the portal border prevents the tophung instruments from providing the desired upstage coverage, though, it may be necessary to ask "Which instrument has the best opportunity to get to the desired focus point?" This may result in ignoring common wisdom and cross-focusing the instruments; the tophung instruments focus to the downstage zone, while the underhung instruments focus upstage, allowing them to shoot under the portal border and reach further upstage.

Front portals (or other soft goods) will occasionally be used for only a portion of a production. When these scenic pieces are in place, their leg opening is typically less wide than the adjacent black masking legs. If any frontlight systems are used while the por-

tal is in place, keeping light off the portal results in the offstage instruments in the system having more extreme side shutter cuts. Offstage instruments in other frontlight systems will provide farther offstage coverage, since their side shutter cuts will remain open to the black masking. If all of the frontlight systems are turned on when the portal is in place, however, common wisdom dictates that the side shutters of all of the offstage instruments must cut off the portal. In that situation, the choice is often made to dedicate the side instruments of only one frontlight system for use when the portal is in place. The alternate solution is to add a duplicate pair of offstage instruments in the same color to the system. The first offstage instruments will be cut off the portal, and used when the portal is present. The added offstage instruments, in the same color, are used instead when the portal is removed, and frontlight coverage is required offstage to the black masking legs.

Box Boom Plotting Analysis

If the light plot contains no area light systems, instruments in the box boom systems can assist in providing facial dimensionality from the front of house. The object of a completed box boom focus is a wash of light, originating from a front diagonal hanging position in the house, which provides even coverage across the stage. The coverage usually begins at the downstage edge of the playing area at the light line. Sometimes this system is continued upstage with instruments hung at matching diagonal frontlight locations in the overhead electrics. Other times the angles and colors used in the system can be continued, with varying degrees of success, using instruments in matching colors mounted on sidelight booms.

Box Boom Focus

Architecture, the height of the hanging location, scenery, and any equipment attached to the proscenium are only a few of the obstacles standing in the

way of allowing this even coverage to occur. In an effort to retain as much light as possible, while shuttering off unwanted distractions, the barrel focus of box boom instruments is typically sharper edged than that of the frontlights.

Figure 9.7 shows channel 30 controlling units #3 and #6 on the stage left box boom. Colored in Roscolux 51, they'll be focused as the stage left lavender box boom system for *Hokey*. The downstage light line spike marks, along with the stage right masking legs, provide the triangulation for the focus points. Unit #3 is a Source Four-26° ellipsoidal, which will focus to the far throw focus point, while unit #6, a 6 × 9 (40° beam spread) ellipsoidal, will focus to the near throw focus point. This focus will be duplicated for channels 40 and 50 on the stage left box boom, and channels 29, 39, and 49 on the stage right box

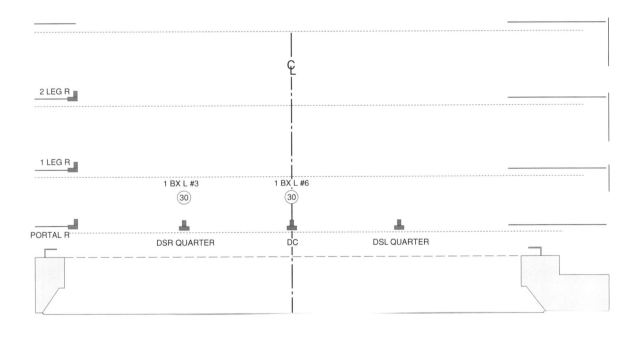

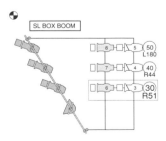

Figure 9.7 The Box Boom Instruments and Their Focus Points

boom. Unit #3's hanging position is more difficult to access by the electrician, so it will be focused first, on the far throw focus point.

Figure 9.8 is an abbreviated focus chart showing that the preliminary focus point for unit #3 is 9'-0" stage right of centerline, and 5'-0" upstage of plaster line. The shutter cuts will eliminate the portions of the beam that splash light onto the black masking or onto the front of the stage. When the instrument is pointed, however, it quickly becomes apparent that shuttering successfully off the black masking legs will mean cutting through the hot spot of the light beam.

Figure 9.9 shows channel 30, after the focus points have been shifted, and the instruments have been pointed. This is the point at which the overlap and blend between the two instruments should be checked. If there's a "dark hole," or a drop in intensity between the two instruments, the focus points and their hot spots should be adjusted closer to each other. When the blend between the two beams is acceptable, the shutters should be applied. Unit #3 will still require shutter cuts to avoid splashing the black mask-

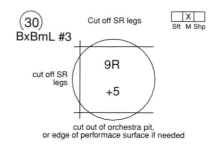

Figure 9.8   Focus Chart for Box Boom Left #3

ing legs, while unit #6 will require a side cut to keep light off the stage left proscenium.

Figure 9.10 shows channel 30 after the shutter cuts have been executed. The side cuts between the two instruments were left open, to provide as much beam overlap as possible. Attempting to provide as much coverage as possible, while keeping light shuttered off the masking and architecture, means that the beam edges may be sharper than the straight front-

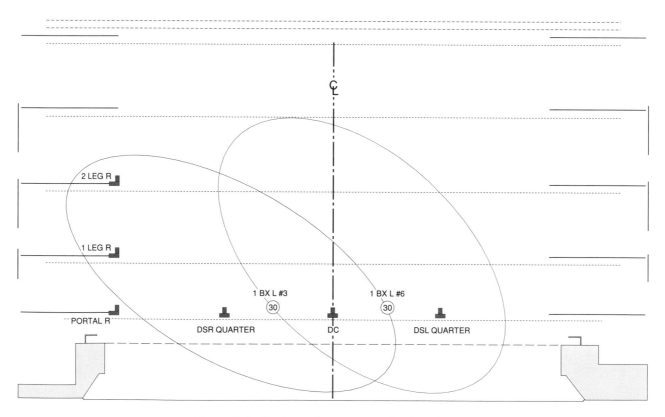

Figure 9.9   The Focused Box Boom Pools Before Shuttering

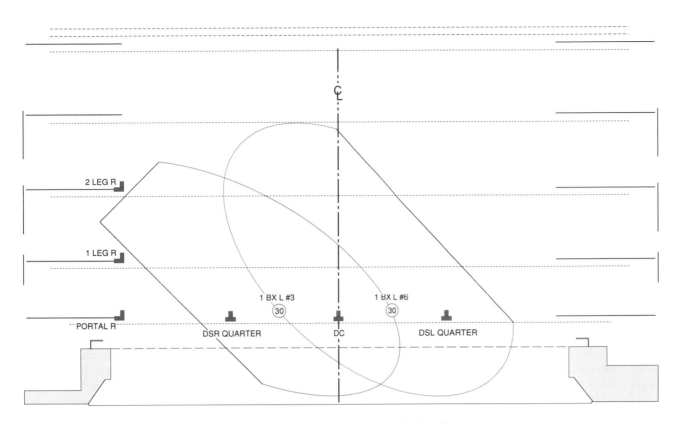

Figure 9.10 The Focused Box Boom Pools After Shuttering

light system. The focus of the stage left lavender box boom system is now complete.

Shelley's Notes: Box Boom Tips and Work-Arounds

No matter how many beam sections are drawn, the final box boom focus may be completely different than what was planned. In theory, the box boom system is often used to provide a wash of frontlight from a different angle than straight frontlight. If reality demands that the focus points be shifted to create an even wash, adapt to the situation and move on. The previous example demonstrated this adaptation. The objective is often reduced to merely using as much of the beam as possible. If the scenery isn't in place during the focus, knowing the placement of all scenic elements becomes important.

Usually, once the focus for the first box boom system is determined, that focus is copied for the other color systems. This will work well for *Hokey*, since the box boom instruments are all hung at the same height above the stage. Many theatres, though, have

box boom positions that stack pairs of instruments below each other. In these situations, the top layer of instruments is usually focused first, so that the electrician "works down" the position. The challenge may develop with the lower layers of instruments. The system of focus points and shutter cuts that worked on the highest layer of instruments may not work at all two or three layers down. Since the lower instruments are at a reduced angle to the stage, duplicating the system of shutter cuts used on the top layer might result in thin slices of light.

If that's a possibility, consider plotting the most unsaturated colors at the top of the box boom, and the more saturated colors at the bottom of the position. While still providing facial coverage, instruments from the lower location create more light (and the resulting shadows from performers) onto the masking legs. If the color is saturated enough, however, the shadows won't be noticed on the masking legs. Of course, if the legs are white, completely different shutter cuts should be considered.

When the location of the hanging position in relation to the stage is awkward, the alternatives may be few and time consuming as well. Choices include rehanging the instruments to a higher position, rehanging the instruments to a different position, or eliminating the instruments altogether. Focusing the instruments in their present position may result in abandoning any structure where the focus points make any sense. The instruments are focused merely to provide as much coverage from that angle as possible, while cutting off the scenery and the architecture. If the choice is made to eliminate the units, and the plot doesn't include area frontlight, quick thinking may be required to provide light in the near corner of the stage if the performers step out of the straight frontlight.

In some theatres, the box boom positions are difficult to access, and the instruments may have been hung there long ago. If that's the case, there's little doubt that they've received little maintenance. Shutters may be "sticky," absent, or just plain immovable. Recognizing this situation can alter the box boom focus priorities from pointing the ideal wash to getting light on the stage with the least movement, the fewest shutter cuts, using the least amount of time. This is a perfect situation to apply the golden rule: "Will there be a cue with this system on by itself?" If the answer given is a confident "no," then the task has been simplified: Get light on the stage, out of the pit, and off the scenery. Remember, there'll probably be backlight in the light cues, which will obliterate the beam edges or the peculiar shutter cuts from the audience's angle of observation.

If top shutter cuts will be inevitable, reducing the number of other cuts in the instrument may mean raising the hot spot of the instrument. This elevation may land the beam edge on the stage, and eliminate the need for a bottom shutter cut. Although the hot spots will no longer be at their designated focus points, the wash will be focused in half the time and the frustration level will remain low. Sometimes the opposite situation occurs; when the focus point is in the middle of the first opening, the hot spot may land on the far masking legs. If the top shutters are sticky, the solution may be to lower the focus point. Though this will "drop the focus," it will eliminate the need for a top shutter cut, and the focus can proceed.

Box Boom Cross Focus

Usually, instruments hung on box booms are assigned focus points so that the light beams from the instruments don't cross. When cross-focusing is attempted, the barrels of the instruments may bump into each other while trying to achieve the focus. This barrel-bumping occurs when

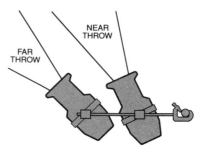

Figure 9.11 Typical Box Boom Focus

the units aren't hung far enough apart, and the focus can be slowed while the electrician rehangs one of the instruments to provide more space between them. In most cases, it's not worth the effort. In some theatres, though, the box boom's location may force a reevaluation of this plotting method.

Figure 9.11 is a groundplan showing the common method of plotting and focus assigned to box boom instruments. Unit #1 is focusing to the far throw focus point, while unit #2 is focusing to the near throw focus point. In some theatres, however, unit #2 can't get focus "around" the near side of the proscenium. Although the beams of the instruments can be focused closer together, unit #2 will still require extensive side shuttering.

Figure 9.12 is a groundplan showing the same two instruments "cross-focusing," contrary to common wisdom. Unit #1 is focusing to the near throw focus point, while unit #2 is focusing to the far throw focus point. The instruments have been hung further apart on the sidearm to prevent the barrels from bumping into each other.

Filling In Box Boom Coverage

Sometimes the box boom position is so close to the proscenium it's not possible to utilize a near instrument. When the continuation of the color is more important to the design

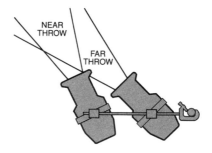

Figure 9.12 Cross Box Boom Focus

than matching the angle, consider using an additional instrument from a different location.

Figure 9.13 is a groundplan showing box boom units #1 and #2 focused to the far and center throw focus points. The near throw focus point coverage is provided by truss unit #3. Although its focused as a straight frontlight to the near side of the stage, its colored to match the same color as the box boom units. Although the angle doesn't match, the color coverage will be consistent across the stage.

✋ Sneaky Tip: Box Booms during Bows

Since it's downstage of the proscenium, box boom light can be used to cover performers during bows, when they're most likely to walk downstage of the light line to the edge of the stage. To allow for this possibility, the shutter cuts of focused box boom lights can be left open downstage of the light line, to provide as much light downstage as possible. It may be possible to leave the bottom of the beam open, which can mean one or two less shutter cuts that have to be made. On the other hand, sometimes the apron is deep, but unused until the bows. Although the downstage side of the box boom light may remain unshuttered to cover the bows, this may result in too much light being seen downstage of the light line for the rest of the performance.

If there's enough instrumentation and hanging space available at the box boom position, focus an additional pair of units specifically for the bows on the apron and put them on a submaster. The rest of the box boom lights can remain shuttered to the light line, and the stage manager can call for the submaster at his or her discretion. The added pair don't need to be recorded as a separate cue.

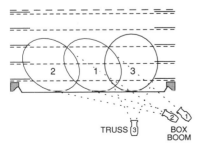

Figure 9.13 Near Fill Box Boom Coverage

Frontlight Drop Wash Analysis

Backdrops in the scenic stack are usually lit from striplights or cyc lights overhead and groundrows below. The combination provides an even wash of light over the entire surface of the backdrop. On the other hand, when a show drop is used instead of a main curtain, the drop is often hung downstage of the first electric. Other situations may find a midstage or upstage drop inserted in such tight quarters that it is impossible to squeeze in a set of striplights to provide any kind of wash. In these cases, the choices are reduced. One solution might be to use footlights or other instrumentation mounted on the apron or in the orchestra pit. When that's not an available solution, the common alternative is to use a frontlight drop wash.

Although drop washes from the box boom position aren't out of the question, the angle of the light to the drop is slanted, or oblique. When a light striking a surface is from an oblique angle, the beam edge will not be the same on the near and far sides. Roughly translated, if the instrument is not shooting straight onto the drop, but from the box boom instead, the shutter cuts will be a different sharpness on either side, due to the difference in the actual throw distance from one side of the beam to the other. Attempting to focus a wash from an angle to produce an even intensity over the entire surface of a drop can be very time consuming, and involve a lot of diffusion.

Since there is no need to provide three dimensionality, the instruments assigned to produce even washes of frontlight on downstage drops are usually located at the balcony rail position, and placed so that they focus straight into the goods. The lower the position, the easier it is to provide light as high as possible on the drop, up under the borders.

Frontlight Drop Wash Focus

When focusing a drop wash, it's advisable to start in the center to be certain that the wash will be symmetrical. To produce an overall wash of equal intensity, the beam edges are softened to blend together. When ellipsoidals are used, consider supplying the focusing electricians with several different kinds of diffusion to blend the beam edges in the middle of the drop.

☑ A list to consider before focusing a drop wash system:

- The drop needs to be at in-trim. Period. This is one system which requires the goods to be seen to ensure an even blend, and eliminate the need for a touch-up.

- Any masking used specifically to mask the drop when it's at playing trim should also be at in-trim. If the drop isn't large enough to "fill" the portal opening, this might include an additional masking border and legs.
- Determine the staging for the scene. The location of the performers in relation to the drop may affect the height of the focus points on the drop, the location of any bottom cuts, or the focus arrangement of a template wash.

Figure 9.14A is a simple front elevation showing a masking border and two masking legs surrounding a downstage drop. The six circles represent pools of light from six instruments hung on the balcony rail. They have been pointed to provide full drop wash coverage. The pools overlap, so that the hot spots of the beams of light almost touch the edges of adjacent pools. The beams of light extend outside the drop area.

Usually the top row is focused first, to reduce the chance that there will be dark spots between the top row and the bottom row. If the bottom row needs to

be raised to achieve smooth coverage, facial frontlight may fill in any darkness at the bottom of the drop. After all of the instruments are pointed and locked, Figure 9.14B shows how the shutters would be cut to the shape of the drop. When the shutter cuts are made, no tiny circular edges from the beams will be left in the corners of the drop.

It's worth noting, however, that anyone standing in front of the drop will cast their shadow onto the drop (Figure 9.14C). If there will be extensive per-former activity, it may make sense to consider raising the focus of the instruments.

Figure 9.15A shows the focus of what will be a partial drop wash. The focus points have been raised so that after shuttering, more light gets out of the in-struments (Figure 9.15B). This provides more light on the drop, and reduces the amount of shutter burn in-side the instrument. When shuttered, the bottom cuts are above the performer's head (Figure 9.15C).

The drop should be investigated before the plot is constructed, and examined before the focus session. If the drop has a painted sky or some other design ele-ment, Figure 9.16A shows how a reduced drop wash using only 3 instruments might be pointed.

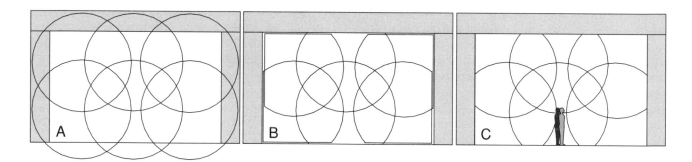

Figure 9.14 A Full Drop Focus Before and After Shuttering

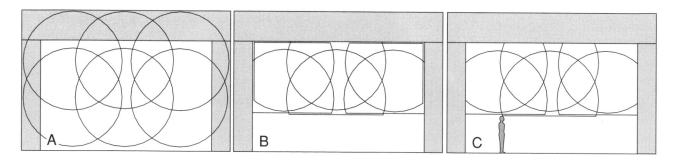

Figure 9.15 A Raised Partial Drop Focus Before and After Shuttering

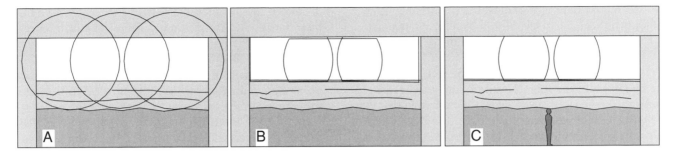

Figure 9.16 A Reduced Drop Focus Before and After Shuttering

Figure 9.16B shows the bottom cuts shuttered in to blend into the horizon line of the drop. After the shutter cuts are complete, the top "sky" of the drop is illuminated, and the bottom cuts are above the performer's head (Figure 9.16C).

Leg Wash Analysis

Unlike black legs that try to disappear, scenic legs contain a design that's intended to be seen. In most cases, scenic legs are hung equidistant from center, so that each pair of legs provides the same width of leg opening. Attempting to cast light onto scenic legs can be frustrating. Attempting to light the legs with instruments hung directly downstage on the balcony rail will result in lighting only the first leg and leaving the rest of the legs in shadow. However, if the same instrument is panned across and focused onto the legs on the opposite side of the stage, all of the legs receive light. To light as much of the legs as far offstage as possible (and reduce the chance of shadows being cast on upstage legs), the instruments used for a leg wash get hung as far from centerline as possible, and focused across the stage.

The same light, focused on the opposite legs, will also cast light on the proscenium or borders, causing sharp shadow lines on the legs. The lowest border is often viewed as the horizontal constraint. So the top shutter, cutting light off the border, eliminates the sharp shadow. Once the light is shuttered off of the borders, the barrel focus may cause the shutter to produce as sharp an edge as the original shadow from the lowest border. For that reason, the barrel of the instrument is typically softened, so that the beam edge is soft and fades into darkness.

Border trims define the top shutter cut, and since they may be lower than drawn on the section, the instruments used for a leg wash are usually hung as low as possible. The bottom of the box boom or the ends of the balcony rail are the typical positions of choice. The lower the better, so that the beams can cast light higher onto the scenic legs, under the lowest border. The bottom cut is defined by the height of whatever shadow-causing objects may pass between the light beams and the scenic legs. Shadow-causing objects can include tall hats, spears, scenery, or performers being lifted during entrances or exits.

The number of instruments required for a leg wash depends on the throw distance, the beam spread of the selected units, the number of legs involved, and the overall depth of the stage occupied by the legs. If there are more than two sets of legs in a typical stage depth, at least two instruments are used from each side. This ensures that the shutter cuts can be achieved, and eliminates the possibility of the curved beam edges being seen.

Leg Wash Focus

A list to consider before focusing a leg wash system:

- Either the scenic leg or spike marks indicating their onstage edges need to be placed prior to focus. If the legs are hung but can't come to their in-trim position during the focus session, the position of the spike marks should be double-checked by standing on each spike mark and looking straight up to confirm the leg's location.
- The borders, whether they're scenic or black, should be at their performance trim. Approximate top cuts can be made, but there may be no time to return to the hanging position for a touch-up focus.
- Whatever is downstage of the first scenic legs needs to be either in position or spiked. This

scenic element is also masking the offstage edge of the scenic leg. Usually, the scenic element is a black portal leg or the proscenium.

In Figure 9.17, two additional Source Four-26° ellipsoidals from the stage left box boom will be focused onto the stage right scenic legs. One formula that can be used to determine the location of the hot spots begins by measuring the distance from the masking downstage of the first scenic leg (in this case, the black portal leg) to the scenic backing (in this case, the black scrim). In the *Hokey* groundplan, that distance is 23'-

3″. When the distance is divided by three, the two intersections will be 7'-9″ apart. These focus references will be spiked in line with the onstage edge of the legs.

Figure 9.18 shows the focus chart for the downstage instrument in the leg wash. Although the focus point is indicated, it will initially be used to indicate the center of the horizontal axis of the beam.

Once the instrument has been pointed towards the focus reference spike mark, the beam will be raised, so that the hot spot is halfway up the scenic leg.

Figure 9.19 shows the leg wash instruments after they have been pointed. When viewed from the front,

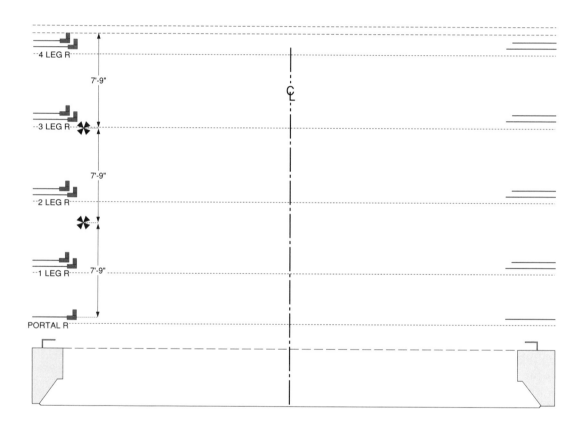

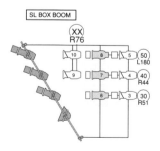

Figure 9.17 The Leg Wash Instruments and Their Focus Points

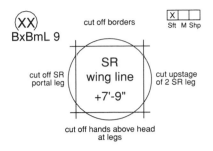

Figure 9.18 Focus Chart for Box Boom Left #9

the beams are pointed approximately halfway up the leg, so that the bottoms of the beams are close to the bottom of the leg. At this point, the overlap and blend between the two instruments should be checked. The instruments will receive side shutter cuts off the black portal masking leg and the black scrim upstage.

Figure 9.20 shows the leg wash instruments after the side shutter cuts have been applied. Top shutter cuts will eliminate light off the borders. Once the top

cuts have been achieved, the designer will stand at the onstage side of the legs, and raise his or her hands above his or her head. The bottom shutters will cut in until they're touching the bottom of all of the legs. While they maintain that angle, the shutters will then continue cutting in until they reach the top of the designer's hands.

Figure 9.21 is a front view showing the completed leg wash focus, indicating where the top and bottom shutters were applied. In reality, the shutter cuts are usually soft and match between the units. The height of the top cut may be adapted if the border trims change height during the show. The bottom cut may be adapted depending on the height of performer traffic moving through the opening.

If shadow-causing objects are tall, the location of the bottom cut may need to be more extreme. Either the bottom cut needs to be pushed further into the instrument, or the intensity of the leg wash will need to be reduced when the shadow-causing objects pass through the beam of light. The focus of one side of the leg wash system is now complete.

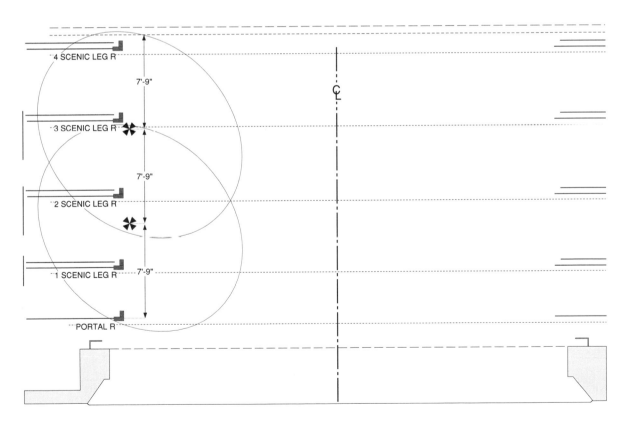

Figure 9.19 The Focused Leg Wash Pools Before Shuttering

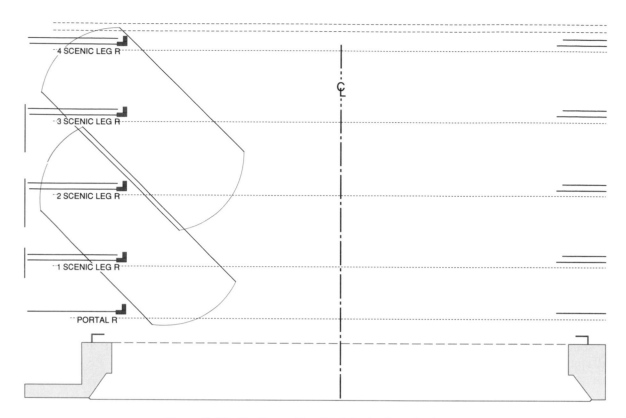

Figure 9.20 The Focused Leg Wash Pools After Side Shuttering

 Shelley's Notes: Leg Wash Work-Arounds

If there's no balcony rail in the theatre, and the box boom doesn't get low enough to provide an adequate shot, the leg wash system can be hung in a third location.

Figure 9.22 is a groundplan showing an instrument mounted on a boom in the first opening stage left, offstage and out of the audience's sightlines. It can provide some light on the scenic legs. The instrument will be mounted higher on the boom than any shadow-causing object. Otherwise, if the object moves through the first opening stage left while the leg wash instrument is on, the object will suddenly be very bright and distract attention from the scene.

Sometimes the leg wash can be placed on a separate boom downstage of the proscenium, though this may require additional masking. Or it may be possible to place a boom in the seating area, though this should

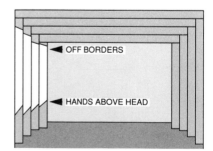

Figure 9.21 The Focused Leg Wash Pools After Top and Bottom Shuttering

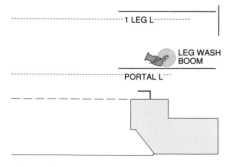

Figure 9.22 A Third Leg Wash Hanging Position

be carefully considered and cleared with the management of the theatre.

Overhead Positions

The focus of the overhead electrics usually involves a focusing electrician perched on top of a ladder, lift, or hoist. The ladder is usually castered so a ladder crew can move it about the stage. In most cases, moving a ladder from one opening to another can take some amount of time. Rather than focusing each instrument in a single system, an overhead electric focus usually addresses each electric, one instrument at a time. The ladder starts at one end of the electric, and moves across the stage as each instrument is focused, finishing at the opposite end of the same electric. Once the final instrument has been completed, the ladder is moved to the next electric position upstage. Instruments in the overhead electrics are often assigned to several different systems that focus to different locations on the stage. Because of that, placing the ladder in a position which allows the electrician to focus each instrument, while staying out of the way of its light

beam, can be complex and time-consuming. Depending on the type of ladder used, minutes can go by merely maneuvering it from the downstage side to the upstage side of the same electric. For that matter, some amount of time is necessary to move the ladder from one side of the stage to the other. The fewer movements taken by the ladder, the faster the focus.

For this reason, the choreography of the ladder must be taken into account. When up or downstage movement of the ladder takes too much time, it makes sense to limit the number of those movements. In many cases, if the ladder is on one side of the electric, it will be faster to focus only those instruments or systems on that electric that require the ladder on that side. Then the ladder gets repositioned to the opposite side of the electric—once. After repositioning, a second pass will be taken to focus the remaining instruments on the same electric.

When the ladder finishes one electric, it may be faster to start the next electric from the same side of the stage, rather than take time to move the ladder across. For example, Figure 9.23 shows the first two overhead electrics. After unit #19 (the final instrument

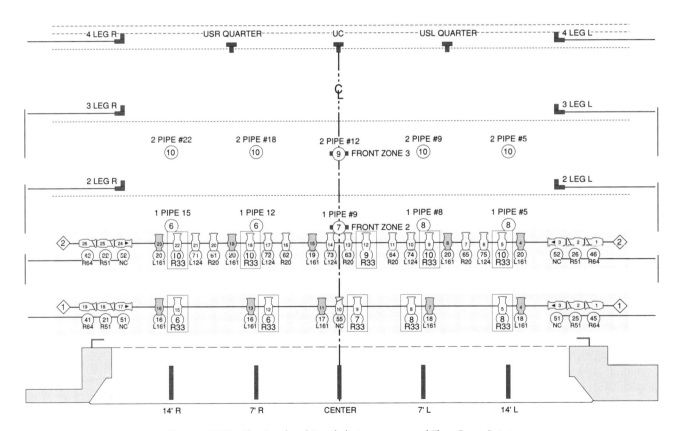

Figure 9.23 The Overhead Frontlight Instruments and Their Focus Points

on the first electric) has been focused, consider moving the ladder directly upstage to unit #26 on the second electric, rather than second electric unit #1.

The prefocus and final focused positions of the instruments should also be considered before the focus begins. Often, the instruments are prefocused while hanging straight down, so that several beams of light from instruments in the same channel don't obliterate the ability to see the beam in question. If there is a series of pipe end sidelights, consider beginning with the most onstage unit of the series. Otherwise, unit #2 may block the focus of unit #1.

This is the portion of the focus when the focus cues can come into play. If that is the plan, then be certain everyone knows the ladder choreography, which has been determined by the order of memories 1 > 100 that were programmed into the lighting console.

✔️ A list to consider before focusing overhead electrics:

- Confirm that the borders are at playing trim.
- Confirm that all legs are at playing trim, or spike marks are present to define their location.
- Confirm that any scenic portals are lowered to trim.
- If any scenery needs to be flown in and out during the focus, a stagehand is assigned to the fly rail, and knows that you may be requiring the movement of flown scenery.
- The stage is clear of nails or screws that might trip the casters under the ladder.
- There are enough stagehands assigned to the bottom of the ladder to move it efficiently.
- The stagehands are listening to the electrician, who's at the top of the ladder, for his or her movement directions.
- Perform a channel check (if one has not yet been performed) of the entire overhead to determine nonfunctioning instruments. If time allows, examine the softpatch for errors to reduce the number of possible explanations for inoperable instruments.

Although the instruments in overhead electrics are realistically focused in sequential order, the focus for each system in the *Hokey* light plot will continue to be individually illustrated. The overhead frontlight focus will be discussed first.

Overhead Frontlight Focus

The overhead frontlight washes may be a continuation of the frontlight system originating from the front of house. In this case, the two frontlight washes for *Hokey* consist of three zones each. The first zone was hung on the front of house truss. The next two zones are hung on the first and second electrics.

Figure 9.23 shows channels 6 > 10, the instruments on the first and second electric, colored in Roscolux 33. When focused, they'll act as the second and third zone in the pink straight frontlight system for *Hokey*. The apron spike marks, along with the front zone 2 and 3 centerline spike marks, provide the triangulation for the focus points. The masking leg spike marks will provide signposts for side shutter cuts if the legs aren't in place during the focus session, while the upstage T's (the light line) provide the signposts for top cuts if the scenic stack is absent. This focus will be duplicated for channels 16 > 20, the Lee 161 blue straight frontlight wash. The first instrument that will be focused is 1 electric unit #9, which will be focused on centerline. This unit will be focused first to ensure that the upstage frontlight will be focused symmetrically.

Figure 9.24 shows the focus chart for unit #9 on the first electric The preliminary focus point is on centerline, 10'-0" upstage of plaster line. The beam is intended to remain open, except for a possible top shutter cut off of the #1 black border upstage of the electric, or the black scrim in the scenic stack.

Before starting the focus of the entire frontlight system on the first electric, the placement of the second zone of focus points should first be double-checked. This is done by standing on the centerline focus point in the second zone, and activating the center channel of the first zone of frontlight. In this case, that would be unit #6 on the truss, controlled by channel 3. If the

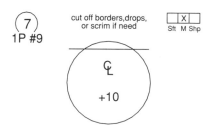

Figure 9.24 Focus Chart for 1 Electric #9

light from channel 3 is hitting the lighting designer above eye level, the first electric beams should adequately overlap, and the placement of the second zone focus points should be correct. If the upstage edge of channel 3 isn't reaching the designer's eyes, the second zone focus points may need to move downstage, or the top cuts in the first zone instruments may need to be opened to retain an up and downstage blend between the two zones. After the focus of 1 Electric #9 has been completed, the combined beams of the two centerline instruments, channels 3 and 7, should result in a blended frontlight system between the two zones. The same double-check should be performed between channels 7 and 9 before the entire frontlight system on the second electric is focused.

Figure 9.25 shows channels 6 > 10 after the 10 instruments have been pointed. The offstage instruments in channels 6, 8, and 10 will require side cuts to keep light off the black masking legs. Channels 9 and 10 will require top cuts to eliminate unwanted portions of the beams from the black scrim.

Figure 9.26 shows channels 6 > 10 after the shutter cuts have been executed. To achieve side-to-side blending, the barrels are all medium soft. Though these diagrams show all of the instruments pointed, and then shuttered in two separate steps, each instrument will be shuttered after it's been pointed during the actual focus. The focus of the second and third zones of pink straight frontlight is now complete. Group 1 can be activated to check the focus and blend of the entire straight frontlight system.

Overhead Sidelight Plotting Analysis

Overhead sidelight systems are often used to provide dimensionality for the performers and three-dimensional scenery. When walls are involved in the scenic design, overhead sidelight can gain even more importance. If backlight can't reach particular areas of the stage, the overhead sidelight may be the only system that can prevent an area from looking "flat," a result of being lit only with frontlight. In many situations, overhead sidelights can be plotted like another

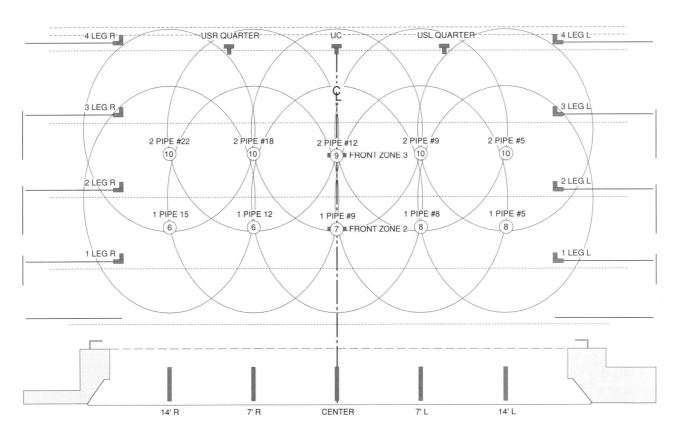

Figure 9.25 The Focused Overhead Frontlight Pools Before Shuttering

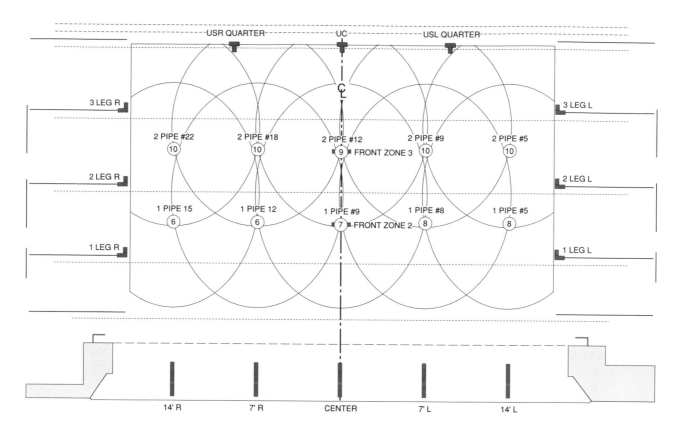

Figure 9.26 The Focused Overhead Frontlight Pools After Shuttering

system of frontlight, with a pair of instruments from each side focusing to the same focus points as the frontlight.

At other times, overhead sidelight can be plotted to provide a wash from either side. This type of plotting can result in the use of fewer instruments. Rather than matching the focus points for frontlights, a front section allows the lighting designer to calculate unique focus points that provide an even blend of coverage. For example, the blend may be achieved with three instruments that are focused to the far quarter line, the centerline, and the near quarter line of each opening. Since the length of battens may vary, this type of wash may combine hanging positions. The far and center instruments may be hung on the overhead electrics, while the near instrument is mounted high on a sidelight boom. The height of the boom unit often duplicates the angle from the other focus points to the overhead units, so that the same angle of light is projected onto the near quarter line of the stage.

Another manner of overhead sidelight plots only a single instrument at the end of a batten to create a single wash of light to the opposite side of the stage. Instead of plotting additional overhead instruments to "complete" the angle of light from the near side, this manner of plotting relies on boom sidelight to "fill in" the coverage from the near side.

When overhead sidelights are used in scenic designs involving side walls, providing coverage at head height invariably implies that the beam will also be splashing onto the wall. Though a top shutter cut can reduce the amount of light on the wall, the beam is usually softened, so that the edge of the beam "fades out," rather than abruptly stopping with a barrel focused to a sharp edge. A stage without scenery, however, presents a different scenario. Often, the instrument focused to the far quarter line also splashes light onto the black masking legs. To reduce halation and retain as much light as possible, the barrel is often focused so that the shutter edge is sharp. To reduce the amount of light hitting the legs, the upstage shutter is then cut off of the black masking leg that defines the upstage side of the opening containing the overhead sidelight.

Producing a high angle sidelight from an overhead electric often results in the instruments being hung as far offstage as possible at the end of the batten. This common hanging location has become another name for the system. Overhead sidelights hung at the end of a batten are also referred to as pipe ends.

Overhead Sidelight Focus

The *Hokey* light plot has two pipe end systems, colored in Roscolux 51 and 64. Although a templated instrument can be seen adjacent to the pair, its focus will be different. The focus of the two pipe end systems will be discussed first.

Figure 9.27 shows the instruments and the focus points for channels 25 > 28, controlling the second instruments on the first, second, fourth, and fifth electrics. Colored in Roscolux 51, they'll be focused as the stage left lavender pipe end system for *Hokey*. The downstage and upstage quarter line spike marks, along with the stage right masking legs, provide the triangulation for the focus points.

The focus points for both the overhead sidelight and the boom sidelight may be shifted up or down-stage, depending on the amount of the black masking that is attempting to be hidden. In this case, the finished focus for the system will attempt to eliminate as much of the light on the black masking legs as possible. To do so, the focus points of the three upstage pipe ends are shifted downstage from the middle of each opening. While the focus point for channel 25 is in the middle of the first opening, the focus points for the rest of the system are located at the intersection between the stage right quarter line and the black masking leg downstage of each electric. The locations of the leg spike marks will be used not only to locate the focus points, they'll also be the objects of the side shutter cuts as well. This focus will be duplicated for channels 45 > 48, the stage left blue pipe end system.

Figure 9.28 shows that the preliminary focus point for unit #2 is 9'-0" stage right of centerline, and in the middle of the first opening. The shutter cuts will eliminate the portions of the beam that splash light onto the black masking on either side of the opening.

It is believed that the performers will not be lifted in the air near the onstage side of the legs, so the top

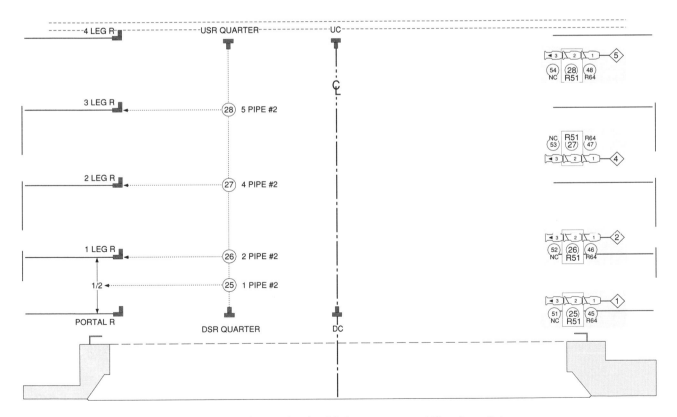

Figure 9.27 The Overhead Sidelight Instruments and Their Focus Points

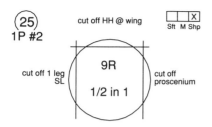

Figure 9.28 Focus Chart for 1 Electric #2

shutter will cut the beam above the top of the tallest performer's head (Head High) standing next to the black legs.

Figure 9.29 shows channels 25 > 28 after the instruments have been pointed. Side cuts will be required on all of the instruments to keep light off the black masking legs. The other three instruments will also receive the same top cut as channel 21.

Figure 9.30 shows channels 25 > 28 after the shutter cuts have been executed. To keep light off the black legs, while using as much of the beam as possible, the units have a sharp focus. The focus of the stage left lavender pipe end system is now complete. Group 4 can be activated to check the focus and blend of the system.

Depending on the relative trims of the electrics and the borders, it may be necessary to cut the shutters even more. If light is hitting the back of a border, it should be shuttered to eliminate that spill. Although some light may be lost, it will prevent light from bouncing off the back of the downstage border, onto the next border upstage of the electric. Not shuttering the light would reduce the effect of a clean black environment. More than that, however, it's also a matter of safety.

Golden Rule: Cut Beams of Light Off Close Combustibles

Sometimes instruments are hung in locations so close that the units are close to soft goods or other objects that can burn. Flame-retardant products can be applied to fabric to reduce the chance that the heat from an instrument could start a fire. In addition, several

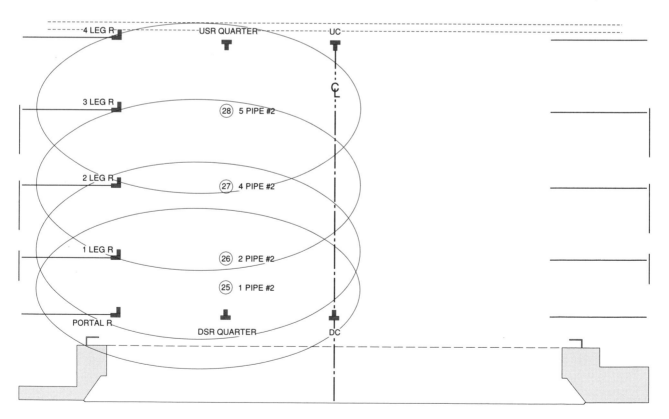

Figure 9.29 The Focused Overhead Sidelight Pools Before Shuttering

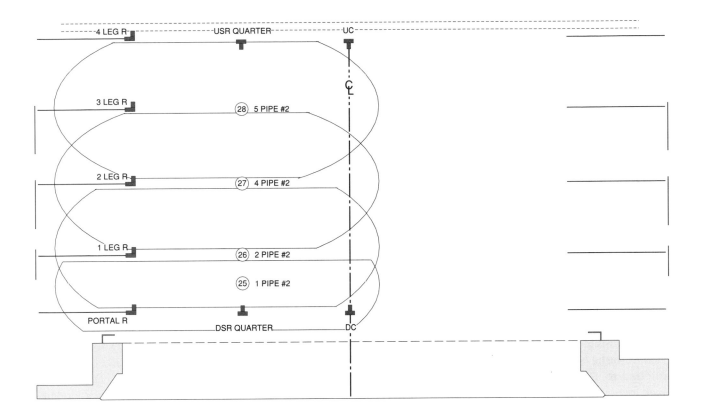

Figure 9.30 The Focused Overhead Sidelight Pools After Shuttering

different fabrics that are constructed of heat-insulating material, can be draped between the instrument and anything combustible.

As the lighting designer, you shouldn't have to worry if the hanging location of the instruments is close to soft goods or scenery. From a perspective of time management, however, it's wise to watch for those potential problems. Unnoticed, fixing fire safety issues can later consume time that was intended to be used completing electrical tasks. Setting the trims can be delayed when the electrics have to be lowered down to the stage so that heat-resistant material can be tied to the batten. Worse yet is losing focus time while the focusing electrician ties heat-insulating material to the batten in the air. If there's no material to insulate the instrument, it may be necessary to rehang the unit or just turn the instrument off.

In addition to the heat of the instrument itself, the heat of the beam coming out of the unit can also be intense enough to start a fire. As such, beams splashing on soft goods close to the instrument can not only be a visual distraction, they can more importantly be a potential fire-starter. Overhead sidelight, downlight, backlight, and boom sidelight are all systems that may require an additional shutter cut to be certain there's no chance that their beams could make the masking smolder. During the focus, be aware of this hazard and address it. Never allow carelessness on your part to contribute to a disaster.

If you're not convinced, look up any of the numbers of tragedies involving fire in the history of theatre. It's sobering and often the cause of the fire was traced to someone who was thoughtless. As a member of the theatrical community, matters of fire safety should be burned deep in your mind. As one of the people in charge, you should contribute to setting safety standards. Strive to be aware of, and address, any potential hazards.

Overhead Template Plotting Analysis

A template is a thin piece of metal containing holes. When inserted into the gate of an ellipsoidal, its beam of light is reshaped to mirror the design of the holes. Since templates "break up" the light coming out of an ellipsoidal, they are perceived as producing "textured" light. Depending on the angle, direction, color, intensity, and movement chosen to be used, templated light can provide dimensionality, define a location, establish a time of day, or evoke a feeling. They are usually used in four main applications.

First, templates can be focused from overhead positions to produce textured light on horizontal surfaces, such as the stage. A templated instrument producing a pattern of light similar to light passing through a window, for example, can define the location of the scene as an interior. If the same instrument is equipped with a different template to produce a pattern of light similar to light passing through trees, it can establish the scene as an exterior. An abstract "breakup" pattern, on the other hand, might be used to merely produce blobs of light on the stage, and affect the perception of the audience.

Second, templates can be used to add texture and dimensionality onto vertical scenery. If a painted backdrop contains a design of a lake, a template can be focused onto the water painted in the drop. After being shuttered to the boundaries of the water in a soft-edged focus, the mottled spots of light will add texture to the lake. If a scenic design consists of several walls, on the other hand, a series of templated instruments can project a breakup pattern high on the walls. At a reduced intensity, the pattern visually adds texture to the flat surfaces.

Third, templates can be used to supply texture and dimensionality to animate or inanimate objects on the stage. One example of this can be seen as a result of templates inserted into low-angled sidelights. When focused as a typical boom sidelight system, the "mottled" light can be seen on the side of performer's bodies as they move about the stage. Another example can be seen when templates are projected onto a unit set centered on the stage. When templated light is projected onto the scenery, it adds dimension to the otherwise flat surfaces.

Finally, templates can be used to apply texture to the air. When an atmospheric generator is used within a confined performance space, it produces a haze that may not be seen until lights strike the particles in the air. Beams of light, otherwise unnoticed, can change the look and perception of an entire scene, shaped by the different shafts of light now seen by the introduction of the haze. The number of beams (defined by the number of holes) from a templated unit can give the appearance of multiple sources of light produced by a single source. When this look is employed, the relative

hanging locations for template systems may be as important a choice as the kind of ellipsoidal or the particular template used. Instruments hung on overhead electrics, for example, are often located at specific distances from centerline, so that their beams will produce symmetrical shafts in the air.

Templated light is often designed to combine these applications. They may be included in a plot to light both the stage and the performers moving through the space, or they may be designed to project light that is both seen in the air and strike objects on the stage.

Occasionally, templates will be used to provide a breakup pattern over an entire backdrop. To produce this effect, initial choices are made to define the hanging position, the beam spread, and the number of ellipsoidals. To maintain a consistent focus for the beam edge of each "hole" in the template, the instruments are often located so that the templates focus straight into the backdrop. As a result of this choice, the instruments are often placed either on the first electric or the balcony rail. Drawing a section from either position shows an accurate spread of coverage using beam spreads of various sizes. Determining which size of beam spread to specify is directly related to the number of instruments that will be used to cover the entire area of the backdrop. The common formula used to make this calculation is based on a general assumption. One cautious assumption states that the beam spread of a typical template will reduce the beam spread of an instrument by approximately 50%. Based on that assumption, the number of instruments of any particular beam spread can be determined.

Since templates are only applicable to ellipsoidals, the beam edge of each hole of light is affected by running the barrel. One typical dilemma faced by designers is caused by templated ellipsoidals whose sharp focus doesn't eliminate halation coming out of the instrument, in addition to the direct beams escaping through the holes. The scattered light diffuses the desired contrast between the holes, and reduces the mottling effect. One common solution to this problem is to insert a donut in front of the lens, or to exchange the instrument for another matching unit.

When template systems are used to "break up" an entire performance surface, they are often designed so that they produce as much patterned light as possible, while requiring the fewest instruments to achieve that coverage. To achieve the maximum actual throw distance for each instrument, the units are often plotted into side galleries, ladders, or overhead hanging positions. In the case of *Hokey*, an overhead pipe end template system contains a template called Dense Leaves. This system will be primarily used in the first scene of Act 2, conceived as a nighttime forest scene. Not only will the system cover the performance surface with this leafy pattern, reduced intensities of other systems will allow the textured light to appear on performers moving through the space as well.

Overhead Template Focus

The *Hokey* light plot has a single overhead template system using Rosco Designer Pattern 7733 templates. The system is hung in a pipe end sidelight configuration. Each unit will be focused to a different area so that the combined instruments cover the entire stage.

Figure 9.31 shows one side of the instruments and the focus points for channels 51 > 54, controlling the third instruments on the first, second, fourth, and fifth electrics. Specified as No Color units, they'll be left ungelled and focused as the stage left side overhead pipe end template system for *Hokey*. The downstage and upstage right quarter line spike marks, along with

the #1 and #3 stage right masking legs provide the focus point triangulation for channels 52 and 54. The same masking legs provide the upstage/downstage placement of channels 51 and 53. During focus, those templates will be focused to overlap at centerline and fill the stage with the pattern.

The focus points for the template system may be shifted on or offstage, so that the beams from channels 52 and 54 can remain as "open" as possible without using shutters. The focus points may also shift so that the pattern reaches as far offstage as possible without striking the downstage side of the black masking legs exposed to the audience. The focus points may also need to shift closer to the center of the stage as well, to ensure overlap coverage between the upstage and downstage zones.

Figure 9.32 shows that the preliminary focus point for unit #3 is 3'-0" stage right of centerline, and in line with the first black masking leg. The beam's task is to cover both the first and the second opening, while overlapping at center and blending with channel 52 farther offstage.

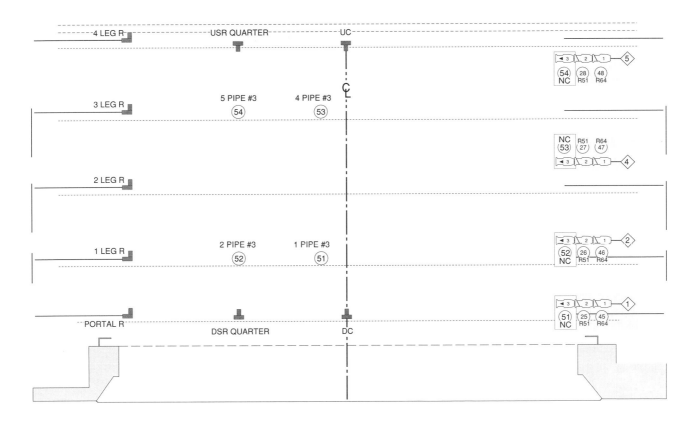

Figure 9.31 The Overhead Template Instruments and Their Focus Points

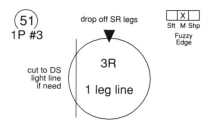

Figure 9.32 Focus Chart for 1 Electric #3

Since the template system's primary purpose is to cover the stage with a consistent pattern, less attention is paid to performer location. When the system is used as a primary source of light in the nighttime forest scene, it's planned that the additional templates inserted in the boom sidelights (channels 109 > 114) will "fill in" any locations not covered by the overhead system.

Figure 9.33 shows one side of channels 51 > 54 after the instruments have been pointed. The individ-

ual holes of light from the templates are not shown. This illustration is shown as if the templates have been removed.

Figure 9.34 shows channels 51 > 54 after the shutter cuts have been executed in the offstage instruments. The shutter cuts are used in the offstage instruments only to keep light off the black legs and the black scrim. The focus of the stage left template pipe end system is now complete. Once the other side of templates are focused, group 15 can be activated to check the focus and blend of the system.

Overhead Downlight Plotting Analysis

Downlight is usually viewed as shafts of light pointing straight down, so that the combined light beams form symmetrical pools, equidistantly overlapping left and right, and up and downstage. In reality, downlights rarely point straight down. An electric doesn't often get placed in the middle of an opening. In many cases, the instruments are hung on electrics which are located in the up or downstage side of an opening. When focused, the downlight instruments are slightly tipped

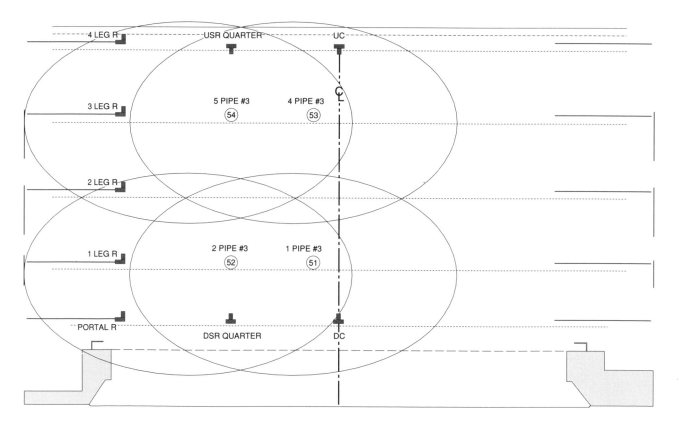

Figure 9.33 The Focused Overhead Template Pools Before Shuttering

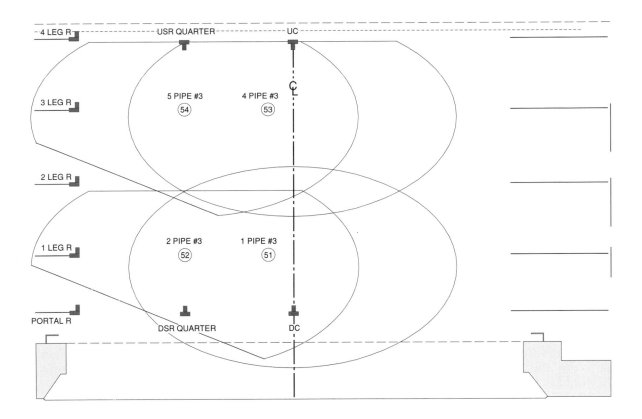

Figure 9.34 The Focused Overhead Template Pools After Shuttering

up or downstage so that the focused pools appear symmetrical to one another, producing that effect. Since this is one of the systems that is more obvious to the audience's angle of observation, however, care must be taken during the hang and the focus to create the illusion that the instruments are focused "straight" down.

While the focus points for downlights in the first zone can be centered in the middle of the opening, they may just as easily be shifted upstage, so that the downstage beam edges land close to the downstage light line. The focus points for downlights in the final zone, on the other hand, are often shifted downstage so that the upstage beam edges land at the upstage light line. If the section is drawn so that accurate trims and beam spreads of the instruments are shown, it will be clearly seen where the beam edges and focus points of intermediate zones will need to be located, so that the pools symmetrically overlap.

The number of downlight zones and the number of instruments used in each zone are different from show to show. When a production is presented on an open stage, the focus and symmetry of a downlight system will be much more apparent to the audience's angle of observation. Depending on the trim heights of the electrics and the instrumentation used, the number of zones is often equal to or less than the number of openings on the stage. Those same parameters are also used to determine a rough number of downlights across each zone. Once that initial coverage is defined, however, the number of instruments is often adjusted to make certain that the final amount of units in a single zone is an odd number, rather than an even one. One reason for this number adjustment is so that side pools can be dimmed, while any stage action at center can be reinforced. Using this method, the most basic system for one zone is considered to be as few as three pools across, focused on the centerline and the two quarter lines.

Typically, the desired appearance of downlight is a series of round pools. If at all possible, any shutter cuts or sharp beam edges from barndoors are avoided unless necessary. The first key to a successful downlight system starts when the instruments are plotted.

The beam spreads drawn in the section show if there's any chance that the edge of the light beams will hit scenery in the air. Sometimes entire electrics are shifted up or downstage to be certain that the beams of the downlights won't strike adjacent borders and thus require the downlight to receive a straight-edged shutter cut. If that's unavoidable, the cuts should match on all of the instruments in that zone. If a particular zone of downlights may need to tip upstage to produce equidistantly spaced pools between zones, it's ill advised to hang the instruments on an electric that has a border on the upstage side.

The second key to producing successful downlight systems relates to the instrument's hanging location on the electric. Units on one side of centerline should be equidistant to each other and to match their counterparts on the other side of centerline. Though they may not end up pointing straight down, their on and offstage hanging location should ideally be directly "in line" with each of the focus points. When that's not possible, the distances should be "mirrored" from one side to the other and matched between electrics.

The third key to the downlight system's success is to match the barrel softness, so that one beam doesn't stand out. If the production involves an atmospheric element like haze, the hanging positions and the beam edges will stand out even more. Care must be taken while focusing to ensure that the appearance of the light shafts are symmetrical.

Finally the success of a downlight system can be seen in the way in which it is controlled. If each instrument is assigned to an independent channel, the units can be used as a series of specials, isolating each portion of the stage. When dimmers or channels become scarce, attention should be paid to the blocking of the production. If there's little need for one side of the stage to be isolated, adjacent instruments in a zone may be combined. Another approach may be to combine the offstage channels of the second and third zones of downlight. Usually, the center instruments of each zone are jealously guarded to remain separate, since they can isolate different portions of the most important area of the stage.

Overhead Downlight Focus

The light plot for *Hokey* contains two downlight systems. Channels 61 > 70 are colored in Roscolux 20, and channels 71 > 80 are colored in Lee 124. Since a separate channel controls every instrument, the intent of the systems is to isolate areas of the stage or combine to wash the entire performance surface with a color. Though the two zones shown in the section cover the depth of the stage on the floor, the fact that there are only two zones, combined with the position of the electrics, doesn't provide any coverage at head height in the upstage side of the fourth opening.

Figure 9.35 shows channels 61 > 70, the instruments on the second and fourth electric, colored in Roscolux 20. When focused, they'll act as the first and second zone in the amber downlight system for *Hokey*. In this figure the positions of the electrics have been moved, so that the focus points can be seen. The apron spike marks and the down zone 1 and 2 centerline spike marks provide the triangulation for the focus points. The masking leg spike marks will again provide signposts for side shutter cuts if the legs aren't in place during the focus session, while the upstage and downstage T's provide the signposts for the edges of the beams. This focus will be duplicated for channels 71 > 80, the Lee 124 green downlight wash. The first instrument that will be focused is 2 electric unit #13, which will be focused on centerline. Again, this unit in the zone will be focused first in order to ensure that the system will have side-to-side symmetry. If circumstances dictated, 4 electric unit #9 could be the first instrument focused, followed by the rest of the instruments on that electric.

Figure 9.36 shows that the preliminary focus point for unit #13 is 8'-6" upstage of plaster line, standing on centerline. An additional note points out that the downstage edge of the beam should land at plaster line. The section has shown that the unit will be able to remain unshuttered. The barrel softness for the entire system will be medium soft.

Figure 9.37 shows channels 61 > 70 after the 10 instruments have been pointed. The offstage instruments in channels 61, 65, 66, and 70 will require side cuts to keep light off the black masking legs. The beam edges have landed in their positions without the beams hitting the borders, and no top or bottom cuts will be required.

Figure 9.38 shows channels 61 > 70 after the side shutter cuts have been executed. The focus of the amber downlight system is now complete. Group 7 can be activated to check the focus and blend of the system.

Overhead Backlight Plotting Analysis

Backlight is generally defined as a source originating above and "behind" a person standing on a stage. This often means that backlight is pointed downstage towards the audience, so that light covers the head and

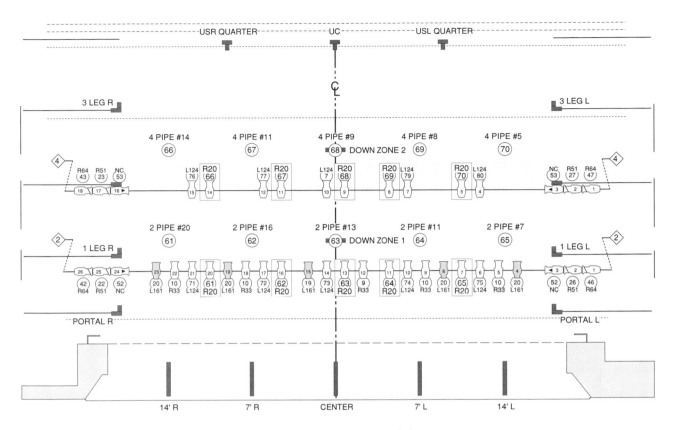

Figure 9.35 The Downlight Instruments and Their Focus Points

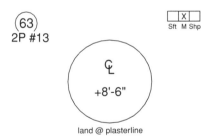

Figure 9.36 Focus Chart for 2 Electric #13

shoulders of the person. A full stage backlight wash in a single color typically covers the entire performance area, from side to side, and from the upstage scenic stack to head height at the downstage light line. To provide coverage at the downstage light line, backlight usually spills onto the apron, into the orchestra pit, or into the first rows of the audience. In many situations, this coverage is successfully achieved when each backlight electric is located in the upstage side of its particular opening between the borders. In that

way, the instruments can tip as far downstage as possible, under the next border closer to the audience, without being in view.

Backlight systems can be plotted in a variety of styles. Straight backlight is hung so that the instruments focus directly downstage to their focus points, while diagonal backlight uses a pair of instruments equidistantly spaced on either side of each focus point. Another style of backlight clusters instruments together near centerline, and then "fan focuses" the units out from center to the sides of the stage to cover the zone. Since each style of system incorporates a different number of instruments to provide coverage, each system creates different amounts of intensity on the performance surface.

Regardless of their plotted style, the number of backlight zones and the number of instruments used in each zone are specific to each situation. The width of the stage opening, the height of the overhead electrics, and the beam spread of the selected instruments are the main parameters that define the number of instruments required for each zone of light. The

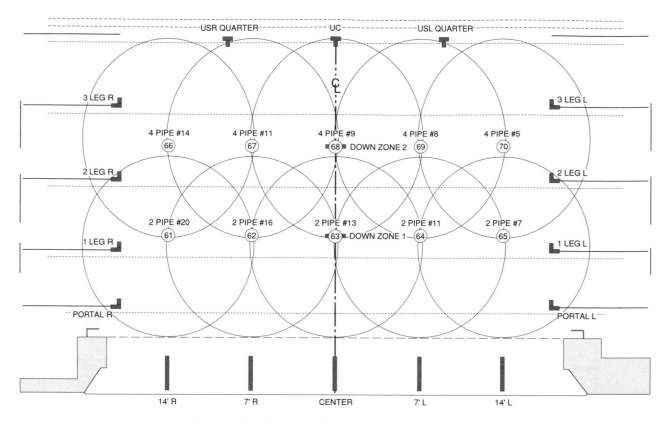

Figure 9.37 The Focused Downlight Pools Before Shuttering

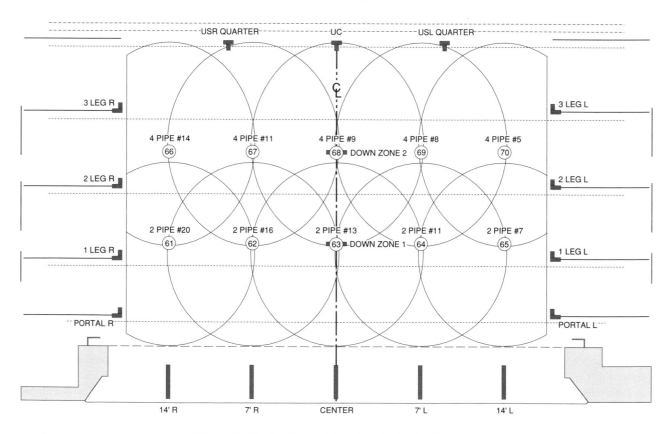

Figure 9.38 The Focused Downlight Pools After Shuttering

first key to a successful full stage backlight system begins with overlapping side-to-side coverage. A front view section, drawn with accurate beam spreads, helps determine the number of instruments required to adequately overlap the beams and provide an even zone of light. That same view also shows the distance required between each instrument and centerline to achieve this equidistant spacing. The distances between centerline and each instrument are often mirrored on all other backlight electrics, so that the beams match between zones. If the system is a straight back focus, then the instruments should be hung on the electrics so that the units merely tip downstage to reach the focus point. If the system is planned to be a diagonal focus, the instruments should be plotted to be consistently equidistant on either side of the focus points.

Providing adequate up and downstage coverage is the second key to a successful full stage backlight system. The combination of stage depth, trim height, and instrument beam spread defines the number of zones that will be required to provide coverage for the entire playing area. From the audience's angle of observation, an even blend of a single color on the floor eliminates the possibility of distractions caused by seeing bright or dark spots on the performance surface. After the trims and instrumentation are defined, the backlight electrics are placed. The upstage zone of a backlight system is often the first zone plotted, because the upstage beam edges of the pools can tip no further upstage without splashing onto the scenic stack. The section, drawn with an accurate beam spread, will clearly show where the downstage edge of the upstage beam drops below head height. That location is often defined as the placement for the next zone of focus points. To accommodate backlight systems, electrics may be shifted up or downstage, so that the borders downstage of an electric don't interfere with the backlight beams.

The third key to a successful full stage backlight system is symmetry in focus. Like downlight, instruments that don't match in size, beam edge, or beam shape can be seen from the audience's angle of observation. Usually, shutter cuts or sharp beam edges from barndoors are avoided, unless necessary to eliminate light off of masking. If a straight edge is required, it's usually matched for the entire zone.

If Fresnels are used in a backlight system, the softness of that instrument's beam edge and the accessories often required to control the beam can combine to make the instrument's use more challenging. If Fresnel backlight isn't carefully plotted, accessories may be required to prevent a portion of the offstage beams from striking the black masking legs high above the stage. Splashing the bottom 8 feet of a leg may be visually admissible, but streaking the leg with backlight color 15 feet above the stage is usually not acceptable. Since there's often no other light at that location, its presence will stand out. One solution to this situation might be to add a tophat in front of the Fresnel's lens. Although a tophat will eliminate scattered light, it can't shutter the beam. Another choice might be to add barndoors to the front lens of the instrument. Once the offstage door is positioned, the light on the leg would be eliminated. If the backlight electric is adjacent to any flying scenery, however, air currents above the stage may create conflicts of interest, which can result in torn soft goods or the opportunity to refocus the instrument.

Finally the success of a backlight system can be seen in how it is controlled. If each instrument is assigned to an independent channel, the units can be used as a series of specials, isolating each area of the stage. When dimmers or channels become scarce, the stage movement within the show should be reviewed. Depending on the locations isolated in the production, the sides of the upstage zone may be able to be joined together. Sometimes the entire upstage zone is controlled by a single channel. The amount of control required by a backlight system can also be affected by the color of the light. For example, a backlight system equipped with a cool or saturated color may be assigned fewer channels of control. A second backlight system, in the same light plot, may contain warmer or more desaturated color. Since that color may provide more intensity, the second system may be assigned more channels of control, and assume the task of providing isolation.

Overhead Backlight Focus

The light plot for *Hokey* contains two backlight washes. Channels 81 > 90 have no color, and channels 91 > 100 are colored in Roscolux 68. Since a separate channel controls every instrument, the intent of both systems is to isolate areas of the stage in either color.

Figure 9.39 shows channels 81 > 90, the instruments on the third and fifth electric using no color. When focused, they'll act as the first and second zone in the no color backlight system for *Hokey*. The apron spike marks and the back zone 1 and 2 centerline spike marks provide the triangulation for the focus points. The masking leg spike marks will again provide signposts for side shutter cuts if the legs aren't in

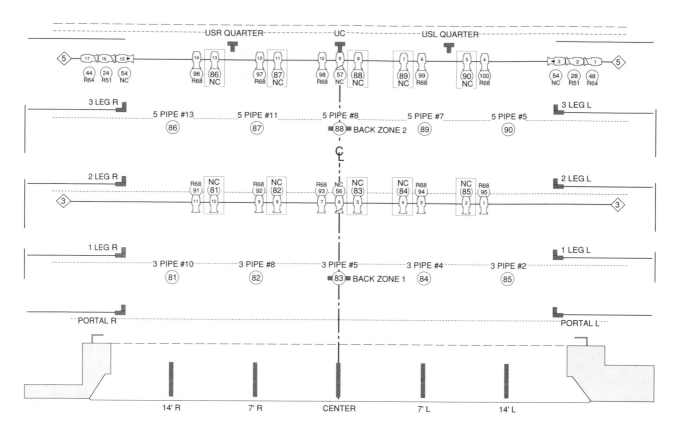

Figure 9.39 The Backlight Instruments and Their Focus Points

place during the focus session, while the upstage T's provide the signposts for the upstage edges of the beams. This focus will be duplicated for channels 91 > 100, the Roscolux 68 blue backlight wash. The first instrument that will be focused is 3 electric unit #5, which will be focused on centerline. Again, this unit in the zone will be focused first to ensure that the system will have side-to-side symmetry.

Figure 9.40 shows that the preliminary focus point for unit #5 is 3'-0" upstage of plaster line, stand-

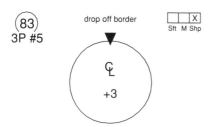

Figure 9.40 Focus Chart for 3 Electric #5

ing on centerline. Although this is the focus for a back-light, the focus chart still views the beam of light from behind the instrument. The note seen at the top of the circle indicates the top of the unshuttered beam should drop off the #1 black border on lineset 9.

While this instrument could be focused by standing on the focus point, an alternate method can also be used. The lighting designer can stand at the down-stage light line, with hands held above his or her head, as the instrument is slowly tipped until the downstage beam edge reaches the hands. When combined with the rest of the downstage zone beams, this should ensure backlight coverage at head height across the light line, and may also provide more light upstage. If the audience seating is close to the stage, a top shutter may be used to cut light below the audience's eyes.

Figure 9.41 shows channels 81 > 90 after the 10 instruments have been pointed. The offstage instruments in channels 81, 85, 66, and 90 will receive side cuts to keep light off the black masking legs. The beam edges have landed as planned, and no top or bottom cuts will be required.

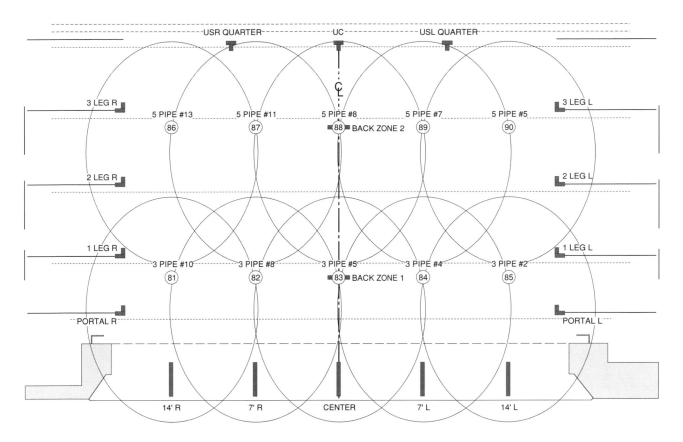

Figure 9.41 The Focused Backlight Pools Before Shuttering

Figure 9.42 shows channels 81 > 90 after the side shutter cuts have been executed. The focus of the no color backlight system is now complete. Group 9 can be activated to check the focus and blend of the system.

Boom Sidelight Positions

Sidelight booms are often the final hanging positions to be addressed in the focus session. Since the positions are closer and more accessible from the deck, more instruments can be simultaneously focused in a shorter amount of time.

If a ladder is required, its position relative to the boom is essential to the speed of the focus. Successfully placing a focusing electrician in the air somewhere near the instrument has little value if the electrician's hands can't get to the focusing apparatus of the instrument. It can also be counterproductive if the ladder placement doesn't allow the electrician to

see the beam of light that he or she is focusing. For those reasons, attention must be paid to the amount of deck equipment that is intended to be stored around the base of the booms. When possible, this equipment should not be placed until the instruments requiring ladder access have been focused. Even without the interference of deck equipment, the lack of backstage space may force the legs to be flown out, so that the ladder can be navigated into a working position for the focus. To accurately define the location for any side shutter cuts in that situation, the spike marks indicating the onstage edge of the black legs can then be used.

If the booms are tall, their height and balance can be a safety concern. When the boom is initially hung, attempts should be made to hang the sidearms and yokes of the instruments as they will be focused. When the boom is then tied off, its center of balance won't radically change as instruments are rehung into performance positions. This will also reduce the time-consuming effort of rehanging instruments during the

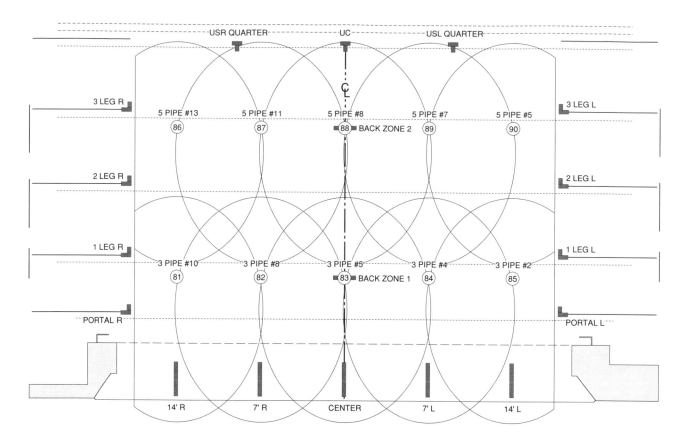

Figure 9.42 The Focused Backlight Pools After Shuttering

focus session. It goes without saying that any stabilizing that must be done to the boom needs to occur prior to the focus. Otherwise, the newly stabilized boom may change the spatial location of the instruments and require the entire position to be focused a second time.

Since booms are the closest major hanging position to the stage, they often become repositories for many other departments. The position is often employed as a location for monitor speakers, either on the ground or hung with the instruments in the air. Booms may also be used to support masking or perform other totally unplanned-for structural functions. Although all departments are working for the same goal, communication between departments will avoid situations where focused booms become involved in a secondary role that results in a need to refocus the entire boom.

Boom Sidelight Plotting Analysis

The introduction of formalized sidelight booms is generally credited to a woman named Jean Rosenthal. Although the kind of light they produced on performers

was originally treated with disdain by reviewers at the time, her contribution to the craft is now utilized by every major American dance company and productions around the world. A boom sidelight system is typically comprised of a series of instruments, one in each opening, that are mounted at matching heights, equipped with matching color, and focused in a matching way. A successful boom sidelight system is generally viewed as an even wash of sidelight that covers the entire depth of a performance space and shapes the sides of performer's bodies.

Over the years, the use of boom sidelight has been refined. Specific hardware has been created to facilitate the construction, placement, and focus of boom sidelight instruments. The modern boom base is often a circular piece of cast iron with a centralized threaded hole that can accept vertical pipe. Not only does it provide a stable base for the vertical pipe, its weight acts as a partial ballast, preventing the natural laws of gravity from tipping the position onto its side. Additional weight, lag bolts, and safety lines from the grid keep gravity at bay. When more floor space is required backstage, the vertical pipe can be screwed into a boiler grade floor flange. Without the ballast of the base plate, rigid stabilization to keep the boom vertical is an absolute. On the other hand, booms can be built with mobility. Boom bases can be equipped with casters, allowing the entire position to be moved during the course of a show. That usually implies that the additional ballast travels with the boom base when it's moved to ensure safe transport.

Pipe manufactured in the United States is produced in stock lengths of 21'-0", which is often used as the upper height limit for the sidelight position. Using a piece of hardware called a sidearm facilitates the focus range of instruments mounted on the vertical pipe. Use of this device, which is a combination of a smaller piece of pipe, a c-clamp, and a sleeved mounting mechanism, allows instruments attached to the vertical pipe to focus on a horizontal plane without having to be "twisted." Over the years, the industry has produced more sophisticated vertical trusses and other structures that allow rapid assembly of the position, and provides a climbing framework so that instruments can be accessed without the assistance of a ladder.

When booms are constructed without sidearms, the yokes of the instruments are usually hung in the same plane from the vertical pipe. In many cases, the up and downstage focus plane for the instruments on a sidelight boom are the same. If all of the instruments are mounted on the same axis, the amount of time required to achieve horizontal movement during focus is reduced.

The type of instrument and focus designation assigned to boom sidelight is unique to every show. Usually, the farther the actual throw distance, the smaller the beam spread and the higher the mounting location on the boom. For example, instruments mounted at the top of a 21'-0" boom are often assigned to focus points between the centerline and the opposite black masking leg. Since their actual throw distance to their focus points is the greatest, their beam spreads are comparably the smallest, often having beam spreads of 12° to 30°. Instruments mounted between 10' and 15' are often assigned to focus points between the two quarter lines. Their beam spreads usually range between 30° and 40°. Units mounted below 10' are often assigned to focus points between the near black masking leg and centerline. The width of the beam is often used to fill the depth of each near opening, so that the performer remains in as much light possible while passing up or downstage. Most units assigned to this function have beam spreads ranging between 30° and 50°. Obviously, the instrumentation available and the needs of the production make this kind of distinction fuzzy. Any number of instrument combinations and focuses can be specified by each design. By assigning the instrumentation and focus so that instruments mounted at the top of the boom focus to the far side, while lower instruments focus to the near side, the focused beams don't "cross," and the possibility of having too much intensity between two instruments in a system is reduced.

Since their beams can be shaped or sharpened, ellipsoidals are the typical instruments chosen for sidelight booms. Although other types of instruments are just as useful to produce sidelight, their beams are often more difficult to control. For example, shaping the beam from a PAR or Fresnel instrument, so that their light doesn't illuminate the near black masking leg, often means that a barndoor or other accessory must be added to the lens of the unit. This often results in more time and effort spent on either instrument during the hang and the focus. In addition to that, the added accessory can alter the center of balance and increase the overall footprint of the sidelight position.

Regardless of what instrument is used for each system, the same type of unit should be duplicated in that same vertical position on each boom. Matching the height of the instruments implies that the angle will be mirrored in each opening. Not only does this mean that the source of light will be consistent between openings, it also means that the performers will contend with the same vertical arrangement of instruments in the offstage environment.

Next, successful boom sidelight is plotted to match the horizontal location of instrumentation at each hanging position. Ideally, the units are hung on the same horizontal plane, in many cases onstage of the vertical support. Not only does this facilitate focus, but it also reduces the up and downstage "thickness" of the boom. This provides more space between the boom and the masking legs for the passage of performers or other objects. Sometimes the height of the vertical support may be lower than desired. When that occurs, the instruments may be double-hung using longer sidearms. The phrase "double-hung" implies that two instruments will stick out further to one or the other side of the boom. Ideally, all double-hung instruments are mounted above head height to preserve the passage space between the masking legs.

Boom Sidelight Focus

When focusing instruments at this position, keep in mind that any sidelight instrument will initially splash light onto the face of the black legs on the opposite side. The shadows of performers on those legs may be a perceived distraction from the audience's angle of observation. The side shutter cuts applied to the sidelight boom instruments focused to the far quarterline are usually the greatest cause for this concern. Although there are many ways to address this issue, one method that can be used matches the side cuts employed by the pipe end systems. Instruments focusing to the near quarter line are sometimes mounted high enough on the boom so that their top shutters are used to cut unwanted light off the legs and the side cuts are left open, thus allowing for better coverage at the near leg opening. Occasionally, the bottom beam edge hitting the stage can appear to be brighter than the light on the performer, and therefore a distraction. Bottom shutter cuts can be used to eliminate this beam edge.

✓ A list to consider before focusing boom sidelights:

- The position of the booms has been checked and approved.
- Confirm that all masking and scenic borders are at performance trim.
- Confirm that all legs are at in-trim, or spike marks are present to define their location.
- If the booms change color during the course of the production, the instruments have been colored with the series of gels that will initially be used during the light cue level setting session. Precoloring the boom instruments will also confirm that all of the instruments have been hung right side up, so that the color won't fall out of the instrument.
- Perform a channel check of the entire boom package to determine which units don't work. Note the nonfunctioning instruments.
- The hardware used to construct the boom is tight and immobilized. Discovering the entire boom can freely pan up or downstage while working on the final instrument may result in the need to refocus the entire position.

The light plot for *Hokey* includes four boom sidelight washes. At the top of the boom, channels 31 > 38 are colored in Roscolux 51, while channels 101 > 108 are colored in Roscolux 64. When focused, these will become the lavender and blue boom sidelight systems. The booms are also equipped with instruments in channels 109 > 114, and channels 115 > 122. Since the light cue setting session for *Hokey* will begin with Act 1, all of these instruments have already been colored, respectively, in Roscolux 76 and No Color, the color used for that act. The separation of control implies that the instruments will be used to isolate zones of the stage or wash the entire performance area.

Figure 9.43 shows the instruments and the focus points for channels 35 > 38, controlling the top instrument on each sidelight boom. Colored in Roscolux 51, they'll be focused as the stage left lavender boom sidelight system for *Hokey*. The stage left quarter line spike marks, along with the stage right masking legs, provide the triangulation for the focus points.

Like the overhead sidelight, the focus points for the boom sidelight may be shifted up or downstage, depending on how important it is to "hide" the black masking. In this case, the finished focus for the system will attempt to eliminate as much light on the black masking legs as possible. To do so, the focus points of the three upstage boom instruments are shifted downstage from the middle of each opening. While the focus point for channel 35 is in the middle of the first opening, the focus points for the rest of the system are located at the intersection between the stage left quarter line and the black masking leg on the opposite side of the stage of each boom. The locations of the far leg spike marks will be used to not only locate the focus points, they'll also become the objects of the side shutter cuts as well. This focus will be duplicated for channels 101 > 108, the stage left blue boom sidelight system.

Figure 9.44 shows that the preliminary focus point for unit #1 is 9'-0" stage left of centerline and in the middle of the first opening. The side shutter cuts will eliminate the portions of the beam that splash light onto the black masking on either side of the opening. The bottom shutter cut will be made to eliminate the near beam edge. It is believed that the performers will not be lifted in the air near the onstage side of the legs, so the top shutter cut will be made to "HH" or "hands above head" (while standing at the opposite leg). To achieve clean shutter cuts, the barrel will be sharp to the shutter.

Figure 9.45 shows channels 35 > 38 after the instruments have been pointed. Upstage side cuts will be required on all of the instruments to keep light off the far black masking legs. Channel 35's downstage cut will be placed in the stage right smoke pocket. The rest of the downstage cuts will remain open, unless they splash on the upstage side of the near leg.

Figure 9.46 shows channels 35 > 38 after the shutter cuts have been executed. To keep the maxi-

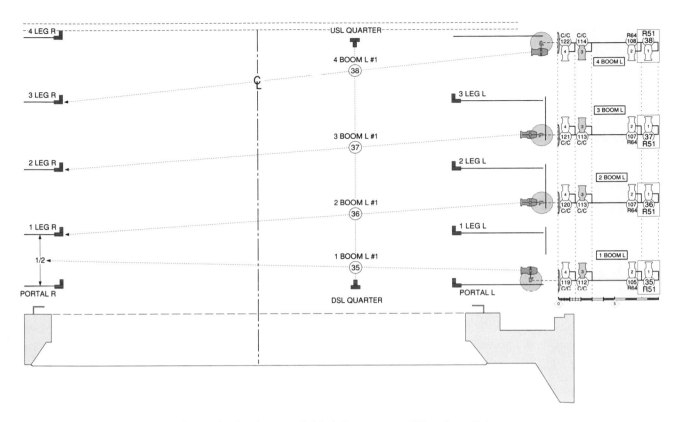

Figure 9.43 The Boom Sidelight Instruments and Their Focus Points

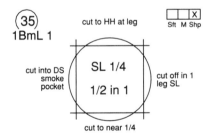

Figure 9.44 Focus Chart for 1 Boom Left #1

mum amount of light off the black legs, while using as much of the beam as possible, the shutter cuts have a sharp focus. The focus of the stage left lavender boom sidelight system is now complete.

The rest of the instruments, mounted on each boom, use the same focus point as the top unit. The bottom pair of instruments, however, will have radically different top and bottom shutter cuts. The bottom instrument on a boom closest to the floor is usually referred to as a **shinbuster,** named for its ability to hobble anyone who runs into it. The unit above

it is commonly referred to as a **mid,** so named because of its location in the middle of the boom.

Figure 9.47 shows that the focus point and the side shutter cuts for unit #3 are the same as unit #1, shown in Figure 9.44. Like unit #1, the shutters are in sharp focus. The top shutter cuts light to the intersection where the leg meets the border on the opposite side, while the bottom shutter is cut off the deck. This focus is duplicated for unit #4 in channel 119.

Figure 9.48 is a front view showing instruments 3 or 4 focused as a system of mids or shinbusters with the top and bottom cuts open.

The top cut is usually shuttered off the borders to eliminate the shadows from performers running in front of the instrument. The bottom cut of the instruments deserves special attention. After the other cuts have been completed, the bottom of the beam could remain unshuttered. A second choice might be to cut the bottom shutter to the near quarter line. The choice in this case, however, will be to cut the bottom shutter just off the deck.

Figure 9.49 is a front view showing the same shinbuster system with top shutter cuts off the borders and

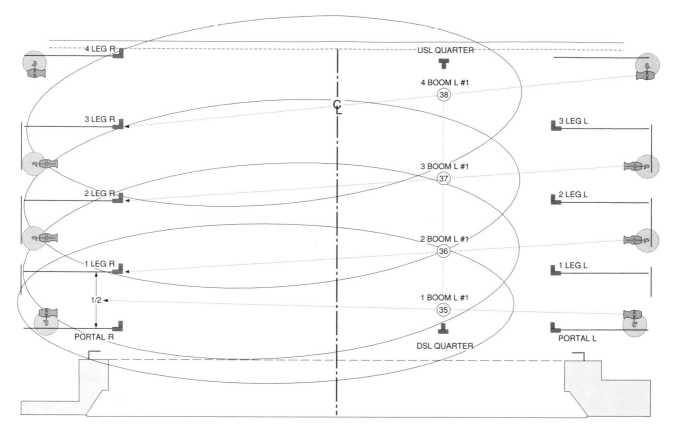

Figure 9.45 The Focused Boom Sidelight Pools Before Shuttering

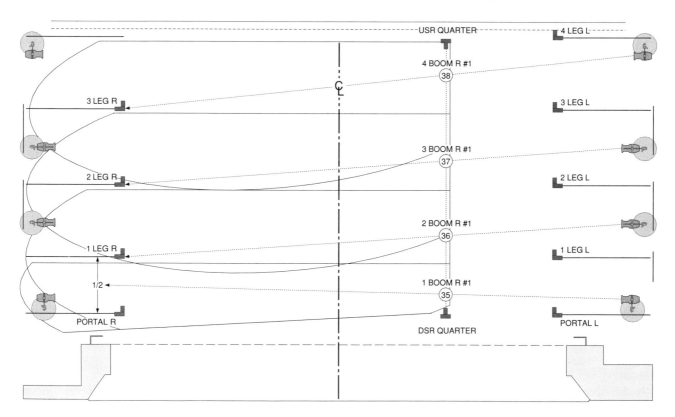

Figure 9.46 The Focused Boom Sidelight Pools After Shuttering

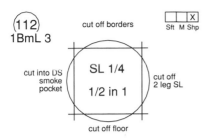

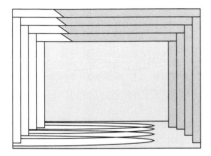

Figure 9.47 Focus Chart for 1 Boom Left #3

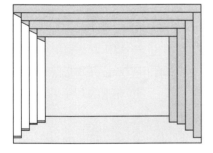

Figure 9.48 The Focused Mid Pools Before Shuttering

Figure 9.49 The Focused Shinbuster Pools After Shuttering

bottom shutter cuts off the deck. With a sharp focus eliminating halation from glazing the deck, this will result in a wash of light that covers the entire stage, but will only illuminate the onstage edge of the opposite black masking legs. Depending on the intensity and the angle of the opposite legs, this system can light performers as if the light were coming from "nowhere." The performance surface can be colored by the backlight in a completely different color than the sidelight.

If this focus is considered, the affected instruments should be mounted as close to the floor as possible to provide the maximum vertical coverage. In addition to that, the barrel focus of the instrument must be as sharp as possible. If sharp-focused instruments produce halation, a donut in front of the lens may be the solution.

Shelley Notes: Boom Sidelight Tips and Work-Arounds

When presented with the choice, consider focusing sidelights requiring ladder access first, leaving instruments accessible from the deck until last. The ladder often requires additional electricians, who can then be available to focus the instruments low on the booms.

When possible, cut the side shutters off any near masking legs. In addition to safety considerations, any light hitting legs upstage of the boom will be seen by the audience, while light splashing legs downstage of the boom will bounce upstage. This is even more apparent when scenic legs are involved. Any scenic legs that are hung without a black backing may show sidelight "bleeding through" if light strikes them on the back side.

Instruments hung high on booms may be targeted to focus points on the opposite quarter line. If there is no visual activity above head height next to the legs on the opposite side, consider cutting the top shutter in to a point above head height while standing next to those legs. This reduces the amount of unnecessary light.

Although matching instruments on opposite booms may always move together as a single channel, attempting to focus those instruments together at the same time can be frustrating. If an instrument from the 1 Boom Left is on at the same time as a unit from 1 Boom Right, both electricians will be blinded, and it will take longer to focus either instrument. When possible, alter the hookup of the sidelight channels so that one side of booms has exclusive control from the opposite side. If this isn't possible, consider switching off the circuits for one side of instruments while the opposite side is focused. If possible, avoid unplugging instruments. Once instruments are unplugged, it may become difficult to find the proper plugs and properly restore the circuitry.

If two electricians are available to focus sidelight, rather than assign each to a single boom on either side of the stage, consider focusing the same instrument on two adjacent booms on one side of the stage. Having both electricians on one side of the stage means that instructions only need to be given to one side. It also reduces the number of instructions: "Both of these instruments will be hot on my head here and here. Paula, your hot spot will be at the top of the 1 Boom Right. Jerry, your hot spot will be at the top of the 2 Boom Right." If four electricians are available for sidelight focus, each of them can be assigned to a different boom on the same side of the stage, one electrician per boom.

If the focus points duplicate between instruments, inform the electricians of their location prior to the focus. If the same system is being simultaneously focused on different booms, focus the hot spot of the first beam, and instruct the rest of the electricians to match the top or bottoms of their beams to the focused instrument. If that's not a possibility, consider running strips of tape up and downstage, giving the focusing electricians a reference location for the bottom of the instrument's beams, or for bottom shutter cuts.

If any infrastructure information has been programmed into the light board, this situation is the perfect time to activate entire matching systems of sidelight. Having this information programmed into submasters will make the activation process even faster.

The Slinky Method of Plotting

Now that the plotting and focus of the *Hokey* lighting systems has been examined, a focusing technique can be discussed that may also be applied to the plotting process. Situations occur during a focus session which require that the focus of a system must be adapted to the physical reality. The focus planned for the system just won't work. At other times, the identity or beam spread of instruments cannot be determined. And then there are those times when every drawing or predetermined focus point can be thrown out the window.

When those situations occur, a method can be adopted to ensure that the adjusted focus of a system will still provide adequate coverage. For reasons that will be explained later, this is called the **slinky method.** To fully understand this method, the method commonly used to determine focus points and zones will be reviewed.

Each theatrical lighting instrument produces a cone of light. The beam spread of the cone can be expressed in increments of degrees. Most theatrical beams of light are made up of two cones, one inside

the other. The field angle is another term describing the overall beam spread of a cone of light, while the beam angle relates to the brighter internal cone.

Figure 9.50 is a section showing the cone of light from a Source Four-36° ellipsoidal hung on the first electric. The field angle of the cone is 36°, creating a pool of light on the stage 18'-0" in diameter. The beam angle is 24°, creating an internal pool of light 10'-6" in diameter. The optical design of most instruments is such that the area of the beam angle is typically at least 50% of the overall field angle. This can be expressed in an equation known as the slinky formula:

$$\frac{\text{field angle}°}{2} = \text{beam angle}°$$

The **slinky formula** states that if the field angle of any instrument is known, dividing that number by 2 results in a number that can be used as an approximate beam angle.

The definition and objective of a system is to produce a consistent intensity of light wider than the

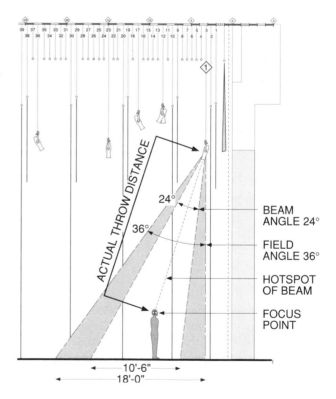

Figure 9.50 Field and Beam Angles of a Source Four Hung on the First Electric

width of a single beam angle. With that in mind, consider the next example.

Figure 9.51 is a groundplan showing the straight frontlight focus of instruments 1, 2, and 3 in a single zone. The dashed lines coming from each instrument trace the edges of each cone to the pool on the floor. Each pool of light (pool A, B, and C) is shown as two circles, one inside the other. The larger shaded circles represent the field angle (edge of the cone) for each light, whereas the white internal circles represent the beam angle within each cone. Three performers (A, B, and C) are standing at their matching focus points within each pool, creating shadows upstage on the floor. The field angles of pools A and B are barely touching, while the field angles of pools B and C are overlapping to the edge of each pool's beam angle.

If performer A walked stage left toward performer B at centerline, he would become dark midway as he walked between the A and B pools of light. If performer B walked stage left towards performer C, she would merely grow darker as she crossed through the overlapping field angles between pools B and C. There would still be a visual "dip" of intensity as she walked towards performer C. To prevent darkness or any visual dip between two pools of light, the pools must be focused so that the *beam angles* are touching or slightly overlapping.

Figure 9.52 shows the result of hanging and focusing the instruments to achieve a blended system. (The performers shadows have been eliminated for clarity.) The hanging position of the three instruments has been shifted so that the cones are still focused as straight frontlight. The field angles are overlapping, but the internal beam angles of the three pools are touching. Performer A can cross stage left to performer C without any visual intensity dip. A consistent level of illumination has been created that is larger than the beam angle of a single instrument. The three instruments have now created a partial straight frontlight system for a single zone.

It's important to note that two relationships have been created by this successful straight frontlight system. First, the edge of pool A overlaps into the *middle* of pool B, bisecting pool B's beam. Second, the edge of pool A is almost *touching* the edge of pool C.

Figure 9.53 shows an entire zone of straight frontlight focused across the stage. To allow the beam angles to touch or overlap, the field edge of pool A is landing in the middle of pool B. As important, however, is the fact that the edge of *every other field pool*

is touching, illustrated by the edges of pools A, C, and E. As a rule of thumb, when every other pool's edge is touching, the combined pools should result in an even wash of light.

Looking at a sharpened focus of a blended system or wash, it's possible to see the overlap of the pools in relation to each other. This is called the **slinky configuration** because of the way the overlapping pools can be drawn with a single line, as shown in Figure 9.54.

The slinky configuration illustrates the formula that presumes the beam angle is half of the overall pool of light. Successfully plotting or focusing instruments into an even wash can be achieved by using the observations illustrated in Figure 9.53:

- *Every other* pool at least touches each other's edge.
- Each pool at least *bisects* the adjacent pool of light.

Based on these two guidelines, it's possible to calculate the overall zone width or depth of a system once the field pool width of a single instrument is known. This is achieved by constructing a beam section, which was detailed in Chapter 1:

1. Define the field angle of the instrument in question.
2. Draw a beam section to determine the actual throw distance.
3. Measure the field pool width at head height.
4. Divide the field pool width by 2, resulting in the formulated width of the internal beam angle pool, or the **beam pool width**.

The beam pool width can now be used to confirm the adequate system coverage created by matching instruments from the same hanging position. First, the beam pool width is multiplied by the number of instruments that are being considered to create a single zone of coverage for that system. The resulting distance is then compared to the width of the leg opening. If the distance is less than the measurement of the leg opening width, the number of considered instruments may not provide adequate head height coverage.

If the depth of the performance space is divided by the same beam pool width, the number of zones required to provide an even depth of coverage can be approximated. When calculating zone-to-zone coverage, the method must take into account that several

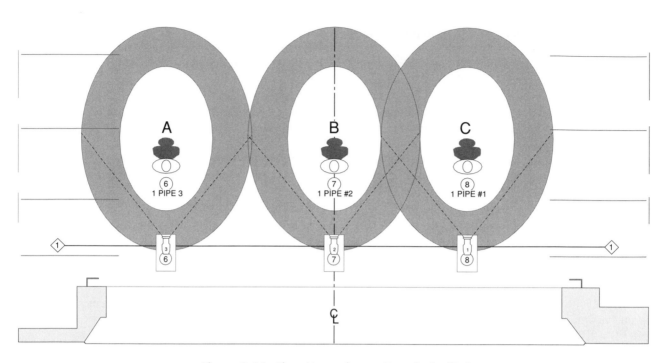

Figure 9.51 Three Nonoverlapping Beam Pools of Light

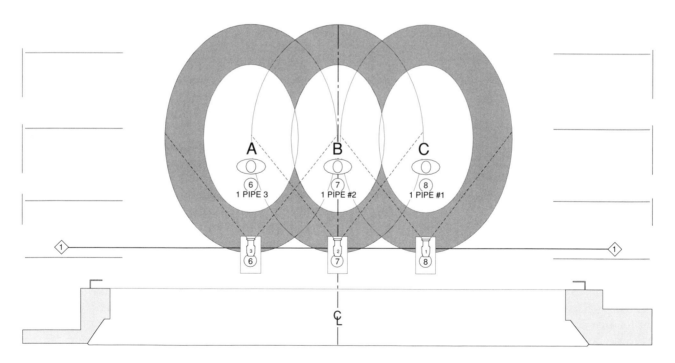

Figure 9.52 Three Overlapping Pools of Light

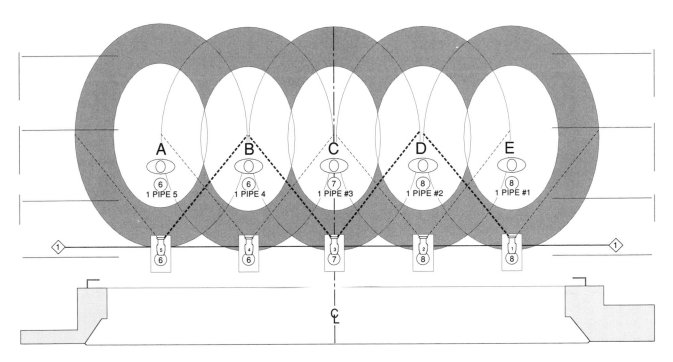

Figure 9.53 Five Overlapping Pools of Light

different hanging positions, trim heights, and possibly more than one type of instrument may be involved.

The Slinky Method of Focusing

Putting the guidelines to practical use, the lighting designer can use the slinky method to calculate approximate focus points and the probability of success for almost any system after focusing only one instrument in the system. In most cases, this can be achieved without even knowing the identity or field angle of the instruments involved. After completing the focus of the first instrument in a system, stand at the edge of that beam and focus the middle of the *second* pool at the

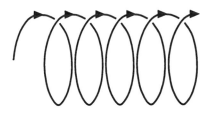

Figure 9.54 The Slinky Configuration

edge of the first pool of light. This technique can also be used to focus different zones of the same system to assure blended up and downstage coverage.

The first example showed the slinky method's use to plot or focus instruments in a single zone of frontlight. This next example illustrates how the method can be used during focus to ensure blended coverage for a single zone of overhead sidelight.

Figure 9.55 shows a front elevation of three 26° instruments, plotted to cover the first zone of one side of overhead pipe end sidelight. This system is focused using this sequence:

- Point the hot spot of the most onstage instrument (unit 3) at the focus point defined as head height at the stage left quarter line in the first opening (C). After instrument 3 is locked off, activate instrument 2.
- Tip the stage left beam edge of instrument 2's pool so that it passes through instrument 3's focus point (C). After instrument 2 is locked off, walk onstage until standing in the hot spot (B), instrument 2's focus point. Activate instrument 1.
- Tip the stage left beam edge of instrument 1's pool so that it passes through instrument 2's

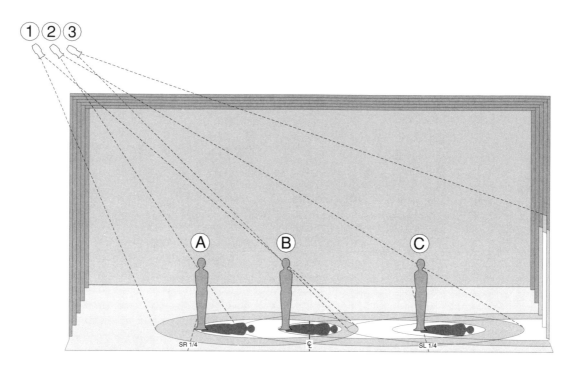

Figure 9.55 The Slinky Method Applied to a Single Zone of Overhead Sidelight

focus point (B). After instrument 1 is locked off, the focus of the overhead sidelight system is complete.

In theory, this will result in the three beam angles touching or overlapping at head height. The intensity of sidelight from stage right should remain consistent while traveling stage left or right in the first opening. If more coverage on the near side is desired, options may include changing the near instrument to a larger beam spread, adding an instrument to the system from the sidelight boom in the same opening, or shifting the focus of the existing three instruments toward stage right.

The slinky method can also be used to confirm up and downstage coverage between overhead sidelight zones.

Figure 9.56 is a section showing the four beam edges from a pipe end sidelight system hung on the first, second, fourth, and fifth electric. Using the slinky method, the four instruments are focused to create a blended zone-to-zone sidelight wash in this sequence:

- Focus the instrument on the first electric while standing at the downstage focus point (A). After

the first electric instrument is locked off, activate the instrument on the second electric (2).
- Tip the downstage edge of the second electric's beam to pass through or overlap the same focus point (A). After the second electric instrument is locked off, walk directly upstage until standing in the hot spot (B) of the second electric's beam.
- The unit on the fourth electric is activated (4). Tip the downstage edge of its beam to pass through the second focus point (B). After the fourth electric instrument is locked off, walk directly upstage until standing in the hot spot (C) of the fourth electric's beam.
- The unit on the fifth electric is activated (5). Tip the downstage edge of its beam to pass through the third focus point (C). After the fifth electric is locked off, the focus of the overhead sidelight system is complete.

The beam angle width of each pool at head height is greater than the distance between any of the focus points. At these trim heights, the beam angles more than overlap between the four pools, and the sidelight intensity at head height will remain consistent up and downstage.

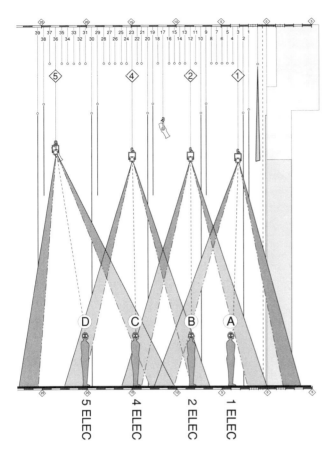

Figure 9.56 The Slinky Method Applied to Overhead Sidelight Zones

Although other methods may be employed during the plotting process to define the focus points, the slinky method can be used in practice, during the focus session, to visually confirm that there are no gaps in the coverage of the system. Once a system has been focused and shaped, the entire system can be activated, allowing the following observations to be made:

- If the edges of *every other* beam aren't touching, the intensity consistency between the beams should be checked; there may be "holes" (or dips of intensity) in the coverage.
- If each beam doesn't overlap into an adjacent pool so that it *bisects* its neighbor's beam of light, the consistency of intensity between the beams should be checked; there may be holes in the coverage.

The slinky method can be applied in this manner to many overhead systems, including downlight or backlight. The next example illustrates how the method can be used while focusing to ensure blended coverage between zones of frontlight.

Figure 9.57 is a section view looking stage left. Using the slinky method, three instruments (one on the truss and two on the overhead electrics) are focused to create a blended up and downstage multizone frontlight wash in this sequence:

- Focus the centerline instrument hung on the truss (T) while standing at the first zone focus point (A). After the truss instrument is locked off, activate the centerline instrument on the first electric (1).
- Tip the downstage beam edge of the first electric's pool (1) at the first zone focus point (A). After the first electric instrument is locked off, activate the matching instrument on the second electric (2).
- Walk directly upstage until standing in the hot spot of the first electric's pool (B), now established as the second zone focus point.
- Tip the downstage beam edge of the second electric's pool (2) at the second zone focus point (B). After the second electric instrument is focused (2), the frontlight system should be accurately focused.

The slinky method states that if the three beam angles overlap at head height, the coverage should remain consistent up and downstage. Due to possible differences in instrumentation type and actual throw distances between zones, the intensity between zones may require balancing.

The slinky method can also be used while focusing diagonal frontlight or backlight. The next example illustrates how the method can be used while focusing to ensure blended coverage between instruments hung in a box boom position.

Figure 9.58 is a front elevation showing three instruments hung at the stage left box boom position. Using the slinky method, the three instruments are focused to create a blended system in this sequence:

- Stand on the far quarter line (A) and focus the hot spot of the far box boom instrument (1) on the focus point. Lock off the first instrument. Activate the second instrument (2).

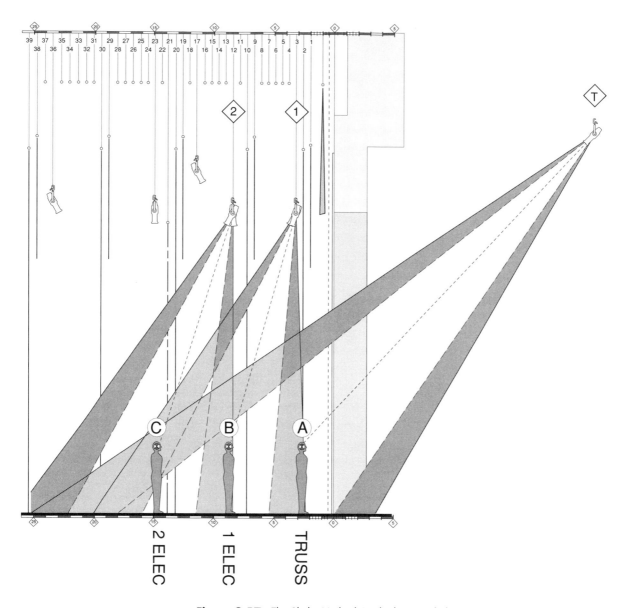

Figure 9.57 The Slinky Method Applied to Frontlight Zones

- Walk to the edge of the first instrument's pool of light (B). Focus the hot spot of the center box boom instrument (2) to that focus point (B), and lock off the second instrument. Activate the third instrument.
- Walk to the edge of the second instrument's pool of light (C). Focus the hot spot of the near box boom instrument (3) to that focus point (C), and lock off the third instrument.

In theory, since the edge of each pool is bisecting the adjacent pool's beam, this should result in the beam angles touching or overlapping at head height, and the intensity of the box boom system should remain consistent. Due to difference in beam spreads of each of the instruments, additional adjustment of the relative beam intensities may be required.

The slinky method can be used as a benchmark to define and adjust washes of light during the plotting

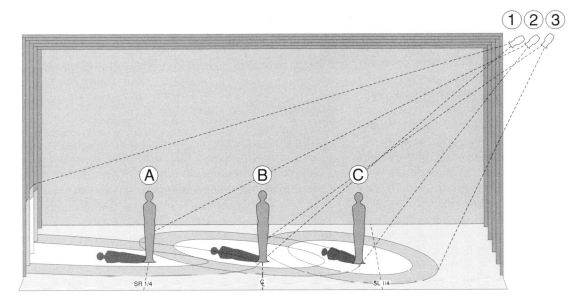

Figure 9.58 The Slinky Method Applied to Box Boom Light in a Single Zone

process or during on-site focus sessions. It can be used to define the distances between focus points in a single zone and distances between adjacent zones.

After a Hanging Position Has Been Focused

It's frustrating to see simple errors after the electrician has left the position. It's even worse to tell the electrician who has just returned to the stage that he or she must return to the just-departed hanging position. Beyond that, it's also time consuming. The time taken by the electrician to return to the focus position, complete the note, and return to the stage is all time during which the electrician could have been doing something else.

After the focus of a hanging position is complete, turn on all the instruments and do a "last look" at all the light beams before the electrician leaves the position.

- If there are similarities in color, rapidly activate the instruments system by system using groups or submasters. This "last check" allows the lighting designer to check beam blending and ensures that the right color is in the right instruments.
- Check for glaring errors. Now is the best time to discover the instrument that slipped after being

focused or the instrument that was skipped and then forgotten.

- The position may be movement sensitive, that is, when the electrician moves the beams of light "bounce." Turn on all the instruments using a hanging position group or submaster while the electrician leaves the position. If the vibration of his or her movement causes the focus of an instrument to drop, it's immediately known.

Shelley Notes: Turn Off the Worklights Before Leaving the Position

If the production electrician is absent when a hanging position has been completed, remind the electrician to turn off the worklights prior to departure. Unnoticed worklights can later cause unexpected delays. The amount of light not seen until the house is dark at the beginning of a technical rehearsal can be surprising. Tech rehearsals can be delayed for no reason other than waiting for those lights to be turned off.

After the Focus Has Concluded

After the final instrument has been focused, work notes taken during the session are given to the production electrician. Combined with his or her own list of notes, the entire scope of work yet to be accomplished can be prioritized and executed at appropriate times.

After the worklights have been turned on, the lighting designer may consider "cleaning up" after him or herself and removing any spike marks. If the focus occurred on top of the performance surface for the show, this action could take place, leaving only the spike marks that the lighting designer may need as reference points. If the performance surface has not yet been installed, however, the lighting designer should reconsider the decision to remove all of the spikes. If there is any delay in the installation of the performance surface, the designer's spike marks may be the only reference points currently placed on the stage. If any other work will be performed that may rely on them as guides, removing any of these spike marks may result in time taken to replace them before the performance surface is installed.

SUMMARY

Once the focus session has been completed, the light plot has now become a fully functional lighting package, and the lighting designer's palette is now prepared. The next step is to create the cues in the light cue level setting session.

10
The Light Cue Level Setting Session and Technical Rehearsals

This chapter examines some of the events that take place during the light cue level setting session and the technical rehearsals. Although they are two distinct events, they are combined into a single chapter. Once the lighting designer begins to create and modify the cues, the activity doesn't stop until the opening of the show.

LIGHT CUE LEVEL SETTING SESSION ANALYSIS

The purpose of the light cue level setting session is to create and record the electrical actions that will occur each time the lights change during the production. Typically, it's also the only scheduled opportunity to discuss and analyze the light cues with the director without the pressure imposed by the technical rehearsals. Any other technical elements that create the different looks of the production are preset to complete each stage picture. Scenery may be changed, properties might be preset, and pieces of wardrobe may be left on stage during different scenes, so that the visual impact of the entire production can be viewed without the performers. Each stage picture and every light change can be created, studied, and analyzed by the director and the design team.

Many people can be involved in a level setting session. The lighting designer directs the activation of the channels or functions of the lighting console, and the board operator executes those directions. Depending on the complexity of the show, there may be one or more assistants recording different facets of the action. One assistant may be assigned to record all of the different cues and actions of the lighting console onto light cue sheets, while a second assistant may be recording the choreography of the followspots on the followspot cue sheets. The stage manager may be present to record the placement of each cue in the call book. The director may be present to collaborate and approve the appearance of the cues. During the cueing process, it may be necessary to see the contrast of light intensities on faces in various locations on the stage. People who may have nothing else to do with the production may be employed as "walkers," and be assigned colored garments to wear that approximate the costumes that will be used in the show. Following the stage directions given by the director, the walkers allow the director to see the different staging compositions that have been blocked with a "substitute" cast. Members of the other departments may also be involved in the cueing session, since this may also be the first time that the each department becomes fully aware of the technical components required for each scene.

This is the period of time when the paperwork included in the cue construction packet comes into prominence. The lighting designer refers to the magic sheet to activate the proper channels at the correct areas of the stage. The cheat sheet is a cross-reference guide, informing him or her of the identity of the channels shown on the monitor display. The cue master is used to inform the lighting designer of the anticipated appearance of each lighting "state." The cue sheets, board operator sheets, repatch sheets, and followspot cue sheets are all used to record the actions of the different lighting elements used in the show. The rest of the paperwork is also present so that it can be updated as the lighting design evolves into a finished product.

Setting light cues begins by activating channels. On manual light boards, channels are activated by manually moving sliders, dials, or handles. On a computer lighting console, this is usually accomplished by typing commands into the keypad of the light board. The sequences of keystrokes used to activate the channels vary between lighting consoles. The combination of channel intensities creates the desired "look." After that look has been approved, the different intensities are recorded, both on paper and as memories within a computer lighting console. A fade time is assigned to the movement of each light cue, defining the length of time that will occur to reach this desired look from the previous look. The light cues are usually created in the same sequence that they'll be seen during the performance. By sequentially following the action of the show, the lighting designer is able to compare the visual changes between each light cue.

With ample time, cueing can be viewed as a slow crafting of the images that were mentally imagined and discussed between the lighting designer, the director, and the design team. On the other hand, if there are many cues to create, and little time to create them, the pace of a cueing session can feel like the visual equivalent of base coating paint, activating systems like broad bristle paintbrushes, and slapping on coats of light.

Whenever light cues are created, the lighting designer plays the roles of artist, programmer, and the time manager. On one level, he or she needs to be able to refine mental images into concrete lighting states that will achieve the objectives of light, assist the production concept, while reinforcing the actions on the stage. At the same time, the lighting designer needs to know how to use the lighting console to produce those looks, and how to communicate to the board operator the actions required to make them happen. Finally, the lighting designer has to keep one eye on the clock to be certain that some form of all of the light cues are created and recorded before the scheduled light cue level setting time has expired.

Before the light cues are physically created, concepts regarding cueing should be discussed. Although cue construction is unique for every show, a number of general concepts hold true in most situations.

General Cueing Concepts and Tactics

In almost every theatrical presentation, the action on the stage is directed to an area of particular focus. It may be one whole side of the stage or it could be a very isolated area. In the course of almost every production, this stage focus shifts between different locations. One of the primary purposes of each light cue in a production, then, is to telegraph these focus shifts to the audience, and thereby reinforce the stage focus. Since the eye is subconsciously drawn to the brightest point on a stage, one basic property of light that is used to direct the stage focus is intensity. Although the other properties of light play as much of a role in each lighting design, the purpose for each light cue is often initially constructed with that in mind; the area of focus, in that light cue, is brighter than the rest of the stage.

From that perspective, every light cue can be constructed based on contrast. A light cue can be "built up," by adding a brighter area of focus to a comparably dim surrounding, or a light cue can be "built down," from a bright focus to a comparably lower intensity. Most light cues are usually constructed using one of these two methods.

Light cues "built up" are constructed by first activating channels at lower intensities, and then adding channels at brighter intensities for stage focus. Light cues for large group scenes often illustrate this method. The general washes are layered in first, to ensure visibility on the stage. Then brighter intensities are added to highlight the lead performers, directing the stage focus. Light cues "built down" reverse the method. The bright focus of the light cue is activated first, followed by adding washes in lower intensities to illuminate the surrounding environment. This method is used to create light cues for highly focused or isolated scenes.

Not only is it important for the designer to understand the focus of each light cue, it's also technically as important to compare the contrast and speed of that look with the light cues that precede and follow it. Cues constructed without being compared to their "neighbors" may not be as visually successful when viewed in sequence during the production.

From a mechanical point of view, time allocated to a cueing session should be spent viewing and discussing completed "looks," rather than deciding how they should appear or how to construct them. Ideally, the look of each cue has been predetermined in the mind of the lighting designer prior to the cueing session, so that the cue can be constructed as rapidly as possible. To expedite the construction process, thought should be given to the handles that will be required to paint the broad strokes. The fewer number of keystrokes required to construct a light cue means more time available to actually look at it. This is one reason to consider programming infrastructure cues, groups, or submasters. They can all be devices used to speed the light cue construction process.

Here are some suggestions to consider before the cueing session that may increase the speed of the cue construction process:

- Decide which cues may be built from other (base) cues, and which cues need to be unique looks built from a clean (black) stage.
- Determine the shortest keystroke combinations to accomplish what needs to be done. Identify series of channel numbers that may be collectively activated. Know how to create and modify handles on that particular lighting console.
- Identify sections of the show that involve transitions or active sequences. Consider padding the cue master with several whole numbers. If the sections later require additional called cues, enough whole-numbered cues will exist. This avoids the possibility of numerous point cues that must be called by the stage manager in rapid succession.

Sometimes, the cueing session is too brief, or the scheduled time is truncated for some reason. Although none of these difficulties may be the fault of the lighting designer, a situation may develop that requires an accelerated pace. The objective may be shifted to making certain that a lack of light cues doesn't stop a technical rehearsal. Although not highly advised, here are some suggestions to consider when faced with that situation:

- Block in the structure. Create, and check, any blackout or fade to black cues.
- Use broad strokes to build light cues. Temporarily lower your standards for visual acceptability so that information is recorded into the light board. Be less concerned with focus and more concerned with visibility. Don't get stuck in the construction of a single light cue.
- Skip internal cues and concentrate on the beginning of scenes, the end of scenes, and the transi-

tion sequences. Attempt to provide the programming so that the transitions can be called in real time.

- If a memory's purpose is to activate a single channel, skip it or record it from the previous cue. Come back later to finish the cue.
- Record cues as other cues. Consult the cue master and "steal" previously recorded cues that are close to the same appearance of cues not yet recorded. If a bright cue has been constructed in Scene 1, it may be completely different than the bright cue required for Scene 2, but it will provide light on the stage.
- When cues are recorded, either assign a default time to all of the cues, or skip entering time fades altogether. After all of the primary cues have been created, go back through the cues and assign all of the time fades at once.
- Keep notes of what you're doing. Check off the cues that have been created. Draw arrows indicating the source of stolen cues. Be able to retrace the steps if there are problems.

Before the Cueing Session

Several things should occur prior to a light cue level setting session. A meeting with the light board operator should occur, and several other items to consider are presented as checklists. Something to drink is suggested, since the lighting designer will be speaking for an extended amount of time.

Meeting with the Light Board Operator

Presumably, a meeting with the board operator occurred during the beginning of the load-in, when the notebook containing disks, paperwork regarding the production, and infrastructure information was exchanged. Prior to the cue level setting session, a second meeting with the board operator may be valuable to discuss the use of the console and the methods that will be employed to construct the light cues.

Ideally, both the lighting designer and the board operator know the command structures, functions, and limitations of the lighting console. A general discussion about the way the console will be used, however, may reveal previously unknown limitations or capabilities of the device. Although both individuals may know the console well, a different version of system software may make a difference in the manner in which cues are constructed.

Here are some basic functions and commands that may be requested during the light cue level setting session and the technical rehearsals.

☑ Functions that are typically required in the operation of a computer lighting console:

- Turn the light board on and off properly.
- Format a disk.
- Record to disk or load memory from disk.
- Use the grand master and submasters.
- Repatch, unpatch, park, or profile dimmers.
- Alter channel information.
- Create or alter groups.
- Create or alter submasters.
- Create, manipulate, and run effect cues.
- Link cues to other cues.
- Print out hardcopy of the light board contents.

☑ Basic commands that may be employed to create and manipulate light cue information in the "live" or "stage" screen:

- Build from a clear fader or cue 0.
- Activate channels, groups, or submasters.
- Record a light cue in track or cue only mode.
- Re-record a light cue in track or cue only mode.
- Assign or alter a time fade.
- Split a time fade (up/down).
- Create a blocker cue.
- Alter a cue to be an autofollow cue.
- Delay a cue.
- Divide a light cue into "parts." (This will be explained during the cueing process.)
- Delete a light cue.
- Initiate a cue in time.

☑ Basic commands that may be employed to create and manipulate light cue information in the "blind" or "preview" screen:

- Build from a clear screen.
- Alter channels, groups, or submasters.
- Create a light cue.
- Alter channel intensities in track or cue only mode.
- Assign or alter a time fade.
- Split a time fade (up/down).
- Create a blocker cue.
- Alter a cue to be an autofollow cue.

- Delay a cue.
- Divide a light cue into "parts." (This will be explained during the cueing process.)
- Delete a light cue.

☑ Basic commands that may be employed to create and manipulate light cue information on a manual light board:

- Activate a dimmer in the active scene.
- Activate a scene.
- Cross-fade between scenes.
- Switch a dimmer to the independent master.
- Preset a nonactive scene.
- Record a preset and a light cue.

Depending on the complexity of the production, other functions may need to be employed. Providing the board operator with a list of the functions that will be used to construct the memories may also help the lighting designer to define each "look." If that list is provided in a timely manner prior to the cueing session, the board operator will have time to study any unfamiliar command language. The functions can then be programmed during the cueing session, eliminating time spent searching in the lighting manual.

This meeting is also the beginning of a working relationship. The lighting designer and board operator will soon be attached to each other through a headset cable. As a coworker, the lighting designer should be considerate. If the designer doesn't anticipate what infrequently used functions may be required, it's impolite to expect a board operator to have the command structure for every function memorized. If neither party is intimate with a light board's operation, a lighting manual close at hand can answer most programming questions. This will allow the session to be devoted to creating the light cues, instead of figuring out how to program them to function properly.

Checklists Before Cueing

 Working Environment

- Is the production table set? Do all of the components work? Are they properly arranged?
- Has other work on stage been completed so that the worklights can be turned off?
- Are there offstage worklights so that other work can continue? Are the worklights controlled so

that they will not be recorded into the light cues?

- Have all doors to the lobby been closed? Have all the curtains, preventing daylight spilling into the space, been closed? Have the theatre tours been canceled?
- Is the scenery, floor surface, and masking in place? Are the correct items in the scenic stack in place? (It's very discouraging to discover the black scrim was accidentally left in through the entire cueing session. When it's correctly removed for the tech, time can be spent altering the channel levels controlling the translucency, rather than observing the flow of the cues.)
- Is the lighting groundrow in place, wrung out, and focused?
- If the performance includes an orchestra, are all of the music stand lights turned on? If there is no music, have pieces of white paper been distributed in their place?
- If costume pieces are to be viewed, are they on site?
- If walkers have been arranged for, are they ready?
- Is the board operator in place?
- Has a channel check been performed? If electrical work notes need to be addressed, can this occur while cues are being constructed? Can dimmers be activated without being recorded into the cues?
- If there are repatches, have all the affected dimmers been checked for their proper contents?
- Have strobes, scrollers, hazers, foggers, or any other special devices been tested and preset?

 Computer Light Board

- Has the system size been defined so that the fewest number of monitor pages will be shown on the channel information display? Have the contents of the RAM been labeled with an alphanumeric keyboard (if available)? Or has a key memory system been loaded into the memories?
- Have all other defaults or system settings (time fade, channel display, mode of tracking, number of channels displayed on a row, etc.) been altered to the preferred setting?
- Are there "handles" in the form of cues, groups, or submasters to quickly control the

worklights? Downstage, upstage, offstage? Have they been checked for accuracy? Are they written down?

- Have the system washes been checked for missing, miscolored, or misfocused instruments? Have any units that appear brighter or dimmer than the rest of the system been noted?
- Are there "handles" in the form of cues, groups, or submasters to build light cues? Have they been checked for accuracy?
- If a disk management system is in place, are the preset cue numbers known?
- If the light board has tracking capability, are blockers built into the cues?
- Have the "time stamp" ghost channels been programmed with information?
- Has the board operator been informed as to what functions of the light board will be required?

 Manual Light Board

- Have the dimmers on the light board been labeled?
- Have all of the sliders and grand master been checked for smoothness of operation?
- Have any submasters, scene masters, or independent masters been checked for smoothness of operation? Have all of the independent switches been checked in their proper scenes? Have any nonfunctioning switches been noted?
- Has the accuracy of repatch dimmers been checked? Have all inactive elements of the repatch been switched off to prevent overloading? Are the repatch sheets ready to be filled out or updated?
- Has the board operator been informed what functions of the light board will be required?
- Does the board operator have enough copies of the board operator sheets or preset sheets?

 Lighting Designer

- Do you know how to use the lighting console? Do you know the limitations and work-arounds, so that the cues can be constructed rapidly with the fewest possible keystrokes?
- Have you preassigned which numerical sequences will be used? Do you know how much

room is available in the RAM? Do you know which numbers to avoid?

- Do you have a plan of attack? Do you know how much time is available to you to program the light cues before the worklights have to be turned on for another task?
- Do you have a method for taking work notes that will be comprehensible?
- Do you have a method for taking cue notes that will be comprehensible?
- Have you determined the amount of time that can be dedicated to each light cue before the session falls behind? Or to each scene? Or to each act?
- If the show is multiscene, has a scene sequence been devised? Has a list been defined showing the order in which the scenes will be lit, involving the fewest possible set changes, concluding with the first scene required in the next call?

 Lighting Designer's Tools

- The magic sheet, the cheat sheet, the cue master
- The support paperwork: color change cards, floor cards, and any additional repertory information
- Enough cue sheets, board operator sheets, followspot cue sheets, or repatch sheets
- Work note sheets
- A keyboard layout sheet and/or a lighting manual.

 Golden Rule: Save Early and Often—Again

Although this was mentioned during the load-in, it's worthwhile to repeat it again while the cues are being created. When the light board is inactive, save the contents of the RAM to the disk. I can't stress enough what effect the loss of board content will have on the tempo of the pre-performance period. The board will crash someday, and no one can say when that moment will occur.

If a storm is brewing outside, save to disk often and remove the disk from the console. There's no telling what lightning can do to electronics. Not only can cues be lost, but enormous amounts of time and effort can also disappear when the light board unexpectedly reboots.

I save to disk at every convenient opportunity. During the cueing session, I've gotten into the habit of making different marks on the cue master, after each time the RAM has been saved to disk. In this way, when the board crashes, I'll know what cues have been lost and where to begin. This technique is especially helpful after the memories have been created. If no additional cues have been created in a notes session, the only signpost that shows which memories have been recorded to disk are my marks on the cue master.

 Golden Rule: Avoiding Blackouts

In almost every production some of the lighting memories are programmed to be blackouts, or cues are built from a black stage. When working with a computer lighting console, the natural inclination is to program the light cues in sequence. Almost all light boards have the ability to remove all light from the stage, and board operators are often well versed in rapidly completing this function. It is common practice to take the stage to black numerous times in the course of a light cue level setting session.

Too often the number of cues that need to be constructed far outweighs the amount of time dedicated to the session. The pace that is required to complete this task often demands the total concentration of the lighting designer.

Throughout the light cue level setting session, however, the lighting designer should remain aware of any personnel who may still be working on the stage. If the worklights have been turned off during the session while people are still working on the deck, the golden rule to remember is this: **Don't take the stage to black if there are people working on stage.**

If the stage lights are abruptly turned off while a crucial action is taking place on stage, the sudden loss of light could potentially cause an injury or accident. If power tools are involved in the on stage activity, the importance of adhering to this golden rule is even greater.

Several methods can be used to avoid that situation, and allow both activities to continue. One method is to program or check all blackout memories while viewing the blind or preview displays, rather than seeing them live onstage. If work on stage is confined to a static area, consider setting up a worklight not controlled by the lighting console. If that's not an option while programming cues that must be built from a black stage, then keep minimal worklight turned on until the stage light in the cue is established. Then turn off the worklights to see the cue. If it's necessary to see the timing of a fade to black, announce to the stage that this is about to happen and wait for clearance from the onstage personnel. Anyone who can't contend with darkness at that moment will give you their opinion regarding your intent.

THE CUEING SESSION BEGINS

Many lighting designers have experienced anxiety at the beginning of a light cue level setting session. That's absolutely normal. Typically, everyone involved in a cueing session can be a little nervous. It's the first time that all of the technical elements will be seen in their proper perspective. The best remedy is to just start. Even if the appearance of the first series of cues isn't satisfactory, take notes and move on. Once a rhythm is established, it will get better. Knowledge will be gained from discussions with the director and the rest of the design team during the course of the session. That knowledge may provide clarity about the appearance of those opening cues. There will be time to address those cues later.

Avoid or delay any unnecessary interruptions to the rhythm of a cueing session. If possible, take notes. Don't turn the time into a work or focus call, unless the problem will affect the cueing process. The cue level setting session should be reserved for the cue construction process.

The Opening: Act 1, Scene 1

The performance of *Hokey* will begin with a short musical introduction with the curtain closed. After the house lights and the curtain warmers have faded out, the curtain will rise to reveal Pookie upstage left in the fourth opening. She performs a series of movements, and then moves to center. She then beckons other members of the group, who join her onstage.

The cue master has been constructed so that memory 100.7 will be the preset that reveals Pookie once the curtain has opened. After Pookie completes her initial movement, memory 101 will build the center area up, and eliminate the opening isolated area up left. When the group joins her, memory 102 will use washes to build a full-stage warm look.

Since the opening look will not be bright, memory 100.7 will be initially built with low intensities of light, and then highlight the point of focus for the cue.

- Constructing memory 100.7 will begin by starting from a clear fader, to be certain that there are no erroneous channel intensities. The time stamp and key memory information, along with any infrastructure channels, are activated so that they will be recorded into all of the cues. If there are many infrastructure channels requiring different levels, this "blank" look may be recorded as memory 100.1, to be used as a template for all other cues that will be built from black.
- The background will be used to establish a location. Initially, the opening look is a quiet, "predawn" moment, and the focus should remain low and close to the stage. With that in mind, the blue groundrow (channel 136) is brought up to 30%. Since the light is being seen through both the black scrim and the translucency, the level of light seen from the audience's angle of observation will be lower.

The next action will be to activate the Roscolux 68 backlight system to 50%. Activating the individual channels is accomplished on the computer lighting console by typing in a series of keystrokes that would appear in this manner on the command line: 91 > 100 @ 5 [Enter]. (On most consoles, when keystroking intensity information, the zero is automatically added. Often this keystroke sequence activates the channels to 50%.) On most consoles, typing this sequence requires nine keystrokes. If this series of channels will be frequently activated and moved together, the group that was programmed for this purpose can be used instead. The keystrokes might appear in this manner on the command line: Group 10 @ 5 [Enter], and would require only six keystrokes.

While that might not seem to make much of a difference, consider the amount of keystroking that is required for a typical show. Presuming that an average production may consist of 100 built memories, it's probable that each memory will consist of at least 20 channel activations to construct each cue. When those two numbers are multiplied, the result is 2000 channel activations. Now consider that during each technical rehearsal, an average of 5 channel intensities are changed for each cue. The number of keystrokes can quickly add up. This is one reason to consider using groups when frequently activating the same series of channels.

For this reason, the group list for *Hokey* was constructed so that each system was given a group assignment. More to the point, the group identity numbers were assigned so that the single-digit groups would activate the largest series of channels that would most frequently be activated together. This is also the reason why the group numbers were so large on the *Hokey* magic sheet. The diamond icon and larger font size were used specifically to allow the group numbers for each system to be easily seen. Instead of activating the series of channels for the Roscolux 68 downlight system, group 10 will be used instead.

- Group 10 is activated to a level of 50%. This washes the performance surface with a blue light.
- Pookie is preset in the fourth opening stage left. The closest downlights (channels 70 and 80) can't be utilized to shape her body, since they aren't focused far enough upstage to provide head high coverage in the fourth opening. Instead, the Roscolux 51 pipe end is used (channel 24), brought up to 50%, to highlight the performer's body from the onstage side.
- To help shape the performer from the offstage side, the stage left shin in the fourth opening is also brought up (channel 122). The performer is close to the boom, so the intensity is only 30%. Since the shinbusters are cut off the deck, the only light that is seen from stage left is on the performer's body.

This "look" is recorded as memory 100.7. Since the cue will be preset on stage before the curtain is raised, it will contain no frontlight downstage of the curtain. The instruments will fade up to their assigned levels in a time of 3 seconds. A time of 0 seconds would bump the instruments to their assigned intensities, but there's no need for that speed; it's potentially jarring to the performers backstage, and the surge in voltage to the filaments might cause lamps to burn out.

Now memory 101 will be constructed. It's been decided that Pookie's cross to center should be a shift in focus on the stage, so the cue will be built from memory 100.7. When the cue is complete, there should no longer be any isolation upstage left. The center area should receive focus instead.

- First, to eliminate the isolation upstage left, channels 24 and 122 are taken to zero.
- To brighten the stage for Pookie and prepare for the following cue, the color in the background and the color on the floor will get a little brighter. Channel 136 is brought up to 50%, and group 10 is brought up to 70%. In addition, channel 133, controlling the blue T-3's at the top of the translucency, is brought up to 30%.
- To isolate center, the NC center backlight special (channel 57) is brought up to 50%.
- To shape the performer and provide color consistency, the Roscolux 51 shinbusters will be activated. To be certain that the performer isn't left in the dark while crossing from upstage left to center, the shinbusters in 2 and in 3 on both sides of the stage (channels 116, 117, 120, and 121) are activated to 50%.

This "look" is recorded as memory 101. Initially, the cue is recorded as a 5-second cross-fade from memory 100.7, but the dimmers don't respond quickly enough. When the cross-fade is run in time, it appears that the "isolation channels" up left fade down too quickly before the performer moves to center. The time is changed to 5 seconds up and 10 seconds down to ensure that there will light on Pookie from the time she leaves up left through the time she stops at center.

The next cue in the sequence, memory 102, will build levels on the entire stage as the group enters, so it could be built from memory 101. On the other hand, it's a unique look. The stage will get much brighter and warmer than the first two cues, so it will be built from a clean black stage.

- Initially, cue 100.1 is loaded into the fader, to retain the infrastructure channels.
- It's been decided that the motivation for the brightness of this cue will be a stylized "dawn." Channel 133, the top blue of the translucency, is brought up to 50%, while channel 131, the NC T-3's, is brought up to 15%. Channel 136, the bottom blue of the translucency, is brought up to 60%, while channel 134, the NC bottom of the translucency, is brought up to 20%.
- Group 7, controlling the Roscolux 20 downlight, is brought up to 50% to color the floor. To shape the bodies of the group, the Roscolux 51 will color them from stage right, while the Roscolux 64 will color them from stage left.

Channels 21 > 24, the stage right lavender pipe ends, are brought up to 50%, along with channels 31 > 34 on the stage right lavender booms. Channels 45 > 48, the stage left blue pipe ends, are brought up to 40%, along with 105 > 108 on the stage left blue booms.

- Frontlight will also be added at a lower intensity to see the group's faces as they enter. Group 1, controlling the Roscolux 33 frontlight, is brought up to 30%. Channels 29 and 30, the Roscolux 51 box booms, are brought up to 50% to fill in the shadows.

This look is recorded as memory 102. Initially assigned a 7-second fade time, it seems too fast when seeing the cross-fade from memory 101 to memory 102 in time. There also seems to be a visual "dip" as the center area fades down and the rest of the cue fades up. To correct these notes, the upfade time is slowed to 10 seconds, while the downfade time is slowed to 13 seconds.

The first three cues for *Hokey* have now been written. The cue list on the monitor display looks like this:

Cue	Time	(Translation)
100	2.5	(Blocker)
100.1	2.5	(Black with infrastructure channels)
100.7	3	(Preset; Pookie USL)
101	5/10	(Center up; USL down)
102	10/13	(Dawn; group enters)
300	2.5	(Blocker)

The Storm

The rest of the cues for the first scene are recorded, concluding with memory 124. That cue will be used for the end of Hokey and Pookie's love song in bright daylight at center center, surrounded by the rest of the group. The show then moves into the second scene of the first act, beginning with the storm conjured by Tee-boo. The choice has been made to not use strobe lights, but to represent the storm with flashes from eillipsoidals. The choice has also been made to use a common visual convention for evil (Tee-boo), the color green.

As the applause dies down at the end of the song, the lights will change into Scene 2 with memory 130, a darker and more foreboding look. The director will choreograph the performers to surround Hokey and Pookie, waving Chinese silk to represent the impending storm, which will be memory 131.

Then, on a sound cue, the director wants the lights to flash, followed by a shifting of the focus to Tee-boo's entrance downstage left. The flash sequence will be programmed into memory 132 and autofollows. Since it's uncertain how many flashes will be needed over what period of time, cue numbers will then be skipped, so that Tee-boo's entrance will be recorded as memory 136. This still gives three whole numbers to record intermediate called cues, if needed, prior to Tee-boo's entrance.

- Since memory 130 will be a different look than memory 124, the cue will be built from black. Again, memory 100.1 (containing the infrastructure channels) is loaded into the fader.
- Memory 130 is an intermediate cue; it's providing the visual punctuation point between the song and the storm. The general feeling of the cue is attempting to be "the storm approaching." With that in mind, channels 135 and 136 are brought up to 50%, to achieve a blue-green mix (evil on the horizon). Group 10 (the Roscolux 68 backlight) is brought up to 70%.
- Since the lovers at center are still the focus, the cue will be built so that the warmth comes from center. Groups 3 and 4, controlling the Roscolux 51 pipe ends, are brought up to 50%, while the cool boom sidelights, assigned to group 12, are also brought up to 50%.
- To provide facial light for the rest of the performers, group 2, controlling the Lee 161 frontlight, is brought up to 50%. If stage focus needs to be directed to a specific person in the group, the followspots will be used, or individual channels in the Roscolux 33 frontlight system may be brought up to a low level so their faces can be seen.
- The cue will be finished by adding specials to center to "punch up" the lovers. Channel 56, controlling the center center downlight, is brought up to 70%. To prevent the lovers faces from being too sharply shadowed, channel 59, controlling the 1 pipe center frontlight, is brought up to 50%.

This look is recorded as memory 130, with a time of 7 seconds. When memory 130 is recorded, most computer consoles recognize that any active channels from the previous memory (in this case memory 124) not reading in memory 130, will automatically be assigned a level of zero. This means that any channel in memory 124 not active in memory 130 will automatically be recorded to fade out to zero in 7 seconds.

Memory 131 will need to be darker and more ominous than memory 130. The initial plan is to use no system frontlight, only sides, downs, and backs.

- First, the background will be addressed. The green bottom of the translucency, channel 135, is brought up to 70%. The blue bottom of the translucency, channel 136, is taken down to 30%.
- The warmth from memory 130 will be taken out. Groups 3 and 4 are taken to zero, and groups 5 and 6, controlling the Roscolux 64 pipe ends, replace them at 30%.
- The color of the floor will shift. Group 10 is taken down to 30%, dimming the blue backlight. In its place, group 8 (controlling the Lee 124 downlight) is brought up to 70%.
- Likewise, the cool booms in group 12 are taken down to 20%, while the blue-green mids in group 13 are brought up to 50%.
- To provide visual contrast to the rest of the scene, the Lee 180 box booms in channels 29 and 30 are brought up to 30% to fill in the front shadows with saturated lavender.

Memory 131 is now recorded, with a time of 10 seconds. Since most of the cue is lower in intensity, it may be necessary to split the time and make the downfade time longer so that there's no visual "dip" as the channels cross-fade. Memory 131 has tinges of green, but is still mixed with other color systems. The saturated colors will be saved for full intensity until the entrance of Tee-boo.

Next, memory 132 will be recorded as the base cue; all of the other cues or effects will be "layered" on top of it. Whenever other cues are not running, memory 132 will provide the basic illumination on stage.

- To make sure that the flashes will be seen, the entire base cue will be a lower version of memory 131. All of the channels are activated (except for the infrastructure channels), and the entire cue is "pulled down" 25%. That look is now recorded

as memory 132, with a time of zero. This means that when the cue is activated, the entire look of the stage will drop down 25% in a bump.

Now for the storm cues. Although the entire sequence could be programmed in an effect loop, the amount of time between the initiation of the storm and Tee-boo's appearance in rehearsal times out to only 5 seconds. Because of that, the sequence will initially be built as a series of autofollows, so that altering the sequence will be easier and more controllable. The memories will skip numbers so that other memories, if need be, can be inserted in between.

- Since the more dramatic angles in this case are perceived to be from the side or the back, the frontlight systems will not be used. To pop through the saturation, the desaturated Roscolux 51 and the Roscolux 64 pipe ends and booms will be employed. Initially a flash will be programmed upstage left and downstage right. Channels 24 and 101 are brought to full. This look is recorded as memory 132.2, with an upfade time of 0 seconds and a downfade time of 1 second.
- Next, a flash midstage right and left will be recorded. Channels 24 and 101 are taken to zero, and channels 23 and 26 are brought up to full. This look is recorded as memory 132.4, also with an upfade time of 0 seconds, and a downfade time of 1 second.
- Now a flash upstage right and downstage left will be recorded. Channels 23 and 26 are taken to zero, and channels 48 and 31 are brought to full.

This look is recorded as memory 132.6, with an upfade time of zero seconds, and a downfade time of 1 second.

On this particular lighting console, a memory that is assigned a delay time indicates that the following cue is an autofollow. The delay time is also defined as the amount of time elapsed between the initiation of the first cue, and the automatic initiation of the second cue. If memory 132 is assigned a delay time of 2 seconds, then memory 132.2 will automatically begin 2 seconds after memory 132 begins. To break up the rhythm of the flashes, the console is programmed with a variety of delay times assigned to memory 132, 132.2, 132.4, and 132.6.

The final cue that needs to be constructed is Tee-boo's entrance, memory 136. Following the director's intent, the stage will be filled with variations of green. Since this is a new look, the memory can be built from black. The fader is cleared, and the infrastructure memory 100.1 is loaded once again.

- The background will become all green by bringing up channel 135 (the green bottom translucency) to full. The floor will also be green by activating group 8 (the Lee 124 downlight) to full. The mids in group 13 (colored in Roscolux 76) are brought to full. Channel 65, the Roscolux 20 downlight downstage left, is brought to 50% to provide focus for Tee-boo. The Roscolux 44 box booms, in channels 39 and 40, are brought up to 50%.

This look is recorded as memory 136, with a time fade of 1 second. The initial sequence is now complete. The cue list on the monitor display looks like this:

Cue	Time	Delay	(Translation)
124	5		(End of love song; applause)
130	7		(Storm on the horizon)
131	10		(Storm about to hit)
132	0	.3	(Thunder crash; base cue)
132.2	0/1	.5	(Flash up left, down right; starts 0.3 seconds after memory 132 begins)
132.4	0/1	.2	(Flash mid left, mid right; starts 0.5 seconds after memory 132.2 begins)
132.6	0/1		(Flash up right, down left; starts 0.2 seconds after memory 132.4 begins)
136	1		(Tee-boo's entrance)

Because the delays are listed on the screen, it's easy to see that the memories between 132 and 136 are auto-follows. Once the stage manager has called cue 132, the board will automatically run through the next three memories until the stage manager calls for cue 136.

Since all of the flash cues are zero count upfades, the total length of time for the entire sequence can be

determined by adding all of the delay times. In this case, the length of time between the initiation of memory 132 through the completion of memory 132.4 will be only 1 second.

Unfortunately, the flashing sequence needs to occupy 5 seconds, so additional action needs to be programmed. Otherwise, after the stage manager calls cue 132, the three flashes will occur and the stage will be static for 4 seconds before Tee-boo enters downstage left. Presuming that the director wants an "active" stage during the thunder crashing, either the delay times between flashes need to be increased so that there's a longer amount of time between flashes, or more memories need to be constructed to fill those 4 seconds. Depending on the timing and choreography, increasing the length of the delay times might be the solution, or it may make the entire sequence look like a mistake.

One solution might be to construct another 12 memories with different channels flashing, which would probably be more visually interesting. If this entire sequence hasn't been thought through prior to the level setting session, however, there may not be enough time to build that sequence.

Another possible solution that would fill the 5-second flash time would be to repeat the sequence or to create a "loop." If the light board has the capability to link memories, a command can be assigned to memory 132.6, instructing the light board to automatically reload memory 132. The memories then progress to the end of the sequence, and then start over again, and repeat indefinitely, until the GO button is pressed to clear the fader and load a new memory. Since there's only one base memory and three flash memories, the rhythm may visually appear too regular.

- The chosen solution is to duplicate the flash cues and alter the delay times to make the times of the flashes irregular. After loading memory 132, record that cue as memory 133, memory 134, and memory 135.
- After loading memory 132.2, record that cue as memory 133.2, 134.2, and memory 135.2.
- Continue the duplication of recording through 135.6, then add and alter the delay times for the entire range of cues between 132 and 135.6, to break up the rhythm of the flashes.

Twelve additional memories have now been created to fill the 5-second sequence. After successfully running the sequence in time, the next problem that becomes apparent is that the instruments don't flash bright enough (bumping up to full in 0 seconds), before they fade out in the down time of 1 second. If this is the case, the solution may be to preheat the filaments.

Preheat is the term applied to a low channel intensity that provides just enough voltage to make the filament in a lamp glow. It's not enough voltage, however, to make the filament create a beam of light. By recording that preheat intensity in every flash cue not involving the active channels, the filaments are warmed up, and can react more quickly to the zero time fade-up command.

First, the preheat intensity is defined for the channels used in the flash sequence (23, 24, 26, 31, 48, and 101). While looking into the lens of each instrument, each channel will be individually brought up to a level somewhere between 09% and 14%, so that the filament of each lamp glows without causing enough light to reach the stage. The channel intensity may be different for each instrument, depending on the dimmers. Each of those preheat intensities is written down.

Next, the board must be programmed. Since there's so little elapsed time between the base cue and the first flash, all of the preheats will be programmed starting with memory 131. While looking at the cue in the blind or preview display, each of the flash channels is programmed with the preheat intensity and recorded in the cue to track. This means the preheat intensities will be at the same levels in memory 132, the base cue. In memory 132.2, channels 24 and 101 come to full, while the rest of the channels continue to track. In memory 132.4, channels 24 and 101 go to zero. Those two channels are reprogrammed to their preheat intensities, again recording to track. This time-consuming process must be repeated through the entire sequence, so that whenever a flash channel is not at full, the channel is only reduced to its preheat intensity, not zero.

One way to avoid this situation is to decide, while building memory 131, which channels will be the flash channels. Those channels are then recorded at preheat intensities in memory 131, which becomes the "template" cue to record all of the other flash cues. The preheat intensity for the nonactive channels is directly recorded into the cues.

After all of the cues are built, the delays assigned, and the preheat intensities programmed, the cue sequence is then run in real time to see its visual effect. Variation to break up the rhythm is achieved by altering the delay time, the up and downfade time, and the

channel intensity in each flash memory. If additional channels are added to the cues, their preheat intensity should first be programmed into memory 131 to track.

Finally, memory 136 is viewed in the blind or preview display. Any of the flash channels that are not used in the cue are programmed to zero and tracked, which eliminates the possibility of the preheat intensities tracking through the rest of the scene. The entire sequence is run again in real time, and finally deemed a success.

It can be seen that elaborate programming sequences are not to be taken lightly. Without proper planning, any programmed linking, looping, effect, or sequential memories can consume extensive programming time. Mentally visualizing the sequence on paper, prior to the level setting session, forces the lighting designer to select the channel numbers, delay times, and memory numbers that will be involved. Otherwise, an entire cue level setting session can easily be reduced to programming one involved sequence for what may possibly be a relatively brief moment during the production. As a result, the rest of the memories may not have been created in the time allotted to the cueing session.

The Beginning of Act 2, Scene 1

The first scene in the second act of *Hokey* is the nighttime forest scene, when the Knotty Piners join Hokey. The sequence will begin with the house lights fading out while intro music is being played. Then the main curtain will rise on a dark stage. With 17 seconds of music, the forest scene will slowly be revealed. Initially the translucency will fade up, followed by the blue light on the floor. Then the leafy templates will appear on the floor, followed by the sidelight fading up. Finally, the frontlight will fade up as Hokey enters the scene.

According to the cue master, memory 200.7 will be recorded as a "black preset" cue, and memory 201 will be called by the stage manager. Memory 201 will be constructed as a five-part cue. Each part will be assigned its own fade and wait time.

When a memory is made up of parts, the visual end result is the same as building a series of overlapping autofollow memories. The difference is that they're all contained in a single memory. To create a single look that consists of five different actions moving at five different speeds, for example, that sequence is typically created by activating a series of channels and recording a separate memory five times with five different time fades. To construct the same sequence using the part feature, the final "look" is created once, recorded once, and then the five components of the memory are separated into parts. Each part is then assigned an individual fade time, wait, or delay to achieve each separate movement.

After creating the typical 5-memory sequence, it's decided that the overhead pipe end templates, for example, should fade up later in the sequence. Typical cue construction requires activating those channels in a later memory, recording that memory, and then deleting the channel levels from the earlier memory. To complete the same action in the part cue, the same channels are merely activated in a later part.

The advantage of a part cue is the fact that it is a single memory. Channels can be "shifted" from part to part with relative ease. The limitation of a part cue, on the other hand, is that it is a single memory. Although channels can easily be shifted, they can only be activated to a single intensity level. If the desired sequence requires the overhead templates to initially fade up to a high intensity, and then immediately fade down to a lower intensity, the sequence must be constructed with two separate memories.

Working with parts may require different methods on different consoles. On some consoles, programming a memory into parts may be restricted to a specific monitor display. Other consoles may require the parts to be created before channels can be assigned to each part. Most consoles that provide this feature are designed to provide at least six parts in any memory.

In this case, memory 201 will be broken into five parts. When the GO button is pushed, the five different parts will automatically occur with individual time fades. The wait times will be programmed to relate to the single push of the GO button. As discussed in Chapter 1, a wait on this lighting console is defined as the amount of time that elapses between the moment that the GO button is pressed, and when the unit of memory (in this case, a part) begins. When programming this amount of complexity, the cue list may not adequately show the time relationships. Sometimes drawing a time map can help illustrate the movement of the cue. Here is one way to illustrate the 5-part memory 201 sequence, using the graphic layout that was shown in Chapter 1.

Figure 10.1 shows the same information as the cue list, but graphically indicates the time line for all of the parts of memory 201. To record this sequence:

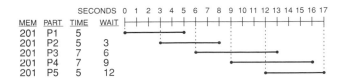

Figure 10.1 A Time Map of Memory 201

- Load memory 100.1, and record that as memory 200.7.
- Now create memory 201. The translucency will be blue green, so channel 136 (blue bottom translucency) is brought up to 50%. Channel 135 (green bottom translucency) is brought up to 25%. The floor will be blue, dappled with templates; group 10 (Roscolux 68 backlight) is brought up to 50%, while group 15 (overhead templates in channels 51 > 54) is brought up to 70%. The blue sidelight booms (in channels 101 > 108) will help shape the initial look of the performers, so group 12 is brought up to 30%. Finally, the blue frontlight will be added; group 2 is brought up to 30% as well.

After this look is recorded as memory 201, the five parts will be created in the preview or blind display.

- Part 1 will bring up the background. After activating channels 135 and 136, part 1 is recorded and assigned a time of 5 seconds.
- Part 2 will bring up the blue backlight. After activating group 10, part 2 is recorded and assigned a time of 5 seconds as well, but with an added wait of 3 seconds. This means that after the GO button is pushed for memory 201, 3 seconds will elapse before part 2 begins its 5-second fade.
- Part 3 will bring up the template system. After activating group 15, part 3 is recorded and assigned a time of 7 seconds, with a wait time of 6 seconds.
- Part 4 will bring up the blue booms. After activating group 12, part 4 is recorded and assigned a time of 7 seconds, with a wait time of 9 seconds.
- Finally, part 5 will bring up the blue frontlight. After group 2 is activated, part 5 is recorded and assigned a time of 7 seconds, with a wait time of 12 seconds.

The programming for the parts of memory 201 is now complete. The cue list on the monitor looks like this:

Cue	Time	Wait	(Translation)
200.7	3		(Preset Act 2-1; black on stage)
201 P1	5		(Blue-green background)
201 P2	5	3	(Blue backlight on the floor)
201 P3	7	6	(Template system)
201 P4	7	9	(Blue booms)
201 P5	5	12	(Blue frontlight)

When the GO button is pressed to load memory 201, part 1 will fade up the background in 5 seconds. Three seconds into that fade, part 2 will begin to fade up the blue backlight on the floor in 5 seconds. Three seconds into that fade, part 3 will begin to fade up the template system in 7 seconds. Three seconds into that fade, part 4 will begin to fade up the blue booms in 7 seconds. Finally, 12 seconds after the GO button was pushed, part 5 will begin to fade up the blue frontlights. The entire cue will be complete in 17 seconds.

If it's necessary to see a single part, on some consoles this can occur by pressing the GOTO button and loading that part into the fade. On other consoles, it may be necessary to search for other workarounds.

The End of Act 2, Scene 1

The end of the forest scene concludes with Hokey and the Knotty Piners singing a rousing song as they agree to join forces in the quest to free Pookie from Tee-boo's spell. The scene has been staged so that the entire group finishes the song down center. After they finish singing, the group remains in a pose as the curtain descends.

Memory 227 has been defined as the cue that will be called as the group assembles downstage. Memory 228 will be called by the stage manager, timed so that all frontlight will have faded out before the curtain descends, leaving the group in light. Constructing this sequence will be relatively simple, by using the inhibitive submaster controlling the front of house channels.

- Memory 227 is currently loaded into the active fader.
- Move the handle for submaster 24 (the front of house inhibitive sub) to zero. All of the front of house lights should now be at zero.
- Record memory 228, assigning a 3-second time fade.
- Restore submaster 24 to full. The front of house lights should remain inactive, since the memory 228 has been recorded with those channels at zero.

After memory 227 is reloaded into the active fader, the cue restores all of the front of house light in the memory. When the GO button is pressed, the channels upstage of the plaster line remain unaffected, while the front of house lights fade to zero in 3 seconds. The cueing for the end of Act 2, Scene 1 is complete.

This is a brief glimpse of some of the methods used to create light cues. There are many other ways to manipulate cue information, using other displays, setups, and command structures such as "rem-dim" or "record minus sub" to expedite cue creation. The manufacturer and model of the computer lighting console that's being used determines the flexibility allowed. Although each lighting console may have its own particular advantages and quirks, the largest limitation may be a lack of understanding on the part of the lighting designer about how to program the lighting console. The lighting designer needs to be prepared.

AFTER THE CUEING SESSION

After the final memory has been recorded, turn on the worklights, change the time stamp, and run the disks. Run the disks. Run the disks. If it's warranted, do a printout. Take the time to be certain that every cue that has been recorded has been marked on the cue master as having been constructed. Note all changes in channeling, submaster assignment, or group identity on the appropriate paperwork. Make note of any cue work that will be delayed until a future time. Give work notes, if needed. If possible, take a moment, get out of the theatre, take some deep breaths, and collect your thoughts. Take something to write on. After seeing the entire show once, inspiration or clarity can strike at any time.

FOLLOWSPOTS

When the followspot cue sheets were prepared, the basic elements of the instruments were mentioned: the iris size, the color boomerang, and the douser. This section will now examine how those elements can be used within a production and provide suggestions to simplify their use.

Followspot Concepts

Before the tasks of the followspots (or spots) are assigned, it may be valuable to consider why and how they're used.

The justification used for followspotting comes from three sources, provided by the world of art and scientific research. Almost any classical painting is a demonstration of the tenet which states that the eye is subconsciously attracted to the brightest point of light. Scientific observation has confirmed that the eye is subconsciously attracted to movement, while research has determined that there's a corollary between visibility and sound, justifying the old adage "what isn't seen, isn't heard."

A followspot can be used to implement those tenets. It directs the stage focus by moving and, by making one area of the stage brighter, it identifies the source of the speech or sound, allowing the performer to be heard. In most cases, though, while providing that focus, the followspot attempts to downplay its existence. To do this, the intensity and the softness of the beam edge are carefully controlled. On the other hand, the need for stage focus may overrule any desire for subtlety. Successfully providing stage focus during bright scenes may result in the followspots being used uncolored and "hard edged." In other situations, the hard edge of a followspot can sometimes be used to define location. An example of this is often seen in productions involving a theatrical setting. When the "performance" occurs, the hard beam edge telegraphs to the audience that the action is taking place "onstage."

Concealing the existence of a followspot is also directly related to the hot spot, speed of fade, and fluidity of movement. In most circumstances, when performers are being followed the hot spot will be on the face. Regardless of the beam's size, the spot needs to remain at least on the head of the performer. To keep the spot hidden, the time fades of the spot should be smooth and unobtrusive. When the spot follows a performer to an exit, the light should fade before the shadow of the performer is seen on the scenic legs. If a followspot's beam movement is inconsistent with the speed of the performer, the followspot's existence will be exposed. This is important when the spot is seen against scenery or a backdrop. The "smooth" followspot will be subconsciously noted, accepted by the audience, and attention will return to the stage focus. The movements of a "jerky" spot will constantly divert attention from the performer. Likewise, if the performer suddenly goes "dark" by moving out of the followspot, the absence of the followspot will steal stage focus.

Followspot Analysis

As has been shown, a followspot directs stage focus by making one area of the stage brighter. Typically, this is accomplished by "irising down," or reducing the size of the beam to a single performer. Although the priority of most followspots is to concentrate on the face, many forms of theatre use followspots in different iris sizes for specific purposes. In dance, spots often use a "full body shot" (the most "open"), which is larger than the body of a rapidly moving dancer. In musicals, the spot beams may be irised slightly smaller to what's referred to as a "body shot," highlighting the entire body of a performer from head to toe during songs and scenes staged with less vigorous movement. Opera spots often tighten the iris to "waist shots" during solos, covering only from above the head to the waist, to direct attention to the singer's face and mouth. In some cases, the spots iris tighter to "head shots," highlighting only the singer's face. "Pin spots" refer to the smallest iris size possible in that particular instrument, and aren't specific to any particular form. Spots in drama are used less frequently in a variety of sizes, often providing focus with a subtly moving frontlight special.

Regardless of the genre of the production, the task typically assigned to followspots is to provide the stage focus without calling attention to their existence. This is usually achieved by softening the edge of the beam, while reducing the intensity with the douser. That being said, manipulating a spot to produce an even field of coverage and a soft beam edge at the same time can be a constant source of frustration. For instance, the focus of the lamp inside the instrument can result in a high-contrast hot spot that may be impossible to center in the reflector. Or, without diffusion, softened lenses can produce exaggerated halation. Even fields of coverage are most frequently achieved after performing a "show and tell," when individual pieces of several different diffusions are held in front of the beam, one at a time. On the other hand, pursuit of the elusive "fuzzy edge" has inspired many tactics, ranging from taping diffusion in or outside of the instrument, to placing petroleum jelly on the individual colors, to taping portions of plastic storage bags purchased at the supermarket in place of diffusion.

Compounding the problem is the fact that many modern followspot lamps possess undesirable color temperatures that stand out in severe contrast to the way the rest of the scene is lit. Uncolored, their light can change the color of a performer's skin tone to an undesirable tint, giving them the appearance of a patient recently released from a hospital. The show and tell period may not only attempt to solve the mystery of the elusive fuzzy edge, it may also strive to determine the best color correction filter for a particular lamp.

The placement of theatrical followspots usually falls within two categories. The first category includes productions which only use spots as frontlight to direct the stage focus. Here, architectural limitations in most theatres typically dictate no more than three spotlights as that is the maximum number of instruments that can fit into the spot booth. The second category includes productions which use followspots from the front and another location, usually the side or rear. In this case, it is possible to balance the intensity from one side of the stage to the other, by employing an even number of spots divided equally on either side of the stage.

While the lighting designer or an assistant may initially choreograph the spots until their cues are set, by the time the show opens the followspot's actions are often called by a stage manager or another electrician. The complexity of the production and the need to call other cues may not afford the stage manager the time to provide direction to the spots, in which case the lead followspot operator provides the cues to the rest of the operators, usually on a separate headset channel.

Followspot Tactics

The three main attributes of a followspot were mentioned when the followspot cue sheets were prepared. Before the technical rehearsals begin, consider assigning followspots a series of "defaults": iris size, color, and fade times (both up and down). If the followspot activity will be constrained to a few lead performers, or "leads," consider assigning default performers to the followspots as well. The cue sheets will then only need to record what is unique to each spot cue, rather than detail the preset for every upfade, or pickup.

Before the rehearsal begins followspots should be assigned an identity number. If only two followspots are used, the brighter instrument typically receives the label "1" and the one spot should be on the number one performer. When three or more front spots are used, common convention is to begin the numbering from stage left using the same numbering system, the same as the instruments on the light plot. If the followspots are scattered around the theatre, the numerical labels are usually assigned in a circular pattern. Starting at one instrument (usually in the front), the instruments are numbered in a continual sweep around the theatre. If stacking occurs, number top to bottom. Use of this system allows the followspot director to refer rapidly to half of the followspots as "odds," and the other half "evens," cueing alternate spots on either side.

Labeling the followspots forces the lighting designer to consider their position. Suppose followspots are located far from centerline, and the performers need to be seen as they appear from the wings. The only option may be to assign the pickup to the followspot on the opposite side of the stage. But employing this tactic may result in abandoning any system assigning followspots to specific performers. Rather, pickups may be determined by which side of the stage a performer makes his or her entrance.

Since the brightest followspot needs to be on the most important focus point, it's important to compare all of the beam intensities before the rehearsal. If the followspots are nonmatching intensities, be certain to determine which one is the brightest. In dance, that spot is usually on the woman. In opera, it's often the highest billed singer. Although the protocol may differ from situation to situation, it's always important to know which spot physically puts out more light so spot usage can be properly allocated.

During bright scenes, if the intensity of a single followspot isn't sufficient to "cut" through the light cue and highlight the focus point, consider adding a second followspot to increase the contrast. When that's still insufficient, it may be necessary to un-gel the spot (commonly known as "drop the color") to succeed.

When there are too many performers requiring stage focus at different times, assigning a default performer may once again not be possible. The wardrobe crew may not be present or willing to risk damaging the costume for a rehearsal, and initially identifying the leads for the followspot pickups may be difficult without the costumes. Describing pickups by name will mean nothing to spot operators unfamiliar with the cast. For that matter, understudies or alternate casts may be leading the rehearsal, rather than the cast who will perform that night. On those occasions, consider identifying the characters by color: red sweats, yellow shirt, and so forth. Building on that idea, consider asking the leads to wear pieces (t-shirts, pants) in their character's colors during initial rehearsals. If future rehearsals are planned to insert understudies into leading roles, investigate the possibility of purchasing two or three t-shirts of related colors to be used specifically for these uncostumed rehearsals.

Designing followspot choreography in a production with constantly shifting points of focus can be an exciting challenge, but the complexity can also create conundrums. Inevitably, there are moments when there are more points of focus required than there are followspots and the lighting designer needs to make choices. First, the most important point of focus must be determined. Once that's defined, the current position of the followspots needs to be considered. If two performers are adjacent to each other, it may be possible to open the iris of one spot to cover both performers, while slowly fading out the second followspot. The now-available followspot can then pick up the additional focus point. Moments can occur when a spot, following one performer, suddenly needs to pick up a different performer. If a moment occurs where the two performers are staged close together, consider using that moment to change (or "swap") the spot's focus to the second performer.

Since followspots can affect the stage focus, their use doesn't have to be constrained to only highlighting performers. They can been viewed as frontlight get-me-out-of-trouble specials. From that perspective, their use can be expanded, providing stage focus for anything on the stage. This may range from highlighting properties, to illuminating entire pieces of "unplanned-for" scenery. When utilized for these types of pickups, the followspot's fade time may need to be carefully matched with the speed of the light cues. Colors may be chosen that have nothing to do with the performers and are used solely to complement the inanimate objects.

Followspots before the First Technical Rehearsal

Meet with the followspot operators before the first encounter on headset. One purpose for the meeting is to allow the lighting designer to explain the numbering, the defaults being used, identify the main performers, and any special pickups. The meeting's second purpose is to allow the lighting designer the opportunity to attach faces to names and establish a working relationship with the operators. With larger shows, this meeting may be the opportunity to distribute the color. The spot operators then have the responsibility to correctly load the color into the boomerang.

When calling followspots on a headset, the first rule to remember is to be brief. The followspot director should rehearse the semantics of his or her directions, so that the largest amount of information can be conveyed in the fewest possible words. The followspot director who chatters away incessantly through a performance may soon discover that he or she is alone on the channel. The operators have grown tired of the banter and have taken off their headsets.

Before giving any instructions, confirm that all operators are on headset and that they can hear the spot director. Unless time is short, giving instructions can wait until everyone is on, so that the instructions only need to be given once. After confirming that all involved know their individual label, have all the followspots turned on, and cast their beams on a common wall to compare the focus and intensity of the instruments. Once the spots are focused, note the units that seem brighter or darker for future work calls. Check the mechanical elements of the instruments, confirm that the colors are loaded in the correct sequence ("run through the colors"), check the largest and smallest iris sizes, and check that the dousers are fully functional in both directions (faded out, faded up).

If people are on stage, have one instrument pick them up, and define any typical iris sizes that will be used for the production, including full body, body, waist, or head shot and physically mark the position of the iris control on the spot itself. Once the instrument has been marked, have it rejoin the other light pools back up on the wall, and mirror the sizes to the other instruments. After all the instruments have been calibrated, explain the location of typical entrances or other areas of the stage where the spots will fade up (commonly known as "pickup points") to be used in the show. Typical pickup points include "in 1" left and right, "in 4" left and right, down center, and center center. Providing the spots with this location information will also confirm that all of the followspot beams can reach each of the pickup points.

If there are any special sequences, consider practicing those sequences before the rehearsal begins. Typical sequences may include a slow opening or closing of the iris on a performer ("Close to a head shot in 7 counts." or "Even spots open to a waist shot in 10 counts.") or changing color in zero counts ("Odd spots swap color to frame three in a bump."). Other sequences may involve individual pickups made in black ("Spot one in a pin spot on the glove down center in three counts."), or swirling patterns on show curtains ("Ballyhoo on the show drop.").

The followspot director and the followspot operators are now ready to begin the technical rehearsal.

THE TECHNICAL REHEARSAL ANALYSIS

It can be said that the primary purpose of the **technical rehearsal** is to add the performers safely to the technical elements of the production. Although that statement is true, from a broader perspective, the technical rehearsal also offers the first real glimpse of the production's visual concept. The technical rehearsal is the opportunity for the director and the design team to clarify the stage picture, and decide if the design choices that have been made will succeed. To achieve this goal, the initial objective of the technical rehearsal is to address every problem that might potentially slow or stop the production in subsequent rehearsals. This may require several repetitions of the same sequence to "work through" a particular transition. The first rehearsal with performers can also be referred to as a "stop and start." Once the flow of the production is achieved, and the performers have refined their performance, it will be possible to see if the overall concept has successfully evolved. Since the amount of time dedicated to this portion of the rehearsal process is finite, the secondary objective of these rehearsals is to complete an entire "work through" of the show in the scheduled amount of time.

In a complex production, different technical rehearsals may be dedicated to different acts of the production. Although the performers attempt to perform the show without interruption in "real time," any

problems that may hamper the production in future rehearsals warrant a stoppage of the action. During these rehearsals, light cues are altered and shaped in their appearance. Together with the other technical elements, the placement and timing of each cue is rehearsed in real time. Simultaneously, many other refinements may be taking place as well. The director may alter staging for the performers, scenery may be repositioned, and properties may be respiked. To an outside observer, it can resemble barely organized chaos.

Often, initial techs occur without adding the additional complexity of wardrobe, or any live music. Sometimes after the entire show has been teched, rehearsals solely addressing transitions can take place, called **cue-to-cue rehearsals.** Rehearsing cues and transitions without the performers is often called a **dry tech.** Costumes, hair pieces, and makeup are added for the **dress rehearsal(s).** When an orchestra is added, and the performers wear their costumes, the rehearsal is known as an **orchestra dress.** After a point, the labels of the rehearsals become confusing, but usually once the performers begin their work on the stage, the light cues will always be rehearsed. Due to that fact, for the purpose of this text, all of these rehearsals will be referred to as the technical rehearsal.

If the number of technical rehearsals is reduced, the need to correct problems immediately becomes intensified. If the first technical rehearsal is also the final orchestra dress, it can be a free-for-all. In this situation, everyone has his or her own agenda. The director and choreographer may think that the rehearsal is solely to allow them to space or stage the performers. Performers may believe the rehearsal is to correct the conductor about the tempos. Conductors may believe the rehearsal is to get the correct tempos, mix, and color from the orchestra. The stage manager is trying to call the transitions and cue sequences correctly. The scenic designer may take advantage of a break in the action to direct the rehanging of a backdrop. Meanwhile, the lighting designer is checking the intensity, blend, and timing of each light cue, while reacting to the numerous demands, requests, and suggestions of everyone around the production table.

Hopefully, those situations are few and far between. *Hokey*'s production schedule is a relatively relaxed one. Now that the light cues have been created, and the elements of the transitions rehearsed, preference is given to the director or choreographer to insert the performers into the stage picture and adapt to their presence. Initially, the stage manager is with the lighting designer at the production table. This allows the pair to discuss the timing or placement of light cues and have face-to-face discussions with the director.

Prior to the Technical Rehearsal

 A list to consider prior to the technical rehearsal:

- Prior to the tech, a check is made to confirm that all of the required components are functioning at the production table. This is very important. Few things get a tech off to a rougher start than discovering at the last minute that the monitor is flickering, the headsets aren't working, or, when the house goes out, the worklight at the table is burned out.
- All of the cue construction paperwork is present, updated, and arranged. Adequate numbers of forms are available. Work note sheets are dated and prepared.
- A channel check has been performed for both instruments and any electrical devices, and any problems have been noted.
- A blackout check has been performed. The running lights and spotting lights are functioning, and unnecessary worklights (including the grid worklights) are turned off.
- Any repertory work has been accomplished (color changes or refocusing in the sidelight booms).
- Repatch is set for the top of the rehearsal and has been checked for accuracy.
- The cue light system is functioning.
- The light board is in the preset cue.
- All members of the electrics department have checked in on headset and know their initial actions.
- The seating area between the stage and the production table has been cleared. (Since the eye is unconsciously attracted to movement, observers sitting in that area may otherwise distract the lighting designer.)
- A path of easy access has been established between backstage and the production table. (The last thing needed 3 minutes prior to the start of the tech is the opportunity to play treasure hunt because the labyrinthine route between the two locations is unknown.)

The lighting designer and the electrics department are now ready to begin the technical rehearsal.

 ## Shelley's Soapbox: Headset Etiquette

The headset is a tool for communication. Although its contribution to theatre can't be stressed enough, wearing even the most comfortable headset for 12 hours can still make anyone's head throb. While trying to work in a fairly intense situation, distractions can often become twice as irritating. If one of your ears is trapped inside of plastic and foam and you have no choice about what comes through the speaker in your ear, the last thing that's needed is unknowing personnel not following proper headset etiquette. The headset is not a telephone for casual conversation—it is a business tool.

 A list of do's and don'ts when wearing a headset:

- If you're not speaking with someone over the headset, turn off your microphone.
- Have the location of the microphone switch of the headset memorized. Use it often. If uncertain, check with the sound department so you know how the microphone switches on the belt-pack work. If the headset has a call button, know how to turn the headset on and off, without accidentally hitting that button instead. If there's any confusion, label the switches or buttons with tape.
- Remain calm, even in emergencies. Don't lose your patience while talking over a headset. Don't ever scream into a headset. Don't even think of taking your headset off in a huff and slamming it onto the table with the microphone on.
- Speak clearly into the headset. Don't talk while the microphone is under your chin or above your head. Do not mumble, hum, whistle, sing, or cluck while the microphone is on. Don't eat, chew gum, drink, sneeze, or yell to someone in the distance while the headset microphone is turned on.
- Don't believe that the headset is its own private confessional. Be aware that your headset conversation may be broadcast on monitor speakers backstage or into green rooms or management offices. Personal opinions about the talent, state

of the show, or any of the individuals with whom you are working should not be expressed over headset.

The Technical Rehearsal Begins

When the technical rehearsal begins, the lighting designer looks at each light cue to see what is right and what needs to be corrected. This may include the channel intensities, the length of the time fades, and the called placement of the cue. At the same time, the designer is also making certain that the visual purpose of the cue is correct and works with the action on the stage. Meanwhile, the stage manager is attempting to run the rehearsal by calling cues for the first time and providing direction. There's usually a lot of activity on the headset.

The most important thing that needs to be remembered by the lighting designer is safety. Certainly, there may be times that require darkness while performers are present onstage. If a cue must be rebuilt from scratch, the most expedient method may be to start from a clean slate; a black stage. The lighting designer must remember, though, that the performers are not used to being in the dark. Rapidly taking the stage to black may cause unnecessary accidents or injury. If a black stage is required, announce the fact loudly to the entire theatre. Extending the golden rule that was presented during the light cue level setting session, there should never be an unexpected or unannounced fade to black or blackout during a technical rehearsal.

The second thing the lighting designer must keep in mind is the overall purpose of the activity. If at all possible, the flow of the technical rehearsal should not be delayed by the lighting designer making changes. If the lighting designer refuses to interrupt cue work for the sake of the rehearsal, consider this thought. Although the corrected light cues may now look better, while that work was performed, the entire cast, crew, and design team was unable to do their jobs while a series of level intensities was altered. Unless those changes drastically affect the sequence to be rehearsed, the lighting designer must stop changing levels when the stage manager is ready to continue, so that the board operator can prepare to run the sequence again.

As the technical rehearsal continues, the number of corrections requiring attention may lead the lighting designer to believe that four things must be done at the same time. Regardless of the tasks involved, the lighting designer must remain aware of the surrounding environment. When someone is trying to address the lighting designer while cues are being changed, the designer may be speaking to the board operator over a headset. If it's in the middle of an involved sequence, be polite. At least acknowledge the person with a wave of the hand or a nod. By acknowledging them, they won't feel like they're being ignored, and they'll be less likely to get impatient. The lighting designer especially needs to be cognizant of the stage manager, who may be patiently waiting for the lighting designer to finish reprogramming before the rehearsal continues. Even more important than the stage manager, the lighting designer should stop whatever he or she is doing whenever the director wants to have a discussion.

In many cases, the lighting designer is on the same channel as the stage manager, so the priority of the moment must be maintained. Although every correction may seem incredibly important, the lighting designer must keep the larger objective in mind. Don't become an obstruction to the flow of the rehearsal. When the stage manager is attempting to call cue sequences, the lighting designer must bite his or her tongue. Be silent and don't vocally get in the way on headset. If possible, have a walkie-talkie to communicate with the electricians backstage to reduce the activity on the headset. Reduce the number of corrections that have to be changed before the sequence is run again. If there are numerous notes, chances are that the other facets involved in the sequence will also need adjusting or will need to run the sequence again as well. Take notes, and if there's no opportune time during the tech, fix light cues during the next break or at another time while viewing the blind or preview screen.

If cues are to be deleted, consider recording the rejected cues into the library block, instead of eliminating them completely. When possible, keep a list of the cues, and use the same numerical sequence so you know where the cues came from. Remember to always record cues into the library block in the correct mode (track or cue only). The mode often used for singular recording is cue only, not track.

When the technical rehearsal is stopped for a requested change in the lighting, come to an understanding of what change is needed, and then react as rapidly as possible. Inform the stage manager of any changes in the cue placement. Rewrite the affected cues. Consider the possibility of using another cue that has already been approved. If the cue must be built from scratch, consider which handles can be used to construct the light cue as rapidly as possible.

While teching involved sequences, there may be confusion about cue placement. Sometimes the simplest solution may be for the lighting designer to call portions of the rehearsal. If the stage manager is unclear about placement of the cues, offer to call sequences in a nonthreatening manner. Whether the sequence is perfect or a complete fiasco, the stage manager has had the opportunity to observe the sequence from a different perspective.

Later rehearsals may be smooth enough to check the cues from other vantage points in the house. Sitting in the back of the house may reveal that a light cue is too dim. The balcony view may allow the designer to see unsightly or misfocused patterns of light on the floor.

Remain conversational and calm at all times. Nervous energy can be easily transferred over a headset, and can lead to a negative atmosphere, or even accidents.

End of the Final Rehearsal

Prior to the beginning of the final rehearsal, the schedule should be examined. Presumably, there will be a portion of time designated for cleanup. The production schedule may read "Tech Notes, 5:30 P.M. to 6:00 P.M." This time is typically scheduled to complete final notes. and clean the house. This time can also be used to make changes in the lighting cues while looking at the stage. Seeing cue changes onstage is always preferable to altering information on paper or in a blind display. If the board notes are separated into two categories (need to see to change, can change blind), prioritizing the board notes that require viewing will be clear. The need to prioritize can be more urgent, though, because the amount of time available probably isn't really 30 minutes. Although the final tech notes period is listed on the schedule as a 30 minute block of time, typical union protocol states that "wash-up" begins 5 to 15 minutes before the end of the call. Therefore, if tech notes are scheduled between 5:30 and 6:00, the lighting designer may really only have until 5:45 to make cue corrections while looking at the stage, before the stagehands arrive to remove the production table.

With that time constraint in mind, as soon as the rehearsal has concluded, inform the production electrician if any refocus or work notes that will be required. A ladder crew will be organized and in place by the time the board notes are complete. If there's a choice between work notes and board notes, work on stage requiring the lighting designer's attention often takes precedence over board work. Depending on the complexity of the preshow check and preset call, it may be difficult to get a ladder crew onstage after half an hour without disrupting the flow of the production. Usually, any incomplete board notes can be addressed after the preshow check is complete, while looking at the blind display. However, depending on the number and severity of cue notes that need to be seen, it may be necessary to continue to work at the production table until the crew is sent out to take the table away.

After the final board note has been recorded and the memory has been run to disk, the console may only be needed to activate channels for work notes. If there are still many board notes, consider using an off-line editing program, if one is available. If this is a possibility, ask the board operator to bring you an up-to-date disk and update the light cues during the dinner break.

Briefly consider a view of the schedule in reverse. Depending on many variables, the stagehands may not be called for the performance until after the house has opened to seat the audience. If that's the case, when the crew leaves the theatre for dinner, all work in the house must be complete. Lighting equipment, color, and focusing ladders all need to be removed. The headsets need to be cleared, the monitors may need to be moved to the stage manager's console, and the production table must be disassembled and removed. The house invariably needs to be cleaned. Prioritize the activities that must take place before the performance can begin. If a front of house instrument requires refocusing, then that should be addressed immediately; the curtain will be closed when the crew returns from dinner, and time may be needed after the final instrument has been refocused to remove the electrician and the ladder.

If you foresee running out of time, consider what could take place after the crew has returned from dinner. Present the situation to the production electrician and the house electrician; they are there to help you manage the time. If there are overhead instruments that require a refocus, that task might be delayed until after half hour, when the crew has returned and the main curtain is closed. On the other hand, it may be possible to refocus the overhead lighting instruments while the tech table is being struck.

In addition to all of these considerations, this period of time is often the last appropriate time to determine the viewing location, the lighting designer's office during the performance.

The Viewing Location

During the course of the show, the lighting designer's role often shifts from being a participant in the production to being an observer with a headset, noting any problems within the electrics department. In a broader sense, however, the lighting designer may be the only person watching the show from the audience's perspective on headset who's not occupied with specific tasks. If that's the case, the lighting designer may be requested to take notes about any other visual or timing aspect of the show. To function in that capacity, the lighting designer should ideally be located with a complete view of the stage and have the ability to hear and speak to the board operator, stage manager, and the followspots. If it is possible to acquire a two-channel headset, the typical request is to be given the ability to both hear and speak to the stage manager and board operator on one channel, and the followspots on the second channel. Since presetting this headset configuration may take some time, the request should be made long before the beginning of the first performance.

Ideally, the viewing location will be somewhere other than in the light booth. Although there may be occasion for the lighting designer to speak to the board operator during the show, in most cases the board operator must concentrate solely on listening to the stage manager. The last thing a board operator needs is a lighting designer attempting to fix light cues live in front of an audience. Unless a situation develops that may involve the safety of someone in the theatre, respect the board operator's role in the performance. When given the choice, the lighting designer should choose to be in a separate location. Live changes made in haste can potentially contribute to opening night crises.

On occasion, the architectural design of the theatre may dictate that the lighting designer has to sit in the audience; no other location exists. Although a headset will inform the lighting designer of the current memory or cue, discretely taking notes with a flashlight is a challenge and little room is available for paperwork. Since the documents may no longer be immediately accessible, notes may be less specific, harder to understand, or completely illegible, which means that the same problems will be repeated in the same cues during the next performance.

Like the route to the production table, the best time to determine the path to the viewing position is not immediately prior to the show. Determine the route to the viewing location and the light booth before the house opens. If the viewing location's perspective is restricted, this time can also be used to determine how to move easily and quietly into the house to see the unobscured stage picture, which may include the top of the scenery, the downstage edge, or one side of the wings. This time can also used to meet the ushers who will allow the lighting designer uninterrupted passage during the performance.

SUMMARY

Once the house has been cleared and all possible work notes have been executed, the stage is often abandoned to a state much like the quiet before a storm. This is an excellent opportunity for the lighting designer to update all of the paperwork that will be used as reference documents during the observation of the performance. If that process is complete, the time can be used to leave the space and do other things—for instance, go eat.

11 The Performance

This chapter examines the typical sequence of events that surround the performance, beginning with preshow checks, and followed by a preset of the technical elements involved in the production. Then the performance begins. At the conclusion of the first act, several changes may occur during the intermission. After the conclusion of the performance, meetings may be arranged to analyze the observations made during the show, and notes are given that will determine the amount of work that will need to be accomplished before the next performance.

Typically, critics who review the show attend a scheduled performance, often declared the "opening." In most situations, once the show opens, changes are no longer made, and the show is "frozen." Once frozen, notes will no longer be given, usually because the director and the rest of the design team have finished their contract and no longer attend the show on a nightly basis. Usually, that point also signals the completion of the lighting designer's contract as well. In preparation for the lighting designer's absence, the show is often staffed so that once the production is open, all tasks are performed without his or her involvement. As such, during the initial performances the lighting designer may solely be an observer, watching the show for light cue and timing notes, and observing the preshow check and intermission to ensure that it flows smoothly and no details are missed.

BEFORE THE PERFORMANCE

The time prior to a union-staffed performance is often broken into two distinct periods of time. The **preshow call** is the time when a reduced crew (if nothing else, the department heads) perform preshow checks to confirm that all technical elements related to the production are operational, and to note anything that must be fixed. Typically, this period of time is strictly confined to only observe and note the status of the technical elements. Nothing can be repaired, adjusted, or preset until the **show call**, when all of the technical personnel are required by contract to be in the theatre (the **show crew**). During the show call, any notes are addressed, and the stage is preset for the performance. Usually, the preshow call is scheduled for 90 minutes prior to the beginning of the performance, while the show call begins 30 minutes before the performance.

The factor that may affect this schedule relates to what the audience sees when entering the theatre, known as the stage "preset." If the production doesn't use a main curtain, then all onstage work must be complete before the scheduled time the audience is to be admitted into the theatre. This moment is often referred to as "the house is open." In most theatres in the United States, the house opens 30 minutes prior to the scheduled beginning of the performance. If the preset for a union show is an open stage without a curtain, then the show call is sometimes moved back at least 30 minutes before the house opens, or one hour before the performance begins.

On the other hand, if the audience is admitted to the theatre with the main curtain in, financial constraints may dictate that the show crew not be called until "half hour," the same time as "house open." When that's the case, the audience is often briefly delayed while the electrics crew quickly checks the front of house channels. Presuming there are no problems, the main curtain is then flown in, the doors are opened to the audience, and the light check continues upstage of the curtain while the audience is seated in the house. In this situation, the ability to rapidly check function and focus of the instruments gains new significance.

Any burnouts downstage of the main curtain need to be rapidly located and identified. Reaching any front of house (FOH) position takes some amount of time. Immediately discovering any FOH problems at least attempts to prevent a delay in opening the house. Unless it's a critical special, the nonfunctional instrument may merely be noted for lamp replacement during the next available work call.

The Preshow Call

The electrics department begins the preshow call by activating each lighting instrument and checking every electrical device used or related to the production. The purpose of this **preshow check** is to be certain that everything is in working order, that the instruments have retained their focus, and that the color media has not faded or burned out. Although the lighting designer may have focus notes and light board corrections, none of those notes can technically be addressed until the lighting system is checked and the show call begins. The reason for this is simple. Performing any notes or corrections makes no sense if the lights aren't functioning and the show can't take place. The only way to determine that the show is preserved and the lighting system is functioning is to do a preshow check. Therefore, the preshow check takes precedence. Besides, the preshow check may uncover other notes that can be addressed at the same time as the designer's work notes. On the other hand, if there are major problems, priority instantly shifts to making certain that the lighting system is functional and the show can go on. In those situations, the designer's notes may be quietly set aside.

Electrics Preshow Check

Although the main curtain is "in" for the stage preset of *Hokey*, the entire show crew has been called to begin work "at hour." Having this extra breathing room allows the preshow checks to be relaxed, and everyone can use the time to double-check everything before the first performance.

Even though the light plot for *Hokey* doesn't include a large number of instruments, the overall list of items that need to be checked involves much more than merely the instruments in the light plot. Many show-related electrical items used on stage are often the responsibility of the electrics department. Worklights, running lights, cueing lights, and any special effects are all checked to confirm that they are opera-

tional. In some cases, house lights, hall lights, or aisle lights may also be part of the electrics department's responsibility.

The preshow light check can have many names, including dimmer check, burnout check, or channel check. Initially, the lighting designer may "run" the preshow check, or observe it and take notes. If nothing else, after the show "opens," the production electrician assumes the responsibility, and the lighting designer becomes another pair of eyes watching the work take place. Once the show opens, there may not be time before every performance to run an extensive preshow check of the entire light plot. Unless the overhead electrics were hit before the end of the technical rehearsal (or there's been an earthquake), it's often assumed that the focus of the instruments won't radically change except for an occasional instrument that drops its focus. Extensive electric preshow checks are often selectively scheduled on an individual show-by-show basis.

It's believed that whenever filaments are quickly activated, the surge in voltage may cause them to prematurely burn out. To avoid this, once the system has been turned on, a programmed memory is often loaded that contains all of the instruments at a low percentage to "warm the filaments." These light cues were programmed in the *Hokey* disk as memories 900.7 and 950.7. All of the channels used in the show fade up to 30% in 10 counts to perform this function.

Before any of checks are performed, some of the worklights are turned off and the house lights are dimmed to improve contrast and visibility of the light. If there are lights in the grid, those are usually left on, so that it's possible to see the silhouette of a nonfunctioning instrument.

Four different methods are commonly used to confirm that the rest of the instruments in the light plot are functional and focused. The **individual channel check** is exactly what it implies, sequentially looking at each channel one by one. Like the check performed after the hang, it's performed to confirm that the contents of each channel works and that the focus of the instruments hasn't changed. Starting with channel 1, each channel is activated to a level of full so that it can be seen. For a large light plot, this may not be time effective. If the time between the preshow call and the house opening is short, this type of preshow check will need to be performed rapidly. The lighting designer should have the focus for the entire show memorized, and the board operator needs to be nimble-fingered.

A second method that only checks for nonfunctioning instruments is referred to as the **burnout check.** Every channel that contains an instrument is activated to the same percentage (25% to 50%). Each position is visually scanned to confirm that every instrument has light coming out of it. Although this is faster than an individual channel check to determine burnouts, it also means that the focus of each instrument isn't addressed. With all of the lighting instruments on at one time, this check often requires a rigid pattern while examining the entire light plot. Otherwise, while attempting to view all of the different locations simultaneously, any distraction may result in an entire position being visually skipped and forgotten.

A third method used to check burnouts is the **position channel check.** This is comprised of a series of cues programmed into computer memory lighting consoles. The cues are constructed so that only one position is activated in each cue. If a channel contains two instruments located in two positions, then the channel will come up in two different cues. This method provides a structure to the burnout check. By activating all of the instruments in a single position, it's possible to rapidly scan the entire position and see a dark spot, which may indicate a burned-out lamp. The intensity of the channels is usually recorded at a lower percentage, so that eyes aren't strained while looking into the lenses of the instruments. Since a single position is the focus of concentration, and every channel involved in the show is programmed into one of the memories, the possibility of accidentally skipping a position or an instrument is reduced. The 900 series of memories were programmed into the console during load-in for this purpose. If this method is considered, any changes or additions to the light plot should be reflected in the cues before they are used. This will prevent the possibility of mistaking an absent channel for a burnout.

Even though this is a more systematic approach to the burnout check, this method still doesn't address the issue of focus. Unless the instrument has completely dropped focus, seeing any focus irregularities will be difficult.

Although the issue of focus isn't addressed, a position channel check still has its advantages. Since all of the channels are programmed into cues, the need to individually activate channels is eliminated. This means that anyone can hit the GO button to advance to the next light cue (and the next hanging position). If the console is in a remote location, the position channel check reduces the need for communication between the production electrician and the board operator. Instead of interpreting numbers shouted over a tiny sound monitor, the board operator only has to listen for the next GO. If the production electrician is the only electrician called to perform a preshow check, the position channel check provides a system for determining burnouts quickly. The cues used in the position channel check can be linked as a series of autofollows. By programming a delay between each cue, the GO button can be pressed once; the production electrician can then move to the stage and scan each position as the cues load in sequence. If more time is required at a single position, the delay time can be lengthened.

A fourth method that allows both burnouts and focus to be checked is called a **system channel check.** This preshow check is also comprised of a series of cues programmed into memory lighting consoles. In this case, the cues are constructed so that only one system of light is activated in each cue. Since the focus of each system involves overlapping and matching beam edges, it's possible to rapidly identify any deviations in focus between instruments. Once the appearance of each system has been memorized, the entire light plot can be checked rapidly for both burnouts and focus. The initial purpose of the 950 series of cues was to provide handles while constructing memories for the show. Their second purpose, however, was to be used in this application. Since matching systems of light are in adjacent memories, seeing burnouts or focus anomalies is relatively simple. Due to the fact that the number of systems is greater than the number of positions, there are more memories in the system channel check. This means that the system channel check will take more time to complete, but a more complete picture of the light plot's current status will be known.

The other advantage of this method is the same as the position channel check. The GO button is the only keystroke used, communication is simplified, and the cues can be linked as autofollows, allowing the check to be performed by a single person. The only time that paperwork may need to be consulted is when memories containing special channels aren't properly updated.

Golden Rule: Complete the Check Before Fixing the Problems

When a nonfunctioning instrument is discovered during the electric preshow check, the first course of action is *not* to check the lamp, swap the plugs, or any other troubleshooting activity. The first thing to do when encountering an instrument that doesn't work is to *finish the electric preshow check.*

Continue through the entire light plot to be certain that all of the problems are known. Then the troubleshooting can begin. Although this seems basic, it can often be overlooked. On more than one occasion, I've seen this basic rule forgotten. While an electric preshow check is being performed, a burnout will be discovered. The preshow check is interrupted to get a ladder onstage. The burnout is replaced and the ladder struck. After this interruption, the preshow check then continues, and a second nonfunctional instrument in the same position is discovered. The ladder must return to the stage, requiring a duplication of effort.

It's worthy to note at this point that a burned-out lamp may not always be the source of a nonfunctioning instrument. A blown component within a dimmer rack may be the culprit, causing several lamps to appear to be burnouts. Repairing a blown component may take little time to complete, but several minutes of troubleshooting may be required to identify the true source of the problem. If the preshow check is interrupted to address a single instrument, some amount of the finite time available may be consumed merely in gaining access to that unit. Only after the replacement lamp also fails to function will it become obvious that a larger problem exists, and time has now been lost that could have been applied to the troubleshooting process.

Finally, it's worth noting that a nonfunctioning lamp may be the least of the problems encountered before a performance. Electronic components can fail at any time, most often when a system is turned on. This action sends a surge of voltage through the entire system. The more electronic devices involved in any production directly translates into that many more possibilities of things not working. Since every action consumes some amount of time, spending that time fixing a single instrument will be shown for the error it is when an entire dimmer rack is later discovered to be nonfunctional. The status of the entire lighting system must first be determined. Time spent interrupting the preshow check to fix a single burnout may delay seeing the larger problem, which could ultimately delay or cause a performance to be lost.

Shelley's Notes: Electrics Preshow Checks

During the electrics preshow check, the worklights often need to remain on so that other tasks can happen at the same time, and it may be difficult to see the focus of the instruments. In these situations, the angle of observation can be used to the lighting designer's advantage. If the lighting designer stands in the path of the reflection of the beam, even under most worklight, the beam edges will be much more visible. As an example, activating channels 1 > 5 would turn on the downstage frontlight zone hung on the truss. To see the edge of the beams, rather than stand downstage facing the backdrop, the lighting designer would stand upstage, facing the instruments, and the reflection of light bouncing upstage off the stage. The downstage side of the multiple beam edges will be seen on the floor. If the beams match, the focus is correct. If one beam edge is in a different plane, the instrument may have dropped and might require refocusing.

If worklights must remain on throughout the entire preshow check, the lighting designer can use this method to check the focus of the systems. By anticipating the direction from which the next system's beams will originate, the designer can move to a position on the stage to see the light reflected from the stage and the beam edges of that particular system.

Although submasters are often assigned to control systems during the performance, their use as preshow checking devices should not be dismissed. If a series of electrical devices are used in the light plot, the submasters can allow many of them to be checked, requiring only the activation of a handle instead of numerous channels. If color scrollers are used in a production, for example, one submaster can be assigned to all of the color scrollers, while a second submaster can be assigned to all of the channels controlling the instruments behind the scrollers. Using this method not only means that all of the color scrolls can be checked at one time, but it also means anyone can run the board instead of a trained console operator.

The Show Call

Once the show call begins, all of the work notes can be addressed, and the stage can be preset for the top of the show. Although the technical departments go about their tasks to preset the stage in a relaxed fashion, the activities are performed with a sense of purpose. Much of this pace is due to the fact that the schedule is finite. Problems may be discovered that were not apparent in the preshow checks, and if they need to be solved, they are rapidly addressed. What's avoided is the possibility of having to delay the beginning of the performance. Not only does this make the evening that much longer, it might possibly extend the overall length of the show call beyond the length of time allowed. When that occurs, members of several different unions may automatically be escalated into the higher additional pay rate of overtime.

Overhead Work Notes

If the notes include any work in the overhead electrics, the request is often politely made that no performers be on stage until all ladder work is complete. Although this varies from production to production, the reason is twofold: First, performers are kept off the stage to be certain that the space is absolutely safe. Second, if the ladder needs to move around the stage, additional people just get in the way. To reduce this inconvenience, effort is made to complete the notes and presets with alacrity. The sooner the stage can be "given over" to the performers, the more relaxed the stage environment.

In this effort to clear the stage, any electrical work notes are addressed first. Because the ladder may be buried behind offstage equipment, some time may be involved in accessing it. While the ladder is being brought to the stage, the work notes are identified by location. The traffic pattern of the ladder is then determined so that it spends as little time as possible on the performance surface, and begins the notes at the farthest location first. In that way, if time runs short, the ladder won't be caught in the most distant location. Unless instruments are hung too high to reach with a regular ladder, any work or focus notes involving the sidelight booms are delayed until the overhead ladder has been returned to its storage area.

Sidelight Check

Once the overhead work notes are complete, the sidelight boom instruments are often then recolored, and any electrical tasks on the deck are performed. These activities are accomplished and checked using the color cards. Usually, the sidelight booms aren't checked until after their color and templates have been preset for the top of the show. Since they're the closest instruments to the stage, sidelights often receive the roughest treatment and require the most attention. More than that, however, waiting to check the sidelights until after they've been recolored means that the color units will match the color cards, and any unintentional refocusing that may have occurred while the units were being prepared will be spotted. Once the

sidelights are checked for focus and color, the rest of the systems, specials, and rovers can be checked for their function and focus using the floor cards.

The key to accelerating these checks is to determine what channels need to be seen, define how to quickly confirm that the instruments are correct, and how to rapidly activate them. If the same collection of channels will be requested in the same order before every performance, consider recording the sequences into cues or groups. Although the sidelights can be checked channel-by-channel, it may be quicker to record groups that activate one side of one system at a time. By matching the shutter cuts and the beam edges, the focused accuracy of an entire sidelight system can more rapidly be checked. A different approach might be to create a handle that contains all of the channels assigned to a single boom. When activated, all of the side shutter cuts can be compared. A third approach is to create a handle that contains all of the instruments on one side of the stage. The *Hokey* light plot has been programmed so that submasters 10 and 11 perform this function.

When one of these two submasters is used to check one side of the boom sidelights, the sub is initially brought up to a low level, so that the focus of the units can be checked. This is achieved by walking up and downstage and looking into the instruments to see the centered filament in the reflector. Afterwards, the submaster is brought to full, to check side shutter cuts off of the scenic backing, and top shutter cuts off of the borders. If it's necessary to check sidelight focus under worklights, consider using the angle of observation to see the edges of the beams. Stand at center and look down at the stage. The bottom beam edges should be visible, along with the side shutter cuts. If the side cuts are compared to the locations of the black masking legs, it's possible to determine which instruments will require a shutter adjustment. To finish the sidelight check, any rovers used for that portion of the performance are activated and focused.

Light Board Notes

If the board notes were corrected with an off-line editing program during dinner, the lighting designer need only view or assist with the preshow checks. He or she can then proceed to the viewing location. On the other hand, if no off-line editing could occur, no board notes should be attempted until the initial checks are complete, and the board operator can listen to the lighting designer give corrections.

Depending on the number of notes and the amount of time available, it may be necessary to prioritize the notes. When the board operator or stage manager says "stop," stop. Allow the board operator a chance to prepare for the show. In addition to that, the lighting designer now needs to move to the viewing location.

When programming board notes, a light cue may need to be seen on stage to determine the problem and apply the correction. Presuming that the problem is coming from an instrument upstage of the main curtain, this is one situation that may utilize the FOH inhibitive submaster. This situation is one reason why the curtain warmers, conductor special, and house lights are not programmed into that sub. Deactivate the front of house inhibitive sub for *Hokey* (sub 24), and then load the cue into the light board. Since no current channels in the front of house are affected, there will be no visual light change from the audience's perspective. Backstage, however, it will be possible to examine the problematic light cue and correct the memory. Once the problem has been determined, it can be recorded into the memory using the blind display, after which the fader can be cleared. If there's front of house light in the cue, it must be recorded in the blind display. If recorded live, the front of house light will be erased from that cue. When the process is complete, don't forget to restore the FOH inhibitive submaster to its show level. Otherwise, the front of house light will remain inactive for the entire act.

Final Light Board Check
At this point, the entire lighting package should be ready for the performance. As a final double check, however, the preset sequence programmed at the beginning of each act is viewed.

In the case of *Hokey,* the following preset sequence has been programmed into the computer console:

- *Memory 100.4* = All of the stage left sidelights (used in the act) brought up to a level of 70%. The intensity isn't so bright that it hurts the eyes to look into the lights, but it's bright enough to see errant shutters spilling on masking or scenery. Comparing the sidelights to a color card will confirm that the instruments have been correctly colored. Standing in the focus points and looking into the reflectors of the instruments will confirm that the lamp is centered in the reflectors.
- *Memory 100.5* = All of the stage right sidelights (used in the act) brought up to a level of 70%.

Again, the colors of the instruments can be checked, along with the focus and the shuttering.
- *Memory 100.6* = All of the cues (used in the act) are "piled on" together. After the cues are combined, the front of house inhibitive submaster (sub 24) is then taken to zero, and the cue is recorded. This cue is known as the super cue, since it contains the highest recorded level for each channel in that specific act. Since the channels in the super cue reflect only their highest intensity in the cues, it's possible to see if a problem warrants immediate attention. As an example, although an errant instrument is discovered while looking at the super cue, the severity of the problem is lessened because its intensity is only 30%. On the other hand, if the channel is reading at 100%, a check of the cues may be warranted. If it appears at a level of full in cues with a reduced number of channels, the problem may be apparent during the performance, and so it should be addressed.

The super cue is often viewed from down center just upstage of the main curtain, the closest approximation of the audience's perspective. From this viewpoint, any abnormalities will be most apparent. If the scenery stack is reset to a translucency and a black scrim, be certain to activate the channels upstage of the translucency before the show begins. Be certain there are no light leaks under the drops, and check that no groundrow instruments have been knocked out of focus. Although other sidelight notes can be addressed once the curtain flies out, when problems involving the translucency are seen in front of the audience, there's little that can be done to fix them.

After these checks have been accomplished, the final preshow check of the lighting system is complete. The light board can now be loaded with the first memory of the show, in this case, memory 100.7. If the preset is a black stage, a submaster containing a backlight or downlight system upstage of the main curtain can be activated. After the worklights have been turned off, the stage manager can ask the board operator for the submaster to be taken to zero to be ready for the first light cue. The light board is ready for the performance.

The Viewing Location
Ideally, when the lighting designer determined the path to the viewing location, it was also possible to check the environment of the space. The headset,

along with the monitors, and the sound feed were all operational. The dimmer controlling the worklights in the space was functional. When returning to the viewing location immediately before the show, consider double-checking all of these elements. If possible, arrive in the viewing area early to arrange the workspace and be ready for the performance.

THE PERFORMANCE

If there's no one else taking notes for the production on headset, the lighting designer should be certain to be in position at the viewing position before the performance begins. During initial performances, the stage manager may be attempting to place the cues for several different elements at once. In that situation, the lighting designer can also be a point of reference. Presuming that the lighting designer and the stage manager now have a working relationship, the lighting designer's separate perspective may be of value to the stage manager to restructure complex calling sequences. Before the show begins, the lighting designer should report to the stage manager on headset, and then say nothing else unless requested.

Notes Taken during the Performance

Most notes taken during the show will be regarding the cues. The documents used to construct the cues now become a portion of the reference material. This packet of information may include the cue master, the magic sheet, the cheat sheet, the color cards, and the floor cards. The light cues or a printout may be used to show the actual cue content for each memory if no monitor is available. The light plot can be used as an instrument schedule.

The last paperwork that will be required is blank paper to take notes. Usually, the notes can be broken down into three categories. Initially, there will be notes taken to change cue content and the timing of the light cues. Since the changes in timing need to be given to both the light board and the stage manager, the single document can be also be used to record placement changes. These notes can then be used to give both board notes and notes to the stage manager. The work notes sheet will be used to take notes regarding changes or tasks that will need to be addressed by the production electrician and the crew in the next work call. If followspots are used in the production, those notes

are usually written directly on the followspot cue sheets, so that they can be updated before the next performance.

Fresh, dated documents should be used for each performance. The notes are written as legibly as possible, since an incomprehensible note merely guarantees that the note will be taken again. The cue number is clearly written for each note. If the note is directed to a specific person, the initial of the person's name may be written next to the note.

As the notes are then given to the proper recipients, a line will be drawn through the note, taking care not to obscure it. Being able to see the note, once it's been given, allows the board and work notes sheets to still be read as archival documents. After the notes are given, they'll be kept in a folder or notebook. Keeping this archival record allows the lighting designer to trace back the changes that were made in each memory or cue. Keeping the archival notes means that when the new board operator makes an honest mistake, time is not lost. If, by accident, the disk is loaded into the just-updated RAM, the notes can still be read, and the changes can be fed back into the light board a second time. If need be, these documents can be photocopied and given to the proper parties prior to the next performance.

 Shelley's Notes: Defining the Mystery Instrument

Sometimes it's impossible to have a monitor showing the actions of the light board in the viewing position. Granted, the stage manager will state the cue number on the call. When watching the show, however, the cue may appear that, for the first time, includes an unwanted hot spot in the middle of the stage. If several systems are involved in the cue, it's frustrating to define the problem instrument.

Presumably, a single instrument is creating the hot spot. If the show is using an extensive instrument inventory, however, even that assumption may be erroneous. Taking a note is certainly recommended, but it may be possible to actually determine the channel. As performers walk through the hot spot, study the shadows on the floor. The number and direction of the shadows will provide clues to the origin of the light that's hitting that portion of the stage. Better yet, the hot instrument is probably causing the darkest shadow. Between the direction and the depth of shadow, an educated guess may be made as to the exact cause of the hot spot.

Intermission

Typically, the lighting designer will go backstage at intermission. Regardless of what happened during the first act, the lighting designer should not give any notes unless requested. Ideally, the only reason for the lighting designer to be backstage at intermission is to answer any questions posed by other personnel.

In some cases, however, the lighting designer may be requested to come backstage and make a design decision during a complex intermission change. Or there may be a different translucent backdrop that should be checked. It may be realized that the note regarding a focus change in a rover may not have been passed on. If any of these scenarios possibly occurs, then the lighting designer must not only return backstage at intermission, he or she needs to be there as soon as the intermission starts. Waltzing in after the work has been completed, only to ask for the same work to be performed again, is not fair to the crew. As soon as the curtain closes on the final cue, leave the viewing location and proceed backstage. Have respect for the crew's time by being on time.

If there is a color change in the sidelights, the preset memories for the second act should allow any instruments requiring a second focus to be seen. The super cue will show any instruments that may be suddenly hitting scenery.

Attempt to return to the viewing position before the second act begins.

The Bows

In many shows, the bow cue involves two memories. Much like the method used to create the memories at the end of Act 2, Scene 1, in *Hokey,* the bow cues at the end of the show utilized the FOH innibitive submaster. Initially, a cue was created that lit the entire stage and included frontlight (memory 486). This was recorded as the bow ride. After the inhibitive FOH submaster was pulled down to zero, the remains of the cue were recorded as the memories prior to and after the bow ride, becoming the bow preset (memory 485) and bow postset (memory 487). If the bows are strictly choreographed, this structure can continue to be recorded into the memories, so that the light cues match each movement of the curtain opening and closing in sequence.

Although it may seem redundant to watch the bows, cues still occur that need to be checked. On opening night, actions may take place that will not only require your perspective for analysis after the fact, but they may possibly demand your active participation.

During opening night bows, people can do funny things. Directors can change their mind without telling anyone. Leads can suddenly be inspired to create their own bow sequence and walk downstage where there is no light. Or the audience may applaud longer than expected. At this point, the bows can suddenly become a free-for-all. The stage manager may have to abandon memory numbers, and for the first time, ask for specific actions instead. When these situations develop, the handles that have been programmed into the computer light board may be able to help prevent the wheels from falling off. If a main curtain is used, the first handle that should be considered is the front of house inhibitive submaster (sub 24), which will fade and restore the front of house light while leaving the rest of the stage unchanged. If the stage manager needs to fade the entire stage to black and then restore, the grand master may be used. If no grand master exists, then the upstage inhibitive submaster (sub 12) can be faded and restored simultaneously with the FOH inhibitive sub (sub 24).

During these moments of intensity, the first thing that the lighting designer should do is get on the headset and not say a word. If the stage manager or the board operator needs help, they'll ask. Unless your perspective allows you to see an accident about to occur, stay out of the way. Your voice will interfere with the stage manager being heard. If you're addressed, give the information requested as succinctly as possible, telling the board operator numbers, not labels, then turn the microphone off. Don't offer advice, encouragement, or comments about the magic of the moment.

Spontaneous moments like these provide excellent examples of why it's not advised to release followspot operators after their final cue. Suddenly there may be the need for the followspots to cover the lead couple in the dark on the apron. In addition, consider that numerous people may be onstage during the bows who aren't used to being blinded by light. Disoriented, they may attempt to exit backstage, but instead go to locations on the stage that are dark. The momentary blindness and disorientation may possibly lead to severe injury if they're close to the edge of the stage. Though the followspots may be used to direct focus during the bows, during moments like these they should be considered beacons, to light the floor in front of people in the dark, so that the edge of the stage can be seen.

If the wheels do indeed fall off, and the board is without any more memories to load, choices must be made on the spot. If there's silence on the headset, find a memory number to load and be ready to give it over the headset. On the other hand, it may make more sense to remain silent, and just leave the board where it is. This may result in the front of house lights crashing onto the main curtain. Or the choice may be made to fade the light board to black as the curtain closes. Let the stage manager make these choices.

AFTER THE SHOW

Presuming that the bows have been uneventful, get backstage as quickly as possible. There may be a production meeting immediately following the performance that may alter the work calls in the morning. In addition to that, the lighting designer must be certain that the director is given the opportunity to give notes. The director may have a limited amount of time available to meet after the show, and if the meeting doesn't take place, there's no guarantee that the notes will be addressed by the next performance. To be able to instigate the notes, some amount of time may be required to analyze, organize, and prioritize the next day.

A private production meeting may be required with the production electrician, to devise a plan of attack for the next work call. Then he or she can prioritize and ask for the proper number of crew people. If the work call has already been previously decided, by the time the lighting designer reaches backstage, it may be deserted. Leave any notes in prespecified locations and leave the theatre.

The Departure

If it's the last night of the lighting designer's contract, notes may still be received. Although they're probably about the performance just seen, they may also be applicable to future incarnations of the same production. Sometimes, they may be desperate notes that require extensive blind programming in the lighting designer's absence. If that's the case, remember that no programming can take place until the next show call. There is time to devise a plan to attempt to meet those demands.

Before the lighting designer's departure, the production electrician must be provided with accurate, up-to-date documentation so that the production runs smoothly in the lighting designer's absence. Even if the paperwork has scribbles on it, the information is then accurate. Although updating archival paperwork may be boring, if or when it's needed, it had best be accurate for the sake of the show.

Distribute any last work notes and board notes. Thank everyone on the crew for his or her help and support in mounting the production. Temper whatever frustration may exist with the fact that the show was not created by you alone. Without everyone's effort and support, the production would never have been possible.

Out of the Theatre

Go home. Analyze what went right and what went wrong. There were many lessons to be learned from the experiences of the day. If time is taken to examine what went wrong, it may be possible to avoid making the same mistakes again in the future.

If you'll be back the next day, analyze, prioritize, and prepare the notes for the next day. The morning work call will begin with any projects that require lots of worklight. If the light board operator isn't involved in those activities, then he or she may be able to program board notes. If an off-line editing program can be utilized, consider using it. If there's a lot of work to be completed before the stage can be set to look at light cues, stay out of the crew's way. After the notes requiring worklight are completed, the stage will be set to look at light cues. Construct a preliminary list of the scenes and light cues to be viewed. Consider scheduling the sequence so that the last scene before lunch will be the first scene worked on in the afternoon rehearsal. After consultation with the carpentry staff, the list will be used to schedule the scene order.

On the other hand, the lighting designer might have seen the show for the last time. On most productions, the lighting designer is present only through the opening. The notes have been distributed and it's time to pack the bags.

SUMMARY

This concludes *A Practical Guide to Stage Lighting*. Though this text has presented one practical viewpoint of the events surrounding the installation of a production, there are many more variations and unknowns that can affect any show.

Experience is the harshest instructor. The willingness to learn is what prevents the same mistake from happening more than once. On the other hand, there are situations when, no matter what the lighting designer may be prepared for, the events can border on the catastrophic. Here is one lesson that the reader will hopefully never have the opportunity to experience.

Tales from the Road: A Lifetime in Italy One Night

One time Ballet Trockadero de Monte Carlo was touring Italy. The Trocks, as they are known, are an all-male dance company that performs parodies of dance classics. As such, all of the guys wear ballet toe shoes, which is no small feat (or feet, in the case of Shannon, who wore 13-1/2 double EEs). When we initially started performing on the Italian raked stages, performances were often punctuated by off-balance pirouettes resulting in spinout sprawls rivaling the Indy 500. By the time we arrived in a small port city in the "heel" of the country, everyone had adjusted to the slanted stage.

I had been told that the theatre owned a dance floor, which was a relief, since we didn't travel with one. I was thrilled with the prospect that, for a change, we were actually going to be performing on a surface that didn't have gaps in the stage, allowing us to see through the floor into the basement. I had also been told that they had all of the lighting equipment that we required. They were mistaken on both counts.

The theatre had a proscenium and a small ante-proscenium, which is essentially a second proscenium opening and a small offstage area downstage of the actual picture frame opening. This is where the curtain was controlled, but the space was not large enough for the huge tripods we had to use for booms. After we arrived, I discovered that the dance floor was actually kitchen linoleum. I also found out that the lighting equipment was being rented from somewhere else (little did I know that meant another part of the country). When Chewie (the interpreter) and I showed up at the theatre, we were greeted by the load-in crew, two carpenters.

I had gotten used to the Italian method of rigging. I ran around the stage placing pieces of wood on the deck, stating as I went "This is a border, this is a leg, this is an electric." The carps nodded, ran up to the grid, and proceeded to nail the Italian version of sheaves (which look a lot like large spools for sewing thread) into the wooden grid. They then proceeded to drop down several lines of 1/4-inch hemp, returned to

the deck, scabbed together several pieces of 1 × 2, tied the 1/4-inch hemp to it, and presto! It's a batten! This is a batten? Certainly this method was adequate for the legs and borders. None of the masking moved during the show, so it didn't' matter if goods weren't counterweighted. There wasn't that much weight on each batten, because the fabric was so lightweight it was translucent at best. Unfortunately, this was also the construction method presented for the electrics. At the time, however, I couldn't get too concerned about that finite point since there were no instruments to hang on the electric battens.

About 10:30 A.M. the electricians came wandering in, after picking up the electrics package from some other province. They had almost completed unloading all of the lighting equipment when the head electrician slapped himself on the forehead. This translates into almost any language: "Damn! I forgot the . . ."

It turned out that what had been left behind were the clamps to hang the instruments from the battens. I was getting a little nervous about the time and didn't want them to leave again, so they suggested gaff taping the instruments to the 1 × 2. I expressed my concern that the focus might not work real well, as well as my lack of confidence that the lights would stay up in the air. This entire train of thought was expressed rather simply: Barely shake head, squint eyes, and say "No." That also translates pretty well into any language. Eventually, someone came up with a spool of metal containing a series of holes that in English is called plumber's tape. After some discussion this became our c-clamps. A piece of plumber's tape was wrapped around the 1 × 2, and then bolted together through the hole in the yoke. Although it wasn't very pretty or secure, it was certainly more functional and a little safer than the gaffer tape. We all laughed and bonded and applauded our new method of hanging instruments.

That's about the time that the head electrician slapped himself on the forehead again, translated into "Damn! The gel frames." Well, we still had a lot of plumber's tape. After four pieces were cut, they were then bolted together. It's a gel frame! Except that the bolts were too large to slip through the color frame holders, and the tape was too stiff to be bent. Well, so much for any color changes. We proceeded to bolt the color into the instruments. The rest of the afternoon was concerned with trying to get the system working, which eventually had to be controlled by saltwater dimmers, and raising the noncounterweighted electrics to something like trim without killing anyone. After some scouring, the somewhat nervous dancers were convinced to perform their onstage warm-up period wearing hard hats.

Our evening opened with confidence; the performance began with *Yes Virginia, another Piano Ballet.* A sendup of Robbins's *Dances at a Gathering,* the original is a pleasant collection of simple dances performed by 10 dancers, a grand piano, and a pianist. The Trocks version approached the piece with a lone piano onstage, one man, and three "ballerinas" with attitude. At one point in the choreography, petty rivalries between two of the ballerinas would result in a moment of slapstick. A line of three dancers was formed upstage, with the man in the middle holding the two ballerinas' hands. This line then swept in an arc around the front of the stage past the piano. One of the women, intent on harming her rival, would purposefully place herself as a pivot during this arc like the children's game crack the whip, which would result in the second woman slamming into the piano.

One of the divas in the company named Zami could play the second woman's role in this moment to perfection. Not only could he come to a screeching halt against the piano without harming himself, he would "mount" the piano and hold himself off the floor, with both legs in the air straddling the keyboard. Since the stage was raked, we had placed chocks under the wheels of the piano to prevent it from moving. What we didn't know was that the chocks weren't very effective. So there we were in mid-performance. I was calling cues from stage right while the threesome joined hands. They swung the arc. The other "woman" whipped Zami into the piano. As expected, there was huge laughter.

And then the piano started to move. With Zami pasted to the corner of the piano like a fly on the windshield, the baby grand imperceptibly shuttered, and then started oh so slowly to inch its way downstage on the rake toward the orchestra pit.

My jaw slacked. Little sounds made their way out of my throat. Then I started looking around. Fast. One of the stagehands standing next to me had a cane. I grabbed it (sorry about that) and reached around the corner of the masking leg with the cane, snaking the hook of the cane around the upstage leg of the piano. This at least slowed it down. Unfortunately, this was an excellent demonstration of the laws of motion. Moreover, the laws were winning. Zami, the piano, the cane, and I were all slowly being dragged into the pit, with Zami still astride the piano.

Chewie grabbed my legs. An electrician grabbed his. Suddenly a human chain was formed backstage, one end clutching the radiator mounted to the side wall. In the back of my mind I began to wonder where the ice was. Finally, Zami got off the piano and continued to dance. Granted, he looked a little terrified; hey, if I had been riding a piano to my certain doom, I would have looked a little funny too.

But we made it to the end of the piece. The piano didn't move any more, we finished the piece, we did bows, we were going to make it out of this mess and regroup at intermission . . . and then the curtain didn't close. Chewie screamed incessantly into the headset without effect. Finally, after some amount of screaming from the electricians on the opposite side, the curtain slowly jerked to a close.

Ralph, the curtain operator, seemed like a nice enough fellow, but either his family tree didn't fork or he was equipped with the attention span of a dinner plate. Regardless, the situation had to be addressed; something had to be done to get the curtain under control. After some amount of discussion, it was determined that his tardiness was due to his inability to pull the ropes controlling the curtain while keeping the telephone handset next to his ear to hear the cues. As intermission ended, I turned around in time to see the crew gaff taping the handset to Ralph's head while Chewie sternly explained to him in no uncertain terms that he should pull his rope any time he heard the word "Go."

The second act started with the Trockadero tribute to the Olympics, a duet for two in Greek togas called *Spring Waters.* During the piece, the sailors in the audience felt it appropriate to throw money at the dancers and scream encouragement in Italian. Since none of us knew any Italian, we thought they were screaming "Bravo." Apparently, though, the sailors were enthusiastically informing the dancers how much fun a sailor could be. Anyway, the dance ended. We did the bows. Ralph and his taped head closed the curtain on cue. We were a hit, but now we had to reset the stage and continue with the next piece.

During the pause, I ran onstage to get the coins swept out of the way, chase the dancers onto the stage who were to perform in the next piece, *Pas de Quatre,* and chase the *Spring Waters* dancers off, who were busy picking up the coins. I met Chewie down center. I said quickly "As soon as we get this cleaned we'll be ready to *go,*" when I looked behind him to see Ralph's taped head snap up at the magic word and pull the curtain open. Chewie dove offstage into the middle of the saltwater dimmers and the tape deck. I was not so fortunate. I ended up diving into the ante-pro with Ralph, who was so busy congratulating himself for finally hearing a cue that he didn't realize that I shouldn't be standing there in his arms.

I almost panicked. Should I just casually walk around the proscenium in full view of the audience? Or do I just trust that Chewie could read my cue sheet? I was stunned like the proverbial deer in the headlights. Suddenly I saw a hole in the wall. I bent over and could see the tape deck through the hole! I shoved my arm into the hole, and could feel my hand sticking out of the other side of the wall.

I looked at the stage, with the four dancers now in preset position, and raised my index finger in the direction of the tape deck. When the proper moment arrived, I dropped my finger . . . and the music started! I then raised my finger in the direction of the saltwater dimmer operators and, at the proper moment, dropped my finger . . . and the lights changed! Using my index finger to call the show, the piece ran flawlessly, even the numerous cues involved in the curtain call. And Ralph even got the curtain right. After the end of the show, Chewie and I sat at the piano and bonded over a flask of tequila.

Glossary

Actual throw distance The measured distance between an instrument and its focus point, which defines the size and intensity of the light beam.

Attribute Quality or characteristic belonging to functions, commands, or structures in a computer lighting environ ronment.

Autofollow A light cue or any action that begins at the moment the previous cue or action has completed its time duration. More loosely, any light cue that is linked to a previous cue. Its initiation may begin before the previous cue has completed its time fade.

Beam angle The internal cone of a light beam created by an instrument. Usually defined in degree increments, it is the area of the light beam where the light is 50% of the intensity of that instrument's hot spot.

Beam spread The overall size or width of a light beam created by an instrument. Often defined in degree increments. See *field angle*.

Blackout A lighting state in which all intensity to all lighting instruments is off; complete darkness. Also referred to in the speed at which the state is achieved, usually in zero seconds.

Blind record The process of altering channel intensity or other information contained within the lighting console without the results being seen on stage.

Blind screen A computer display showing the channel level information of a light cue without the channels being activated to their displayed levels. Also shortened to *blind*. Depending on the console, also called *preview*.

Blocker cue A cue that contains hard commands for all channels from previous cues. Tracking channels recognize the hard command and assume the level programmed in the cue. The same channel following the blocker cue assumes the level provided within the blocker.

Center center A reference point in the middle of the playing area. Typically located on centerline midway between the up and downstage light lines.

Chromatic aberration The prismatic fringe seen at the edge of a pool of light like a rainbow; often seen when an ellipsoidal is focused to a sharp edge.

Column Vertical row of information.

Command line Location on a computer display reflecting keypad function instructions given to lighting console.

Console An electronic mechanism containing the CPU, RAM, and control apparatus that, when connected to dimmers, remotely controls their voltage output to instruments and other devices.

Continuity hour Phrase used in union labor, to indicate physical labor other than typical work involved in show call taking place for 1 hour. Typically applied to a separate hour of pay, either immediately prior to the half-hour show call, or immediately following the performance.

Cross-fade Act of moving to a new look on stage. Using a manual preset board, the term often means moving a master fader between two banks or rows of dimmers preset in different configurations. When using a computer console, often means loading a new memory into a fader.

Cue A single lighting state, also called a look, usually assigned a fade time. For a manual light board, the specific level assignments for dimmers. For a computer light board, a unit of memory containing specific channel intensities. Also used as the command given, usually by a stage manager, to initiate a predetermined action.

Cue content The level intensity information for all channels in a cue.

Cue information The level intensity information for all channels in a single cue and any other associated time or function attributes of the same cue.

Cue list screen A computer display listing sequential list of recorded cues and any associated attributes.

Cue only Type of recording function that memorizes the change in channel intensity for only the affected cue. Channels changed in the cue revert to intensity from previous cue in the next cue.

Cue screen   Usually refers to the monitor display showing the level assignments for each channel.

Cue to cue   Period of time when technical elements, sequences, and transitions of production are rehearsed, with or without performers. Stage action is abbreviated to the action solely required to provide a timed standby before a cue. See *dry tech*.

Default   Parameters initially presented within a lighting console that contains no programmed information. These settings are typically set at the factory.

Delay   Dependent on software platform, one of the two time durations that can occur with the initiation of a memory on a computer lighting console. Usually defined as amount of time between initiation of first memory (pressing the GO button), and automatic initiation of next programmed memory. See *wait*.

Dimmer   Device that regulates voltage to other devices. Usually controls brightness of lighting instruments.

Display   A specific arrangement of information on a computer monitor.

Donut   Metal insert placed in ellipsoidal color frame holders to eliminate halation or chromatic aberration outside edge of beam pool. The hole in the donut is typically the same diameter as the gate of the instrument on which it will be used.

Downfade   Any channel intensities in a fade that are decreasing from previous state or cue, often related to in terms of time.

Dress rehearsal   Period of time when all elements of the production are rehearsed with performers in costume.

Dry tech   Period of time when technical elements, sequences, and transitions of production are rehearsed without performer involvement. See *cue to cue*.

Electrical path   The singular electric and electronic route for each lighting instrument or device in a light plot, defined by the intersections in the route. Usually includes a circuit, dimmer, and sometimes a control channel.

Fade   A gradual change of channel intensities from one lighting state to another.

Fader   In manual light boards, a physical handle that controls the levels of a series of dimmers. In computer lighting consoles, a portion of the electronics and software controlling predetermined contents of a single cue.

Feeding the cues   Programming previously existing cues into a computer lighting console.

Field angle   The overall size or width of a light beam created by an instrument. Usually defined in degree increments, it is the area of the light beam where the light is

10% of the intensity of that instrument's hot spot. See *beam spread*.

Focus point   The location on the stage, scenery, or in space where the hot spot of an instrument's beam is pointed. When instruments are assigned to illuminate performers, the location on the stage or the location of the designer's head used to define the placement of the instrument's hot spot can be both referred to as the focus point.

Focus session   Period of time when the lighting instruments are aimed at specific locations from directions given by the lighting designer.

Footer   Bottom line of information that is duplicated on separate pages of a single document.

Four wall theatre   A theatre empty and void of all equipment. The only things contained are the four walls. All support equipment necessary for the production will have to be brought from remote locations.

Frozen   Usually referred to as the moment when no more changes will be made or sometimes allowed to the production. May or may not be associated with opening night. See *liquid*.

Full   The channel intensity of 100%.

Ghost channel   A channel without an assigned dimmer. The level intensity displayed by the channel provides information about the current contents of the RAM contained in the lighting console.

Go   The command given to initiate a cue or action. Also refers to the button on lighting consoles that is pressed to load a memory into a fader.

Grand master   A fader that overrides all other intensity levels.

Groundplan zero point   The architectural point of reference from which all relative measurements are made. Typically, the intersection of the centerline and the plaster line.

Group   Software function given to a unit of memory containing unrelated channels at any intensity level. Software equivalent of a submaster, but intensity level is controlled by keypad on light board. As such, a group can act as either pile-on or inhibitive.

Halation   Unwanted scattered light bouncing off inside of ellipsoidal. Often solved by using a donut.

Half hour   The 30-minute period of time prior to a performance. Often the same time as *house open*.

Hard command   Phrase used in computer light boards, referring to tracking systems. Describes a new level intensity assigned to a channel in a particular cue. The "hard command" instruction forces the channel to assume the new level intensity.

Hardpatch   The act of physically plugging cables or circuits into dimmers, manually assigning the control of an instrument or electrical device.

Head height   The horizontal plane in space above a stage defined by the lighting designer as the generic height used to determine focus points. Most often shown in section view drawings to illustrate beam overlap of different zones within a single system.

Header   Top line of information that is duplicated on separate pages of a single document.

Hot spot   The brightest portion of a light beam created by an instrument, usually in the center of the beam.

Hour before half hour   A 1-hour period of time prior to half hour, used to perform preshow checks of the technical elements of the production. Not to be confused with continuity hour.

House   Term used to refer to the entire audience seating area.

House open   The moment when the doors to the theatre are opened, allowing the audience to be seated.

Infrastructure cues   Light cues, other than memories created to play back "looks" in a production, that are used to provide additional handles or other functions in a computer lighting console.

Inhibitive   An attribute often associated with submasters that overrides the intensity of its contents. Like a grand master. See *pile-on* or *timed.*

Integer   A whole number that has no fraction or numbers following a decimal point.

Intensity   The actual brightness of light generated by the lamp inside the instrument.

Key memory number   A numeric system used to identify a portion of, or entire contents of RAM within a computer lighting console. When a recorded level from a designated ghost channel is visually combined with the initial memory number of a collection of light cues, the resulting key memory number identifies not only the intended purpose of those light cues, but also the disk where the light cues are stored.

Light board   Device that controls intensity of instruments or other devices. Can be manual, preset, or computer. See *console.*

Light line   Imaginary boundary defining the collective edge of coverage for primary lighting systems.

Link   A jump to any other memory recorded in the lighting console, usually other than the next sequential numeric memory.

Liquid   The period of time before decisions have been made defining what will technically occur during each moment of a production. Every option is examined as a stage moment before the final version is decided on. See *frozen.*

Live screen   The monitor display showing the present levels of the channels, reflecting the current output of all active faders. Also known as *stage screen.*

Load-in   Beginning the installation or mounting of equipment for a production. May or may not involve equipment being "loaded into" the theatre. The term is applied to a time increment that may affect the amount of money and people required for labor. A loose call dependent on the management in charge.

Load-out   The period of time following the final performance. Typically begins when equipment starts being disassembled and ends when the performance facility has been restored to the same state of existence before production loaded in. Often concludes with final truck pulling away from the loading dock. Sometimes also referred to as *strike.*

Macro   A recorded series of keystrokes or actions that performs a repeated effect. Can be initiated on different contents.

Memory   A single unit of information within the RAM of a lighting console, also referred to as a *cue.*

Monitor   A computer display device.

Non-dim   A physical device controlling the voltage output to another device or instrument controlled by a computer lighting console. Often limited to only outputting zero or full voltage in zero seconds.

Notes session   Period of time following end of rehearsal session spent analyzing rehearsal, coordinating solutions, and deciding future production schedule.

Opaque   The visual state seen when light is not transmitted nor objects seen through a material. See *translucent* and *transparent.*

Opening night   The first performance viewed by a paid audience, or reviewed by critics.

Orchestra dress   Period of time when all elements of a production are rehearsed with a live orchestra and wardrobe.

Orchestra tech   Period of time when all elements of a production, except for wardrobe, are rehearsed with a live orchestra.

Overtime   An escalation of pay rates, after a set number of labor hours have concluded.

Park   A software command or state that overrides all other commands or handles, often associated with dimmers. If a dimmer is "parked" at a level, its intensity cannot be altered. By "parking" dimmers containing worklight at full, memories can still be recorded without programming the worklight channels into the cue.

Part A recorded lighting state that is assigned unique time durations within a single light cue. Often several parts can exist in any lighting memory.

Patch Specifies the control assigned to each instrument. See *hardpatch* and *softpatch*.

Patch screen The monitor screen that shows the dimmer assignments to the channels.

Perishables Consumable items such as tape, pens, markers, or gel, templates, and special effects fluids. Once used, the items cannot be returned for refund.

Pile-on Term describing the action of "highest level takes precedence," so that the higher intensity level overrides other level information. The higher level is being "piled on" to the existing level. Pile-on is an attribute often associated with submasters. See *inhibitive* or *timed*.

Playback The act of loading a preexisting memory into a fader, activating the contents of the memory.

Postset The appearance seen on stage, or the sound heard by the audience, after the bows have been completed and the performers have left the stage.

Prehang Period of time prior to official beginning of load-in, usually performing reduced scenic or electrical activities and requiring less labor. Typically involves only electrics or rigging equipment.

Preset The state when activity, spatial location, or actions are in a state of readiness and preparation for a production or a specific moment. Can also refer to a type of manual light board, or a single row of controllers for that light board.

Preshow The period of scheduled time prior to a performance. May or may not be the same as half hour. Can also refer to actions that take place before the actual production begins.

Previews Performances given to nonpaying audience, or prior to the arrival of critics.

Production meeting Period of time when production technical information is shared among different departments.

Profile patch Commands instructing a dimmer to alter its perception of what is "full" or any other portion within the curve of the dimmer.

Pull the order Physical act of assembling a lighting inventory from a light rental shop.

Record Giving a label to a particular state of light. On a manual light board, writing the level intensities for the dimmers. On a computer light board, assigning a numeric label to a particular arrangement of channel levels.

Rental shop An organization often containing all of the components required to package a light plot. May also provide service, support, maintenance, and sales of equipment and perishables.

Replug The physical act of altering the circuit and connected instrument to a dimmer. May be performed by pulling one plug out of a dimmer input and inserting a second plug in its place. May also be achieved by switches that control separate inputs.

Row Horizontal line of information.

Scene master Physical handle on light board that controls a bank or row of sliders controlling dimmers.

Show call Period of time defined in union labor for presetting of all equipment for performance. Often does not involve other labor associated with maintenance or work call. Typically refers to the number of stagehands required to run the technical elements during a performance.

Slider Physical handle on light board that controls a range of functions, ranging from a single dimmer to a series of channels.

Softpatch The act of assigning dimmer control to a channel on a computer lighting console using software; often achieved with a keypad.

Standby The heightened moment or preparatory command given prior to the command to initiate a cue (go).

Step A sequential repetitive action. Step through cues, step through channels, etc. Also refers to unit of memory associated with effect packages in computer light boards.

Strike See *load-out*.

Submaster Physical handle, usually containing unrelated channels. On lighting computer consoles, can be programmed to have different attributes, including pile-on, inhibitive, or timed.

Super group Collection of related channels in a single system, or a whole bunch of channels.

System At least two instruments equipped with matching color filters that are focused to different or adjacent areas of the stage. When overlapping light beams in the same color create a consistent intensity wider than the width of a single beam angle, can also be referred to as a wash. The term is also used to refer to an entire lighting package.

Technical rehearsal Period of time when technical elements of the production are combined with performers to define timing and effect. Usually doesn't include wardrobe or orchestra. Often called a tech.

Template Thin pieces of metal containing holes. When a template is inserted into an ellipsoidal, light projected through the lens of the instrument mirrors the shape of the holes. Also called gobos or patterns.

Time fade   Duration of seconds for a light cue or action to be completed.

Time stamp channel   Ghost channel designated to display a calendar date or time not associated with the time clock chip contained in a computer lighting console. Used to define the last date that the contents of the RAM was altered.

Timed   An attribute often associated with submasters which, when activated, automatically fades up its contents, maintains a preprogrammed intensity, and fades the contents back out. See *pile-on* or *inhibitive.*

Title block   Area of logistical information that may or may not be confined in a particular area. In paperwork, often found in headers or footers.

Track   To keep track of something; to track light cues. Also, type of recording function that memorizes the change in channel intensity and instructs the channel to continue through succeeding cues until it encounters a hard command.

Track screen   Usually refers to the monitor display arranged in a grid or spreadsheet format; rows indicate each sequential cue, while columns indicate an individual channel. Contents of each row of the grid show the channel levels for each cue, while contents of each column show the level progression for each channel.

Translucent   The visual state seen when light is transmitted but objects are not distinctly seen through a material. See *transparent* and *opaque.*

Transparent   The visual state seen when light passes through or objects are distinctly seen on the other side of a material. See *translucent* and *opaque.*

Trim   The act of physically moving objects in the air to a predetermined distance or to a visual location from a sightline point. Also a reference to a specific vertical location.

Upfade   Any channel intensities in a fade that are increasing to a higher level than the previous cue, often related to in terms of time.

Venue   Location or site of performance usually involving an audience.

Wait   Dependent on software platform and can mean one of two things. Either the duration of time between the initiation of a memory (pressing the GO button) and the initiation of the following memory in a sequence, or the duration of time between the initiation of a memory (pressing the GO button) and the actual moment at which the same memory begins to load into the fader. See *delay.*

Walk-away   Phrase indicating that no stage work will commence following a performance. The only official stage activity is "walking away" from the stage.

Warning   A preparatory command given prior to, or in place of, a standby.

Wash   At least two instruments focused so that their overlapping beams create a consistent hue and intensity over a portion, or all of, a performance area. Can also be referred to as a *system.*

Wheels fall off   The point in a technical rehearsal when all coherence and direction is lost.

Zone   At least two light beams focused to create a single band of light aimed at focus points equidistant from plaster line, so that the overlapping beams create a consistent hue and intensity across the width of a stage. Overlapping zones are often combined to create a system or a wash.

Bibliography

A Method of Lighting the Stage
Stanley McCandless
Theatre Arts Books
333 Sixth Avenue
New York, NY 10014

Designing with Light, Second Edition
J. Michael Gillette
Mayfield Publishing Company
1240 Villa Street
Mountain View, CA 94041

Lighting Handbook
Westinghouse Electric Corporation
Lamp Divisions
Bloomfield, New Jersey 07003

Lighting the Stage
Willard F. Bellman
Chandler Publishing Company
257 Park Avenue South
New York, NY 10010

Photometrics Handbook
Robert C. Mumm
Broadway Press
3001 Sprintcrest Drive
Louisville, KY 40241

Pocket Ref
Thomas J. Glover
Sequoia Publishing
Aggeon Cal, Inc.
123-33T Gray Avenue
Santa Barbara, CA 93101

Scenery for the Theatre
Harold Burris-Meyer & Edward C. Cole
Little, Brown and Company
3 Center Plaza, Floor 3
Boston, MA 02108

Stage Lighting
Richard Pilbrow
Von Nostrand Reinhold Company
450 West 33rd Street
New York, NY 10001

Stage Scenery
A. S. Gillette
HarperCollins Publishers
10 East 53rd Street
New York, NY 10022

The Dramatic Imagination
Robert Edmond Jones
Theatre Arts Books
333 Sixth Avenue
New York, NY 10014

The Magic of Light
Jean Rosenthal and Lael Wertenbaker
Little, Brown and Company, Boston-Toronto
In association with Theatre Arts Books
333 Sixth Avenue
New York, NY 10014

Index